D1487016

FRONTIERS OF CIVIL LIBERTIES

WITH A PREFACE BY

Senator Robert F. Kennedy

AND

AN INTRODUCTION BY

Louis H. Pollak

Dean of Yale University Law School

FRONTIERS OF CIVIL LIBERTIES

BY

NORMAN DORSEN

PANTHEON BOOKS

A Division of Random House New York

FIRST PRINTING

 Published in the United States by Pantheon Books, a division of Random House, Inc., New York, and simultaneously in Canada by Random House of Canada Limited, Toronto.

Library of Congress Catalog Card Number: 67-13321

Manufactured in the United States of America
by The Haddon Craftsmen, Inc., Scranton, Pennsylvania
Designed by Vincent Torre

To my mother and father

Preface

We are often tempted, and sometimes constrained, by the complexity of our nation's problems to consider them only in broad compass. Our economy produces nearly $800 billion in goods and services each year; more than 30,000,000 Americans live in poverty; whole cities of new homes, schools and hospitals must be built; the turbulent world in which we live seems beyond control.

But in concentrating on the scale of our problems, we risk losing sight of the fact that our national purpose—our reason for national existence—is rooted in the dignity and liberty of the individual human being. The founding of the United States was premised on the belief that men must be left to think, to speak, to believe and to act according to their own lights.

In this book, Norman Dorsen, a respected young teacher and scholar, reminds us of the problems and achievements of our time in fostering individual liberty. He recounts the hard battles we have fought over the rights of men and points out the battles yet to be won. His book discusses the Negro's efforts to win full political equality, analyzes the struggles of government employees against degrading attempts to legislate belief, and dramatizes the link between economic and political justice. Yet through these accounts runs a single theme: that the rights of American citizens are indivisible, and that the liberty of our nation is threatened when even one of us is denied his freedom.

Men like Norman Dorsen have shown us that these issues are not academic—indeed, that scholars and teachers have a critical role to play in the heat of battle. Their activities in the courts and other arenas of action have won for all Americans a greater share of political freedom. Professor Dorsen himself, as advocate in the Supreme Court and other tribunals, has helped to shape many of the constitutional rulings which over the past few years have made freedom a reality for more of our citizens. In civil rights, in reapportionment, in loyalty oath cases and now in the attempts to secure the rights of the poor, scholar-advocates such as he have demonstrated the link between intellect and action.

With this book, Professor Dorsen adds to these achievements a substantial scholarly accomplishment, carefully surveying the present territory of American liberty—and describing the future which will be won only through the continued commitment and energy of us all.

ROBERT F. KENNEDY

The late Senator Kennedy wrote the above preface in the fall of 1967.

Contents

SECTION III

SECTION IV

Introduction

In a volume which will endure, the introduction should be constructed of materials as lasting as those which give permanence to the intellectual abode to which it is the entryway. This is a volume which will endure, both because the process of giving definition to a free society is an ever-continuing one and because Professor Dorsen has addressed himself to that process with a subtlety and a length of perspective that will do service for years to come. Nonetheless, this Introduction—at the hazard of seeming merely topical—will take as a point of departure a brief and entirely ceremonial event which has, as these words are written, only just transpired, and which will, by the time this volume is published, be not only months past but in all likelihood largely forgotten by anyone other than a few immediate participants.

I

The event took place at ten o'clock on Monday morning, October 2, 1967. The Justices of the Supreme Court of the United States, led by the Chief Justice, convened in public session to open the Court's October Term, 1967. At that session, which was attended by the President, Thurgood Marshall took the judicial oath—to "administer justice without respect to persons, and do equal right to the poor and to the rich, and . . . faithfully and impartially discharge and perform all the duties incumbent upon [him] . . . according to the best of [his] abilities and understanding, agreeably to the Constitution and the laws of the United States . . ."—and took his seat; he is the ninety-sixth Justice to be installed since the Court was established 178 years ago.

It is respectfully submitted that what is enduringly important about the event is not the sentimental symbolism attaching to the installation of the first Negro member of the Supreme Court. For if our nation at last recognizes the truth of what the elder Justice Harlan insisted upon in vain in 1896—that the Constitution is color-blind—then surely it is fair to expect that soon we will be blind to the color of the Justices.

The enduring importance of the event lies elsewhere. It lies in the fact that Justice Marshall—son of a Pullman porter and great-grandson of a slave—embodies in his own person the capacity of our legal system to vindicate the rights of the people. As chief strategist and victorious field commander of the *School Segregation Cases*, he rescued from outlawry those who, until 1964, were simply the objects of American law's indignity and not, as whites have been since the Revolution, joint proprietors of the law. Today Marshall sits on the bench, in direct lineal succession and direct constitutional rebuff to Justice Joseph Bradley, author of the prevailing opinion—in the ill-named *Civil Rights Cases*—from whose myopia so much misfortune arose.

But the point is not simply that legally ordained racial segregation is no longer countenanced by the Constitution, nor even that the way is now open to Congress and to state legislatures to move directly against private racial discrimination which has public consequences (in employment, housing, education, medical care, etc.). The point is less dramatic and more important. It is that American law has shown that it is capable of beginning to work itself pure, first in the courts and then in the political arena. And a society which is at last making inroads—far too slowly, to be sure, but inroads nonetheless—on the most corrosive of its ills is not beyond redemption; nor are its corrective processes to be dismissed as hopelessly inadequate to the tasks ahead.

A society whose corrective processes are long stultified is ripe for, and invites, revolution. It is in that sense, and very likely only in that sense, that revolution is an abiding and honorable ingredient of the American democratic tradition. Today, with racial segregation by law a thing of the past, with the numbers of the enfranchised steadily expanding, and with legislative reapportionment gaining momentum, there is perhaps less occasion to doubt the capacity of our federal and state governments to promote the liberties of the people than at any other time in our history. And yet, to speak of the integrity of our governmental processes in the face of this nation's ever-mounting frustrations—frustrations born of despair in the black slums and of widespread doubts about why we are at war and whither the war is tending—is to run the risk of being written off as a Pollyanna. It is essential that we recognize that we face problems of greater complexity, more deeply felt and more vigorously complained of by larger and more varied constituencies, than at any time in our history since the Civil War. People and problems, and correlative impatience, are multiplying with dire rapidity. If it is true that we have proved ourselves possessed of the capacity to govern responsibly, we must utilize that capacity fully and without delay.

This means that unrest in the slums must be met with strategies more comprehensive than police dogs and antiriot laws—strategies, that is to say, addressed not to symptoms but to the underlying pathology.

It also means that those who romanticize violence, or rationalize it as an effective and hence acceptable political tactic, are practicing on themselves and others a deception of calamitous and perhaps catastrophic dimension. This is not to say that there is no place in American jurisprudence, past and present, for deliberate disobedience to law. There is, and it is a revered place. But as the unfolding history of American civil liberty demonstrates, that revered place is reserved for the peaceful testing of asserted abuse of official authority; a testing which invokes and acquiesces in the higher arbitrament of the Constitution; a testing which differs *toto caelo* from the insurrection which overturns, or the massive recalcitrance which chokes, the due processes of law.

When Madison, on June 8, 1789, urged on his fellow members of the House of Representatives the wisdom of amending the Constitution by adding to it a bill of rights, he pointed out that if the proposed amendments carried, "independent tribunals of justice will consider themselves in a peculiar manner the guardians of those rights; they will be an impenetrable bulwark against every assumption of power in the legislative or executive; they will be naturally led to resist every encroachment upon rights expressly stipulated for in the Constitution by the Declaration of Rights." A century and a quarter later Holmes took occasion to remind his judicial colleagues —and his fellow countrymen—"that legislatures are ultimate guardians of the liberties and welfare of the people in quite as great a degree as the courts." The installation of Thurgood Marshall as a Justice of the Supreme Court can serve to remind us of the wisdom of both sentiments, and of the high courage which fidelity to these sentiments requires of us.

II

In the pages which follow, Professor Dorsen canvasses a number of major problems of freedom—problems which have been at the forefront in the past twenty years, or which are even now at the law's cutting edge. And we are particularly in Professor Dorsen's debt because even those problems which are familiar are presented through documents which the ordinary citizen never sees. Thus, Professor Dorsen does not fill his book with the landmark Supreme Court opinions, but instead shows us the briefs which shaped the opinions, the conferences whose tactical and policy choices informed the briefs, and the exploratory memoranda which sketched out guidelines for the conferences. And the validity of this pragmatic perspective is attested to by the fact that many of the documents are work-products of Professor Dorsen and his colleagues at the Arthur Garfield Hays Civil Liberties Program at New York University Law School.

The first section of the book poses fundamental questions about the capacity of our legal institutions to fulfill the liberating roles assigned to them by the Constitution. There are, for example, important lessons of which one is reminded by Professor Dorsen's retrospective look at the vulgarities and cruelties of McCarthyism: for three or four troubled years, cherished constitutional rights seemed to have been eroded, and neither Holmes's faith in legislators nor Madison's faith in judges seemed much more than whimsey. Of course, Professor Dorsen does not limit his inquiry to the practices of those who wield official power; he also asks the right questions about the readiness of the bar to translate into reality the obligation, so prized in the profession's rhetoric, to push the hard cases which seriously challenge the status quo.

In the second section of the book, Professor Dorsen samples a number of deeply disturbing problems which probe our society's professed tolerance of dissent. Included here are such diverse issues as the retribution visited upon a state university professor who attempted to make a public case for premarital sexual relationships; the attempt of the armed forces to censor a servicemen's newspaper; and the blacklisting by private employers of assertedly "subversive" writers and performers.

In Section III, Professor Dorsen turns a critical eye on the fairness of the processes through which our legal institutions operate. The criminal trial, whose glaring publicness is aided and abetted by press and television, poses certain dangers, and opportunities. The adjudication of delinquency, whose benevolent privacy blunts that opportunity for full inquiry which is the boast of the adversary system, poses other dangers and opportunities. In this section of the book Professor Dorsen also considers the role of sanctions—and especially the ultimate sanction—in a civilized society's system of social controls. Again in this portion of the book there surfaces the insistent question of how rights can be meaningfully asserted without more and better lawyers, single-mindedly devoted to the client's interest without regard to his color, ideology or ability to pay.

The closing section of the book treats of the persistent and pervasive problems of racial discrimination which—nearly fourteen years after the *School Segregation Cases*—remain the central testing ground of our professed commitment to democracy. Here Professor Dorsen maps out the legal avenues which need to be pursued in assaults upon *de facto* school segregation, segregation in residential housing and discrimination in employment. And in this same context of racial oppression, Professor Dorsen appropriately turns his attention to the degrading design and callous administration of the categories of public assistance which are denominated "welfare" programs.

Taken in its entirety, Professor Dorsen's book is a national agenda of real questions which require real answers, if we are serious about being and becoming a free society. They are questions for Thurgood Marshall and his colleagues, for all their fellow public officials, for all their fellow lawyers, and for all their fellow citizens.

LOUIS H. POLLAK

October 1967

Preliminary Remarks

The chief object of this book is to alert the public to the diversity, subtlety and importance of civil liberties problems in the United States. Every one of us has a personal stake in how these problems are resolved.

The book contains selected examples of my work as a civil liberties lawyer while serving as Director of the Arthur Garfield Hays Civil Liberties Program at New York University School of Law. The Hays Program was established in September 1958 in honor of the late Arthur Garfield Hays, who served for many years as General Counsel of the American Civil Liberties Union. The program carries on research concerning human rights, provides practical assistance to action organizations, conducts special projects and conferences, and above all trains law students for public service in the protection of individual liberty in the United States.

Arthur Hays once summed up his personal philosophy as follows:

After his capture, John Brown said that he was worth more for hanging than for any other purpose. For myself it may well be that I have been worth more for the rights of others to express themselves than any other purpose. . . . I hate to see people pushed around. I vent my emotions in trying to help them from being pushed.

This philosophy, which animates the program honoring Hays's name, is a response to the fact that civil liberties are never secure;

there is always someone trying to "push people around." Professor Charles A. Reich has expressed an important reason for this state of affairs: civil liberties, he says, are "an unnatural state for man or for society because in a short-range way they are essentially contrary to the self-interest of the majority. They require the majority to restrain itself, to say No to its immediate impulses, and to allow things to go on that threaten it."

Because it is natural for any group to attempt to maintain a dominant position, the independence and legal rights of minorities and other vulnerable sectors of society need protection. The first line of defense is the political branches of government. Legislators and administrators alike must be trained to recognize and protect fundamental rights, and especially not to sacrifice them to the supposed needs of the nation as a whole.

But this is often not easy. Political pressures on elected representatives are great. They are greatest at times of national crisis, and thus the stress on liberty is most acute at such times. Moreover, as the selections in this book should make clear, there are numerous ways in which individuals can be hurt. Legislators and administrators do not and realistically cannot be expected to do the full job.

It is therefore necessary to turn to the second line of defense—the courts. In a country with a written Bill of Rights that catalogues the essential civil liberties, and a tradition whereby federal and state statutes, as well as other official acts, are scrutinized judicially for constitutional defects, the courts are the last barrier to arbitrary governmental action. Short of constitutional amendment, they are the ultimate definers of our liberties.

The second line of defense is maintained through what is commonly known as the "test case." These cases present to the courts, and ultimately to the Supreme Court, claims by individuals that government representatives have impaired fundamental rights. These test cases are not artificial or staged, as they are sometimes thought to be, but rather involve real grievances at the hands of officials; they are the accepted means by which statutes and ordinances and administrative action are reviewed for possible constitutional infirmity.

The test case is usually conducted by a relatively new breed of advocate, the civil liberties lawyer. The swift pace of constitutional change in recent years has called forth attorneys who bridge the gap between government and law, who, for example, must be as aware of the nuances of our federal system as of the technical rules of pleading and evidence. Required to master both constitutional doctrine and complex federal and state legislation, the civil liberties lawyer has emerged as an important new factor in the legal profession, a recognized specialist like the domestic relations or tax lawyer.

There is abundant evidence of this development. In 1966 the American Bar Association established a Section of Individual Rights and Responsibilities to serve as a national forum for practitioners working in this field. Three years earlier a group of imaginative law students, who had acted as volunteers in the South during the civil rights summer of 1963, formed the Law Students Civil Rights Research Council, which now provides enthusiastic and skillful assistance to attorneys of record and trains students for the time when they will take their place in the front lines. The law schools, too, have played a part as advanced courses in civil liberties and civil rights have appeared in the curriculum of all major institutions. Finally, the emergence to full maturity of the legal staffs of the great national organizations—the ACLU, the NAACP Legal Defense and Educational Fund, the American Jewish Congress and others—as well as the development of active federal agencies—the Civil Rights Commission, the Civil Rights Division of the Department of Justice and the Equal Employment Opportunity Commission—has enabled the willing young advocate eschewing a commercial career to move directly into constitutional litigation.

The civil liberties lawyer and his role in safeguarding individual liberty are important to this book for several reasons. Ten chapters involve briefs in litigated cases, and the reader should appreciate the context in which the work was done. In addition, the rest of the book—the conferences, the memoranda for the ACLU and even the articles and speeches—all reveal how the advocate, or at least the academic advocate, plies his trade. These varied products nicely suggest, moreover, the diverse ways in which the law of civil liberties develops: through direct appeals to government agencies, through the policy pronouncements of concerned organizations and through the formulation and exchange of ideas at scholarly meetings.

All the briefs presented here involve cases in the Supreme Court of the United States. Two types of distinctions among these briefs deserve special notice. First, there is the difference between the full-blown brief on the merits of a case and the preliminary brief, known as the Petition for Certiorari or the Jurisdictional Statement. The preliminary brief, an example of which can be found in Chapter 10, is directed solely to persuading the Supreme Court that a substantial constitutional issue exists that requires plenary consideration. If the Court agrees, a full brief on the merits is then prepared.

The second distinction is between briefs involving direct representation of an individual claiming a constitutional right and briefs *amicus curiae,* in which a civil liberties organization acting as a "friend of the court" urges a particular result based on its special interest and competence. Chapters 7, 14, 17, 19 and 25 are examples of direct representation, while Chapters 13, 15, 16 and 22 exemplify the brief *amicus curiae.* There is sometimes a very important practical difference between the two situations. When a civil liberties lawyer undertakes direct representation, it is his case from the beginning and he is charged with raising all available legal arguments on behalf of his client. The lawyer acting as *amicus curiae* ordinarily enters the case only at the appellate stage, and even then his brief is confined to issues of particular concern to the organization on whose behalf he is acting.

The reader should bear in mind, while reading the briefs, that they represent but one side of a legal dispute. In every civil liberties case, as in all other cases, there are lawyers on both sides. In particular, in each of the cases presented in this book, there were advocates—usually representing an agency of the government—who attempted to persuade the Supreme Court that there had been no infringement of constitutional rights. On one occasion these efforts met with success (Chapter 15), and on two others the Court declined to hear the case and thus permitted the judgment of the lower court to stand (Chapters 10 and 19). The important fact is that in brief-writing, unlike scholarly work, the context is an adversary proceeding, and the lawyer—including the civil liberties lawyer—has the obligation to express the strongest possible argument on behalf of his client.

A pervasive question that arises in connection with much civil liberties litigation is whether the so-called test case really results in lasting gains, or whether the effect of these victories is merely sporadic and must be relitigated continually as government officials repeat a forbidden transgression on individual rights. This problem has been notably presented in recent years in connection with the Supreme Court decisions in the *School Segregation Cases* and the *School Prayer Cases.* In both situations there has been widespread reluctance on the part of officials to comply with either the letter or the spirit of the Court's pronouncements.

This is indeed a serious problem. Unless court victories are followed up, there will frequently be backsliding due either to ignorance of the new judicial rule or to bureaucratic resistance to a change in established policies. The central problem is not that of establishing rights; rather it is in ensuring that these rights will be recognized and honored in the everyday affairs of men. Most constitutional rights can be nullified by illegal police actions in the streets, by the actions of unyielding public officials in their defense of the status quo, and by massive resistance or even mere indifference from the populace at large. This difficulty is most pronounced in the area of civil liberties, but it occurs in other types of litigation.

The remedy seems to me to be in two stages. First, government agencies should promptly disseminate information concerning new legal requirements and check periodically as to whether administrative practices have been modified accordingly. Secondly, if these internal controls either are lacking or are ineffective because of widespread lack of sympathy on the part of officials and members of the public for a new legal requirement, the civil liberties lawyer must try to force compliance, usually by instituting new suits. When the opposition to a judicial decision is particularly strong, as with the *School Prayer* or *School Desegregation Cases,* this becomes a long-drawn-out process, and it may be years or even decades before persistent efforts crumble the illegal resistance and secure rights that previously were won only on paper.

The general reader should be alerted to the way in which case references are used in briefs and the other legal writing contained in this book. There is nothing mysterious about the process. Each decided case stands for one or more propositions of law that have been determined by a court. In trying to establish a new proposition, it is obviously useful for a lawyer to rely on analogous existing decisions and to try to "distinguish" as resting on irrelevant grounds decisions that are inconsistent with the new proposition. Because courts ordinarily do not wish to deviate from earlier rulings, it is frequently necessary for lawyers—especially civil liberties lawyers seeking to break new ground—to engage in this procedure of rational distinction of earlier cases.

The problem is most acute when there is an inconsistent decision standing squarely in the path of the new proposition. This occurred, for example, in connection with the brief in the *Gideon* case (Chapter 13). In this event the civil liberties lawyer must try to persuade the court that the earlier decision should be overruled, either because it was decided erroneously in the first instance or because new circumstances have revealed its undesirability.

This difficulty is somewhat mitigated in civil liberties litigation, however, because the general rules regarding adherence to prior decisions are relaxed when an interpretation of the Constitution is involved. The reason for this is that short of constitutional amendment, only the courts can change a rule that experience has revealed to be erroneous or outdated. In cases that do not involve constitutional points, on the other hand, the legislature is always able to enact a new rule if there is reason to believe that a particular judicial decision was unwise. For this reason the Supreme Court has always been more willing to re-examine civil liberties cases, and this in turn gives greater scope to lawyers seeking to establish new protections for individual rights.

A few words should be added about the form of the material. As already indicated, the selections were adapted for this book from court briefs, memoranda and articles. In most instances adaptation has meant shortening, and in the interest of easy reading I have not indicated where cuts and modifications have been made in text or footnotes. In addition, footnotes have been renumbered. Those who may be interested in the original version should refer to the citations in the notes following each selection; briefs are on file at the United States Supreme Court and selected law libraries.

These preliminary remarks are intended to acquaint the reader with some aspects of the work of the civil liberties lawyer, especially one operating from a base in a law school. The chapters that follow will, it is hoped, provide concrete evidence of the range and importance of the constitutional issues that the American people regularly present for resolution by all institutions of government, but above all by the Supreme Court. If new light is thereby shed on the nature and fragility of liberty in a complex and turbulent society, a chief goal of this book will have been achieved.

N.D.

Acknowledgments

The notes to each chapter list my many collaborators, both lawyers and law students, to all of whom I am deeply indebted. They lent their efforts because of a conviction that they were engaged in important work on behalf of civil liberty. I can think of no other motivation that could have led to more dedicated service.

Among the most valuable of my associates have been the Arthur Garfield Hays and Robert Marshall Civil Liberties Fellows of the Hays Program. Long before it became common for civil liberties lawyers to use law students widely, I had learned to my great advantage, and I hope to theirs, that bright and enthusiastic students can be of enormous assistance in countless ways, whether the project at hand is a brief, a speech, an article or a memorandum. Appendix A contains the names of those who have become Civil Liberties Fellows since the inception of the Hays Program. The reader should recognize that although the work of only some of the Fellows is reflected in this book, the others made important contributions to other projects of the program.

Appendix B is a roster of the Advisory Committee to the Hays Program, including those who, as the Hays Memorial Committee, were mainly responsible for establishing this unit at the New York University School of Law. Included are many of the most brilliant civil liberties lawyers in the nation. Their counsel and company have added considerably to the professional and personal satisfaction that I have derived from my work.

Even at the risk of unjustified omissions, I must acknowledge certain special obligations. Melvin L. Wulf, Legal Director of the American Civil Liberties Union, and Leonard B. Boudin, General Counsel of the Emergency Civil Liberties Committee, have been my colleagues on numerous occasions, and I have profited from their experience and wisdom. Three other members of the ACLU family have earned my gratitude: John de J. Pemberton, the effective and modest Executive Director of the Union; Associate Director Alan Reitman, who has had a vital influence on civil liberties for two decades; and Roger Baldwin, a founder of the ACLU, a founder of the Hays Program and a tireless, joyous and humane person.

Several students and former students assisted in adapting the various selections for this volume. I am, in particular, greatly in debt to David Rudovsky. He is not only co-author of Chapter 6 and a valued contributor to other chapters, but he efficiently and imaginatively participated in every aspect of the editing process. In addition, Norman J. Chachkin, Alan D. Freeman and Michael D. Kaufman all rendered valuable help in editing and preparing introductions for some chapters, and John C. Gray, Jr., and Stephen Gillers tried to assure technical accuracy throughout the book.

Finally, I am grateful to Miss Dede Fuchs, Mrs. Arlene Tolopko and Miss Dorothy Waleski for their excellent secretarial work, often under chaotic conditions.

N. D.

September 1967

FRONTIERS OF CIVIL LIBERTIES

SECTION I

GENERAL PROBLEMS OF CIVIL LIBERTY

Civil liberty comprises generally the conditions of individual freedom. A free society attempts to secure individual autonomy, self-development and self-expression, and the protection of all persons and groups from unjustified coercive action by the government and private parties. Although these goals are general and incapable of absolute achievement, and although the civil liberties designed to accommodate them are subject to redefinition, the latter include at least freedom of speech, thought and religion, the right to fair procedures in judicial and other proceedings, and the right to equal treatment at the hands of government. And as ideas of human freedom have altered and enlarged, civil liberty, for many, has come to include two other important rights: the assurance of minimal economic subsistence for an individual and his family, and protection by the government against privately wielded power which may destroy his freedom. The ultimate aim, it should be stressed again, is the realization by each person of his full intellectual, political and spiritual potentialities.

A distinctive feature of civil liberties is that, in the United States at least, they do not depend on the grace or discretion of a legislative or popular majority, but rather belong to each person, in the words of the Declaration of Independence, as "inalienable rights" that transcend the politics and passions of the day. As Justice Robert H. Jackson expressed the idea in a leading case:

The very purpose of a Bill of Rights was to withdraw certain subjects from the vicissitudes of political controversy, to place them beyond the reach of majorities and officials and to establish them as legal principles to be applied by the courts. One's right to life, liberty, and property, to free speech, a free press, freedom of worship and assembly, and other fundamental rights may not be submitted to vote; they depend on the outcome of no elections.

Because civil liberties are beyond the reach of the majority and their legislative representatives, they are in a sense inconsistent with democratic theory—that government policy is shaped by the dominant political group. Thus, whether it is tax policy, labor policy or foreign policy, the number of votes in Congress, or in the state legislatures, ordinarily determines official action. The exceptional status of civil liberties therefore requires some justification.

The first two chapters in this section deal with this problem and the closely related issue of the role of the Supreme Court in American government. Chapter 1 focuses on the source of individual liberty in the United States, the Bill of Rights, with a view to ascertaining whether a written charter of liberty is essential by comparing the experience under it with the situation in countries with similar traditions that lack a bill of rights. This chapter also examines the justification for judicial review—the doctrine that empowers the courts to treat as legal nullities statutes and other official acts that are inconsistent with a provision of the Constitution. It is this doctrine that gives the American judiciary its enormous influence on public issues that elsewhere would be within the sole prerogative of the political branches of government. This is true even though the courts will often be responsive to public opinion in constitutional cases, perhaps out of a desire to achieve a national consensus, perhaps out of a desire to maintain its goodwill with the general public, and perhaps out of self-protection against the retribution of an aroused Congress, which controls the judiciary's purse and at least some of its jurisdiction.

Chapter 2 concentrates on the Supreme Court, which has final responsibility for interpreting the Bill of Rights, and therefore final responsibility—subject to constitutional amendment—for defining civil liberty. The discussion, built around recent controversial cases, analyzes the sources and nature of civil liberty and presents competing views about the manner in which the Supreme Court should exercise its awesome powers.

The third and fourth chapters illustrate different ways in which the system can go wrong. Chapter 3 focuses on an example of congressional criticism, but one that was hardly constructive. It contains a detailed answer to the charge of Senator James Eastland, Chairman of the Senate Judiciary Committee, that certain Supreme Court decisions were "pro-Communist." As Professors Paul Bator and Alexander Bickel point out in Chapter 2, there are substantial grounds to challenge the wisdom of many of the Court's decisions. But the kind of attack leveled by Senator Eastland not only was without basis in fact, it also made the task of serious critics of the Court more difficult and subject to popular misinterpretation.

Chapter 4 deals with the phenomenon of McCarthyism from an angle that has been largely unexplored. Although it is well known that Senator McCarthy was casual about individual liberties and did much to perpetuate a cold-war climate in the United States during the early 1950s, it has not often been noticed that McCarthy himself was without the actual power to harm individuals. For this he had to rely on the agencies of government with authority to act, and all too frequently he was not disappointed in the consequences. How and why the United States Army capitulated to him, and the effect on the civil liberties of Army employees and military personnel, are the basic themes of this chapter.

The chapter on McCarthy and the Army considers one way in which problems of civil liberty arise from the actions of legislators and government officials. Chapter 5 approaches this issue from another perspective: the effect that a high state officer, the New York Attorney General, can have on the rights of the individual citizen through the development of state policy, legislation and law enforcement.

Chapter 6, the final chapter in this section, explores an issue of utmost contemporary importance: civil liberties in wartime. Under the stress of war, governments have traditionally disrespected the rights of individuals who dissent from official policy. And though the Vietnam war has not been accompanied so far by repression on a large scale, some instances have recently come to light. This problem of free speech and two other novel issues of civil liberty that have emerged during the war are the subjects of this chapter.

1

Civil Liberties and the Bill of Rights

A fundamental question concerning the American Constitution is whether its reduction to written form, and particularly the incorporation of a bill of rights, has served to expand the freedom of the people. The problem has intrigued many scholars, who have compared the American experience with that of other nations which share common traditions but lack a written constitution. It is of considerable contemporary importance as new nations of Africa and Asia wrestle with the question whether to draft a bill of rights to guarantee basic freedoms to their citizens. A related controversy, which has persisted in the United States for more than 150 years, concerns the legitimacy of the power of judges to invalidate action by the federal and state governments that is found to be inconsistent with a provision of the Constitution. Although this power is essential to the operation of the Bill of Rights in the United States, it is nowhere expressed in the Constitution and has frequently been challenged as judicial usurpation at the expense of the other branches of government. These themes are the subject of the following essay.

An analysis of the implications for civil liberty of a bill of rights is an appropriate one as we meet to recall the first issuance of Magna Carta 750 years ago. The Great Writ, as it came to be known, was the initial and indispensable document of individual freedom under Anglo-American law. Derivable from it are our basic liberties—among them the security of private property, the security of the person, the right to judgment by one's peers, the right to seek redress of grievances from the sovereign, and the great and mysterious concept of due process of law—then called "the law of the land." It would be possible, therefore, to consider the precise ways in which the Charter laid the groundwork for American liberty and how its clauses are linked umbilically to our Constitution. But I shall resist the temptation to canvass the history in detail and instead shall venture certain views on two more general issues of contemporary concern—first, the origins and premises of a functioning and effective bill of rights, and second, the practical consequences for freedom, if any, of a *written* constitution containing a bill of rights.

I

The first question demands insistent inquiry into the original decision in 1791 to incorporate a written pledge of rights in the American Constitution. If we recognize that the historical foundations for individual liberty by then had been laid in England, that that nation had eschewed a written constitution, that the concept of freedom might easily have been rigidified in a document at the expense of organic growth of principle at the hands of right-minded judges, we swiftly perceive that the decision to promulgate a bill of rights in the United States was far from inevitable.

Indeed, there were powerful voices among the framers who were opposed to the Bill of Rights. Chief among them was Hamilton. He thought such guarantees "less applicable" to a constitution "like that under consideration, which is merely intended to regulate the general political interests of the nation, than to a constitution which has the regulation of every species of personal and private concerns."[1] Hamilton believed that a bill of rights was suitable for the constitutions of the states, which retained residual legislative power, but not for the federal government, because of the danger that enumeration of the powers denied to the central government would suggest that these were merely exceptions to a general federal power to deal with the subject matter. For example, he maintained "that the provision against restraining the liberty of the press afforded a clear implication that a power to prescribe proper regulations concerning [the press] was intended to be vested in the national government."[2]

The Constitutional Convention rejected—and in my view properly—Hamilton's fear of what he called the "doctrine of constructive powers." The answer to Hamilton is, I think, that no one ever supposed the government to have been granted powers *for the purpose of* interfering with individual liberties. The real problem, as history has shown, is that the liberty of the people might be infringed through the exercise of otherwise legitimate governmental powers such as the power to regulate commerce or to provide for the national defense.

Hamilton had a stronger argument against the inclusion of a written bill of rights. Building on the canon of statutory construction *expressio unius, exclusio alterius*—to include one is to exclude any other—he could say that enumeration of particular liberties "would disparage those rights which were not placed in that enumeration."[3]

That there was such a risk is clear. The example of modern India reveals the perils of statutory definiteness in a constitutional document. Article 14 of the Indian Constitution contains a general guarantee of equal protection of the laws similar to our own Fourteenth Amendment. But article 15 elaborates the general protection as follows: "(1) The State shall not discriminate against any citizen on grounds only of religion, race, caste, sex, place of birth or any of them."[4] The incompleteness of this list is apparent from recent cases in the United States Supreme Court that have applied the equal protection clause on behalf of the class of indigent criminal defendants. Could similar decisions be reached under the particularized Indian Bill of Rights? Probably not—even if the word "only" were omitted from the document. No doubt there are other arbitrary classifications omitted from the Indian list which would be more difficult to establish because of the specificity of article 15.

The framers of the American Constitution wisely refrained from potentially strangling specification. On the contrary, the general phrases "equal protection of the laws," "due process" and "privileges and immunities" were inserted so that the Constitution "intended to endure for ages to come" and "to be adapted to the various crises of human affairs"[5] would not embody the means for its own emasculation.

Yet another device was utilized to assure that the detailing of certain rights would not exclude all others. James Madison, believing Hamilton's position "one of the most plausible arguments"[6] made against the Bill of Rights, responded with the Ninth Amendment, which tersely provides that "The enumeration in the Constitution, of certain rights, shall not be construed to deny or disparage others retained by the people." As prophesied by my colleague Professor Norman Redlich, the Supreme Court, in the *Connecticut Birth Control Case,* has finally returned a dividend on Madison's investment.[7] Three Justices turned to this half-forgotten provision to secure a right to privacy in the intimate aspects of the marriage relationship.[8]

We must now examine an unspoken premise of our discussion of a written constitution—the existence of an independent judiciary with the power and duty to invalidate statutes and official acts found to be inconsistent with the document. Without such a conceded power on behalf of the judiciary, the written words will have an admonitory influence rather than a legal consequence. It will be the task of the second portion of this paper to examine the importance of this distinction between admonition and rule of law, but for the present we shall assume that judicially enforced guarantees do make a difference to liberty and consider instead the *right* of judges to exercise the awesome and, for all practical purposes under our constitutional scheme, final power of judicial review.

This is not an idle inquiry. On its result depends the legitimacy of the entire institution of judicial review, and only from this legitimacy can one mobilize popular and professional support for an arguably undemocratic doctrine that permits appointive judges serving for life to invalidate decisions of the political representatives of the people.

It will be recalled that as early as 1803, in the leading case of *Marbury v. Madison,* Chief Justice Marshall ruled that the federal courts possessed the vital power to declare acts of the legislature inoperative if they were found to be inconsistent with the written Constitution. Marshall cleverly chose a highly technical case in which to make this important pronouncement increasing judicial power. Moreover, he made sure that the actual result of the case—it denied the former Federalist President John Adams the right to pack local courts with last-minute appointees—would please the new administration of Republican Thomas Jefferson, thus tempering their criticism of Marshall's opinion.

Throughout our history there have been those who denied the existence of the power. Not two decades after *Marbury v. Madison,* a leading state judge vigorously contended that "the foundation of every argument in favor of the right of the judiciary, is found, at last, to be an assumption of the whole ground in dispute."[9] This view of the matter was not idiosyncratic. As recently as 1938, the respected Professor Morris Cohen maintained that Marshall's reasoning in *Marbury v. Madison* was "baseless," that the existence of power was "by no means generally understood" at the time of the Convention, that the Union would not be imperiled if the power were lacking, and that the arguments supporting the restriction of "the democratic will by the judgment of a few elderly gentlemen" (as Cohen put it) were "precisely those which the adherents of Hitler and Mussolini use against the frailty of democratically representative or elective government."[10]

More recently, Judge Learned Hand lent his powerful voice to those who doubted the general grant of judicial review in the Constitution, although he conceded at last that it was "essential to prevent the defeat of the venture at hand"—i.e., the new government—for the Supreme Court to assume at least some of this power.[11] Judge Hand was not playing with words. From his approach there naturally emerged a theory of limited judicial review that cautioned the Supreme Court not to exercise its prerogative whenever it "sees, or thinks that it sees, an invasion of the Constitution."[12] With this conclusion Judge Hand placed himself in the constitutional tradition spearheaded in the last century by Professor James B. Thayer of the Harvard Law School, who opined that a court can only disregard a statute when those "who have the right to make laws have not merely made a mistake, but have made a very clear one—so clear that it is not open to rational question."[13] Judge Hand, in short, by grudgingly recognizing a right of judicial review, implicitly cautioned judges to exercise the power with extreme reluctance if at all.

The difficulty, with all respect, is that Judge Hand, Professor Cohen and the others were wrong, and their error greatly weakens the dependent theory of limited judicial review. I hasten to add that if the evidence were really doubtful or if this were a conclusion drawn by me alone, I should hesitate long before uttering such a flat statement. But the evidence is bountiful and the weight of authority sufficient to justify such seeming impudence.

For example, Dean Roscoe Pound concluded, after full examination of the evidence, that the claim that judicial review is judicial usurpation is abundantly refuted by the

clear understanding of American lawyers before the Revolution, based on the seventeenth-century books in which they had been taught, the unanimous course of decision after independence and down to the adoption of the Constitution, not to speak of the writings of the two prime movers in the convention which drafted the instrument.[14]

Some of the abundant evidence for judicial review traces to the relationship between the English mother country and her far-flung possessions. The "Instrument of Government," drawn up in 1653, provided for certain fundamental rights in the colonies, and stated further that "all laws, statutes, ordinances, and clauses in any law statute and ordinance to the contrary of the aforesaid liberty shall be esteemed null and void."[15] This century-old statute was of course a cornerstone of colonial jurisprudence easily assimilated by the new American government.

Finally, as Dean Pound demonstrated through his researches, the course of decision in the Americas *before* as well as after independence lent strong support to his conclusion. Perhaps the earliest instance was the celebrated trial of John Peter Zenger for publishing a newspaper criticizing the royal governor in New York. In the manner of tyrants high and petty, then and always, the governor sought to still the independent voice, and he arranged for Zenger's indictment for seditious libel. Andrew Hamilton, a leading Philadelphia lawyer, defended Zenger and secured an acquittal relying on Magna Carta, the concept of the "law of the land," and the liberty of the subject. In those days issues of law as well as fact could be argued to the jury, so the victory of Zenger in a case in which the facts were essentially undisputed was as much a victory for the primacy of the courts as for freedom of the press and opinion.[16]

The gist of it is that there seems to be ample justification for Professor Herbert Wechsler's statement, "I have not the slightest doubt respecting the legitimacy of judicial review, whether the action called in question in a case which otherwise is proper for adjudication is legislative or executive, federal or state."[17]

II

The origins and premises of the Bill of Rights are important, but practical men may take a more pragmatic approach. What is the actual effect of a written constitution? What difference does it make to civil liberty, and exactly how?

It will be useful to deal with two preliminary issues. First we must ask ourselves, what is "liberty" or "civil liberty"? Even partial research discloses a plethora of definitions, both legal and philosophical,[18] but from the sea of words there seem to emerge two broad positions of relevance to lawyers. Each suggests a particular line of inquiry and a particular purpose of law.

The first focuses on the liberty of the subject in relation to the state—his personal freedom from the arbitrary exercise of power by those authorized in a politically organized society to adjust relations and order conduct, and so who are able to apply the force of that society to individuals.[19] The second approach is quite different; it concentrates on the potentially liberating force of government. In the words of Professor Joseph Snee, the goal of law is to assist individuals "to realize" themselves, that is, to create "a society rationally organized for the purpose of establishing, maintaining and perfecting the conditions necessary and appropriate for community life to perform its role in the complete development of man."[20]

To many the latter definition may seem utopian, and to some even dangerously paternalistic. And although we shall not dwell on it, it is a view of the nature of liberty and of law that is increasingly being recognized as pertinent to individual development in a complex, urban society.

To choose as our touchstone "negative liberty"—freedom from arbitrary state power—does not solve all problems of definition. An especially tough question is whether we mean to protect under the concept "civil liberty" only what have come to be known as "personal rights," or whether we should pay heed also to "property rights"?

The covers of many books have been stretched by this theme, and I would not presume in a paragraph to do more than pose the issue. But I should like to do so by quoting once more from Judge Learned Hand, who two decades ago said that "when 'personal rights' were in issue [in the Supreme Court], something strangely akin to the discredited attitude toward the Bill of Rights of the old apostles of the institution of property was gaining recognition." Judge Hand then observed, "Just why property itself was not a 'personal right' nobody took the time to explain."[21] Professor Paul A. Freund, selecting one of several possible readings of these Delphic words, later wrote:

> *Judge Hand has contributed to clarity of analysis by reminding us that the relevant comparison is not between the enduring values of free inquiry and expression on the one hand, and transitory measures for the control of property on the other; the problem is harder than that. We are obliged to compare the ultimate values of property with those of free inquiry and expression, or to compare the legislative compromises in the two realms.*[22]

It is possible to reply to Professor Freund that the issue of the constitutional protection afforded "property" and "personal" rights need not turn on their imponderable long-term value to society, but rather on more practical legal considerations. For example, the Bill of Rights contains a detailed list of protected "personal rights" but makes only a vague, general reference to the right of property.

Moreover, "personal rights" relate mainly to questions of procedure in which judges presumably have special expertness, and enforcement of these rights requires little or no resort to economic and social facts that may be beyond the ability of the judicial process to establish. This is not to say that rights to personal property are to be disregarded. It is rather to suggest that the now established Supreme Court practice of upholding legislation that incidentally reduces the value of property while it regulates economic and social conditions rests on a sound basis.

The second preliminary issue is, if anything, even thornier, and it brings us but a step away from our central inquiry into the value of a written constitution and bill of rights. The issue will be familiar to practicing lawyers—what are the relevant standards for deciding the question and where do they come from? Should we ask, which is the freest society, even assuming we could determine this fact? Or would it be possible to estimate how any given nation with a written constitution would have developed without one, or vice versa? In the absence of materials with which to make these judgments, we are, it seems to me, thrown back upon specific instances and general estimates.

Fortunately, there are others who have blazed the trail and lighted the way. Chief among these is the late Professor Edmond Cahn, who, in a thoughtful essay appropriately entitled "The Parchment Barriers," faced up to this problem.[23]

The main theme of the paper on "parchment barriers" is that no matter how courageous the man, "without an authoritative text the modern democratic judge . . . will certainly decline to overrule or annul a legislative decision."[24] On the other hand, the judge with a written constitutional text is in an entirely different position. "He feels equipped with legitimate standards of decision and ready to perform his function independently and manfully."[25]

There is much support for Professor Cahn's thesis. In the United States, the courts, particularly in recent years, have voided both federal and state enactments that impinged on civil liberty. The reports contain many cases upholding claims that freedom of expression, freedom of religion or the right to due process has been denied.[26] And there are other decisions in which courts have vindicated the right to equal protection of the laws at the instance of those wishing their ballots to be counted at par or their horizons not to be limited by the color of their skins.[27]

Furthermore, we should not make the mistake of looking only to instances in which the judiciary has actually invalidated legislation or executive action. There is another, perhaps more important, category of cases in which the power of judicial review is manifested. I refer to the numerous decisions in which statutes and administrative orders have been construed, sometimes artificially, with an eye to avoiding serious constitutional questions. One example must suffice. In *United States v. Rumely*,[28] the Supreme Court limited the meaning of the phrase "lobbying activities intended to influence, promote or retard legislation" which was found in a congressional resolution authorizing a committee investigation. The Court held that the phrase merely covered representations made directly to members of Congress rather than all attempts to influence public opinion concerning legislation. The reason? Following traditional practice, the Court thought its function best fulfilled by deciding constitutional questions only if absolutely necessary to determine the controversy before it. And *Rumely*, to put it mildly, did involve a sticky constitutional issue: whether a congressional investigating committee was interfering with freedom of expression and the press by interrogating a publisher who had disseminated certain unpopular ideas. By construing the lobbying phrase narrowly, the Court relieved the witness from committee questions without the need for a constitutional decision. But there is no doubt that the Bill of Rights did the trick by encouraging a narrow interpretation.

Despite the substantial support for the importance of "parchment barriers," there is another side to the story. Among others, Professor A. V. Dicey, the nineteenth-century fountainhead of modern British constitutional law, ridiculed the "mere paper affirmations"[29] of a bill of rights. Who can say that Professor Dicey's judgment has not been buttressed by twentieth-century history? The German Weimar Republic had a written constitution and bill of rights, and this not only was the vehicle for the rise of Nazism, but was used after 1932 to provide an air of macabre legality to that venal government. Even today Communist Rumania and Falangist Spain boast written documents guaranteeing the rights of their peoples to free expression and religion as well as relief from arbitrary police practices.

These barriers have, as I understand it, proved to be parchment indeed.

But perhaps we should not look so far afield. How have the other English-speaking nations fared—those countries that share our legal tradition but whose courts do not possess the power of judicial review? Three instances involving three different countries may lead the all-out advocate of written constitutions to give the matter a second thought.

The first two suggest that courts can reach common decisions irrespective of the existence of a legally enforceable bill of rights. Thus, the Supreme Court of Canada about a decade ago refused in a 5–4 decision to apply a bylaw of the City of Quebec forbidding distribution in the streets of any book, pamphlet or tract without written prior permission of the chief of police.[30] The bylaw was challenged, appropriately enough, by a member of Jehovah's Witnesses, a group whose propensity to litigate has contributed so much to our own constitutional development. One Justice of the Supreme Court decided in favor of the witness as a matter of statutory construction, but his four concurring colleagues in effect exercised a power of judicial review by denying Quebec the power to authorize the ordinance on a theory that smacked of a natural-law freedom of religion.[31] The result would be the same in the United States,[32] of course, but the point is that our northern neighbor managed very well without an entrenched bill of rights, at least as to provincial legislation.

A second instance suggests that decisions in tandem may go *counter* to civil liberty. The celebrated English decision in 1942 in *Liversidge v. Anderson*[33] upheld the power of the Home Secretary to detain any person if the secretary had "reasonable cause to believe [him] to be of hostile origin or associations or to have been recently concerned in acts prejudicial to the public safety or the defense of the realm." The court did not wish to embarrass the executive in time of war, even though the vague standard authorizing detention was hardly comforting to those who revered the rule of law. But before we smugly condemn what to some may appear the lapse of a system unblessed with a bill of rights, we should recall our own *Japanese Internment Case,* in which the United States Supreme Court in 1944 sustained the indiscriminate rounding up and confinement of persons of Japanese blood on the West Coast during the early years of World War II.[34]

My final example casts us in even a darker light. The case of the "First-String Communists" was decided in the Supreme Court in 1951, and the upshot was that individuals could be sentenced to long prison terms under a law that prohibited not any act to overthrow the government, nor indeed advocacy of such overthrow, but conspiracy to advocate the overthrow of the government.[35] Thus speech twice removed from action was criminally punished despite the injunction of the First Amendment that "Congress shall make no law abridging the freedom of speech." In contrast with this result, the Supreme Court of Australia, operating *without* a bill of rights, found it possible in the same cold-war year of 1951 to render ineffective the Australian Communist Party Dissolution Act, which was introduced with the stated aim of dissolving the party and preventing Communists from holding office in trade unions and in the government service.[36] A narrow statutory construction was the device employed in Australia, but a major theme underlying the judges' opinions was that a statute that attaches legal incapacities to individuals independent of standards of personal responsibility runs counter to fundamental principles inherent in the common law.

So there we have a pair of cases in which the nation without the bill of rights fared very well, at least insofar as traditional canons of civil liberty are concerned.

Does this history serve to invalidate Professor Cahn's conclusion that a written bill of rights is indispensable to liberty, or at least a prime prerequisite to an independent and sturdy judiciary? Was Dicey therefore correct in disparaging "mere paper affirmations"?

Some of our most eminent judges have suggested this conclusion by strongly doubting the power of courts to protect the people from tyranny. As Justice Frankfurter put it, "Self-discipline and the voters [not the courts] must be the ultimate reliance for discouraging or correcting . . . abuses."[37] The same idea was expressed by Justice Robert Jackson shortly before his death:

> *. . . I know of no modern instance in which any judiciary has saved a whole people from the great currents of intolerance, passion, usurpation, and tyranny which have threatened liberty and free institutions. . . . I doubt that any court, whatever its powers, could have saved Louis XVI*

or Marie Antoinette. None could have avoided the French Revolution, none could have stopped its excesses, and none could have prevented its culmination in the dictatorship of Napoleon.[38]

But for the classic statement of the position we again turn to Judge Learned Hand, who said:

Liberty lies in the hearts of men and women; when it dies there, no constitution, no law, no court can save it; no constitution, no law, no court can even do much to help it. While it lies there it needs no constitution, no law, no court to save it.[39]

Are these jurists correct? Do the protections of the Bill of Rights come virtually to naught? I do not think so.

The Supreme Court may not always have acted in the libertarian tradition, and it certainly has not solved, nor could it solve, all problems of freedom and discrimination. But we must not be blind to what it has achieved. To mention only the obvious, it has played an enormously constructive role in securing for the Negro the right to vote, to travel, to educate his children, in short, to participate fully in the life of the nation. In addition, after default by the political branches of government, the Court has taken the lead in the sensitive task of trying to assure each citizen that his vote will not be discounted because of invidious apportionment of legislative districts. Finally, the Court has been a major force in reforming the rules governing criminal trials by establishing minimum standards to protect the accused. These exercises of judicial power will not, of course, be to everyone's taste, but the critical impact of the Bill of Rights coupled with judicial review is there for all to see.

Finally, I shall lean on a quotation from Professor Henry M. Hart to try to show why Judge Hand and those aligned with him are guilty of a logical fallacy as well as of underestimating the practical importance of a functioning bill of rights. Professor Hart has pointed out that Judge Hand's statement quoted above

assumes that there are two kinds of societies—one kind, over here, in which the spirit of moderation flourishes, and another kind, over here, which is riven by dissension. Neither kind, Judge Hand says, can be helped very much by the courts. But, of course, that isn't what societies are like. In particular, it isn't what American society is like. A society is a something in process—in process of becoming. It has always within it, as ours does, seeds of dissension. And it has also within it forces making for moderation and mutual accommodation. The question—the relevant question—is whether the courts have a significant contribution to make in pushing American society in the direction of moderation—not by themselves; of course they can't save us by themselves; but in combination with other institutions. Once the question is put that way, the answer, it seems to me, has to be yes.[40]

And with that I agree.

NOTES

This paper was delivered in October 1965 at a convocation at the New York University School of Law celebrating the 750th anniversary of Magna Carta. It was subsequently published with the title "Civil Liberty Under a Constitutional Document," in 21 *The Record* (The Association of the Bar of the City of New York) 73 (February 1966) and in 66 *New York University Arts and Sciences* No. 24 at 16 (Spring 1966). The author received research assistance from Douglas S. Liebhafsky.

1. *The Federalist* No. 8 (Mentor ed. 1961).
2. *Ibid.*
3. *Ibid.*
4. As quoted in Franck, *Comparative Constitutional Process* (tent. ed. 1965). Cf. article 37 of the Constitution of Nigeria, quoted in *id.*
5. McCulloch v. Maryland, 17 U.S. (4 Wheat.) 316, 415 (1819).
6. 1 *Annals of Cong.* 456 (1789).
7. Redlich, "Are There Certain Rights . . . Retained by the People?" 37 *N.Y.U.L. Rev.* 787 (1962).
8. Griswold v. Connecticut, 381 U.S. 479 (1965).
9. Eakin v. Raub, 12 S. & R. 330 (Pa. 1825).
10. Cohen, *The Faith of a Liberal* 182–85, 192 (1946).
11. Hand, *The Bill of Rights* 10–15 (1958).
12. *Id.* at 15.
13. Thayer, "The Origin and Scope of the American Doctrine of Constitutional Law," 7 *Harv. L. Rev.* 129, 144 (1893).
14. Pound, *The Development of Constitutional Guarantees of Liberty* 110 (1957).
15. As quoted in *id.* at 62.
16. For a discussion of the case, see *id.* at 183–84.
17. Wechsler, *Principles, Politics, and Fundamental Law* 4 (1960).

18. For a collection of some of these, see Deutsch, "Strategies of Freedom: The Widening of Choices and the Change of Goals," in *Nomos IV, Liberty* (Friedrich ed. 1962).

19. Pound, *op. cit. supra* note 14 at 1.

20. See *Government under Law* 96, 142 (Sutherland ed. 1956).

21. Hand, "Chief Justice Stone's Conception of the Judicial Function," 46 *Colum. L. Rev.* 696, 698 (1946).

22. Freund, *The Supreme Court of the United States* 34–35 (1961).

23. Printed in 32 *American Scholar* 21 (Winter 1962–63).

24. *Id.* at 34.

25. *Id.* at 35.

26. E.g., Near v. Minnesota, 283 U.S. 697 (1931); Sherbert v. Verner, 374 U.S. 398 (1963); Rochin v. California, 352 U.S. 165 (1952).

27. E.g., Wesberry v. Sanders, 376 U.S. 1 (1964); Brown v. Board of Education, 347 U.S. 483 (1954).

28. 345 U.S. 41 (1953).

29. See generally Dicey, *The Law of the Constitution* 341 *et seq.* (1st ed. 1885).

30. Saumur v. City of Quebec and Attorney General of Canada, [1953] 4 D.L.R. 641.

31. *Id.* at 670. On Canada's civil liberties, see generally Tarnopolsky, *The Canadian Bill of Rights* (1966).

32. See, e.g., Cantwell v. Connecticut, 310 U.S. 296 (1940).

33. [1942] A.C. 206.

34. Korematsu v. United States, 323 U.S. 214 (1944).

35. Dennis v. United States, 341 U.S. 494 (1951).

36. Australian Communist Party v. Commonwealth, [1951] 83 C.L.R. 1.

37. See Tenney v. Brandhove, 341 U.S. 367, 378 (1951).

38. Jackson, *The Supreme Court in the American System of Government* 80 (1955).

39. Hand, *The Spirit of Liberty* 190 (Dilliard ed. 1953).

40. See the remarks of Professor Hart in *Government under Law* 140–41 (Sutherland ed. 1956).

2

The United States Supreme Court and Civil Liberties

A Conference

The proper role of the Supreme Court in civil liberties cases, while always hotly disputed, rarely was put in sharper focus than during the 1962 Term of Court. Accordingly, despite the generality of the topic, in March 1963 the Arthur Garfield Hays Civil Liberties Program organized a conference on this subject. The participants were Professor Paul M. Bator of Harvard Law School, Professor Caleb Foote, then of Pennsylvania Law School and now of the University of California Law School at Berkeley, and Professors Alexander M. Bickel and Charles A. Reich of Yale Law School.

I / Introduction (Norman Dorsen)

For purposes of convenience, the broad question that was the subject of the conference was divided into two parts. The first, to which Professors Paul Bator and Caleb Foote addressed themselves, centered on the Supreme Court's role in deciding constitutional issues arising from the administration of the criminal law. The second involved what Professor Alexander Bickel described as "more exciting subject matter." There will certainly be a difference of opinion about this, but in any event he and Professor Charles Reich spoke on a wider front. As I followed the discussion of both parts, an overriding theme appeared time and again—the pervasive and remarkable changes that have recently occurred in the Court's approach to constitutional problems, and the induced change in orientation by students of the Court's work. Justice Harlan drew public attention to this phenomenon when he recently wrote, with no particular enthusiasm, of "the swift pace of current constitutional adjudication."[1]

What is the explanation? In his remarks, Professor Reich presented his thumbnail view of the matter in terms of the rapid changes that have occurred in our society over the past fifty years. Yet this offers only a partial answer. It may explain long-range trends, but it provides no clear insight into the causes of the accelerated doctrinal change that began soon after the accession of the present Chief Justice. A climax was reached on March 18, 1963, less than two weeks after the Hays Conference, when the Supreme Court overruled no fewer than four earlier decisions.[2]

Explanations aside, it is a fact that the Court is moving at a rapid rate. Perhaps it is keeping pace with the movement and the mood in the country and in the legal profession, and perhaps not. And this may not even be a fair question concerning an institution charged with the constitutional responsibility to curb excesses of the political majority as they threaten, in myriad ways, minorities of all stripes and shades.

This quiet judicial revolution is associated in the popular mind with the not quite so quiet Negro revolution, in which men and women of color are attempting to secure for themselves and their posterity rights and privileges long denied. *Brown v. Board of Education,*[3] its predecessors and its progeny, of course provide the basis for this view. Indeed, one wonders whether gains made through direct action and through the efforts of other branches of government would have been forthcoming without the impetus of Supreme Court decisions and the intangible but nonetheless real moral support the Court provides to the Negro as the governmental institution most generally held to embody the ethical norms of the society.

But the chief hallmark of the quiet revolution has not, so it seems, been the Court's participation in the struggle of the American Negro for equality, nor even its bold entry into the arena of political apportionment,[4] but rather its reformulation of constitutional standards in criminal cases, particularly on behalf of the penniless defendant. The seminal case was *Griffin v. Illinois*,[5] where the Court ruled that a state is required under the Fourteenth Amendment to provide a transcript free of charge to a defendant who cannot afford one if the transcript is necessary to the perfection of an appeal available to the defendant of means. This decision has been steadily applied to other aspects of the criminal process.[6] In this light, *Gideon v. Wainwright*[7] and *Douglas v. California*,[8] requiring states to appoint counsel on behalf of indigent defendants at trial and on appeal, appeared almost inevitable. This is true not only because of the unworkability of the "fundamental unfairness" rule of *Betts v. Brady*,[9] but because of the all but unanimous recognition that the nation as a whole has a duty to equalize, as far as possible, the standing of its people before the criminal bar if "evenhandedness of justice" is to be anything more than a slogan.

The Court has not limited its reformulation of constitutional standards in the criminal law to cases in which the poor are seeking assistance in overcoming their handicapped position. Thus, the Fourth Amendment's prohibition of unreasonable searches and seizures now carries with it the remedy of exclusion of the tainted evidence from state trials,[10] and federal standards are to govern the question of the validity of the search.[11] In a no less important development, the law governing review of state convictions through collateral attack in the federal courts has been thoroughly revamped.[12] The end is not in sight as the Court increasingly devotes attention to assuring the fairness of trials both federal and state.

It may be thought that these doctrinal revisions would be of concern during our conference only to panelists Bator and Foote. But this is not so, for the pertinent cases in the criminal field reflect the resolution of conflicting principles of wider applicability. Thus, Professor Bator's concern over the limits of the Court's usefulness once it has set the basic outlines of due process in the administration of criminal justice is, it seems to me, but a variant of the position taken by Professor Bickel that the Supreme Court must flex its muscles only rarely if the democratic character of our constitutional system is to be preserved. In other words, both Professors Bickel and Bator approached the role of the Court with marked caution—the former because of doubts arising from his conception of the nature of the institution, the latter because of a belief in the practical limitations on its administrative or supervisory power.[13]

The other two participants held a different view. Professor Reich tackled the problem along broad lines, arguing that the prime constitutional responsibility of the Supreme Court is the defense of individual freedom whenever it is threatened by government or the other power groups in the society. He maintained, moreover, that the Court has shown itself a most effective agency for this purpose. The poor, as the largest of our oppressed minorities, must look to the Court as must the Negro, the religious and political dissenter, and the disenfranchised urban voter. Professor Foote likewise puts faith in the Supreme Court, although in the conference he concentrated on a question often slighted—the validity of the factual premises underlying the Court's value judgments. In selecting as his chief example the right of indigent defendants to assigned counsel, shortly to be made a reality in the *Gideon* case, Professor Foote could not be accused of ducking the tough question. His concern that the Supreme Court act only with full awareness of the facts reflects confidence in the Court's power and efficacy, but also a skeptical aloofness from too easy commitment to its judgments, even those that appear most welcome.

The conferees would be the first to agree that their respective statements are not the last word on the work of the Supreme Court. The problems involved are too large, too difficult and (fortunately for the profession) perhaps insoluble. But each of them, I think, has made a distinct contribution to the understanding of the Court's role as it copes with claims of civil liberty under the Constitution.

II / (Paul Bator)

Speculating broadly about the role of the Court in the administration of criminal justice, it is perhaps fair to conclude that we are now reaching the end of one era and entering upon another.

The era we have been in has been striking because of the very prominence of the role played by the Court. If you look at the reports of the Supreme Court fifty years ago, you will find that what might be called the law of due process in the administration of criminal justice was a very rudimentary and meager law indeed. During these fifty years, the Court has, almost singlehandedly, formulated a broad and ambitious "system" of constitutional law. We have, therefore, been going through an era of large-scale movement, of sweeping and creative shifts and growth in doctrine, of basic structural reorientations. The Court has, in this period, established beyond cavil its role as formulator of the basic standards of decency and fairness in the administration of the criminal law. It has outlined these constitutional standards of due process in terms with which you are all familiar: the right to be free from the third degree, the exclusionary rules in connection with search and seizure, the right to have legal representation, the right to have a fair trial before an unbiased tribunal, one not dominated by a mob or hostile community, and all the rest.

I wonder whether one cannot hazard the guess that this era of radical change, of large movements and sweeping alterations of constitutional doctrine, may be drawing to a close? Can we not foresee a period in which the basic outlines of the law of due process in the administration of criminal justice will become stabilized, in which the rate of advance and change will slow considerably?

It seems to me that if one views the field in the large, one senses that the *basic* pattern or structure of great doctrine is largely complete. *Wolf v. Colorado*[14] is dead. I don't think it will be long before *Betts v. Brady*[15] is dead. The major reforms are in place. There remain a few areas where we may still see rather radical shifts in doctrine: self-incrimination perhaps, and double jeopardy. More striking is a field in which the law is still in a wholly rudimentary state: due process of law in postconviction procedures, in sentencing and treatment, where we continue to live in a jungle of total discretion. But with such exceptions acknowledged, it seems to me that we can now expect stabilization in the basic structure of the law of due process in criminal administration.

Where does that leave us? I think there is probably a very broad consensus now on the soundness of this basic structure. There continue to be isolated complaints about *Mapp v. Ohio*;[16] there will be some complaints if *Betts v. Brady* is overruled. But in general there is no *serious* dispute about the correctness of the great doctrines which today embody the notion of what process is "due" in the administration of criminal justice. On the other hand, in this era of large change and movement, the Court has, without doubt, left in its wake what might be called messy areas in the law. If we turn, in other words, from the general structure of doctrine to questions of detail, to particular applications and particular balancings, we will find many places where the situation is not very satisfactory.

The basic task, it seems to me, for those interested in civil rights and liberties in the administration of justice, is that of cleaning up the messes which the Court has left in its wake and of building the general standards of fairness and decency embodied in the great due process doctrines into the day-to-day operations of the criminal law. And the basic question I want to put is this: To what extent should we rely or can we rely on the Court itself to undertake these tasks? The Court has performed admirably in creating what I have called the basic structure of due process, in formulating the large doctrines and general propositions. Can it go much further now that the task is basically no longer a doctrinal one, but rather the one of building an operating system of criminal justice which in its daily workings really does respect liberty and privacy and yet which can cope with the problem of law enforcement?

My general proposition is that it would be a great mistake, a tremendous mistake, to place our only reliance, even our chief reliance, on the Court, because it seems to me that in the field of administration of criminal justice, the principal task we have before us today is not a task of supervision, or of doctrinal building, but rather a task of planning, research, education, legislation and administrative reform at the local level; in other words, a task which is basically *political*.

Why do I say this? If we look at the messy areas created or left by the Court, the striking thing we discover is that very often they are not the result of the fact that the Court has decided a particular case badly or that its reasoning was sloppy here or there. It seems to me that the messy areas, the failure to create a really decent operating system of criminal administration, are basically the product of the inherent crudity of the method of constitutional adjudication as a means of solving detailed questions of application or as a way of building operating systems of criminal administration.

The Court operates in an episodic way. It skims along the surface of a going system and its operations have "bite" only on occasion. More important, the intellectual and analytical tools available to the Court in case-by-case adjudication, the tools of precedent and analogy, and even more important, the research available to the Court and the research it can undertake, are of a very limited range.

Let me give one or two examples. The first is the problem of surveillance, or eavesdropping. We face here a very radical problem because technology is advancing so rapidly that perhaps invasion, and even abolition, of privacy will soon be enormously easy and inexpensive. The technology is such that the things we all know about, wiretapping and spike mikes, will soon be considered medieval in their crudity compared to what is now coming on the market and what will soon be on the market in inexpensive form.

My question is this: Are we really going to place our chief reliance for solution of the problems posed for the administration of criminal justice by this fantastic technology on the Supreme Court and its method of constitutional adjudication? How is the Court going to cope with the terrifying problems of meshing a decent system of criminal-law administration with this technology? Is it an adequate response to this problem to ask the Court to create *ad hoc* rules of evidence derived from the ambiguities of the Fourth Amendment? The problem of privacy and its relation to law enforcement in a day of advanced technology is a highly complicated and basically social and political problem, and I think that the Fourth Amendment will prove to be a very limited kind of tool for dealing with it. Case-by-case constitutional adjudication is not going to answer the question of how we are going to deal with the threats to civil liberties created by modern techniques of surveillance. In other words, the real operating need in this field is for research, for education and for legislation and administrative reform and experimentation, that is, action at the local political level.

I think very much the same kind of analysis could be made in the field of arrest, where again the basic problem is to build up a day-to-day ongoing system of decent law and practice. The present situation in the field of arrest and investigation seems to be, insofar as we know anything about it, that we have a great network of going practice which is largely invisible and probably largely illegal, with the Supreme Court occasionally swooping down here and there and excoriating a particular abuse and reversing a particular conviction. But the practice and the theory diverge radically. And here again the Court's analytical tools are crude; we are not going to get a decent system of law and practice governing the investigation of crime derived from the eighteenth-century law of arrest.

It seems to me that we have a moral here for lawyers and citizens interested in civil liberties. I think it is a great mistake to put all our eggs in the Supreme Court's basket. What we need is basically political system-building and reform and action at the local level if we really want respect for civil liberties to be built into the administration of justice. In other words, if we want a decent system, if we want a world where civil liberties are respected in the actual operations of the criminal law, if that is what we want rather than simply the pleasure of having the Supreme Court swoop down occasionally to chastise a police chief, then the effort must be made at the local level to build a decent system through what I call political action, in which I include the notions of research and education. And if we succeed at the local level in building a decent system, that in turn is going to give the Supreme Court great illumination when it has to solve its problems. After all, the Court, too, is going to have to continue to decide cases under the Constitution. But the Supreme Court cannot get all its illumination from above. Even Mr. Justice Black's fundamentalist vision of the good life will not give the Court all the answers to every detailed problem of control and balance and application. But if at least some of the states at the local level manage to incorporate respect for civil rights into their operating systems of criminal justice, this will help the Court immeasurably in deciding just what it is that the Constitution demands.

This, therefore, is why I think that the main effort for those of us interested in civil rights in connection with the criminal process will have to shift, at least partially, from concern with constitutional litigation to the great task of political action and reform at the local operating level.

III / (Caleb Foote)

The great stoic philosopher Epictetus in one of his writings imagined himself facing a wrestler. The strong man boasted to him "See my dumbbells," to which the philosopher impatiently retorted, "Your dumbbells are your own affair. I desire to see their effect." We should like to be able to supply this kind of standard to our subject, to be able to see beyond the decisions of the Supreme Court and to gain a comprehensive picture of the effect of the Court's custodianship of our civil liberties.

I want to invite your attention to some of the factual problems which are posed when one tries to make such an assessment. An evaluation of these problems seems to me an essential prerequisite to any understanding of the "Supreme Court's proper role." I would suppose, incidentally, that our problems are only just beginning.

When we measure the effectiveness of a public health campaign such as that against polio or venereal disease, we can say that the incidence of the disease ten years ago when the campaign began was such and such; that now it is so and so; that the difference represents a measurable decline; and thus by the use of controls we may be able to attribute that decline to certain specific factors. Such an empirical validation is as important for civil liberties as for science. We all know from sad experience that any form of government can hold out the promise of a bill of rights, and that what is critical is to look behind the promise to see if its principles are available in practice to most clients of the police and of the criminal law.

Consider first an important question which is now before the United States Supreme Court relating to the scope of the requirement to provide counsel for indigents under the due process clause in state criminal cases. The rule we have been following, at least since *Betts v. Brady*[17] was decided, has invited a case-by-case adjudication. Counsel is required only where special circumstances would make a trial without counsel "fundamentally unfair." It would be of both extraordinary interest and significance if we could have any sort of reliable empirical data on how this rule worked in practice, and how it compares with practice under the varying rules that are applied in different jurisdictions.

In the right-to-counsel cases, I think we can all agree with *Betts v. Brady* that some defendants can and will be fairly tried without counsel; can agree with the civil libertarians that in some cases denial of counsel outrages our basic concept of a fair trial; and agree with the skeptics that even in a required-counsel jurisdiction, some defendants represented by court-appointed counsel are nonetheless denied the minimum representation necessary for a fair trial. The critical factor is the relative frequency of these three kinds of cases. Indeed, if there are a substantial number of cases in required-counsel jurisdictions where the defendant is prejudiced because of the laxity of the waiver rule or because of merely superficial representation by appointed counsel, then the liberals may be grossly overestimating the civil liberties importance of overruling *Betts v. Brady*.

Consider also some of the other relative unknowns which the Supreme Court is going to have to deal with in deciding the right-to-counsel cases. We have little other than opinion evidence and armchair speculation with which to evaluate the relative merits of different methods by which counsel may be provided to indigents or what the cost of each of these different methods would be to the states. We do not know whether or in what ways the incidence of civil liberties violations is related to the stage of the case at which counsel is appointed. We do not know how critical it is to extend counsel to minor or petty offenders or what the cost of such an extension would be. We do not know to what extent, if any, provision of competent counsel in all cases immediately after arrest and before any interrogation, which would be the fullest implementation of the Sixth Amendment, would impair police ability to control crime or to what extent it would increase the proportion of assumedly guilty but unconvictable individuals. We do not know in what proportion of cases where counsel is appointed for an indigent or where a run-of-the-mill defendant obtains a run-of-the-mill private attorney, the representation which is afforded meets even the minimum standards suggested for effectiveness in *Powell v. Alabama*.[18] This last is an especially disturbing unknown when both common knowledge and recent sociological studies tell us that the lawyers who engage in criminal cases are not representative of high or even of average competence within the bar.[19]

It is said that 80 percent of our defendants are indigent, not merely financially limited but financially incompetent. If this is true—I think it is just a guess, but surely we ought to ascertain whether or not it is true—doesn't it follow that adversary procedure as a self-generating protector of civil liberties is likely to be critically defective? As to bail, we already have documentation of the ineffectiveness of our system to achieve its stated goal and know that the provision of the Eighth Amendment on bail is as meaningless a piece of verbiage to many and probably most American criminal defendants as we assume some of the platitudes of the Soviet Constitution to be.[20] The situation in regard to our other problems may or may not be as aggravated, but until we have data we will not know.

In any event, it seems to me that the Supreme Court is in urgent need of assistance in the kind of fact-finding that will allow it to make better evaluations of the state of our civil liberties, and which will allow us to make a better assessment of what the Court is doing. Indeed, it is hard to understand why so little empirical research has been done. While the kinds of research I have noted would be costly and would involve complex research problems, cost and technical difficulty do not seem to be the reasons for our continued acceptance of ignorance in the civil liberties field. A country which conquered polio with a March of Dimes could certainly afford a March of Pennies for the Bill of Rights, and a spirit willing to gamble millions against the unknown of cancer would not be deterred by research obstacles if it really wanted answers.

The underlying explanation, I am afraid, is that both those who take an expansive view of civil liberty protection and those who wish to see a restricted application of the Bill of Rights have assumed the factual premises which underlie their positions. Each approach the possibility of getting concrete factual data with the trepidation with which one regards Pandora's box. On the prosecutor's side, for example, at neither state nor federal levels have the departments of justice begun to assume the responsibilities implicit in their names: the promotion of justice and civil liberty by long-range planning, by research, by an aggressive initiative in rule-making and legislation in a manner parallel to that pursued, for example, by the Department of Health, Education and Welfare. On the other side, our unofficial guardians of the public conscience, like the American Civil Liberties Union, have paralleled the methodology of the departments of justice, going from case to case and problem to problem in the hurly-burly of daily affairs. This critical and essential function is not to be deprecated, but standing by itself it is woefully incomplete. Unless problems are anticipated in advance and the facts necessary for their intelligent resolution methodically amassed, we will continue to guess where we could have known. Nor has the Court begun to get the kind of assistance and prodding it deserves from the bar, from legal education, or from the critical articles which spring up around its decisions.

So far I have been dealing only with those areas in which factual data is largely unobtainable. A more complex problem, and one which will arise with increasing frequency as we start to accumulate more factual data, concerns the relevance of underlying empirical data to the Court's decision-making process. Some past decisions will give us an inkling of the kind of difficulties that have arisen. Consider first *Skinner v. Oklahoma*,[21] a 1942 decision in which a state statute for the involuntary sterilization of certain classes of habitual criminals was held unconstitutional. In the earlier case of *Buck v. Bell*,[22] the Court had sustained compulsory sterilization for mental defectives. Whatever excuses may have existed for the cavalier misuse of empirical data which characterized *Buck v. Bell* were not present in 1942 when the *Skinner* case was decided. The basic scientific defects in the case for involuntary sterilization were presented and the Court itself noted sufficient reference to the biological literature to virtually compel the conclusion that *Buck v. Bell* was gross error.[23] The Court, however, dodged the basic question and decided the case by introducing what can only be described as a fanciful equal protection theory. Only Mr. Justice Jackson even mentioned the key issue, and he favored postponing its resolution to another day.[24]

Skinner presented the simpler of the empirical problems, a purely scientific question of the relationship of heredity and habitual criminality, and the biological evidence was overwhelmingly against the reasonableness of the statute. The question was squarely posed, it was briefed and argued, and it has not become any riper for decision in the twenty-one years since the Court dodged the question. What, then, was gained by postponing decision? The Court has hardly begun to face the question of how it should evaluate empirical evidence that could be critical to the solution of civil liberties cases.

There will, of course, be those who will defend the Court by the application of the time-honored standard that it should properly decide no more than absolutely necessary to dispose of the case before it. Yet twenty-one years after *Skinner* the Court is still waiting for that compulsory sterilization case; similarly, it has had no further occasion to deal with criminal registration ordinances. One justification for holding back in constitutional adjudication is reliance upon the adversary process to bring forth cases. As I have already noted, this reliance may be wholly unjustified in the human rights arena. Potential litigants in compulsory sterilization cases are the institutionalized mentally defective or mentally ill, and they don't get into court very often. Thus, although only one litigant was directly before the Court in *Skinner* and although the Court's equal protection vagary saved him from sterilization, behind him were thousands of institutional inmates in some twenty or twenty-five states who were and are subject to sterilization under laws most of which would not be voided by the vague *Skinner* formulation. As a practical matter, *Skinner* represented their only hope for a constitutional adjudication of their rights. To apply a conceptual theory of the narrowest possible decision-making in the face of such facts seems to me an abdication of the Court's responsibility.

Similarly, aside from atypical cases like *Lanzetta v. New Jersey*[25] or *Thompson v. City of Louisville*[26] the light from Washington never reaches either the vast grey area of illegal arrest or the summary criminal processes from which tens of thousands of people go to jail annually after trials which, we may suspect, lack the most elementary fairness, often under charge of vagrancy or disorderly conduct pursuant to statutes of the most dubious constitutionality. A few years ago, when Dancing Sam Thompson's Kentucky lawyers got his disorderly conduct conviction reversed in the Supreme Court, there was an editorial back-patting around the country because even such a two-bit case as this could go straight from the

Louisville Police Court to those hallowed halls in Washington. The facts of life are that while *Thompson* stands alone in the Supreme Court, there is a vast army of Thompsons on skid rows or in police detention pens, jails, penitentiaries, or mental institutions who are penniless, friendless, lawyerless and without any of the resources required to set the processes of the law in motion.

When by happenstance a case from this vast unseen reservoir does make its way to the Supreme Court, the bar and the profession have an obligation to see that the empirical data is obtained and is presented, and the Court has an obligation of guidance and breadth of adjudication quite different from that applicable to most cases on its docket. With empirical fact-finding sensitizing our awareness of the problems of poverty and ignorance, the Court could play a much more significant part in developing corrective measures against a glaring deficiency in our scheme of criminal justice.

IV / (Alexander M. Bickel)

First, let me say that I am delighted about one thing and that is that I am under no obligation to address myself to the staggering list of problems Mr. Foote has left with us. I do not by any means wish to indicate that they are not all terribly real. I am just glad that my branch of the subject does not oblige me to address myself to them.

I will intrude only so far as to remark that it struck me—not being attuned to this branch of the subject tonight—that Mr. Foote was sort of proving Mr. Bator's point. If it is true that the problems are quite this staggering, that they are quite as rooted in complex social, psychological and medical facts, is not Professor Bator right that they may well be beyond the competence of a Court both in that they must surely be dealt with by some more continuous process than the Court can provide, and in that they call for resources which, rich as the government of the United States is, are normally less at the disposal of the Supreme Court of the United States than they are of the Arthur Garfield Hays Civil Liberties Program and many others? But that is to intrude on a subject that is not for me to discuss tonight.

I am rather to address myself to the Court's function in respect of issues which, meaning no offense, I think we would all agree are larger and more fundamental, at least in the sense that they reach farther. When the Court decides whether or not children may pray in classrooms, or whether or not children must go to the same schools rather than separate ones, or when it decides even so relatively trivial a matter as whether the Congress may take one's citizenship away, it is deciding a broader, more ultimate issue than some of the procedural issues that were touched on before.

I thought the only fair thing I could do in the short time allotted was to state one or two premises that are at the basis of my thought on the subject. I hopefully accept for my premises the description "orthodox." I hope these premises have been and remain generally shared, which is what I choose to read the word as meaning.

There are a number of premises abroad about the work of the Court, some more articulate, some less, but I assure you, as a student of the literature, that they are present. And I should like to list three of them by way of preface to a statement of my own.

One is that the Constitution of the United States prescribes in reasonably clear—if not chemically pure, as one of my colleagues says—and precise language the rules of conduct which it is the obligation and function of the Supreme Court to enforce in our society.

The second premise, a variant from this one, is that as we look about us, those of us who have had the benefit of an education, who are informed, who are sensitive, thoughtful, reflective, intelligent people, those of us of that sort naturally develop ideas about how we would like to see society run. Indeed, we have a kind of obligation—I mean to the unenlightened others—to develop such ideas. When we have developed ideas of this sort, it becomes the duty of the Supreme Court of the United States to enforce them as law. There is room in this second hypothesis for error. There is room for difference of opinion. We do not mean to be dogmatic about it. But there is no room for egregious error, and in any event, the arena in which the differences of opinion are to be played out is the arena of ourselves, the educated, the sensitive.

The third of the premises that float about is a combination of the other two. It is that the notions we sensitive, reflective people develop about how we should govern society are usually, if we look hard enough, to be found in the Constitution.

I do not hold with any of these premises. I do not hold with the first, that the rules are laid out in the Constitution, because I do not believe there is any such Constitution. I do not believe any such document exists which solves problems upon ready reference. To be sure there are some core provisions which are clear. There are, unfortunately, two things to be said about such provisions. One is that most of them never get litigated. They are the sort that do not, by tradition, come to decision in the Supreme Court. Secondly, even those that tradition will allow to be adjucated will be found to be reasonably clear at the core because they are unquestioned.

Addressing myself to questions that do get litigated, I must say again that I do not think there is any Constitution which solves them just like that. If there were, I would find myself most uncomfortable, I think, living under it—living under a document which in matters by hypothesis of fundamental importance governs me without recourse, saving only the improbability of a ridiculous amendment procedure. I would feel terribly uncomfortable living in a society in which that was true, in which a document governs conduct beyond the possibility of the exercise of contemporary human judgment.

As for the second premise—and they are not straw premises really; they may not be stated very often, and I daresay they are never stated the way I stated them, but they are there—I can only say that it seems to me uncommonly arrogant and authoritarian. I do not think that I have enough of the de Gaulle in me to wish to be governed by even a number of de Gaulles, even if I were to be one of the number. I believe more firmly than that in the notion of government by consent. While I am fully aware of all the difficulties that the political scientists have been able to figure out about the simpleminded notions of representative government that used to be current half a century ago, I somehow cannot free myself of the feeling that the policy-making function of representative institutions is the hallmark of this system; it is the hallmark of a government that may be designated by this or that symbol—government by consent, or democracy, call it what you please—nevertheless the hallmark of our form of government. This is the chief characteristic that makes our system unlike, say, the current French Republic, that makes it unlike various other forms of government which are equally free with ourselves in using all sorts of phrases, certainly including democracy and not even excluding rule of law. I believe in that characteristic of our system, and it seems to me that any attitude that attributes either to a constitution or to a small appointive body of men freely ranging governmental powers is profoundly and fatally inconsistent with any such belief.

I am sure they will be delighted to hear this in Washington. I wholeheartedly support the Supreme Court of the United States. But it follows from my premises that I support it, as I say, in a state of tension. I am able not to explode because seeing as I do both the value of the judicial process and its necessary limitations, viewing it both as valuable and with an extreme sense of caution, guardedly, I think I can find and I think I can confirm out of the history of the Court that not all so-called constitutional judgments are alike. There are, in other words, many things the Court does. Most of the procedural matters, I think, fall into the category which does not provoke a direct clash between the judicial and the political branches. Procedure most often does not affect those large ends of government with which alone majorities of our people and legislative majorities can realistically be said to be intelligently concerned.

Most constitutional decisions concern the "hows" of government, not the "whats." They concern the ways and not the ends. And I am most often quite satisfied to have that function performed. Nevertheless, it would be nonsense to pretend that the Court has not in the past rendered, and that we do not expect it in the future to render, judgments that do reach the largest ends of government, the purposes of our society. And I am satisfied to have that so, although, I must say, rarely.

Before you arrive at any qualitative judgment, there is a pure, simple and arbitrary quantitative one to be made. We were all glad that the Court spoke on May 17, 1954. Yet a court that decided the equivalent of five cases such as *Brown v. Board of Education*[27] in a single year would have seen the end of the institution, I am sure.

The Court is our greatest educational institution. It may bring a question up to the forefront of public consciousness, reduce it and play with it—sort of a cat-and-mouse game, perhaps—until there comes a moment of inarticulable judgment, of political feel, not at all different from the sense of timing that other political officers have, when the time seems ripe for a final adjudication. And the Court will then act.

What I have described is the history of the *Segregation Cases.* When that is not done, when the judgment is a bolt out of the blue—as was true, for example, with the *School Prayer Case*[28] last year, as was true with the *McCollum* released-time case[29] fifteen years ago—the judgment is ineffective. It is, in a word, disobeyed. Not disobeyed the way Governor Barnett disobeys. The decree is not disobeyed, but the judgment remains an *ad hoc* disposition of a single case and nobody else bothers to follow it.

Why then worry about the Court's function? Why worry if, when the process is not properly pursued, the Court is ineffective? I do worry because I value the Court's process, and I think when it renders ineffective judgments, when it pursues the process in a wrong way, what it does is to harm—and one fine day it may be fatal—its value in society both as to those numerous problems which it can handle and handle well without much of a clash with the political institutions, and as to those few—I do not suppose there have been a dozen in our history—as to which it can, if it does its job properly, renew and make effective the moral judgment of the community, which is indeed a very high function.

V / (Charles A. Reich)

My point of view in a nutshell is that the Supreme Court ought to and can take a leading and active role both in the field Mr. Bator and Mr. Foote talked about and in the broader field Mr. Bickel and I are speaking about. My view is based, like Mr. Bickel's, on assumptions. Perhaps they are assumptions that I cannot prove, but I will state them for you and I will say in advance not only that I agree with these assumptions but that I regard them as being more orthodox than anything we have heard up to now.

The first three assumptions relate to civil liberties at any time and in any place. To begin with, I think civil liberties are in a sense an unnatural state for man or for society because in a short-range way they are essentially contrary to the self-interest of the majority. They require the majority to restrain itself, to say No to its immediate impulses, and to allow things to go on that threaten it. At all times the natural state would be contrary to civil liberties if the majority had its immediate way. Even the great friends of civil liberties have their troubles when somebody uses free speech in an attempt to suppress civil liberties and free speech.

The second point is that civil liberties are a very sophisticated concept. It takes a little knowledge and a little thought to understand why we should let a man remain silent because he says that he may incriminate himself. The natural thing to think is, "Well, if he is innocent, he ought to tell us, and if he is guilty, why should we bother with him?" Civil liberties involve quite a bit of sophistication in many, many areas. The thought that we should exclude from evidence a valid confession is also very difficult for many people to understand. When we become sophisticated we understand that what seems to be a true confession may not be. I could mention a lot of other examples. Essentially, I am suggesting that it takes more than good will to understand and be for civil liberties.

Third—and here I disagree wholly with Professor Bator—it seems to me that civil liberties are never firmly established, never secure. On the contrary, because they are opposed to fundamental forces in society, you have to keep shoring them up and maintaining them. The job by its very nature can never be finished.

The three things I have mentioned are, it seems to me, true of society at any time. There are also many things about our society that were not true when the Constitution was adopted. Some are familiar. They relate to the great pressures of our complex society toward conformity and away from individualistic expression of ideas and beliefs. All of you are familiar with them. I will list a few. The mass society that we live in and the consequent pressures that it generates. The fact that we have big organizations, big government, big business and so forth. The resulting bureaucracy that tends to make everybody follow a general line of thought. Our continuing state of military insecurity. The dominance of mass communications, with our ideas coming to us after they have gone through many different filters which let pass only a dulling sameness. And the disappearance in our modern society of some of the sociological factors that favor independence, such as small-property owning, small business and so forth.

These things, it seems to me, bring far more pressure against civil liberties than those things that existed when the Constitution was adopted, so that my view about civil liberties today is a little on the pessimistic side.

These assumptions lead me to three conclusions. The first is that if you are to have civil liberty, it must be primarily created and maintained by law. Second, the law has to be principally maintained and enforced by courts, at least in the social structure that we have. Third, the courts should be very active in the way they do this job.

As to the law, it seems to me that if you have all these forces in society working against civil liberties, you need a very strong and very firm force to stand against them. You cannot expect that forces in society weaker than law or legal institutions are very likely to do this job. We need a powerful self-restraint upon ourselves, and that is the special function law performs. I think the framers of the Constitution felt this; and I think that they therefore wrote the basic notion of civil liberties into the Constitution as law. I disagree with Mr. Bickel on this point. I think we do have a very explicit Constitution governing civil liberties and that it was written for the purpose of counteracting the forces against liberty that existed even at that time and are so much stronger today. If law was necessary to protect civil liberties in 1789, it is even more necessary today.

The question that comes up next is, What kind of institution shall take over the keeping of this law, or the interpretation of it at any given time? The suggestion has been made by Mr. Bickel, and also by Mr. Bator, that something in the nature of the political process can be depended on to do this job primarily, leaving the Supreme Court to do the job only secondarily. I just do not think that the political process is adequate to the task. In the first place, it seems that the political process produces responses to immediate needs, and immediate needs are often contrary to civil liberties. Civil liberty is a long-range concept. You must permit somebody to speak today because you want the chance to speak another day. Legislators or executive officials who have to respond to immediate pressures find it difficult to do this kind of long-range thinking.

In addition, legislators and executives have to act to solve immediate problems. That duty is likely to reduce their ability to think in long-range terms. Further, I see no evidence that our legislators or executives, or the people who elect them, have the kind of historical knowledge and sophistication that will allow them to see what the answer is in a particular, complex situation. I do not see how we can expect in the Congress, which I suppose is our best legislative body, the kind of debate and thought and understanding that we expect of the Supreme Court concerning a question of, say, self-incrimination. And even if we were to have that thoughtfulness in the Congress or in the state legislatures, it seems that the fact that legislators are subject to the political process, and not insulated from it as judges are, makes it far more difficult for them to act on the basis of long-range views. They are likely to get removed from office whereas the Justices are there for life; and this was a reason for putting them there for life.

All of these points strike me as important in considering the role of the Court, but I have yet to mention the most fundamental one. We must remember that the democratic political process requires the existence of civil liberties in order to function. If we do not have the vote, if we do not have the right to speak, if we do not have the right to hear others, then the political process cannot function, and then you cannot look to it to correct evils that may grow up. I do not see how we can count on a self-corrective process in the legislature or in the executive branch to deal with suppression of liberty. On the contrary, we never accomplished reform in the field of apportionment from Congress, from the state legislators, from the President. We could only get reform by having the Supreme Court, an outside insulated body, interpret the Constitution, and thereby make possible the vote of the people. So I say that no political process can be effectively self-correcting in the sense that Mr. Bickel and Mr. Bator have suggested.

The fact that I do not fully trust the political process to guarantee civil liberties leads me to feel that the Supreme Court must do its share to enforce longer-range considerations in our society. The Court itself must not be the reluctant, passive creature that Mr. Bickel describes, because if it is that, it will really not be doing the kind of job that it must do. It cannot always defer to the legislature because, as I have said, the legislature is not the safe repository of long-range thinking. The Court cannot wait for popular consent, because the consent may not be available due to the defects in civil liberties which prevent such consent from ever being formed. The Court cannot make a practice of putting off decisions because if it puts them off, things are going to be embedded in society that are almost impossible to uproot. The Court cannot accept the legal status quo, because the situation is changing so rapidly that it must constantly be asking itself, "Is this legal doctrine a doctrine that faithfully reflects the purposes that the Constitution was supposed to achieve in this area?" And the Court cannot simply abdicate in the hope that other forces in society will do its job for it. It must sometimes get out there and educate. Mr. Bickel said the Supreme Court was a great educator. I agree, and I say that it ought to do more. Sometimes we have got to educate where there is no public opinion at all.

Now, let us look at the objections to giving the Supreme Court these functions. In the first place, it is said that the Court cannot do very much because (*a*) its doctrines are not very flexible, and (*b*) it is not a very effective body anyway. It is "the least dangerous branch."

As to doctrines, it seems to me that the Court has tools at its hand to fashion doctrines that will meet any of the problems that a changing society brings up. I am not worried about the doctrinal problem. The Court has done many amazing things on the basis of doctrine and I expect it will do many more.

As for the alleged ineffectiveness, if the Court is able to uproot a whole society, as it is doing in the *Segregation Cases* and their progeny, and if the Court can uproot a whole political system, as it is now doing in the *Reapportionment Cases*, it seems to me that we have evidence that it is a rather effective body. And I submit that those two kinds of uprooting are more difficult in some ways than an uprooting in the field of free speech which may not go to the fundamentals of social relations as the *Segregation Cases* did.

The question of danger to the Court as an institution has only been hinted at. The fear is that if the Court tried to do things without popular consent it might get into terrible trouble. I feel that the Court has always been on the brink of trouble. Many Justices have been threatened with impeachment, but they have gone on and done their work. The Court-packing plan failed. The segregationist elements in Congress did not succeed in any of their plans to limit the power of the Court. The reason is that the people, although they have not consented to any particular decisions of the Court, do consent to the Court as an institution and to its function. That is the only consent we need in order to have a Court that functions—the basic consent of the people that this institution shall interpret the Constitution. If you have that consent, I do not feel that you have to worry about consent for each decision. That will come in time, and I just do not believe the Court will be overthrown as a result of hostility to any particular decision.

It is also suggested that there is something that is vaguely undemocratic about the Court—that it is not an institution really based upon consent, or that its decisions do not necessarily reflect the view of the people at any given moment. But democracy is a very different thing from popular consensus at a given time. Democracy, on the contrary, is a limitation upon a transient consensus, plus a controlled method of changing the fundamental law if those changes are deemed desirable. The very essence of our system is long-range limitations upon the power of the majority to act, because a democracy is concerned not just with majority rights but also with minority rights.

Despite all that I have said, ultimately the people have to be the custodians of freedom. That surely is what Mr. Bickel believes and Mr. Bator and Mr. Foote. My point here in essence is that without information, without the freedom to hear and to speak, without the freedom to associate, even people who believe in freedom, who have it in their hearts, are likely to end up living under some sort of tyranny.

It seems to me that the framers of the Constitution knew this, and they therefore built our liberties into a structure of law. And it seems to me further that the highest duty of the Court is to enforce the Constitution's guarantees so that the democratic process can function. Only when the Court does its job, only when the Bill of Rights is made into something that is real, will the people have the knowledge and the means to do their own job of maintaining their freedom.[30]

Since the 1963 Hays Conference the Supreme Court has often acted to protect individual rights, both in criminal cases and in the more general category of "civil liberties." For example, the Court recently found in the "emanations and penumbra" of the Bill of Rights a right of privacy which it used to strike down a Connecticut anti-birth-control law,[31] and a national debate has been touched off by decisions placing restrictions on police interrogation of persons suspected of crime.[32] One consequence of this debate was the formation by President Johnson of a National Crime Commission to examine the causes of mounting crime in the United States and to recommend remedial measures. Among other notable contributions of the Commission was its heavy reliance on the kind of empirical data that Professor Foote said was of such potential importance to courts and law enforcement officials.

At the same time, scholars as well as the general public continued to differ about whether the Court was overstepping its proper constitutional bounds. These developments come as no surprise, however, because the Court has been the subject of controversy at least since the power of judicial review was established in 1803.

NOTES

The full conference proceedings were published in 10 *Wayne Law Review* 457 (Spring 1964) with the title "Arthur Garfield Hays Conference: The Proper Role of the United States Supreme Court in Civil Liberties Cases."

1. Gray v. Sanders, 372 U.S. 368, 383 (1963) (dissenting opinion).
2. Betts v. Brady, 316 U.S. 445 (1942), overruled by Gideon v. Wainwright, 372 U.S. 335 (1963); South v. Peters, 339 U.S. 276 (1950), overruled by Gray v. Sanders, 372 U.S. 368 (1963); and Darr v. Burford, 339 U.S. 200 (1950), and Daniels v. Allan, 344 U.S. 443 (1953), overruled by Fay v. Noia, 372 U.S. 391 (1963).
3. 347 U.S. 483 (1954).
4. Baker v. Carr, 369 U.S. 186 (1962).
5. 351 U.S. 12 (1956).
6. Smith v. Bennett, 365 U.S. 708 (1961); McCrary v. Indiana, 364 U.S. 277 (1960); Douglas v. Green, 363 U.S. 192 (1960); Burns v. Ohio,

360 U.S. 252 (1959); Ross v. Schneckloth, 357 U.S. 575 (1958); see also Eskridge v. Washington State Board, 357 U.S. 214 (1958).

7. 372 U.S. 335 (1963).

8. 373 U.S. 353 (1963).

9. 316 U.S. 445 (1942).

10. Mapp v. Ohio, 367 U.S. 643 (1961).

11. Ker v. California, 374 U.S. 23 (1963).

12. See Fay v. Noia, 372 U.S. 391 (1963); Townsend v. Sain, 372 U.S. 293 (1963); Sanders v. United States, 373 U.S. 1 (1963).

13. Professor Bator's views are developed in "Finality in Criminal Law and Federal Habeas for State Prisoners," 76 *Harv. L. Rev.* 441 (1963).

14. 338 U.S. 25 (1948), overruled by Mapp v. Ohio, 367 U.S. 643 (1961).

15. 316 U.S. 445 (1942). As predicted, within two weeks from the date of the conference, this case was overruled by Gideon v. Wainwright, 372 U.S. 335 (1963).

16. 367 U.S. 643 (1961).

17. 316 U.S. 445 (1942).

18. 287 U.S. 45 (1932).

19. See, e.g., Ladinsky, "The Impact of Social Backgrounds of Lawyers on Law Practice and the Law," 16 *J. Legal Ed.* 127 (1963).

20. Ares, Rankin & Sturz, "The Manhattan Bail Project: An Interim Report on the Use of Pre-Trial Parole," 38 *N.Y.U.L. Rev.* 67 (1963).

21. 316 U.S. 535 (1942).

22. 274 U.S. 200 (1927).

23. 316 U.S. at 538 n. 1.

24. *Id.* at 546–57 (concurring opinion).

25. 306 U.S. 451 (1939).

26. 362 U.S. 199 (1960).

27. 347 U.S. 483 (1954).

28. Engel v. Vitale, 370 U.S. 421 (1962), subsequently followed in decisions handed down after the conference. See, e.g., School District of Abington Township v. Schempp, 374 U.S. 203 (1963).

29. McCollum v. Board of Education, 333 U.S. 203 (1948).

30. See, generally, Reich, "Mr. Justice Black and the Living Constitution," 76 *Harv. L. Rev.* 673 (1963).

31. Griswold v. Connecticut, 381 U.S. 479 (1965).

32. See, e.g., Escobedo v. Illinois, 378 U.S. 478 (1964); Miranda v. Arizona, 384 U.S. 456 (1966).

3

A Senator Attacks the Supreme Court

On May 2, 1962, Senator James O. Eastland of Mississippi, Chairman of the Senate Judiciary Committee, made an extended attack on the Supreme Court. He charged that in a large number of cases the Justices of the Court had voted "pro-Communist," thus threatening "fundamentally the basic security of our country from the onslaught of the Communist conspiracy." In support of his remarks, the Senator inserted in the Congressional Record a chart of selected cases, which indicated how the individual Justices had voted. In Senator Eastland's words: "If the decision of the individual judge was in favor of the position advocated by the Communist Party, or the Communist sympathizer involved in the particular case, it was scored as pro, meaning pro-Communist. If the judge's decision was contrary to this position, he was scored as con—or contrary."

Shortly thereafter, Senator Jacob K. Javits of New York requested the author to prepare a response to Senator Eastland. Senator Javits said that he "was not satisfied to let the matter stand . . . with the Congressional Record showing only the attack on the Supreme Court, a body that is in no position under the Constitution to defend itself." The author then prepared the memorandum that is *printed below, and Senator Javits inserted it in the* Congressional Record, *stating that he "fully agreed with its documented conclusion."*

I / The Supreme Court Decisions Referred to by Senator Eastland

Several years ago, one of this country's greatest jurists, the late Learned Hand, counseled us wisely on the subject of criticism of the judges of the Supreme Court and other courts, whether federal or state. Judge Hand said:

> *While it is proper that people should find fault when their judges fail, it is only reasonable that they should recognize the difficulties. Perhaps it is also fair to ask that before the judges are blamed they shall be given the credit of having tried to do their best. Let them be severely brought to book, when they go wrong, but by those who will take the trouble to understand.*[1]

The valid technique for evaluating the work of the Supreme Court is scrupulous legal analysis of the decisions themselves in light of their historical antecedents. Senator Eastland's charges against the members of the Supreme Court represent an entirely inconsistent approach. They are completely unrelated to legal doctrine or historical context. Instead, they focus solely on the results of cases, and measure these results by a distorting and oversimplified standard. A subsequent section of this memorandum contains comment on certain unfortunate consequences of Senator Eastland's method of criticism. This section will concentrate on legal analysis of the Supreme Court cases referred to by Senator Eastland in his attack on the Court.

As Judge Learned Hand indicated, it is not a simple matter to evaluate the work of the Supreme Court. The complexities of law and fact make treacherous any but the most comprehensive analysis. Nevertheless, inspection of a certain number of decisions may be helpful in demonstrating that the members of the Supreme Court, in the cases singled out by Senator Eastland, used well-established legal doctrines in reaching their conclusions. That individual Justices can differ as to the applicability of a legal doctrine in a particular case is merely further proof of the difficulty of the judicial task assigned the Supreme Court.

In view of limitations on space, only two methods of analysis will be employed. These show (*a*) that many of the cases cited by Senator Eastland were decided on the basis of judicial precedent and therefore obviously did not represent a break with the past; and (*b*) that doctrines employed by the Court in cases involving national security (Communism) are also employed in other types of cases.

A. *Legal Precedent*

In *Curcio v. United States,*[2] the question was whether the petitioner's personal privilege against self-incrimination under the Fifth Amendment attached to questions relating to the whereabouts of certain union books and records which he declined to produce pursuant to a grand jury subpoena. The Court unanimously held that it did.

It was well established by prior cases that custodians of the documents of associations, whether incorporated or unincorporated, had no privilege with respect to such records.[3] It was equally well established that the custodian had a constitutional privilege to decline *to answer questions* about the whereabouts of such records when they were no longer in his possession. Thus, in *Wilson v. United States,* Justice (later Chief Justice) Hughes said: "They [the custodians of records] may decline to utter upon the witness stand a single self-criminating word. They may demand that any accusation against them individually be established without the aid of their oral testimony. . . ."[4] And in *Shapiro v. United States,* the Court said: "Of course all *oral* testimony by individuals can properly be compelled only by exchange of immunity for waiver of privilege."[5] In view of these precedents, it is clear that the decision of the unanimous Court in the *Curcio* case was solidly grounded.

In the area of fair administration of justice, *Gold v. United States*[6] is squarely based on *Remmer v. United States,*[7] which involved income tax fraud. Gold had been convicted of filing a false non-Communist affidavit and the district court judgment had been affirmed by an equally divided court of appeals. One of the issues was whether Gold had been deprived of a fair trial because "an F.B.I. agent, investigating another case in which falsity of a non-Communist affidavit was also charged,"[8] had asked three members of the jury whether they had received propaganda literature, and also because other members of the jury had heard of the FBI contacts.

In a 6 to 3 *per curiam* decision, the Supreme Court held that a new trial should be granted, "because of official intrusion into the privacy of the jury."[9] It is true, as the dissenters stated in *Gold,* that the earlier *Remmer* opinion had said that tampering with a juror was only "presumptively prejudicial."[10] However, the Supreme Court in its second opinion in the *Remmer* case had ruled that intrusion on a jury could be deemed nonprejudicial only in the rarest instances. The decision in the *Gold* case seems a highly appropriate application of the *Remmer* doctrine; indeed, the facts indicate that there was at least as much likelihood of prejudice in *Gold* as in *Remmer.*

A series of cases illustrating both the principle of *stare decisis* and the fact that it is often difficult of application are *Galvan v. Press,*[11] *Rowoldt v. Perfetto,*[12] and *Niukkanen v. McAlexander.*[13] In *Galvan v. Press,* it was held that an alien was properly ordered deported under section 22 of the Internal Security Act of 1950,[14] two Justices dissenting on the ground that the provision was unconstitutional. In the *Rowoldt* case, after a careful review of the legislative history of the 1951 amendments to the Internal Security Act, a majority of the Court concluded that Congress did not intend the deportation of former members of the Communist Party unless their association was "meaningful" and had "political implications." The majority concluded that the one-year membership of the petitioner in the party during which he "didn't get a penny" nor betrayed any ideological identification with the party's unlawful aims was insufficient to warrant deportation. The dissenting Justices disagreed that the 1951 amendments required a "meaningful association" with the Communist Party, and thought that mere membership (which was conceded) was sufficient.

In the third case, *Niukkanen v. McAlexander,*[15] the petitioner was an alien who had been brought to this country when less than a year old and who had lived here for over fifty years. Although he was briefly a member of the party in the late 1930s, the testimony showed that he never was an officeholder, never was employed by the party and never represented the party on any occasion. There was also testimony, as in the *Rowoldt* case, that the petitioner's sole interest in joining during the depression was in "bread and butter" and the "sufferings of the people." A majority of the Court held that because the trial examiner disbelieved certain testimony of the petitioner, the *Rowoldt* rule did not apply. Four Justices disagreed on the ground that undisputed evidence put the case squarely within the "meaningful association" rule of *Rowoldt v. Perfetto.*

Ignoring the complex factual and legal issues in these cases, Senator Eastland simply counts as "pro-Communist" the votes of the dissenters in the *Galvan* and *Niukkanen* cases, and the majority in the *Rowoldt* case.[16]

B. *Application of Legal Doctrine to Non-Communist Cases*

Some of the cases discussed immediately above had precedents not involving national security. Many other cases referred to by Senator Eastland involve doctrines that have been applied across the board, irrespective of the nature of the litigant before the Court.

1. CONTEMPT CASES

Sacher v. United States[17] involved a contempt citation of defense counsel for eleven Communist leaders who were convicted of violating the Smith Act after a turbulent nine-month trial. During the Smith Act trial the judge repeatedly warned counsel that their conduct was contemptuous. Immediately upon receiving the jury's verdict of guilty, the judge, without further notice or hearing, found counsel guilty of criminal contempt and sentenced them to prison. On appeal, a majority of the Supreme Court affirmed the contempt conviction. The dissenting Justices contended that the citation for contempt should have been tried before a jury; that it should not in any event have been tried before the same judge who conducted the Smith Act trial; and that a full hearing was essential to due process of law. Senator Eastland has characterized the dissenters' votes as "pro-Communist," presumably because the defense counsel had been representing Communists on trial under the Smith Act.

But procedural protections have been jealously guarded in all kinds of contempt cases having nothing remotely to do with national security. Just last term, the Supreme Court reversed the conviction of an attorney held in contempt for his conduct during a civil antitrust suit.[18] Also last term, the Court held that the summary contempt power could not be used to punish out-of-court statements of a sheriff attacking as "agitation" and "intimidation" a grand jury investigation into alleged bloc voting by Negroes.[19]

There are many other decisions in favor of individuals on trial under the summary contempt power. In none of them could it fairly be said that the Court, or the individual Justices, were doing more than their duty to oversee the judiciary's awesome contempt power. Likewise, there is no basis for the conclusion that any sympathy existed for the cause of the defendant, or with his conduct. As Justice Frankfurter said in dissent in the *Sacher* case itself:

> *I would not remotely minimize the gravity of the conduct of which the petitioners have been found guilty, let alone condone it. But their intrinsic guilt is not relevant to the issue before us. This Court brought the case here in order to consider whether the trial court followed the proper procedure in determining that the misconduct of the petitioners subjected them to punishment. . . . Time out of mind this Court has reversed convictions for the most heinous offenses, even though no doubt about the guilt of the defendants was entertained. It reversed because the mode by which guilt was established disregarded those standards of procedure which are so precious and so important for our society.*[20]

2. FREE SPEECH CASES

Many of the cases cited by Senator Eastland involve freedom of expression. In all of them the votes in favor of the individual's right to speak or publish are regarded as "pro-Communist."[21]

Many of the same constitutional arguments urged by the dissenting Justices in the above cases, in all of which a majority ruled that no First Amendment violation occurred, were equally pressed in cases not involving Communism.

Thus, in *Beauharnais v. Illinois*,[22] a majority of the Court upheld a conviction under a state criminal libel law against a speaker who was exposing Negroes to "contempt, derision and obloquy." The dissenting Justices claimed that the conviction was unconstitutional as invading the defendant's right to freedom of speech. In *Terminiello v. Chicago*,[23] a majority of the Court reversed a conviction for breach of the peace based on the defendant's speech attacking Jews, Catholics and Negroes. The majority held that the defendant had a constitutional right to express his views, no matter how unpopular and how odious.

It makes as much sense to say that the votes selected by Senator Eastland were "pro-Communist" as to say that the Justices voting in favor of the First Amendment in the *Beauharnais* and *Terminiello* cases were anti-Negro, anti-Jewish and anti-Catholic.

3. STATUTORY INTERPRETATION

Many of the cases referred to by Senator Eastland involve questions of statutory interpretation. He characterizes as "pro-Communist" certain votes in those cases without regard to their validity under established canons of interpretation.

a. Construction of Statutes to Avoid Constitutional Issues. It is well established that courts will attempt to interpret statutes so as not to require a judicial ruling on constitutional questions. In the words of Chief Justice Taft, "it is our duty in the interpretation of federal statutes to reach a conclusion which will avoid serious doubt of their constitutionality."[24] Again, as Justice (later Chief Justice) Stone wrote, what Congress has written "must be construed with an eye to possible constitutional limitations so as to avoid doubts as to its validity."[25] A recent decision resting on this rule of statutory construction is *United States v. Rumely*,[26] in which the Court narrowly construed a congressional resolution authorizing an investigation of "lobbying activities" so as to include only "representations made directly to the Congress, its Members or its committees" and not all activities intending "to influence, encourage, promote or retard legislation." As a result, a contempt conviction of a purveyor of literature of a conservative persuasion was overturned.

In *United States v. Witkovich,*[27] the Court interpreted section 242(d) of the Immigration and Nationality Act[28] so as to deny authorities the power to require an alien under a final order of deportation to furnish information except with respect to his availability for deportation. A majority of the Court believed that serious constitutional questions under the First Amendment would be presented by a contrary interpretation. Since the language of section 242(d) could fairly be construed to limit the authority to request information, the Court did so.

Senator Eastland counts the votes in favor of a narrow interpretation of the statute in *Witkovich* as pro-Communist,[29] presumably because many of the questions asked by immigration officials related to Witkovich's possible membership in the Communist Party and activities on behalf of the party. Such a conclusion ignores the rule of statutory construction, as illustrated by the cases discussed above, that was in fact the basis for the decision.

b. Strict Construction of Penal Laws. A long-standing maxim of statutory interpretation cautions judges to interpret criminal statutes strictly in order to be sure, before a person is convicted and perhaps imprisoned, that defendants are punished only for violations that they could have avoided. As Chief Justice Marshall said over a century ago:

> *The rule that penal laws are to be construed strictly, is perhaps not much less old than construction itself. It is founded on the tenderness of the law for the rights of individuals; and on the plain principle, that the power of punishment is vested in the legislative, not in the judicial department. It is the legislature, not the court, which is to define a crime, and ordain its punishment.*[30]

More recently, in *United States v. Universal C.I.T. Credit Corp.,*[31] involving a prosecution for violation of minimum wage, overtime and record-keeping provisions of the Fair Labor Standards Act, the Court reversed a conviction by applying this doctrine. The Court said:

> *Very early Mr. Chief Justice Marshall told us, "Where the mind labours to discover the design of the legislature, it seizes every thing from which aid can be derived. . . ."* United States v. Fisher, 2 *Cranch* 358, 386.

Particularly is this so when we construe statutes defining conduct which entail stigma and penalties and prison. Not that penal statutes are not subject to the basic consideration that legislation like all other writings should be given, insofar as the language permits, a commonsensical meaning. But when choice has to be made between two readings of what conduct Congress has made a crime, it is appropriate, before we choose the harsher alternative, to require that Congress should have spoken in language that is clear and definite. We should not derive criminal outlawry from some ambiguous implication.[32]

Senator Eastland lists among the votes labeled "pro-Communist" cases in which certain Justices employed the canon of strictly construing penal statutes.[33] Whether or not they were correct in doing so is a difficult question of law in each case. What is not difficult is to see that the doctrine is a confirmed part of the law of legislative interpretation; that its use is common in the Supreme Court in a wide variety of contexts; and that to brand Justices who use it in a case that happens to involve national security as voting "pro-Communist" is totally unjustified.

II / The Good Faith of the Justices

As has already been mentioned, the proper basis for criticism of decisions of the Supreme Court is a rigorous legal and historical analysis of the cases themselves. But because Senator Eastland did not content himself with making charges based on such a standard, it is necessary to go beyond the decisions and show the weaknesses of his allegations in other respects.

In the course of his remarks, despite certain intimations in the language employed, Senator Eastland at no point charged that individual members of the Supreme Court or the Court as an institution ever had the motive of advancing the Communist cause of weakening this country's ability to preserve its democratic form of government.

This is not surprising. To impute such motives to the men sitting on the Supreme Court would be ridiculous—tantamount to the assertion, in a wide variety of other cases, that a vote in favor of a particular result necessarily coincided with sympathy on the part of the individual Justice for the litigant for whom he voted. Thus, to suggest a "pro-Communist" purpose to the Justices of the Court would be to make a similar charge in the following cases, among many others:

(1) That the votes of Justices Black, Douglas, Murphy and Rutledge in *Adamson v. California*[34] indicate their sympathy for murderers because they voted in favor of the position advocated by counsel for accused murderers. The real question in that case was whether the due process clause of the Fourteenth Amendment to the Constitution prohibited a state prosecutor from commenting on the fact that a criminal defendant did not take the stand to testify on his own behalf.

(2) That the votes of Justices Frankfurter, Black, Reed, Douglas, Jackson, Burton, Vinson and Clark in *Rochin v. California*[35] indicate their sympathy for narcotics peddlers because they voted in favor of the position advocated by counsel for alleged narcotics peddlers. The real question was whether the due process clause of the Fourteenth Amendment to the Constitution permitted police to obtain evidence of a narcotics violation by forcing an emetic solution through a tube inserted in a man's stomach.

(3) That the votes of Justices Clark, Black, Frankfurter, Douglas, Jackson, Burton, Vinson and Minton in *Hoffman v. United States*[36] indicate their sympathy for racketeers because they voted in favor of a position advocated by counsel for alleged racketeers. The real question was whether an individual properly declined to answer questions during a grand jury investigation on the ground that the privilege against self-incrimination of the Fifth Amendment to the Constitution justified the refusal.

(4) That the votes of Justices Black, Douglas, Reed and Jackson in *Beauharnais v. Illinois*[37] indicate their sympathy with racists because they voted in favor of a position taken by certain avowed racists. The real question was whether the liberty of speech and of the press guaranteed as against the states by the due process clause of the Fourteenth Amendment to the Constitution prohibited a conviction for portraying "depravity, criminality, unchastity, or lack of virtue of citizens of the Negro race."

(5) That the votes of Justices Douglas, Black, Reed, Burton and

Vinson in *Terminiello v. Chicago*[38] indicate their sympathy with Nazis because they voted in favor of a position taken by a Nazi sympathizer. The real question again involved the scope of the protection offered, even to words calculated to invite sharp dispute and anger, by the free-speech guarantees of the Constitution.

(6) That the votes of Justices Douglas and Black in *Hannah v. Larche*[39] indicate their sympathy with segregationists because they voted in favor of a position restricting investigative rights of the United States Commission on Civil Rights. The real question was whether the Commission's rules of procedure denying to persons against whom complaints have been filed the right of cross-examination of witnesses are consistent with the protection offered by the due process clause of the Fifth Amendment to the Constitution.

It is no more bizarre to suggest that the present and past Justices of the Supreme Court sympathize with the causes of the parties in the above cases than to make the same suggestion in cases involving national security. Accordingly, it should be no surprise that Senator Eastland refrained from charging that members of the Court were purposefully advancing the cause of Communism by their votes in the cases he selected.

III / Senator Eastland's Underlying Assumptions

If Senator Eastland did not mean to accuse the Supreme Court of lending conscious aid to enemies of the United States, then he meant that the effect of the Court decisions and the votes of individual Justices aided Communism. This position, when analyzed, discloses a particular attitude toward two distinct and important matters of government: (1) the function of the Supreme Court of the United States, including the proper basis for criticism of its rulings, and (2) the nature of the constitutional democracy known as the United States of America. On both issues Senator Eastland's assumptions are subject to severe criticism.

A. *The Supreme Court*

At the outset, let it be made clear that the Supreme Court should no more be immune from criticism than any other governmental organization in a functioning democracy. Such criticism is vital if the Court is to reflect the general will of the people. But not all criticism stands on an equal footing, and the charges leveled by Senator Eastland neither fairly assess the work of the Court nor make any contribution to its improvement.

Senator Eastland evaluates decisions of the Supreme Court according to their result and in so doing considers only one criterion —whether the decision is "pro-Communist" or "anti-Communist." Professor Robert Girard has pointed out that such epithets

> *signifiy nothing more than that their author either agrees or does not agree with a particular decision or group of decisions by the Court. If he thinks the Court should not have interfered as it did, then you have "judicial legislation" or, even worse, "judicial usurpation," depending upon the intensity of the author's conviction. If the Court should have stepped in when it did not the result is "judicial abnegation." On the other hand if the Court's response meets his fancy then you are blessed with "judicial restraint" or "judicial statesmanship."*[40]

Professor Henry M. Hart has pungently parodied the kind of result-oriented criticism that Senator Eastland has engaged in: " 'One up (or one down) for subversion,' 'One up (or one down) for civil liberties.' "[41]

Result-oriented criticism like the accusations of Senator Eastland is unfair and narrow. It ignores the law governing a particular legal or constitutional issue, and the reasoning by which a particular result is reached.

Before a ruling of the Supreme Court can be properly evaluated, it is necessary to know more than which side won. It is necessary to study the facts and the law governing a particular controversy, including the arguments prepared by counsel versed in the case. A proper respect for the Court requires such candid recognition of the competing legal claims and constitutional values. Proper criticism takes account of this, and judges the Court according to professional standards appropriate to its work.

Once again, it must be repeated, the Supreme Court does not and should not stand above criticism. But the criticism must be intelligent and discriminating, fitting to the high function of our highest Court. Perhaps the true standard for critics of the Court should be the same as that to which we expect the Justices themselves to adhere. In the words of Dean Griswold of Harvard Law School:

> *It is a process requiring great intellectual power, an open and inquiring and resourceful mind, and often courage, especially intellectual courage, and the power to rise above oneself. Even more than intellectual acumen, it requires intellectual detachment and disinterestedness, rare qualities approached only through constant awareness of their elusiveness, and constant striving to attain them.*[42]

Senator Eastland's criticism surely does not measure up to this exacting and high standard.

B. *Constitutional Philosophy*

As already mentioned, the sole guide to Supreme Court decisions, according to Senator Eastland, is whether the ruling is or is not "pro-Communist."[43] The fallaciousness of this standard as a means of judging the work of the Supreme Court has already been discussed. This portion of the memorandum will deal with some implications of this standard for our constitutional democracy.

In almost every case cited by Senator Eastland, an individual, several individuals or an organization was asserting a claim under the Constitution of the United States. In some of these cases the claim was accepted by the Court, on other occasions it was rejected. Senator Eastland's view is that when the claim was recognized by a Justice, his vote was "pro-Communist." This is an incorrect and dangerous attitude in terms of the high purposes of the Constitution and the Bill of Rights.

Why should not a vote in favor of a constitutional claim be counted "pro-American" rather than "pro-Communist"? Do not such votes serve to extend the liberties protected by the Constitution? Why could it not be said, with fervor at least equal to that of Senator Eastland's, that when a vote is cast in favor of freedom of speech or of the press or of religion, or to protect individuals against unwarranted searches of their homes or person, or to assure criminal defendants a fair trial, or to invalidate governmental action that discriminates on the basis of race, creed or color, that the Justice is fulfilling the high trust imposed upon him by his oath to "uphold the Constitution of the United States"?

The precedent for this view, contrary to Senator Eastland's, is long and weighty. The principal architect of the Constitution, James Madison, said in the very first Congress that "independent tribunals of justice will consider themselves in a peculiar manner the guardians of those rights."[44] Madison was speaking of rights guaranteed to the people by the Bill of Rights.

The decisive importance to this country of the freedoms guaranteed by the Bill of Rights can be illustrated by taking two brief excerpts from talks recently delivered by members of the Harvard Law School faculty to audiences abroad in which they described the essence of the American system. Senator Eastland's chart includes different types of cases involving the Bill of Rights; a high proportion of these cases concern freedom of speech and the rights of those accused of crime. Professor Livingston Hall had this to say about the rights of the accused:

Our traditional and cultural heritage of due process of law has greatly inspired and influenced the lives and activities of the millions of individuals, living and dead, who have made up Anglo-American *society. Rules of criminal procedure which treat human beings as individuals, and hold each one individually responsible only for his own acts, leave them free to go about their business, secure in the knowledge that they will not be unjustly punished by the State. This had a great effect in releasing their energy for productive and imaginative ends.*[45]

And in discussing the pivotal right of free expression, Professor Roger Fisher said:

Fundamental among the purposes of the first amendment is the role of free expression in the democratic process. Free expression is a means of developing public opinion. Free expression is an aid to an intelligent choice. And free expression provides an opportunity to make a choice. New and better ideas are most likely to be developed in a community which allows free discussion of any ideas. Without discussion who can be sure which ideas are right and which ideas are wrong? Finally, free-

dom of expression serves as an outlet for resentments and hostilities that otherwise might find more dangerous expression.[46]

A particularly moving statement of the enduring value of the freedoms guaranteed by the Constitution has been made by Professor Charles Black of the Yale Law School. It capsulizes the reasons for believing that decisions of the Supreme Court and votes by individual Justices in favor of enforcing the provisions of the Bill of Rights are patriotic in the most meaningful sense.

Consider the place of these phrases "equal protection," "freedom of speech," and the rest in the moral life of our Nation. They state our highest aspirations. They are our political reason for being; they are the things we talk about when we would persuade ourselves or others that our country deserves well of history, deserves to be rallied to in its present struggle with a system in which "freedom of speech" is freedom to say what is welcome to authority, and "equal protection" is the equality of the cemetery. Surely such words, standing where they do and serving such a function are to be construed with the utmost breadth.[47]

Wholeheartedly as one may subscribe to the above views, it is well to recall that they do not decide concrete cases. To decide properly, as has been emphasized above, one must study and reflect upon the law, the facts and the contentions of the parties.

The point here is different, but no less important. It is that Senator Eastland's methodology depreciates the constitutional protections that all Americans enjoy. It is impossible to accept the facile label "pro-Communist" without recognizing that the Senator includes within that definition Supreme Court decisions and votes of individual Justices that enforce the Bill of Rights—decisions and votes that do not seem alien to our heritage, but on the contrary are in the finest American tradition.

The attack by Senator Eastland on the Supreme Court and its members has now been analyzed from several points of view. Examination of a sample of the pertinent cases indicates that the rulings of the Court rest on solid ground. Moreover, there is no basis for any possible claim that in their rulings the Justices were motivated by sympathy for Communism. Finally, the simplistic criterion employed by Senator Eastland in evaluating the work of the Supreme Court ("pro-Communist" or "anti-Communist" decisions) has no validity in terms of the Court's complex constitutional role. Accordingly, it must be concluded that Senator Eastland's charges are wholly without foundation.

Since Senator Eastland's attack the High Court has continued to deal with the legal ramifications of a number of politically sensitive issues, including racial discrimination, reapportionment and religion in the public schools. Some of the Court's decisions, particularly those striking down laws requiring segregation and school prayers, have led to further charges of Communist influence and widely publicized efforts to "impeach Earl Warren." Fortunately, the vast majority of Americans give little credence to these attacks, however much some of them may disagree with the Court's rulings. The good sense of the people may be tested further in the near future if the Court takes under advisement a number of civil liberty issues emanating from protests against the Vietnam war and renders decisions that provoke the kind of unjustified criticism that Senator Eastland resorted to in 1962.

NOTES

The foregoing memorandum was published in 108 *Congressional Record* 22017–75 (October 12, 1962). It also appeared, in a somewhat revised form, in 111 *University of Pennsylvania Law Review* 693 (1963), with the title "Senator Eastland's Attack on the United States Supreme Court: An Analysis and Response." The author received research assistance from Civil Liberties Fellow Jeffrey M. Albert.

1. Hand, "How Far Is a Judge Free in Rendering a Decision?" in *The Spirit of Liberty* 103, 110 (3d ed. 1960).
2. 354 U.S. 118 (1957). See Senator Eastland's Tabulation, 108 *Cong. Rec.* 7028 (May 2, 1962) [hereinafter cited as Tabulation].
3. United States v. White, 322 U.S. 694 (1944); Hale v. Henkel, 201 U.S. 43 (1906).
4. 221 U.S. 361, 385 (1911).
5. 335 U.S. 1, 27 (1948).

6. 352 U.S. 985 (1957), cited in Tabulation.
7. 347 U.S. 227 (1954), 350 U.S. 377 (1956).
8. Gold v. United States, 237 F.2d 764, 775 (D.C. Cir. 1956) (Bazelon, J., dissenting), *rev'd per curiam*, 352 U.S. 985 (1957).
9. 352 U.S. 985 (1957).
10. *Id.* at 985–86 (Reed, J., dissenting), quoting Remmer v. United States, 347 U.S. 227, 229 (1954).
11. 347 U.S. 522 (1954), cited in Tabulation.
12. 355 U.S. 115 (1957), cited in Tabulation.
13. 362 U.S. 390 (1960), cited in Tabulation.
14. Internal Security Act of 1950, §22, 64 Stat. 1006, as amended, 8 U.S.C. §1182 (1958).
15. 362 U.S. 390 (1960).
16. See Tabulation.
17. 343 U.S. 1 (1952), cited in Tabulation.
18. *In re* McConnell, 370 U.S. 230 (1962).
19. Wood v. Georgia, 370 U.S. 375 (1962).
20. 343 U.S. at 27–28.
21. Tabulation, citing Scales v. United States, 367 U.S. 203 (1961); Barenblatt v. United States, 360 U.S. 109 (1959); Dennis v. United States, 341 U.S. 494 (1951).
22. 343 U.S. 250 (1952).
23. 337 U.S. 1 (1949).
24. Richmond Screw Anchor Co. v. United States, 275 U.S. 331, 346 (1928).
25. Lucas v. Alexander, 279 U.S. 573, 577 (1929).
26. 345 U.S. 41 (1953).
27. 353 U.S. 194 (1957).
28. Immigration and Nationality Act of 1952, §242(d), 66 Stat. 211, as amended, 8 U.S.C. §1252(d) (1958).
29. Tabulation.
30. United States v. Wiltberger, 18 U.S. (5 Wheat.) 35, 43 (1820).
31. 344 U.S. 218 (1952).
32. *Id.* at 221–22.
33. Tabulation, citing, e.g., Yates v. United States, 354 U.S. 298 (1957); United States v. Fleischman, 339 U.S. 349 (1950).
34. 332 U.S. 46 (1947).
35. 342 U.S. 165 (1952).
36. 341 U.S. 479 (1951).
37. 343 U.S. 250 (1952).
38. 337 U.S. 1 (1949).
39. 363 U.S. 420 (1960).
40. Girard, Book Review, 11 *Stan. L. Rev.* 800, 804 (1959).
41. Hart, "The Time Chart of the Justices," 73 *Harv. L. Rev.* 84, 125 (1959).

42. Griswold, "Of Time and Attitudes—Professor Hart and Judge Arnold," 74 *Harv. L. Rev.* 81, 94 (1960).

43. 108 *Cong. Rec.* 7027 (May 2, 1962).

44. 1 *Annals of Cong.* 439 (1789).

45. Hall, "The Rights of the Accused in Criminal Cases," in *Talks on American Law* 55, 68–69 (Berman ed. 1961).

46. Fisher, "The Constitutional Right of Freedom of Speech," in *id.* at 85, 88–89.

47. Black, *Old and New Ways in Judicial Review* 11 (Bowdoin College Bulletin No. 328, 1958).

4

McCarthy and the Army

(With John G. Simon)

"McCarthyism" has now entered the English language as a noun signifying political intolerance and the use of official power to harass and destroy one's political enemies. The man responsible for the word was Senator Joseph McCarthy, who terrorized leftists, liberals and just plain opponents during the early 1950s. He made wild and general charges, usually of "Communism," which had the dual effect of eliminating opposition and muting protest. The charges bore a strong similarity to those leveled by Senator Eastland against the Supreme Court in 1962, which were the subject of the preceding chapter. In both cases not only were the accusations, because of their nature, almost impossible to refute clearly before the bar of public opinion, but there was no judicial forum in which those accused could get legal satisfaction.

In the spring of 1954 the American people watched their television sets with fascination as Senator McCarthy and the United States Army bitterly clashed before a Senate investigating committee. The stakes—both personal and political—were enormous. It is now widely agreed that the Senator's constant exposure to the public during two months of hearings helped to erode his immense power and led eventually to his censure by the Senate in the fall of

1954. As the article that follows indicates, there was much more to the encounter than appeared over TV, and the Army was far from blameless in not earlier taking a principled stand against Senator McCarthy.

During this period the authors, fresh out of law school, were Assistants to the General Counsel of the Army, who was the official chiefly responsible for conducting relations between the Army and the Senator. They participated in many of the events that led to the hearings, and served as aides to Joseph Welch once the hearings began. Their article, with the title "McCarthy and the Army—a Fight on the Wrong Front," was published in the fall 1964 issue of the Columbia University Forum *on the tenth anniversary of the controversy. Mr. Simon is a Professor of Law at Yale University.*

The Army-McCarthy affair, which a decade ago left the nation confused and concerned about the men who were guiding its fortunes, returned to the news this year with the release of *Point of Order,* the filmed highlights of the celebrated hearings. The motion picture suggests a re-examination of the case, for it has reinforced ten-year-old recollections that the contest was merely a violent and unseemly power struggle between two leviathans. One of them, the junior Senator from Wisconsin, was charged with demanding special favors for a well-connected Army private. The other, the United States Army, was accused of using the youth as a hostage to halt an embarrassing Senate investigation. In the televised spectacular that ensued, Senator McCarthy and his chief counsel, Roy Cohn, vied against Secretary of the Army Robert Stevens, Army General Counsel John Adams, and Army Special Counsel Joseph Welch, with many other colorful supporting players—the Under Secretary of State, FBI agents, several generals, staff assistants accused of phone-tapping and photo-cropping, and the *casus belli,* Private Gerard David Schine.

The televised extravaganza, however, revealed only one facet of a complex controversy that encompassed issues far graver than the saga of Private Schine. One issue was the Army's loyalty-security program and its response to McCarthyism; the other was the right of a Senate committee to obtain Army secrets and question Army witnesses. On the first of these issues the Army hardly fought at all. On the other, it fought fitfully and in attempted privacy, and it was this sporadic engagement that led, by a winding path, to the televised hearings. Both of these campaigns represented, far more than the case of Private Schine, the nation's involvement with Senator McCarthy.

Throughout this troubled period, the Wisconsin Senator's supporters heard in his anguished cries a klaxon alerting the nation to a Communist "knife held against America's jugular vein"; his detractors heard in them a barbarous assault against the American traditions of fair play and due process. These positions reflected opposing reactions to the major premise underlying the Senator's public acts and utterances—the premise that a man who had any past association with Communists was a threat to the nation and had no claim to civilized treatment at the hands of his government. The premise was not Senator McCarthy's alone. It was shared by many other citizens during the years of the Senator's prominence, for these were the years of the Korean War, of Communist expansion and aggression, and of the conviction of Soviet agents in America and England. To some the premise was particularly attractive because many of the individual targets of McCarthyism came from the ranks of New Deal intellectuals who had complicated life for so long and who now seemed responsible for the latest threat to tranquillity posed by Communism.

But what made Senator McCarthy notable among the millions who shared his premise was the sweep and recklessness of his pronouncements. He used larger numbers ("fifty-seven Communists . . . in the State Department") and attacked more respectable figures (General George C. Marshall "serving the world policy of the Kremlin") than anyone else in public life.

Of all the Senator's targets, the one that sustained the heaviest siege was the most respectable—the United States Army. Senator McCarthy began his assault on the Army in the fall of 1953 at Fort Monmouth, New Jersey, the site of the Signal Corps Engineering Laboratories. Many of the engineers and technicians there had had some exposure during the depression to left-wing groups, some in the penumbra of Communism, and these men had been the subject of loyalty proceedings during the Truman administration. They had been cleared, but when the Eisenhower administration took office, an Executive Order was issued substituting a stricter security test for government employment and requiring reconsideration of all earlier cases in the light of the new standards. These cases were being reviewed when Senator McCarthy, armed with Pentagon intelligence documents that "named names," burst onto the scene.

With a succession of committee hearings and public pronouncements, he swiftly mounted a campaign designed to create the impression that there existed "current espionage" at Fort Monmouth. One technique was to hold an executive session of the Senate Special Subcommittee on Investigations (meaning a session attended by Chairman McCarthy, Counsel Roy Cohn and one or two staff assistants) and then provide a hungry press with a distorted and often inflammatory version of what had taken place. In one of the Senator's accounts to the press, for example, a witness was said to have testified that he was a close personal friend and an apartment mate of Julius Rosenberg; in fact, the verbatim transcript (not available to the press) disclosed merely that the man had casually known Rosenberg ten or fifteen years before and that he once had lived in an apartment into which Rosenberg moved *after* the witness had departed.

Another of the Senator's techniques was to use his congressional immunity to make exaggerated claims on the Senate floor. On one occasion, he asserted that he had received sworn testimony of current espionage at Monmouth. The only evidence he could muster, however, was that two individuals had pleaded the Fifth Amendment before the subcommittee on all subjects, and that one of them had made a large number of unexplained telephone calls to Fort Monmouth. In fact, they had never worked at Monmouth; they were former employees of a private firm that had done some government contracting.

These techniques yielded headlines—2 IN SIGNAL CORPS STILL SPY, MCCARTHY SAYS and SUSPECT FT. MONMOUTH AIDES GAVE REDS A-DATA—but the truth of the matter is that Senator McCarthy came up with exactly nothing in his Fort Monmouth investigation. Not one current or even recent employee was proved to be a past or present member of the Communist Party, and not one declined to answer any question put to him by the government or the subcommittee. If Senator McCarthy had information of "current espionage" at Monmouth, it died with him.

The public was thus deceived, but it was the Monmouth scientists who bore the brunt of the McCarthy siege. The publicity was only part of their torment. Senator McCarthy added a cruel personalized touch by telling at least one scientist that his denial of Communist association was in direct conflict with "other sworn testimony"—a complete misrepresentation, but the scientist did not know it—and then by announcing that the testimony would go to the Justice Department for perjury investigation.

Yet the critical disservice to these employees was rendered not by Senator McCarthy but by the Army. The Army loyalty-security hearing boards were attempting to judge the strength of current loyalties to the nation in the light of ten- or twenty-year-old social relationships or attendance at front-group meetings during the 1930s. Few of the cases involved any allegations more serious or more recent in time. In allowing the men to remain at work while their cases were carefully reappraised under the new Eisenhower criteria, the Army took the view that the existing derogatory information was not serious enough to require precipitate action. Under pressure, the Army abandoned this position.

During the few weeks when Senator McCarthy's investigation was at its height, more than thirty of the Fort Monmouth employees were suddenly suspended—many by the Monmouth Commanding General shortly before they appeared before the McCarthy subcommittee. Most of these men could not be restored to their positions until many months of security hearings had been completed—a period during which they suffered severe financial and personal injury. At the same time, despite efforts by Army Counsel John Adams to halt the process, another group of scientists were denied security clearance and assigned to routine nonsensitive work on the basis of minimal evidence; they labored—or rather, were permitted to vegetate—in what came to be known as the "leper colony" while awaiting issuance of charges or a belated decision that their cases did not warrant prosecution.

Sooner or later, it is true, suspensions and denials of clearance would have been imposed on a few of these men under the new standards even without the stimulus of the McCarthy campaign. But the sudden rush of mass suspensions and assignments to the "leper colony" could only have reflected an acceptance of Senator McCarthy's premise that exposure to Communism meant contamination and that contaminated men deserved little or no consideration.

At no point during the Army's controversy with Senator McCarthy, even during the later televised hearings on the Schine case, was the McCarthy premise openly opposed. Instead, the Army sat silent while Senator McCarthy boasted of his contribution to the nation's security. At times the Army acknowledged that he had expedited the suspensions, at times it asserted it was as speedy and vigorous as he, but all the time it maintained that the way it had handled the Monmouth cases had served the national purpose. What was perhaps most revealing was that the Army consistently denied that it had tried to stop the McCarthy investigations. Why *not* try to stop them? The abuse the McCarthy method visited upon the Army's civilian employees was intolerable, unless, of course, one accepted Senator McCarthy's premise and its implied rejection of an American tradition of fairness in the treatment of government employees.

The Pentagon accepted and applied the McCarthy premise even more strenuously in its treatment of *uniformed* men of the services. Here, as in the Fort Monmouth civilian cases, the Defense Department acted in direct response to a McCarthy campaign—this time, the campaign over Major Irving Peress, a dentist brought into the Army under the doctors' and dentists' draft. On his Army loyalty questionnaire and later before the subcommittee, Major Peress pleaded the Fifth Amendment on all questions relating to Communism; Senator McCarthy declared he was "part of the Communist conspiracy." Under the routine implementation of an act of Congress requiring grade readjustments for military doctors and dentists in accordance with "professional education, experience and ability," Dr. Peress's rank had been readjusted from captain to major, despite his pending security investigation. Thereafter, despite a pending request by Senator McCarthy that Dr. Peress be court-martialed for alleged subversive activities and for pleading the Fifth

Amendment, the Army gave him an early honorable discharge to be rid of him.

The Senator's reaction was ferocious. "Who promoted Peress?" he cried over and over, and what "Commie coddler" gave "this Fifth Amendment Communist" an honorable discharge? The Senator's rage over the Peress case created a fierce and instantaneous clamor at the Pentagon for immediate discharge of all soldier "security risks." As translated by the military personnel machinery in early 1954, this meant removal of soldiers with any derogatory information in their files, no matter how vague, ancient or indirect. In scores of cases it meant not only speedy discharge, but a damning undesirable discharge, even where the security information pertained solely to civilian life. Because the draft inevitably catches up a heterodox group of young men, the Army's traffic in soldier security cases had always been vastly greater—though considerably less publicized—than the security program of any other agency of the government. Now, as the Defense Department hastened to act upon Senator McCarthy's premise that an alleged risk deserves rough as well as speedy treatment, this program became not only the most active but also the most unfair.

In short, during the months that Senator McCarthy was on the attack, the Army and the rest of the military establishment retreated before him, taking his standards as their own and injuring a large number of citizens in the process. This, then, was the front on which the Army never really fought.

Why did the Army not fight? One explanation is that, the national temper being what it was, administration officials were loath to be thought "soft on Communism." Neither did they want the Republican Party damaged by a split; it seemed important to close ranks. Another reason some of these officials did not choose to fight Senator McCarthy was that they could not easily identify with his victims. This inability was perhaps understandable in view of the wide gulf between the executive-suite background of many administration officials and the less genteel minority-group origins of the average Monmouth scientist or Army draftee in security trouble. Moreover, few of these officials were sufficiently curious about the world of ideas to have any understanding of those who had explored the radical notions of the thirties and forties. Many of them fit

George Kennan's description of young security officers: they were "too virginal intellectually . . . to have known temptation." These were some of the men who translated McCarthyism from angry rhetoric into a program of action for the United States government.

At length, other voices prevailed within the Army, and where they did not the courts stepped in. On the civilian side, all but a few of the Monmouth employees eventually were cleared at hearings or by security review boards. On the military side, the Army later provided better procedural protection for accused soldiers and readjudicated the security discharges issued to several hundred men; still other ex-soldiers received improved discharges as the result of a Supreme Court decision holding that the Army could not issue a less-than-honorable discharge on the basis of preinduction activities.

The fact that most Monmouth employees were ultimately cleared resulted in part from what took place on another Army-McCarthy battleground.

Throughout the investigation of Fort Monmouth, the McCarthy subcommittee repeatedly demanded that the Army make available for questioning the members of the civilian loyalty boards that had "cleared Communists." John Adams resisted these demands, believing that the fair administration of the security program would be jeopardized if security "judges" were forced to account to the Senator. The protection thus afforded Army loyalty board members, and the confidence it stimulated in their ranks, may have made the difference between bold and cowed decision-making and thus affected the eventual outcome of many of the Monmouth cases.

Underlying the loyalty board controversy between the Army and Senator McCarthy was an issue of constitutional importance; it is one aspect of the doctrine of "separation of powers" between the executive and legislative branches of the government. The question is whether the Congress, when investigating the executive, is entitled to all the information it wants, or whether the executive is privileged to reject demands to inspect its papers or interrogate its employees when rejection appears to be in the national interest. This issue—one that was first raised when George Washington prevented Congress from investigating the negotiation of the Jay Treaty—cropped up again and again during Senator McCarthy's probes of the Army. This was the issue that the administration tried to settle in privacy, and the one that led indirectly to the Army-McCarthy hearings.

Trouble began in September 1953, soon after the Monmouth investigation opened, when Senator McCarthy demanded details from security files. The Army refused to comply, invoking a directive that President Truman had issued in 1948 forbidding dissemination of such information outside the executive branch in order to protect the reputations of individuals and the independence of security boards. In the face of Senator McCarthy's bitter protests (during which he persisted in referring to the "Truman-Acheson blackout order"), the Army stuck to its guns and continued to do so in later months.

The executive privilege fight broke out soon again with Senator McCarthy's demand for the appearance before his committee of Army loyalty board members. Because there was little direct precedent to support a refusal, John Adams called upon the Justice Department for guidance and also for reaffirmation of President Truman's 1948 directive. On both points the Justice Department privately supported the Army, but offered nothing in writing and nothing that could be quoted.

Several weeks later, the McCarthy committee suddenly and urgently renewed the demand. On January 18, 1954, while Roy Cohn and David Schine were vacationing together in Florida, John Adams informed Mr. Cohn by telephone that Private Schine's tour of duty at Camp Gordon, Georgia, would last four months or more, instead of eight weeks as Mr. Cohn had hoped. Mr. Cohn terminated his vacation and flew back to Washington that night. The next morning the subcommittee ordered Mr. Adams to produce the members of the loyalty board at 2 P.M. the same day.

The administration deftly headed off a collision. John Adams attended a strategy meeting with Sherman Adams, Assistant to the President, Attorney General Herbert Brownell, his deputy William Rogers, and Ambassador Henry Cabot Lodge. They decided to explain to the Republican Senators on the subcommittee how the new loyalty board demand had developed directly out of Mr. Cohn's interest in Private Schine's Army tour. Alarmed at the prospect of scandal, the Republican Senators remonstrated with Senator Mc-

Carthy. Although Senator McCarthy and Mr. Cohn called this "blackmail," Senator McCarthy called off the subpoenas. Meanwhile, Sherman Adams asked John Adams for a written history of the McCarthy-Cohn efforts to obtain special handling for Private Schine.

A month later, in February 1954, the executive privilege battle flared up again—this time over the Peress case. Shortly after the dentist's honorable discharge, Senator McCarthy called Dr. Peress's commanding officer, Brigadier General Ralph Zwicker, before the subcommittee and took him to task for not preventing the discharge. He told General Zwicker he was "not fit to wear that uniform" and that he was either dishonest or unintelligent; next he asked for details of the Peress matter, which General Zwicker declined to give on the basis of the 1948 Truman directive. The Senator then angrily demanded that General Zwicker show up at a later hearing ready to "tell us the truth."

Back at the Pentagon, there was outrage over the Senator's abuse of a general—abuse no worse than that earlier tolerated when it was inflicted on the Monmouth employees. Secretary of the Army Stevens stated publicly that he would allow neither General Zwicker nor any other officer to be subjected to further harassment; he would go to the hearing in their place. At last an issue—even if not quite the right issue—would be joined. But suddenly, as the Army was preparing for the great clash, the Associated Press ticker brought news of what came to be known as the "chicken luncheon." The Secretary had attended—alone and in secrecy—a luncheon meeting with the Republican members of the subcommittee. In the resulting Memo of Understanding, Mr. Stevens did an abrupt about-face by promising General Zwicker's appearance and the appearance of all other officers involved in the Peress case. Senator McCarthy capped the story by telling the press that Mr. Stevens had "got down on his knees." The resulting groan was deafening and global. One British paper said that McCarthy had won what Cornwallis never achieved—the surrender of the American Army.

At this point, in the words of President Eisenhower, "the Army moved over to the attack." But the issue on which the Army joined battle was not the fair operation of the loyalty-security program (the Pentagon had already given way on that) or any of the executive privilege questions. Instead it was the case of G. David Schine. Prodded by Congressmen and newspapermen who had gotten wind of the Schine affair, the Army sent to Capitol Hill a few copies of the Schine case chronology, which Sherman Adams earlier had asked John Adams to prepare. Eight hours later, the full text was in the hands of the public; the next day Senator McCarthy issued countercharges; and shortly thereafter twenty million Americans settled down to observe a marathon television spectacular that was stranger than fiction.

The Schine affair had begun almost a year before its appearance on television. In February 1953, David Schine, aged twenty-five, was appointed the unpaid chief consultant to Senator McCarthy's subcommittee on the recommendation of his good friend Roy Cohn, the subcommittee's new chief counsel. Mr. Schine's credentials were sparse. He had written a brief pamphlet entitled "Definition of Communism," which was distributed by his father throughout the Schine hotel chain. His knowledge of internal security had never led to his employment by the government or anyone else. He did not have legal training or any previous experience in investigation.

In the spring of 1953, Messrs. Schine and Cohn made a fast, well-publicized tour of Europe to investigate the "political reliability" of American information officers overseas. Shortly after their return, Mr. Schine learned that his local draft board had reclassified him 1-A. According to Senator McCarthy, this action was a response to pressure from "extreme left-wing writers," who hated the subcommittee. Whether Mr. Cohn shared this view of the Selective Service System or whether, as the Senator later put it, "[Cohn] thinks Dave should be a general and work from the penthouse of the Waldorf," the fact is that Mr. Schine's bad news precipitated seven months of incessant activity by Mr. Cohn, sometimes assisted (but sometimes secretly sabotaged) by Senator McCarthy. The campaign sought to avoid or at least mitigate the rigors of Mr. Schine's induction by:

(1) Obtaining a direct commission for Mr. Schine in the Army, Navy or Air Force (July–September 1953)—no success;

(2) Obtaining employment in the Central Intelligence Agency in lieu of Army service (October 1953)—no success;

(3) Excusing him from basic training so he could be a special assistant on Communist problems to the Secretary of the Army (October 1953)—no success;

(4) Excusing him from basic training so he could work for the subcommittee at some post in New York City (October–November 1953)—no success (Senator McCarthy privately opposed it);

(5) Obtaining a two-week delay in the start of basic training (October–November 1953)—success (but curtailed at Senator McCarthy's request);

(6) Obtaining passes from basic training at Fort Dix, New Jersey, and excusing him from duty to confer with the subcommittee staff in person or by phone (November 1953–January 1954)—success (passes on 34 out of 68 training days, 86 long-distance telephone calls placed and dozens received during duty hours);

(7) Obtaining a New York City assignment for Private Schine after basic training so that he could check West Point textbooks for subversive leanings (November 1953–January 1954)—no success;

(8) Canceling his assignment to Camp Gordon, Georgia, on the ground that it was "too far away" (December 1953)—no success;

(9) Attempting to shorten the length of Private Schine's training at Camp Gordon from four or five months to eight weeks (January 1954)—no success;

(10) Obtaining a New York City assignment for Private Schine after his Camp Gordon training (December 1953–January 1954)—no success.

In retrospect, there never was any serious possibility that Mr. Schine would obtain the commission that he so ardently pursued. The CIA and all branches of the armed services that considered the commission question agreed that he had no special training or other qualifications. But the attempts to free him from the duties of an Army draftee were another matter. They could not be repulsed so easily, because the avowed reason for most of these intercessions was "subcommittee business."

What Mr. Schine actually did during his evenings and weekends away from Fort Dix on special pass is a nice question. At the hearings, the McCarthy side asserted he had provided the subcommittee with valuable information, but this was contradicted by earlier statements of the Senator's. On one occasion he said that Mr. Schine was "a good boy, but there is nothing indispensable about him"; on another he described him as "completely useless"; and on still another, the eve of Mr. Schine's induction, he told Secretary Stevens:

> *I think for Roy's sake, if you can let him come back for weekends or something so his girls won't get too lonesome—maybe if they shave off his hair, he won't want to come back.*

Moreover, there was virtually no evidence of Mr. Schine's off-duty efforts. When Mr. Cohn was asked to produce all drafts or notes prepared by Mr. Schine, he came forward with only two and one-half pages, plus a few marginal notes. As the Democratic members of the subcommittee, Senators McClellan, Jackson and Symington, concluded, "It is hardly credible that such an allegedly prodigious worker could leave such minute traces of his labor."

More important than the question of Mr. Schine's indispensability was whether his Army service was somehow linked to the subcommittee's concentration on Army security. The hearings on alleged espionage at Fort Monmouth opened in August 1953, shortly after the Schine controversy began. That investigation was soon joined by other aggressive probes directed at the Army—into alleged subversion at the Quartermaster Depot in Brooklyn and at a Pentagon cafeteria, into alleged incompetence of the chief of Army Intelligence, into the case of Major Peress and other "Fifth Amendment" doctors and dentists in the Army, and even into the question of whether certain Army files pertaining to soldiers' Communist affiliations had been destroyed during World War II.

There was more than a chronological link between Mr. Schine and these investigations. The Army charged that attempts of subcommittee personnel to obtain favoritism for their colleagues were coupled with explicit or veiled promises or threats relating to subcommittee inquiries, and considerable evidence supported the charge. For example, there was the way the subcommittee's demand for the appearance of loyalty board members was peremptorily renewed as soon as Mr. Cohn got the bad news about Private Schine's tour of duty at Camp Gordon. Moreover, the link between the private's fate and the subcommittee's activities was reinforced by the late columnist George Sokolsky, who, playing the role of peacemaker, told the Army that if Private Schine were given a certain assignment, Mr. Sokolsky would "move in and stop this investigation of the Army."

Senator McCarthy and his aides attempted to meet the evidence by saying that the Army had it all backwards; the Army had held Mr. Schine as hostage to force cancellation of the subcommittee's investigation, and the Army had offered to supply "dirt" on the other services in order to turn away the subcommittee. These countercharges were emphatically denied by the Army witnesses and gingerly supported at the hearings by some, but not all, of the McCarthy witnesses.

The major evidence presented in support of the countercharges consisted of eleven memoranda of subcommittee conversations with Secretary Stevens or John Adams in 1953 and early 1954, which, if they actually took place, would bear out the countercharges. The McCarthy side asserted that the memoranda were written and filed immediately after the meetings at which the alleged conversations occurred, but Army cross-examination of McCarthy witnesses pointed up certain bewildering anachronisms in the documents. The Army's further inquiry into the contemporaneity of the memos was wholly frustrated by the McCarthy side. Senator McCarthy's personal secretary testified that she had typed all the memos herself but then declared she could not tell whether a single one of the documents in evidence was an original memo or a later copy; as for her stenographic notebooks, they had all been destroyed. Joseph Welch concluded that the authenticity of the memos was "a riddle . . . wrapped in an enigma that we won't be able to solve."

The hearings lasted from April 22 to June 17, 1954. More than two million words of testimony were recorded, but the undisputed high point occurred about a week before the end. Senator McCarthy, perhaps sensing that his grip on the television audience was slipping, cited a young law associate of Joseph Welch as a former member of "the legal arm of the Communist party." This attack proved to be the Senator's undoing when Mr. Welch, in sorrow and anger, excoriated Senator McCarthy's "cruelty and recklessness" for inflicting needless harm on a respected Boston lawyer. Roy Cohn vainly signaled the Senator to stop the attack. But it was too late—

the country had seen McCarthyism at work, and it would not forget.

More testimony and points of order followed this incident, but for practical purposes the hearings were over. Two months later, the special subcommittee that had conducted the hearings released its findings. The Republicans found that Mr. Cohn had been "unduly aggressive and persistent" on behalf of Private Schine but that the Monmouth investigation had not been used as a lever for this purpose; that the Army had tried to "placate" and "appease" Mr. Cohn; that the Army had tried to "terminate or influence" the investigation in unspecified ways; and that no one on either side was guilty of "dishonesty or bad faith." The Democrats came down harder on Mr. Cohn (he had "misrepresented the need of Private Schine's services") and on Senator McCarthy (he had "condoned" Mr. Cohn's actions). They criticized Messrs. Stevens and Adams for "appeasement" of Senator McCarthy and Mr. Cohn, but found "baseless" the McCarthy-Cohn countercharge that the Army had held Private Schine as a hostage.

Neither the press nor the public, however, seemed to pay much attention to the special subcommittee's apportionment of blame, for, in the last analysis, nobody really cared. No matter where the truth lay, the subject in focus was G. David Schine—or, more accurately, improper pressure applied by a Senate committee to achieve personal ends or applied by a military department to achieve bureaucratic ends. It was a subject that involved the personal integrity of certain public servants at a particular moment in history, but, as the special subcommittee must have known, it did not touch upon any of the basic principles of the Republic. As to such matters—the issue of fairness involved in the loyalty-security program, the constitutional issues involved in the executive-privilege conflict—the Army-McCarthy hearings had nothing to say.

There are those who contend that it all worked out for the best. They argue that if the Army had chosen to battle the Senator publicly on the loyalty-security front or on the executive-privilege front, the contest would only have strengthened McCarthyism in a citizenry nervous about subversives and looking for an uncomplicated approach to problems of national security. By fighting on the Schine front, the argument goes, the Army chose an issue divorced from the Communist question and yet one that would discredit the integrity of Senator McCarthy and his circle.

Certainly the Senator's decline and fall date from the hearings. It may have been coincidental, an early by-product of a nascent thaw, which culminated in the 1955 "Spirit of Geneva." But the hearings no doubt contributed. Unlike the classic demagogue, McCarthy met neither a violent end nor defeat on a momentous issue. Instead, a side affair—indeed a farcical one—brought him to the forefront, and there he perished. Prolonged exposure to the public weakened his position as a man on horseback and sent him a horseless rider down the road to Senate censure and lonely obscurity.

Yet the "all for the best" argument is singularly unappealing. It assumes that the public cannot be trusted on the big issues; that it can be expected to indulge its anxieties as a demagogue fans them; that, in this case, the public would not have respected reason and fair play, even if these concepts had been urged by such an impeccable advocate as the United States Army.

More important, the "all for the best" argument misses a major point about McCarthyism. It was not Senator McCarthy who damaged Monmouth employees and Army draftees so much as their Pentagon superiors. McCarthyism could injure individuals only to the extent that those in power cooperated with it. Thus, destroying Senator McCarthy was not alone what the country needed. It also needed public officials who had the instinct, intelligence and courage to do the right thing at the time when the issue arose—not two or three years later, when shelving McCarthyism would no longer create a storm. Senator McCarthy did present the ultimate test of the administration's mettle, and the administration, by eliminating him, eliminated the challenge. But that should never have been necessary.

5

The New York Attorney General and Civil Liberties

The rapidly accelerating demand for advanced, efficient and prompt services has placed tremendous stress upon state and local government. Many persons now realize that additional tax revenue is not in itself a sufficient answer, and that the organization of governmental units also determines the nature of services which are ultimately provided. Accordingly, the structure of government, on all levels, is undergoing close scrutiny and re-evaluation.

One particular area where empirical evidence of institutional obsolescence abounds is that of the organization and dispersal of state legal services. The problem is especially acute here because what at first seems to be a question merely of organization and efficiency, upon closer examination is seen to be important to individual liberties. It is no mere coincidence that federal law enforcement and federal legal services generally accord greater protection to individual rights than do those of the states, very few of which have adopted the federal model of an integrated department of justice.

In New York the 1967 Constitutional Convention provided that state with the rare opportunity of remodeling its governmental structure. A major issue was the organization of the legal depart-

ment. The Democratic State Committee on the Constitutional Convention requested the author's views on the office of the New York Attorney General and his recommendations for change. His paper, which was also submitted to the Committee on the Executive Branch of the Constitutional Convention, follows.

The forthcoming Constitutional Convention in New York will offer the delegates and the citizens of the state a rare opportunity to evaluate the existing charter of government and to fashion a new and hopefully more effective basic document. Many difficult problems of policy and draftsmanship will arise involving a host of subjects. The purpose of this paper is to draw professional attention to a subject that merits thorough re-examination—the office of the New York Attorney General and the Department of Law which he heads.

A review of the state's highest legal office is particularly appropriate at this time. During the past decade the quality and scope of the legal services performed in the United States Department of Justice have steadily progressed. There is generally little public evidence of the work of the Attorney General, but lawyers and others familiar with the Department of Justice can testify to its important and expanding role in the councils of the federal government. At the municipal level, too, there have been recent advances. New York City Corporation Counsel J. Lee Rankin and his chief aides have taken steps to improve the effectiveness of the office and to assure a leading voice in the Lindsay administration of highly qualified legal advisers.

The New York State Attorney General, in contrast, has lagged behind. It is true that certain responsibilities of the office have been handled creditably. The Civil Rights Bureau, in particular, deserves high praise. But overall there is a large gap between what exists and what the people have a right to expect.

In my judgment, the 1967 Constitutional Convention should revise the basic law of New York to provide for a department of justice headed by an attorney general who is appointed by the Governor, subject to state confirmation. In support of this position, I shall point to three areas of present deficiency—lagging law reform, the failure of the Attorney General to adhere to federal constitutional standards, and most important, the need for fundamental reorganization of the state's legal services.

I / Law Reform

The responsibility for discovering defects in the common and statutory law of New York and recommending changes to the legislature rests chiefly with the Law Revision Commission, created in 1934. Notwithstanding this arrangement, the Department of Law, through its Legislative Bureau, is also attempting to perform a similar role, at least in certain substantive areas, and is often asked by the Governor for an opinion on bills passed by the legislature and sent to him for signature.

This division of responsibility is plainly inefficient. The agency in the executive branch which is responsible for reviewing existing law and recommending legislation should also be the one which advises the Governor on the advisability of signing bills passed by the legislature. To this end, the Department of Law should be given full responsibility in the law revision field, and the legal research staff of the Law Revision Commission should be transferred to and work under the supervision of the Attorney General.

The limited role of the Attorney General in this field is also destructive of his task as chief legal officer. Rather than being expressly charged with constant review of the adequacy and fairness of existing law, he is bound only to defend the constitutionality of state statutes. While an orderly system of government requires that the Attorney General act as chief law enforcement officer, the performance of this duty should involve a critical review of existing laws. The law is, and must be, ever changing. The Attorney General should be at the forefront of this change, helping to mold the law to the needs of a modern society.

The defects of the present system can be appreciated by a cursory examination of four important areas of law reform that have been neglected in New York State.

The first is consumer credit, where sharp practices are capable of inflicting great harm upon the individual consumer and the national economy. New York has never joined other states in requiring lenders to disclose the finance charges of loans, in terms of dollars and cents and in terms of the percentage cost of a particular extension of credit. The failure of New York to enact an adequate "truth in lending" law can be explained only by the absence of responsibility at the level of law revision. Without the benefit of uniform rules for the expression of interest rates, the average consumer has no means of comparing available credit terms or realistically computing the annual cost of credit. As one of the most urbanized, credit-oriented states in the nation, New York should be a leader in efforts to provide protection to consumers. That it has lagged is partly due to the divided responsibility for law reform that characterizes our governmental structure.

A second important question for potential law reform that has gone unanswered is whether the state's "fair trade" or resale-price-fixing law, the 1935 Feld-Crawford Act, should be continued. A special exception to the state and federal antitrust laws, the act enables manufacturers and retailers to agree to keep prices above competitive levels, and the New York courts must enforce the agreement even against retailers who do not sign it. There are presently only seventeen states in the United States which allow fair trade agreements to be fully enforced in their courts—that is, against nonsigning retailers. The New York State Moreland Commission in 1964 recommended abolition of "fair trade" in alcoholic beverages on the ground that it results in higher consumer prices than in neighboring states. As early as 1955, the United States Attorney General's National Committee to Study the Antitrust Laws recommended repeal of the special exception in federal law which permits New York's "fair trade" legislation. It is time for New York, and especially its chief legal officer, to re-evaluate "fair trade" in light of the principles of a dynamic free enterprise system and the interests of the consumers of the state.

A third important area in which the Attorney General could play a paramount role is the emerging field of welfare law. The legal profession has become increasingly alert to the wide range of problems associated with defining and securing the substantive and procedural rights of persons entitled to public benefits and protections, such as unemployment insurance, workmen's compensation, social security insurance, public assistance, public housing, and child and welfare services. In addition, there is evidence of unlawful infringements of individual rights in the administration of welfare programs, such as arbitrary eligibility requirements, use of "midnight" searches, release of privileged information, and restrictions on freedom of movement. The Attorney General should have the power and the resources to conduct a much needed comprehensive study of these important problems, which affect the lives of millions of residents of the state.

Similarly, the Attorney General should systematically explore the thorny issues of law enforcement and criminal justice that are the subject of widespread controversy throughout the nation. Just as the federal government has embarked on a broad analysis of legal protections for persons accused of crime, New York should take the lead in providing a state perspective on these problems.

These four examples are merely a few of the many areas of law reform that have been neglected by the New York Attorney General as he attempts to function under an outmoded constitutional system.

II / Adherence to Federal Standards

Whatever one's opinion may be concerning the responsibility of the Attorney General for law reform, there would seem to be little room for dispute about his obligation to assure that state law is in harmony with the latest changes in federal law. But even here there is evidence of the passive concept which presently governs the role of the office of Attorney General.

Consider the Federal Voting Rights Act of 1965. Section 1973(e)(2) of the act provides that any person who is able to demonstrate that he has successfully completed the sixth grade of public school in the Commonwealth of Puerto Rico, even though the classroom language was not English, shall be entitled to vote in any federal, state or local election. Having met this schooling requirement, no person may be denied the right to vote because of an inability to read, write, understand or interpret material printed in the English language.

At the time the federal legislation was passed, New York State law prescribed a literacy standard in direct conflict with the requirements set out above. Article 2, section 1 of the Constitution of the State of New York required that every person be able to read and write English in order to be eligible to vote. Section 168(2) of the New York State Election Law expanded upon the constitutional requirement. The Election Law required that the prospective voter either pass an English literacy test or present proof that he had completed the sixth grade of a public school in the mainland United States or of a public school in the Commonwealth of Puerto Rico in which instruction was carried on "predominantly" in the English language.

Had the role of the office of Attorney General enjoyed a more dynamic interpretation, the legislature would have been encouraged to bring the New York Constitution and complementary legislation into harmony with the new federal voting standards. Instead, the Attorney General moved for and on April 4, 1966, was granted leave to participate as *amicus curiae* in a case then pending before the United States Supreme Court in which the appellees were challenging the federal legislation and seeking to retain the far more restrictive New York standard of voter literacy. When the case was argued before the Court on April 18, 1966, a representative of the Attorney General's office appeared to argue the unconstitutionality of the federal law and the legality of the state standards.

It is interesting to note that the New York City Corporation Counsel took a far less restrictive view of his function in the continued evolvement of state law. Appearing in the same case as *amicus curiae* in behalf of the appellant, Corporation Counsel J. Lee Rankin presented an argument in favor of the reform of New York law and the abandonment of the English literacy test.[1]

Another example of the need to accomplish a basic change in the concept of the Attorney General's office concerns legislative apportionment and districting. From the moment the United States Supreme Court held in 1962 that these are proper subjects for judicial inquiry, the Attorney General has fought to preserve New

York's unrepresentative legislative and congressional districts without, so far as the public record shows, proposing alternatives or suggesting improved machinery to extricate the state from the legal impasse created by conflicting state and federal court reapportionment decisions. Although the Supreme Court rejected the contention that New York's legislative districts met federal standards in June 1964,[2] it was not until two years later that the New York Court of Appeals finally imposed a constitutional reapportionment plan. That two-year period saw the Governor call a special session of a lame-duck legislature in December 1965 which enacted four plans, three of which were held violative of the State Constitution.

Nor has the Attorney General taken any steps to conform New York's congressional districts to the federal standards established by the Supreme Court in *Wesberry v. Sanders*.[3] The present districts (Laws of 1961, chapter 980) are based upon the now erroneous assumption that there is an "absence of Federal and State Constitutional and statutory standards governing the creation of Congressional districts."[4] Yet New York's congressional districts clearly violate federal standards since they are grossly unequal in population and among the most grotesquely gerrymandered in the country. As pointed out in a series of editorials in *The New York Times* for January 23–25, 1962, the present districting results from an attempt to permit a minority party to elect a majority of the state's congressional delegation.

The Attorney General has not put forward a permanent solution to the reapportionment and districting problems in the state. On the contrary, he apparently acquiesced in the veto by the Governor of a bill enacted by the legislature in 1965 which would have established a permanent bipartisan commissioner, the solution widely advocated by leading reapportionment experts.

The Constitutional Convention will be called upon to set forth valid standards and an appropriate mechanism with periodic apportionment and districting. The Attorney General should be taking a leading role in this enterprise.

III / Organization of State Legal Services

New York State's legal activities are now dispersed among a number of independent bodies, including the Temporary Commission of Investigation, the Law Revision Commission and many others. Most of the functions now performed by such independent bodies could be carried out more effectively if they were entrusted to a single department, with a centralized, highly trained investigatory staff and with full responsibility not only for enforcing the state's laws but also for proposing changes in them. The need for such a unified department is even more urgent today than when it was recommended in 1959 in the Ronan Report.

The anomaly of dividing responsibility for law reform between the Attorney General and the Law Revision Commission has already been discussed. The convention should surely consider carefully whether a division of functions is either administratively efficient or an appropriate means of assuring continuous review of state law.

Similarly, the "Temporary" Commission on Investigation owes its independent existence to factors largely unrelated to the wise distribution of legal services within the state. It was created, not because there was any reason to suppose that its duties would be better performed by an independent agency, but instead, to quote the 1959 Report of the Secretary to the Governor, William J. Ronan, proposing a reorganization of the executive branch of the New York State government, "in considerable measure [because of] . . . the awkwardness and uncertainty of the relationship between Governor and Attorney General"—meaning, apparently, that at the time the Governor and the Attorney General were of different political parties. Its principal duties are to investigate law enforcement activities, the conduct of public employees and other matters concerning the "public peace, public safety and public justice," duties already entrusted by law to the Attorney General (who must, in some cases, act with the approval or at the direction of the Governor). All present indications are that the commission, now in its tenth year, is temporary in name only.

There are other units of state government that now provide legal services that raise similar questions. These include the State Police and the Criminal Identification and Statistics Unit of the Department of Correction.

This is not to say that all independent legal entities should be absorbed by the office of Attorney General. In some instances there may be solid substantive reasons for independence. For example, the State Commission for Human Rights (formerly the State Commission Against Discrimination) investigates violations of the Law Against Discrimination. When a complaint is filed, it is assigned to one of the commissioners for investigation. If there is probable cause to credit the allegations, he may endeavor to eliminate the unlawful discriminatory practice by conference, conciliation and persuasion or assign the case to a hearing before a panel of three other members of the commission. The commission may order the respondent to cease and desist from unlawful practices and to take affirmative actions of compliance.

The Attorney General has independent powers to investigate violations of the Law Against Discrimination, to file complaints with the commission, and to prosecute criminal cases arising under various antidiscrimination laws. Within the Department of Law, there is a separate bureau to carry out these and other functions relating to racial and religious discrimination.

To the extent that the State Commission for Human Rights has a conciliatory role in eliminating discriminatory practices and a quasi-judicial role in holding hearings, it is no doubt reasonable to retain its independence. The question remains whether its investigative and enforcement functions should be handled by an integrated department or whether the duplicating work of the Attorney General could be eliminated by transferring its responsibilities in this field to the Commission on Human Rights.

IV / A Proposal: A New York State Department of Justice

The foregoing analysis has pointed to some serious deficiencies in the way in which legal services are being provided to the citizens of New York. Law reform has lagged, federal standards have been resisted, and overall organization has been inefficient. The Attorney General has simply not had the necessary power or the full responsibility to do the job.

The solution, in my judgment, is to grant him the power and hold him responsible for its proper exercise. This means that there should be established a department of justice, patterned on the federal model, which would centralize legal services by abolishing old bureaus or merging them into the new department, and where this is not desirable, nevertheless proclaim the ultimate responsibility of the Attorney General. Only in this way will the public receive an efficient and workable system in which the state's top legal officer can be held to book for the full range of state legal services.

There is a further matter of importance. As head of the Department of Justice the Attorney General should not be elected, but should be appointed by the Governor, subject to Senate confirmation. He thus will be the Governor's lawyer, responsive and responsible to him, an integral part of the administration that is politically responsible to the electorate. At the same time, the people will stand a better chance of receiving a *professional* law officer rather than a *political* head of the office. At present, the individual is chosen for the state ticket every four years, not on the basis of proven performance as a lawyer, but in order to balance the ticket or otherwise assure his election and the election of his running mates. This is not to say that good lawyers have not held the office of Attorney General, or that appointment would guarantee professionalism; it merely recognizes that the present system is not designed to produce the best available legal talent, because extraneous nonprofessional criteria dominate the selection process.

As *The New York Times* said in an editorial-page column last April, "the tasks facing the Constitutional Convention are complex, difficult, and of tremendous importance to the future." Study of the office of the New York Attorney General suggests that a thorough re-examination is called for, and the convention seems the appropriate occasion. The delegates should carefully evaluate the present system of electing the state's chief legal officer. They should also take steps to formulate an organization of legal activity along systematic lines that will lead to a modern and effective legal structure in New York. No better opportunity will arise in our generation.

The Attorney General of New York took exception to the above statement, and he defended his record in a letter to the author. He maintained that several of his actions, including the establishment of the first Consumer Frauds Bureau, the first Charity Frauds Bureau, and a Charitable Foundations and Trusts Division which protects investors, "demonstrate more than a passive interest by the Attorney General in carrying out his responsibility as the 'People's Lawyer.'"

The author responded by pointing out, first, that the Attorney General did not dispute the accuracy of any of the examples used to buttress the author's conclusions, and second, that except for the Consumer Frauds Bureau, the contributions of the Attorney General were primarily of interest to middle and upper income groups. That is, while reforms relating to charity, investment and theater-ticket frauds are to be welcomed, they do not protect the bulk of the people in their essential interests.

The New York Constitutional Convention gave much consideration to the future of the office of Attorney General. The convention finally decided to retain the elective character of the office but to try to consolidate some of the legal services in the state, thus approaching somewhat the federal model of a department of justice. Even this reform was aborted when the voters of New York rejected the proposed new constitution by an overwhelming majority on November 7, 1967.

NOTES

James M. Edwards, Anthony Gooch and Roger Thomas participated in the preparation of the paper.

1. The new federal standard prevailed over New York State law. Katzenbach v. Morgan, 384 U.S. 641 (1966).
2. WMCA, Inc. v. Lorenzo, 377 U.S. 633 (1964).
3. 376 U.S. 1 (1964).
4. McKinney's N.Y. Laws 1961 (Second Extraordinary Session 64).

6

Some Thoughts on Dissent, Personal Liberty and War

(With David Rudovsky)

Civil liberties in the United States have been most critically threatened during times of war or international stress. At such times there are added strains upon traditional forms of protest, induced both by fear for national security and by emotional appeals to patriotism. This perennial problem is accentuated when a substantial body of citizens does not confine itself to mere verbal protest but refuses to participate in the wartime effort. This stand is ordinarily predicated on a belief that a particular war is unjust, immoral or illegal, and it is bound to be profoundly unpopular. Almost inevitably, various forms of repression follow.

A difficult problem is presented: how to accommodate the claims of individual conscience with the recognized need of society to further its national goals and preserve its existence and power. Traditionally, the courts have been a major bulwark against efforts to erode individual freedoms. But in wartime situations the judiciary has demonstrated reluctance to interfere with government decisions, even those that seem callous to personal liberty. For example, during World War II the Supreme Court upheld the government's decision to relocate thousands of West Coast Japanese-Americans into camps despite the absence of a showing that those dispossessed presented a clearly defined threat to national security.

In view of this history, the reader should consider what the role of the courts should be in resolving the civil liberties issues discussed below, as well as the responsibility of the President and Congress in the absence of active intervention by the judiciary.

It is difficult to recall any issue which has so dramatically divided opinion in this nation as the war in Vietnam. Attitudes on both sides of the debate have become intractable, perhaps reflecting the positions of the protagonists on the battlefield and in the diplomatic arena. As the war has widened, further hardening of lines and escalation of opinion have kept pace. The recent shift—"From Dissent to Resistance"—by some protesters is indicative of the new mood.

It is not our purpose to explore the worth or wisdom of current foreign or military policies. The war's enormous toll of human and physical resources is fully documented. Equally obvious, we think, is the substantial effect that diversion of vast national resources from constructive pursuits to Vietnam has had upon domestic programs designed to foster full political, social and economic equality for the poor, the sick, the Negro, the oppressed.

On a different level, the conflict has also had sad consequences flowing from the fact that the extreme emotions generated during wartime are bound to threaten individual liberty. The pages of history are filled with accounts of repression of personal freedoms for which the justification invariably hinges on the alleged requirements of national security. In retrospect, few of these denials of liberty—which were the product of war-fever and of a narrow chauvinism—seem justified. Thus, the "Red scare" after World War I and the period of McCarthyism during the Korean conflict are examples of suppression that prejudiced high interests of the nation.

The concept of dissent in wartime often extends far beyond expressions of opposition, and ultimately presents some philosophic and political issues of considerable complexity.

The first problem involves the curtailment of dissent in its traditional form—the right to protest and criticize government policy. Although these acts of "higher patriotism"[1] may represent the most fundamental civil liberty endangered during a time of national crisis, the right of protest against our Vietnam policy—or any other policy of government—should be easy to resolve at this point in our history.

The courts have provided some protection for the protester. The United States Supreme Court, in the first case to reach it involving opposition to the Vietnam war, ruled that Julian Bond could not be excluded from the Georgia House of Representatives for uttering his sharp disagreements with national policy.[2] And the Court has agreed to decide whether the draft may properly be used as a punishment.[3]

Despite these developments, it is difficult to be sanguine. Earlier signs that the Court will not vindicate acts of protest which carry beyond the traditional confines of free speech[4] were confirmed in its recent decision declaring that the draft-card-burning statute is constitutional.[5] More ominously, large segments of the public still tend to equate dissent with disloyalty and nonconformity with treason. To many, protest and dissent only encourage the North Vietnamese and the Viet Cong to continue their fight. It is not very subtly suggested that if only the United States would present a united front, a quick resolution of the war would be possible.

Moreover, government officials have acted to still dissent. For example, the Director of the Selective Service System, Lieutenant General Lewis B. Hershey, has "suggested" that all local draft boards revoke the deferment of anyone engaging in "illegal activity which interferes with recruiting or causes refusal of duty in the military." Aside from the fact that this ambiguous directive is broad enough to cover speech protected under the First Amendment, it is extremely unlikely that local draft boards can constitutionally be the agents of a punitive governmental policy. Nevertheless, local boards have proceeded to make *ex parte* determinations that certain activity was illegal and have invoked Hershey's directive to reclassify scores of registrants. A judicial ruling that the practice of punitive reclassification is unconstitutional[6] and strong criticism from numerous members of Congress have not deterred Selective Service officials from this course of action.[7]

Of greater significance are the recent convictions secured against Benjamin Spock, Sloane Coffin and three other prominent antiwar figures. While raising several issues of civil liberty, the government's action has been viewed on a broader level as a warning to those who would dissent from the war, the draft and other aspects of public policy.

Despite these developments, we should like to assume that the cruder forms of intolerance will be rejected or at least confined, and we therefore turn to two issues of individual conscience and responsibility that are more subtle and more complex than the basic right to protest.

Specifically, we shall consider the problems of (1) compulsory military service and (2) conscientious objection to a particular war, including the meaning and pertinence of the Nuremberg judgments.

I

The Vietnam war has rekindled a latent national hostility to conscription and in so doing has thrown together the most diverse political elements on the American scene. The fact that usually disparate political voices have found common ground in condemnation of the draft indicates the depth of the issues involved. Like the proverbial iceberg, the draft's effects are often obscured by its relative position in the turbulent sea of war, politics and international crisis.

We would like to approach conscription from the vantage point of individual freedom. Taking this view, it is plain that compulsory military service constitutes a severe deprivation of civil liberty. It removes young men from their homes, occupations, education and family for long periods of time and deprives them of an intrinsic condition of freedom: the direction and control of their lives. It inhibits liberty of movement, residence and travel. It restricts the right of privacy. It limits the right to engage in one's occupation. Once he is in the military an individual's Fourth Amendment rights to be free from unreasonable searches and seizures is severely curtailed. If accused of a crime, he is denied his Sixth Amendment right to a jury and other constitutional rights basic to a fair trial.

Furthermore, even though the courts have protected the First Amendment rights of civilians to criticize the policy of the government during the Vietnam crisis, men in the military do not fare so well. For example, the Court of Military Appeals—the nation's highest military court—has sustained the court-martial conviction of Army Lieutenant Henry H. Howe for "conduct unbecoming an officer" and "contemptuous words against the President." The charges were based on Howe's participation in a peace demonstration, while off duty and in civilian clothes.[8] Private Andrew D. Stapp was convicted for refusing to obey an order to open his foot locker and disclose the allegedly radical reading material inside.[9] And in the most notorious case, Captain Howard B. Levy, a dermatologist at Fort Jackson, Georgia, was court-martialed for actions "prejudicial to the good order and discipline in the armed forces," "conduct unbecoming an officer" and disobeying an order. The charges against Levy were based on his refusal to train Special Forces personnel, and on letters and statements he had made criticizing the war in Vietnam and racial discrimination in the United States.[10]

Not only does the draft restrict liberty; it also subjects the individual to the risks of severe bodily injury and in many instances exposes him to the ultimate deprivation—loss of life. Furthermore, it makes him an instrument of the foreign and military policy of a government with which he may disagree. Yet he has no choice but to obey. For all these reasons it is proper to approach conscription as a program that inherently deprives men of freedom and therefore as one that should be viewed with deep suspicion and normally opposed.

One important way to oppose conscription—like other government programs inhibiting freedom—is to challenge it in the courts. The question is therefore presented whether the draft could be invalidated on constitutional grounds. There are cases rejecting such an approach.[11] They declare that the constitutional provisions authorizing Congress "to declare war" and "to raise and support armies" explicitly support a system of military conscription whether or not the nation is at war. In 1918, in the *Selective Draft Law*

Cases, the Supreme Court enunciated the theoretical justification for this position:

It may not be doubted that the very conception of a just government and its duty to the citizen includes the reciprocal obligation of the citizen to render military service in case of need and the right to compel it.[12]

Despite this sweeping language, constitutional arguments may be made attacking the power of the government to implement military conscription. The *Selective Draft Law Cases* rested primarily on a historical analysis of the intentions of the framers of the Constitution. But the Constitution itself is ambiguous. That Congress shall have the power "to raise armies" does not necessarily imply that armies may be raised through conscription. And the constitutional history contains evidence to the contrary. For example, a leading authority has noted that the framers of the Constitution expressed "substantial opposition to standing armies in time of peace."[13] But the most important evidence is the clause of article I, section 8, which gives Congress the power to call up the militia, the compulsory citizens' army of the eighteenth century. The traditional militia served only three purposes: to enforce the laws, to suppress insurrections, and to repel invasions. The clause further provides for dual federal-state control over the regulation and training of the militia. If the federal government can bypass these careful limitations, the militia clause becomes almost meaningless, in conflict with the clear intent of the framers, who considered the limits on the militia power of Congress a bulwark for personal liberty.[13a]

A second line of attack on the power of the government to order military conscription lies in an examination of a question apparently not considered in 1918. The Supreme Court asked only whether the Constitution gives Congress the power to conscript, and it answered that question affirmatively. But we suggest that even if Congress has the power to order conscription under article 1, this does not settle the matter. Justice Harlan stated the issue well in *Reid v. Covert,*[14] the case holding that Congress could not constitutionally give the military the power to court-martial civilians traveling with the armed forces. He said that two questions were involved.

First, is there any rational connection between the trial of these army wives by court martial and the power of Congress to make rules for the governance of the land and naval forces; in other words is there any initial power here at all? Second, if there is such a rational connection, to what extent does this statute, though reasonably calculated to subserve an enumerated power, collide with other expressed limitations on congressional power; in other words, can this statute, however appropriate to the Article I power looked at in isolation, survive the requirements of Article III and the 5th and 6th Amendments?

The Court in the *Selective Draft Law Cases* considered only the first question presented by Justice Harlan, concluding that conscription was reasonably related to the power to declare war and to raise armies. The decision failed to examine the possible collision of conscription with expressed limitations on congressional power. The restrictions which conscription places upon the draftee's civilian constitutional rights are, as described above, enormous. Thus, the failure to consider the Constitution as a whole in upholding the original Selective Service Act considerably weakens the World War I precedent.

Another line of attack on the constitutionality of military conscription would rely on an important constitutional principle embodied in recent decisions of the Supreme Court. This principle is that the government is not permitted to achieve even a legitimate purpose through means that broadly stifle personal liberties, when the government's objective can be more narrowly achieved. Implementing this concept of the less burdensome alternative, the Supreme Court has invalidated federal and state action impairing the freedoms of speech and travel,[15] and in an important opinion by Justice Clark it has even used the principle to strike down state legislation that burdened interstate commerce.[16] It is at least arguable that the principle is equally applicable to the case of compulsory military service in view of the substantial impairment of liberty that inevitably accompanies it.

But what are the less burdensome alternatives to the draft? The one most frequently mentioned would satisfy the nation's commitments through voluntary recruitment supported by adequate pay and other employment incentives. In view of the draft's interference with personal liberty, it seems fair to impose on its proponents the burden of demonstrating that a volunteer army is not an effective or realistic alternative. The argument is usually made that a volunteer army would place too great a burden on the taxpayers.[17] But it must be remembered that the draft itself is a form of tax on young men, who are forced to work at a salary well under the free market value of their services. Moreover, the draft is a particularly regressive tax since it weighs most heavily on the young and the poor. But most important, the choice between the draft and a volunteer army is a choice between two "expensive" forms of taxation, one of which is less costly to individual freedom—the end, after all, for which military manpower has been chosen as a means.

This is not to ignore the problems such an approach raises. First, the principle of the less burdensome alternative requires a difficult determination as to the legitimate needs of national security. Few would deny that conscription is justified if the continued existence of the nation is at stake. This is what James Madison termed "the impulse of self-preservation."[18] Put another way, it is consistent with a devotion to civil liberty for citizens to deprive themselves of freedom temporarily in the interest of meeting a graver evil. But the justification of pressing national security tends to lose credibility with the passage of time, and a nation that has deprived itself of liberty in order to meet a greater evil must be expected to minimize the period of deprivation.

Second, who is to decide the question of when the national security is threatened and what means are most appropriate to satisfy defense requirements? This is not a wholly new question to constitutional law. Some of the early cases held that the judiciary should pay great deference to legislative judgments on matters touching national security which were based on explicit legislative fact-findings. For example, in *Communist Party v. Subversive Activities Control Board*,[19] in upholding the registration requirements of the Subversive Activities Control Act of 1950, the Court stated that "the legislative judgment as to how the [Communist] threat may best be met consistently with the safeguarding of personal freedom is not to be set aside merely because the judgment of judges would, in the first instance, have chosen other methods."[20] But in a long series of cases decided since *Communist Party v. S.A.C.B.*, the principle of the less burdensome alternative has been used in such a way as to cast doubt on the viability of the analysis in that case.[21]

It should be emphasized, however, that none of the "alternatives" cases involved the wide range of political questions at stake here: national security, war, peace, congressional appropriations, and presumably expert decisions by government officials in both the legislative and executive branches.[22] Accordingly, despite the fact that the constitutionality of the draft is technically "justiciable" and presents a substantial question, there is realistically little likelihood that the courts will entertain cases presenting it, and a favorable decision is an even more remote possibility.[23] But whether or not the courts ultimately act, the fundamental question remains. This means that the legislature must take chief responsibility for revision of current law, bearing in mind that in a nation where concern for personal freedom is the ostensible basis for its existence, the elected officials are also obligated to achieve national goals through methods that least burden civil liberty. And if the Congress undertakes its responsibility in this respect, it could act in a more deliberate manner, more comprehensively and, as direct representatives of the people, with a greater warrant to broad acceptance of its proposals.

Finally, whether consideration of a volunteer army is undertaken on a judicial or legislative level, two additional problems remain. First, some maintain that a career army is likely to be less democratic than the present mixed army. But this is a dubious suggestion. The fact is that the officer class which determines policy in the present army is composed largely of career men. Further, the real political danger seems to be in what former President Eisenhower called the "military-industrial complex" and not in the manner in which men enter the army. Recent military takeovers in Greece and Argentina were staged by armies manned by conscripts, and Napoleon rose to power at the head of such an army.

A second objection to a volunteer army is based on the contention that it would attract, and retain through reinlistment, even a larger number of poor people than the present system and thus would have a disproportionately high number of Negroes. Even if this is true, we believe it is outweighed by the factors discussed above, especially when it is considered that each man would be free to make his individual choice as to an army career. In addition, what indirect discrimination exists against the poor and the Negro should be remedied through urgent reforms in the society at large, which is the true source of the evil.

Even if the power of the government to raise armies by conscription cannot be denied, this does not necessarily mean that the application of the draft law to particular individuals is also immune from attack. An individual's objection to a draft call may take many forms. One approach is based on the contention that the procedure employed by Selective Service in determining whether a young man comes within one of the statutory exemptions or deferments does not meet the requirements of due process. In view of the impact on individual freedom, it might be expected that the highest degree of procedural fairness would be guaranteed in Selective Service determinations. This is unfortunately not the case. As the Report of the National Advisory Commission on Selective Service[24] has documented, there are serious inadequacies in the procedures employed. Most boards do not allow an individual to be represented by counsel. They do not allow the registrant to introduce witnesses in his own behalf. They do not permit confrontation with adverse witnesses. They do not inform registrants of their rights under the law. Many boards are so understaffed that only a few minutes are typically devoted to each case. No record is made of the proceedings and the registrant is not allowed to bring a tape recorder or a stenographer. And the time for taking an appeal is strictly limited.[25]

Furthermore, the courts have been reluctant to review the determinations of Selective Service boards, on the grounds that Congress has provided that board decisions are final[26] and that the decisions rest on nonreviewable determinations of fact by an administrative agency with presumed expertise.[27] It is difficult to justify these restrictions on judicial review, which immunize Selective Service determinations unless they are shown to be arbitrary or capricious, and without any basis in fact.[28]

There are other aspects of the system that are open to challenge. For example, it is strongly arguable that where Negroes are systematically excluded from draft boards, Negro registrants are deprived of equal protection of the laws. This view has support in the *Jury Exclusion Cases*[29] and is presently being litigated.[30] Members of economically disadvantaged groups generally may also raise equal protection objections to the system of deferments. For example, research by Representative Augustus Hawkins of southern California reveals that only 5 percent of the Negroes who physically and mentally qualify for military service can obtain deferment as college students, whereas 95 percent of the whites are so deferred.[31] This issue is also being litigated; a three-judge federal court has recently been convened in New York to consider whether the system of student deferments constitutes economic discrimination in violation of the equal protection clause of the Fourteenth Amendment.[32]

We have not attempted to catalogue the entire range of civil liberty issues raised by a system of conscription. It seems plain, however, that the draft—both conceptually and as administered by Selective Service—is an inherently coercive system, and that to date the response of government officials to these issues has not been commensurate with their grave significance.

II

A second issue of civil liberty has been precipitated for the first time in this country by the war in Vietnam: selective conscientious objection. It is presently being urged in several courts that federal statutes and the Constitution itself support conscientious objector status based upon a refusal to participate in a particular war, specifically the war in Vietnam.[33]

Despite widespread belief to the contrary, the issue of whether one must abjure participation in all wars to be entitled to conscientious objector status is not concluded either by a fair reading of the applicable statute and its legislative history or by judicial construction of the relevant language. The statute exempts those who by reason of religious training and belief are "conscientiously opposed to participation in war in any form."[34] It is certainly arguable, as two courts have already held, that the words "in any form" relate to "participation" by the individual concerned and not to "war."[35] Moreover, if this language is interpreted to exclude the selective conscientious objector, the issue is then raised whether

Congress has discriminated against certain varieties of religious belief. For if only those whose religion compels them to oppose *all* wars are granted CO status, is there not a patent discrimination against the individual whose religion compels opposition to only a certain type of war?

It is increasingly recognized that sincere objection to engaging in a particular war may stem from the same depth of conscience as that which compels resistance to participation in all wars; that it need not be mere political protest; that it can, for example, be based on an ethical or religious revulsion against a war of aggression or a nuclear or genocidal war.[36]

Traditionally, of course, conscience has been regarded as congruent with the precepts of organized religion. But recently, in a landmark ruling, the Supreme Court extended this concept to those who do not express themselves in these terms. In *United States v. Seeger,*[37] the Court was faced with the issue whether the conscientious objector exemption granted by the Selective Service law to those who oppose participation in war by reason of their "religious training and belief"[38] was unconstitutional because it discriminated against different forms of religious expression. In order to save the statute, the Court construed it to include a wide range of religious beliefs, including those of persons who do not belong to an orthodox religious sect. The Court ruled that

> *The test of belief . . . is whether a given belief that is sincere and meaningful occupies a place in the life of its possessor parallel to that filled by [the] orthodox belief in God of one who clearly qualifies for the exemption.*[39]

The *Seeger* case logically implies that claims of conscience may rest on considerations other than those of organized religion. Ethical, humanist, moral or philosophic principles which are central to man's belief and tradition must now be recognized as worthy of the same respect—and the same protection—as those based on conventional religion. Indeed, most branches of Christianity, from the time of Constantine, have accepted a theory of the "just" war.[40] The obvious corollary is that certain wars may be unjust.

At this point let it be emphasized that it is only a "great society"

—and that term is used nonpolitically—which can implement the concept of selective conscientious objection. But ours would not be the first to do so. In 1940, while absorbing the terrible brunt of the Nazi war machine, England glorified her finest hour by recognizing selective claims of conscience.

Fear has been expressed that extension of CO status to selective objectors will operate to condone and encourage civil disobedience. There is simply no necessary relationship between the two. Congressional recognition of the conscientious objector, even in its limited form, reflects agreement that there is a fundamental difference between disobedience of laws generally and conscientious disobedience to laws which require the taking of another's life.

Exemption in this very narrow area need not be and has not been a precedent for refusal to obey any other law. More important, experience under the traditional exemption of our present Selective Service law negates this inference. Civil disobedience has not been promoted by the exemption; in fact, it may have been neutralized. For by recognizing legitimate claims of conscience, the government has relieved conscientious objectors of their quandary and thus forestalled the disobedient acts which frequently would have followed.

One other fear should also be allayed: the understandable concern that spurious claims would flourish if selective objection were to be recognized. But the British experience indicates that few men will apply for selective conscientious exemption. Furthermore, men seeking this exemption from military service must undergo a rigid investigation. Feigning of conscience is difficult, and is not the likely avenue of escape for those who, if they wished, might evade the draft through loopholes in the law. Even were this not so, a nation centrally concerned with the individual, it seems to us, can afford the risk of exempting a few "unconscientious" persons in order to ensure the protection of sincere claims.

The question of selective objection to a particular war leads to consideration of a closely related but separate problem: the meaning and possible relevance of the judgments rendered at Nuremberg against German war criminals. The Nuremberg decrees established as principles of international law that each individual has a duty to determine for himself the legality of his country's actions and that he must refuse to comply with orders which, if followed, would involve complicity in war crimes, crimes against peace or crimes against humanity. In other words, Nuremberg means that an individual ordered by his government to take certain wrongful action was not thereby absolved from personal responsibility. Specifically, the tribunal said:

> *. . . those who execute the plan do not avoid the responsibility by showing that they acted under the direction of the man who conceived it. Hitler could not make aggressive war by himself. He had to have the cooperation of statesmen, military leaders, diplomats, and business men.*[41]

A number of young men have attempted to invoke this doctrine during the Vietnam war, the most noteworthy being Captain Howard B. Levy during his recent court-martial for refusing to train Green Berets in certain medical practices. In a precedent-making decision, the military tribunal recognized the acceptability of such a defense by hearing evidence based upon the Nuremberg war-crime rationale.[42] To date, however, the civilian courts have refused to entertain the issue.[43]

It may seem curious that the Nuremberg judgments are now sought to be invoked as binding precedent upon one of the states that prosecuted the Nazi war criminals. Yet this development was clearly anticipated at the time. The late Justice Jackson, our chief representative at Nuremberg, said:

> *. . . while this law is first applied against German aggressors . . . it must condemn aggression by any other nations, including those which sit here now in judgment.*[44]

Some would assert that Nuremberg amounts to little more than a historical incident, that its position in the corpus of international law is at best tenuous, and that it merely represents the *ex post facto* judgment of the victors over perpetrators of perhaps the most atrocious crimes man has yet dealt his fellow man. Surely, though, Nuremberg's significance is greater than this. It attempts to resolve by an appeal to better instincts the high tension induced in a democratic society by the conflict between two sovereigns—the state and personal conscience—and it denies the individual the right to absolve himself by delegating this responsibility to the state. It is on this level that the selective objection and the Nuremberg principles coincide.

The President's Commission on Selective Service and other authorities have said that to leave the resolution of this conflict to the individual would be too dangerous. But can this be accepted? Can a democratic people admit that the exercise of individual moral and legal responsibility is a threat to our existence? If moral revulsion to a specific national policy becomes widespread, we might examine the possibility that selective conscientious objection, based on Nuremberg or otherwise, might serve as a *political* check on the arbitrary use of governmental power. This, indeed, may well be the most significant implication of Nuremberg.

Our discussion of the Nuremberg judgments should not be taken to imply that the proper relationship between freedom and order is simple. There are no easy answers to many difficult questions. For example, what constitutes a violation of the Nuremberg law? Must the degree of atrocity equal that perpetrated by the Nazis? And how far down the ranks of officials and participants does the Nuremberg rationale extend? However these questions are answered, the widening debate over the nature of our involvement in Vietnam indicates that the citizens of this nation are not prepared to regard the Nuremberg judgments as purely political expressions of military victory, or merely as historical curiosities.

The Vietnam war requires the United States, during a period of external crisis and internal strain, to confront its historic ideals and reaffirm its commitment to certain fundamental values. Since we have been forced to shoulder this responsibility, let us make the self-examination a serious and searching process. In doing so the nation should recall that the degree to which it will protect individual liberty during a period of crisis may well be the ultimate test of its political morality.

NOTES

An earlier version of this paper was delivered by the author in June 1967 at the commencement exercises of Point Park College, Pittsburgh. It was subsequently published in the August 1968 *American Bar Association Journal.* Dr. Irwin Feinberg, a member of the Hays Advisory Committee, and Civil Liberties Fellows Sylvia Law and John C. Gray, Jr., made helpful suggestions.

1. Fulbright, *The Arrogance of Power,* "Part I" (1966).
2. Bond v. Floyd, 385 U.S. 116 (1966).
3. Oestereich v. Selective Service System, Local Bd., No. 11, 280 F. Supp. 78 (D. Wyo. 1968), *cert. granted,* May 20, 1968.
4. See, e.g., Levy v. Corcoran, 389 U.S. 960 (1967); Turner v. New York, 389 U.S. 1056 (1967); Brothman v. Michigan, 389 U.S. 1044 (1968).
5. O'Brien v. United States, *decided* May 27, 1968.
6. Several suits based on the rationale of *Wolff* have been filed challenging the spate of reclassifications following the Hershey directive. Wolff v. Selective Service Local Board, *supra* note 2.
7. Punitive reclassification is not the sole method by which Selective Service regulates the lives of its registrants. More coercive, if less obvious to the public, is its practice of "channeling" individuals into "desirable activities" through the threat of loss of deferment. This psychology is described by Selective Service as "the American or indirect way of achieving what is done in foreign countries where choice is not permitted." Selective Service System, *Memorandum on Channeling* (1965).
8. United States v. Howe, U.S.C.M.A., No. 19846, decided August 6, 1967.
9. See *N.Y. Times,* May 31, 1967, p. 53, col. 5; June 2, 1967, p. 6, col. 4.
10. *Ibid.,* June 5, 1967, p. 1, col. 3; June 5, 1967, p. 22, col. 4.
11. Selective Draft Law Cases, 245 U.S. 366 (1918); United States v. Henderson, 180 F.2d 711 (7th Cir. 1950).
12. 245 U.S. at 378.
13. Henderson, "Courts Martial and the Constitution: The Original Understanding," 71 *Harv. L. Rev.* 293, 299 (1957).

13a. See generally Black, "The Selective Draft Law Cases—a Judicial Milestone on the Road to Absolutism," 11 *B.U.L. Rev.* 37 (1931); Wiener, "The Militia Clause of the Constitution," 54 *Harv. L. Rev.* 181 (1940); Freeman, "The Constitutionality of the Peacetime Draft," 31 *Va. L. Rev.* 40 (1944).

14. 354 U.S. 1, 70 (1954).
15. Keyishian v. Board of Regents, 385 U.S. 589 (1967); Lamont v.

Postmaster General, 381 U.S. 301 (1965); Shelton v. Tucker, 364 U.S. 479 (1960); Lovell v. Griffin, 303 U.S. 444 (1938).

16. Dean Milk Co. v. City of Madison, 340 U.S. 349 (1951).

17. Several studies of the economic feasibility of a volunteer army were done in preparation for the passage of the 1967 Selective Service Act. In April 1964, a study of the draft was initiated by the Department of Defense at the direction of the President. The study, completed before the Vietnam buildup, was never released. Assistant Secretary of Defense Thomas D. Morris, testifying before the House Armed Services Subcommittee in June 1966, concluded on the basis of the study that a volunteer army was prohibitively expensive. See 46 *Cong. Digest* 131–60 (May 1967). On the other hand Dr. Walter Y. Oi, one of the economists who participated in the Defense Department study, has concluded on the basis of the same data that a volunteer army would cost less than the lowest estimate given by the Defense Department and may under one theory of cost computation cost less than a conscripted army. A summary of Dr. Oi's estimates is given in Dr. Milton Friedman, "The Case for an All Volunteer Army," *N.Y. Times Magazine,* May 14, 1967, p. 23.

18. Madison, *The Federalist Papers,* No. 41 at 257 (New American Library ed., 1961).

19. 367 U.S. 1 (1961).

20. *Id.* at 96–97.

21. See cases cited *supra* note 15. See also United States v. Brown, 381 U.S. 437 (1965); United States v. Robel, 389 U.S. 258 (1967).

22. In United States v. Butler, 389 F.2d 172 (6th Cir. 1968), decided February 1968, a case arising before the Vietnam buildup, the court dismissed a challenge to the constitutionality of the draft on the ground that a volunteer army was at the time a less burdensome alternative.

23. But see the dissenting opinions of Justices Stewart and Douglas from the denial of certiorari in Mora v. McNamara, 389 U.S. 934 (1967), in which they stated that the question of the "legality" of the Vietnam war was one of "great magnitude" deserving of Supreme Court consideration.

24. *In Pursuit of Equity: Who Serves When Not All Serve* (February 1967).

25. See generally *ibid.*

26. The Military Selective Service Act of 1967, §10(b)(3), provides that there be no judicial review of the "classification" or processing of any registrant "except by way of a criminal defense in prosecution for failure to report for induction." And see National Student Association v. Hershey, C.A. No. 3078–67, D.C.D.C. (March 1968).

27. See, e.g., United States v. Falbo, 320 U.S. 549 (1944).

28. See, e.g., Estep v. United States, 327 U.S. 114 (1946); Dickinson v. United States, 346 U.S. 389 (1953).

29. Whitus v. Georgia, 385 U.S. 545 (1967); Labat v. Bennett, 365 F.2d 698 (5th Cir. 1966) (en banc).

30. See *N.Y. Times*, March 29, 1968, p. 15, col. 1.

31. 113 *Cong. Rec.* 4283 (April 18, 1967).

32. Boyd v. Clark, Civil No. 2529 (S.D.N.Y., filed Aug. 16, 1967). See also note "Student Deferment and Equal Protection," *1 Colum. Survey of Human Rights L.* 68 (1968).

33. Noyd v. McNamara, 267 F. Supp. 701 (D. Colo. 1967), *aff'd per curiam*, 378 F.2d 538 (10th Cir. 1967), *cert. denied*, 389 U.S. 1022 (1967). See also United States v. Kauten, 133 F.2d 703 (2d Cir. 1943).

34. 50 U.S.C. App. Sec. 456(j), as amended (1967).

35. Taffs v. United States, 208 F.2d 329 (8th Cir. 1953), *cert. denied*, 347 U.S. 928 (1954); United States v. Hartman, 209 F.2d 366 (2d Cir. 1954). See also Sicurella v. United States, 348 U.S. 385 (1955).

36. See generally Hochstadt, "The Right to Exemption from Military Service of a Constitutional Objector to a Particular War," 3 *Harv. Civil Liberties–Civil Rights L. Rev.* 1 (1967).

37. 380 U.S. 163 (1965).

38. 50 U.S.C. App. Sec. 456(j), as amended (1967).

39. 380 U.S. at 166.

40. Selective Service System, 1 *Conscientious Objection* 8 (Special Monograph No. 11, 1950).

41. 6 F.R.D. 69, 112 (1946).

42. See *N.Y. Times*, May 25, 1967, p. 2, col. 4.

43. See, e.g., Mitchell v. United States, 369 F.2d 329 (2d Cir. 1966), *cert. denied*, 386 U.S. 972 (1967).

44. 1 *Nazi Conspiracy and Aggression* 172 (1946).

SECTION II

THE FIRST AMENDMENT

In deceptively simple language the First Amendment provides that "Congress . . . shall make no law abridging the freedom of speech." The meaning of this clause, which was ratified in 1791 as part of the original Bill of Rights, has perplexed both courts and scholars, and there is a wide area of uncertainty about just what speech it protects.

Until relatively recently there was very little judicial authority interpreting the First Amendment. It was not until 1919 that the Supreme Court, in a case involving opposition to the World War I draft, first ruled on a claim that a federal statute unconstitutionally interfered with free expression; not until 1925 that the Court indicated that the states were also bound—under the due process clause of the Fourteenth Amendment—not to "abridge the freedom of speech," and not until 1965 that a federal statute was actually declared invalid on this ground. Particularly with respect to federal statutes, the Court has either avoided decision under the First Amendment or—as in cases involving the anti-Communist Smith Act and the House Un-American Activities Committee—it has found a formula to sustain the government action, even while conceding that some inhibition on free speech has occurred. Over the strong dissent of a minority of Justices, the Court has "balanced" the values of free speech against the value of proceeding against alleged conspiracies to advocate the overthrow of the government by force (as with the Smith Act) or of permitting untrammeled legislative investigations, even into political beliefs (as with HUAC).

In all these cases, of course, politics and constitutional law become intertwined and the legal issues blurred as the government uses the courts to bolster or create new power positions against real or imagined enemies of the state. Accordingly, the development of First Amendment doctrine has proceeded untidily, with Supeme Court decisions inevitably reflecting not only differing judicial views on complex issues of law but also the political mood of the country when a particular case arises.

The first chapter in this section involves the case of *Lamont v. Postmaster General*, which was the first Supreme Court decision invalidating federal legislation for abridging free speech. The reader should note that there was no claim that the Post Office was completely suppressing "foreign Communist propaganda," but only that for the government to require a signed receipt from an individual before he could receive such alleged literature was sufficiently burdensome to render the statute unconstitutional.

The next two chapters also involve censorship, but of a different character. Chapter 8 concerns restrictions imposed by the Army on newspapers operating within the jurisdiction of a military command. Among the problems presented are the exact scope of the First Amendment in such areas and just what role the courts can play in resolving a matter that has traditionally been handled through executive action. Chapter 9 discusses the political tests imposed on performers by the private networks, and the government is involved primarily through the Federal Communications Commission. As the pertinent regulatory agency, the Commission was the appropriate forum for blacklisted individuals to seek relief in the first instance.

There are special reasons to protect the freedom of expression of the academic community, which has traditionally been permitted, indeed encouraged, to explore the world of ideas in novel and unpopular ways, without fear of losing position or income. These reasons have led to the concept of academic tenure, under which professors cannot be dismissed or demoted except for misconduct of a serious kind. Chapter 10 deals with the validity of a dismissal by a state university of a professor who did not have tenure because of the unpopularity of his views. The chapter also illustrates, as does the *Lamont* case in Chapter 7, how problems of fair procedure, considered more fully in Section III, are closely intertwined with the protections accorded free speech by the First Amendment.

During the early 1960s, in an attempt to secure equal rights for Negroes, a wave of sit-ins and other forms of protests swept through the South. These efforts raised a number of legal questions, but none more difficult than distinguishing between speech that is protected by the First Amendment and action that is not. It has long been clear that symbolic speech, through signals or similar means of communication, is at least partly protected, and the Supreme Court has developed special rules for picketing in labor disputes. The same problem is at the heart of the current controversy over draft-card burning; the burning of the card is an act, but the purpose of the burning is to communicate an idea. Although the memorandum contained in Chapter 11 was occasioned by racial discrimination and therefore could have been placed in Section IV, the underlying issue it discusses is the degree to which various forms of protest are protected by the First Amendment, and it has accordingly been included in this section.

The final chapter in the section deals with a different clause of the First Amendment, which provides that "Congress shall make no law respecting an establishment of religion, or prohibiting the free exercise thereof." In 1940 this clause, which has come to symbolize the separation of church and state in the United States, was held by the Supreme Court to be binding on the states through the Fourteenth Amendment due process clause. It is now at the core of a national controversy over federal and state aid to education, the question being whether direct aid to church schools or even indirect aid, such as provision of teaching materials, violates the constitutional provision. The conference in Chapter 12 brings together a variety of viewpoints on this issue.

7

Censorship of "Foreign Communist Propaganda"

Censorship can take many forms. It can proscribe literature deemed "pornographic" as well as political views, and it can be carried on by civic and religious organizations as well as by the government. It has existed in almost all societies from the beginning of time, as those in power seek to ban ideas they consider unpalatable, in particular those which threaten the regime or one of its vital interests. This chapter deals with an example of political censorship that potentially affected millions of American readers: the efforts by the Post Office to limit the availability of unpopular political literature from abroad.

Beginning in 1951 the government undertook a program to stop the flow of "foreign Communist propaganda" into the United States. At first the material was confiscated upon entry. In 1956 the policy was changed to allow persons who requested the material to receive it. The program was justified on the theory that persons abroad who sent propaganda into the United States could be treated as foreign agents under the Foreign Agents Registration Act. President Kennedy ordered the practice ended in March 1961, but the following year Congress passed legislation to reinstitute the system. The new statute, 39 U.S.C. § 4008, provided that mailed matter, except *sealed letters, originating in a foreign country and determined by the Secretary of the Treasury to be "Communist political propaganda" was to be "detained" by the Postmaster General and "delivered only upon the addressee's request," with certain exceptions, and "disposed of" in the absence of a request for delivery.*

Corliss Lamont was engaged in the business of publishing and distributing pamphlets and other literature on subjects of public interest. In July 1963 he received a notice from the Post Office Department in San Francisco, California, that mail addressed to him, consisting of "Peking Review #12, 1963, 1 copy," was being detained as "Communist political propaganda," pursuant to the statute. The notice advised him that unless a specific request was received for the mail, it would be destroyed. Without responding to the notice, Lamont brought an action to declare the statute unconstitutional. A lower court rejected the claim, and the case was then taken to the United States Supreme Court. Excerpts from Lamont's brief follow.

I / The statute impairs freedom of expression.

The broad right to distribute literature, protected by the First Amendment, has been affirmed in this Court on many occasions. In *Martin v. Struthers*,[1] which declared invalid an ordinance prohibiting door-to-door distribution of handbills, the Court stated:

> *The right of freedom of speech and press has broad scope. The authors of the First Amendment knew that novel and unconventional ideas might disturb the complacent, but they chose to encourage a freedom which they believed essential if vigorous enlightment was ever to triumph over slothful ignorance. This freedom embraces the right to distribute literature, and necessarily protects the right to receive it.*

The right to receive information is included in the scope of the protection because the receipt of information furthers the primary policies embedded in the Amendment, those described by Professor Thomas I. Emerson as the public's attainment of truth and widespread participation in decision-making.[2] That the rights have generally been vindicated by the efforts of distributors does not detract from the fact that an essential concern of the Amendment is for the recipient.

The importance of the First Amendment in our society and its preferred constitutional position have been reiterated again and again in decisions of the Court. Mr. Justice Stewart described the protected rights as being "at the foundation of a government based upon the consent of an informed citizenry."[3]

And in a classic statement, the Court carefully explained the reasons for the preferred status of the First Amendment:

> *The freedom of speech and of the press guaranteed by the Constitution embraces at the least the liberty to discuss publicly and truthfully all matters of public concern without previous restraint or fear of subsequent punishment.*
>
> *Freedom of discussion, if it would fulfill its historic function in this nation, must embrace all issues about which information is needed or appropriate to enable the members of society to cope with the exigencies of their period.*[4]

That the material in question may be described as "Communist political propaganda" does not derogate from the individual's right to receive it, for "the Constitution protects expression and association without regard . . . to the truth, popularity or social utility of the ideas and beliefs which are offered."[5] There is "a profound national commitment to the principle that debate on public issues should be uninhibited, robust, and wide-open, and that it may well include vehement, caustic, and sometimes unpleasantly sharp attacks on government and public officials."[6]

The mails are of course subject to the control of Congress, under article I, section 8 of the Constitution, and some of the earlier cases either held or suggested that this congressional power was not limited by the First Amendment. That view is no longer tenable. Thus, "Congress may not by withdrawal of mailing privileges place limitations upon the freedom of speech which if directly attempted would be unconstitutional."[7]

A. *The statute establishes an unconstitutional licensing system that abridges the free delivery of the mails.*

It is well established that registration and licensing as conditions for the distribution of literature are invalid under the First Amendment. In striking down a municipal ordinance forbidding the distribution of literature without first obtaining written permission from the city manager, the Court said:

> *Whatever the motive which induced its adoption, its character is such that it strikes at the very foundation of the freedom of the press by subjecting it to license and censorship. The struggle for the freedom of the press was primarily directed against the power of the licensor. It was against that power that John Milton directed his assault by his "Appeal for the Liberty of Unlicensed Printing." And the liberty of the press became initially a right to publish* "without *a license what formerly could be published only* with *one*."[8]

The broad principle reflected by these cases, that governmental licensing is wholly inconsistent with the First Amendment, has been applied to similar restraints on a person scheduled to make a speech, and to a 2 percent license tax on newspaper advertising revenue.[9]

The statute here establishes the kind of governmental registration and licensing scheme that has consistently been declared invalid by this Court. Pursuant to the statute, an official in the bureaucracy seizes incoming literature, makes a determination as to whether it falls within the vague standard of "Communist political propaganda," then writes the addressee inquiring whether the mail is desired, and delivers it only upon such an expression of desire.

The restraints on freedom of speech are plain. First, there is the inevitable delay while a government official inspects the mail, makes a necessarily imprecise judgment about it, writes the addressee, and then awaits a response before dispatching it. The hand of officialdom is present at every step. Just as the licensing authority in the earlier cases controlled the flow of ideas to the public, so here the government regulates the transmittal of mail to addressees throughout the United States.

A second and more serious obstacle that the statute poses to the exercise of First Amendment rights arises out of the fact that unless the addressee of literature expresses a "desire" to receive it, the mail is never delivered. Quite apart from the consequences of listing individuals who express such a "desire" to receive "Communist political propaganda" (which will be treated in section B below), there is an obvious restraint on the free flow of mail by so conditioning its release. There is a substantial possibility that the mail will not be delivered. First, the addressee must go to the trouble of requesting the mail—an affirmative obligation which the government may not constitutionally impose upon the citizen. In addition, the addressee is bound to feel some inhibition about dealing with the government on an issue as sensitive as the receipt of alleged Communist political propaganda. If a man must be a martyr, or is made to think he may be one, before being allowed by the government to read what is sent to him through the mails, the people surely do not enjoy the "uninhibited, robust, and wide-open"[10] debate contemplated by the First Amendment.

B. *The listing procedure established under the statute impairs protected rights of anonymity by exposing those listed to governmental and private reprisals.*

In a series of cases over the past decade the Court has afforded constitutional protection to those seeking to maintain anonymity in the face of threatened disclosure of identity that would impair rights protected by the Bill of Rights. It is difficult to imagine a case in which the loss of anonymity is more likely to lead to injury than the present one, and where the injury is more directly related to the exercise of liberties safeguarded by the First Amendment.

In *NAACP v. Alabama* and *Bates v. Little Rock,*[11] the Court protected the important interest underlying anonymity by refusing to countenance the enforced disclosure of membership lists where it appeared likely that injury would result from the loss of anonymity. And in *Talley v. California*[12] the Court invalidated an ordinance requiring that handbills show the name of the distributor, saying:

"There can be no doubt that such an identification requirement would tend to restrict freedom to distribute information and thereby freedom of expression."[13] Or as Justice Felix Frankfurter said in *Sweezy v. New Hampshire:*

> *In the political realm, as in the academic, thought and action are presumptively immune from inquisition by political authority. It cannot require argument that inquiry would be barred to ascertain whether a citizen had voted for one or the other of the two major parties.*[14]

The primary danger inherent in maintaining lists under section 4008 becomes plain in the light of the history of the screening process before the enactment of the statute. During that period of enforcement, information about individuals that was obtained by executive agencies was routinely turned over to congressional committees, which on several occasions used it in interrogating witnesses. The authors of the most comprehensive study of the program, observing this pattern, commented on the "close liaison between the Un-American Activities Committee and enforcement officials."[15] Thus, frank acknowledgment of disclosure of the recipients of "Communist propaganda" is found in the transcripts of many congressional hearings.[16]

But the potential injury to those seeking to receive what an official considers Communist political propaganda is not limited to the excesses of congressional committees. The lists established pursuant to the statute have many of the "blacklist" attributes of the Attorney General's list of subversive organizations,[17] and like it can be used to probe the reading habits of Americans under investigation by loyalty and security boards concerned with employees of the government, government contractors and international organizations.[18] The fact of desiring Communist propaganda also might be considered evidence of Communist Party membership or of Communist Front membership under the Internal Security Act of 1950; for example, in proceedings before the Subversive Activities Control Board, literature regarded as Communist propaganda has furnished a considerable part of the evidence against the respondent organizations.[19]

In view of this recent history, the Court below turned its back on the realities of contemporary life in finding that "classification as a person desiring to receive communist political propaganda . . . need not connote disapprobation."

Furthermore, the conclusion of the Court below is dubious as a practical estimate of the consequences of listing because, even if a good-faith effort were made to keep the lists confidential, the risk of disclosure would be great. Not only is there no assurance from customs officials, who administer the program and who were responsible for past disclosures, but the lists are permanent, while administrations and policies change.

But even if the risk of disclosure were less than it patently is, the deterrent effects of listing all those who express a desire to receive "Communist political propaganda" are bound to be severe. The ordinary citizen does not know whether such lists have ever been made public in the past or may be in the future. Nor can he know whether the government will use the lists to prejudice him. Certainly the notice sent to addressees contains no assurance of anonymity. In our contemporary political society, where loyalty and security programs affect millions of governmental and nongovernmental employees, it can safely be assumed that large numbers of persons—not merely the timid—will refrain from taking a step which in any way identifies them as having an interest in "Communist political propaganda."

C. *There is no justification for the significant infringement of freedom of expression by the statute.*

Under the appropriate constitutional standard, "First Amendment rights are beyond abridgment either by legislation that directly restrains their exercise or by suppression or impairment through harassment, humiliation or exposure by government."[20] Or as the Court recently stated: "It is basic that no showing merely of a rational relationship to some colorable state interest would suffice; in this highly sensitive constitutional area, 'only the gravest abuses, endangering paramount interests, give occasion for permissible limitation.' "[21]

Under this standard, section 4008 is clearly invalid under the First Amendment. It imposes a direct restraint on free expression, both as a licensing mechanism and through enforced disclosure of all those desiring "Communist political propaganda." And there are hardly the kind of "paramount interests" present that would justify any limitation of these principles. Adequate statutory authority already exists for coping with any true emergency. 18 U.S.C. § 1717 provides criminal sanctions for the mailing of matter which is treasonous or insurrectionary, and 19 U.S.C. § 1305(a) prevents its importation from abroad. Accordingly, under the appropriate constitutional standard, the decision below should be reversed.

Even if the Court evaluates the constitutionality of section 4008 according to a more permissive standard, whether by a "balancing test" or similar criterion, the result should be the same because no state interest has been shown that would remotely suffice to support the encroachment on First Amendment rights under section 4008.

Various justifications have been offered at times, including the saving of the taxpayer's money, the benefit to American foreign policy and the protection of persons from receipt of Communist propaganda. But no facts have been offered that tend to support these contentions. As the *Heilberg* court concluded, "[the government's] interests, while 'compelling' in theory, are insubstantial, illusory in fact and ignore available alternatives."

D. *The statute stifles freedom of expression more broadly than necessary in the light of available alternative means of achieving the legislative purpose.*

It is now beyond dispute that the Congress may not employ means more drastic than necessary to achieve its purposes when the result is broad impairment of free expression. As the Court said in *Shelton v. Tucker*:[22]

> [E]*ven though the governmental purpose be legitimate and substantial, that purpose cannot be pursued by means that broadly stifle fundamental personal liberties when the end can be more narrowly achieved. The breadth of legislative abridgment must be viewed in the light of less drastic means for achieving the same basic purpose.*

The principle of the *Shelton* case was recently applied in *Aptheker v. Rusk*,[23] where the Court invalidated broad travel restrictions on members of the Communist Party imposed by section 6 of the Subversive Activities Control Act. Noting that "Congress [had] within its power 'less drastic' means of achieving the congressional objective of safeguarding our national security," the Court went on to say:

> *The section therefore is patently not a regulation "narrowly drawn to prevent the supposed evil,"* cf. Cantwell v. Connecticut, 310 *U.S. at* 307, *yet here, as elsewhere, precision must be the touchstone of legislation so affecting basic freedoms.*[24]

Even assuming some proper legislative end that involves protecting Americans from an influx of "Communist political propaganda," it is plain that "less drastic" alternatives are available that would achieve this goal without the vast encroachment on freedom of expression sanctioned by section 4008.

The simplest alternative is embodied in the recommendation of the late Congressman Walter, who introduced H.R. 5751, 87th Cong., 1st Sess. Mr. Walter, who was not noted for his friendly attitude toward Communism, was satisfied with a bill which, as reported out, merely would have authorized the Postmaster either to place notices in post offices informing the public or to notify recipients directly that Communist propaganda in quantity was being sent through the mails. The bill provided that in cases where recipients decided on their own initiative that such propaganda was unwanted, it could be returned to the post office free of charge. If Congress believes that a problem warranting legislative action exists, it is obvious that the Walter proposal is a far more careful and less dangerous means of achieving that goal than section 4008. Indeed, the existing post office regulations already contain an effective remedy. 39 C.F.R. 44.1(a) provides that any person may authorize the Postmaster to withhold the delivery of specifically described classes of foreign printed matter and to substitute his judgment as to classification for that of the addressee.

Undoubtedly there are other ways that Congress could, if it wishes, deal with "Communist political propaganda." The one clear fact is that the method chosen is impermissible because it "broadly stifle[s] fundamental personal liberties when the end can be more narrowly achieved."[25]

II / The statute is void because the term "Communist political propaganda" is unconstitutionally vague and there are no adequate standards to guide those charged with its administration.

The term "Communist political propaganda" in section 4008 means political propaganda as defined in section 1(j) of the Foreign Agents Registration Act of 1938, issued by or on behalf of certain countries, particularly those in the Communist bloc. Section 1(j) of the Foreign Agents Registration Act defines political propaganda as any communication adapted to or intended to influence the public

(i) "with reference to the political or public interests, policies or relations of a government of a foreign country or a foreign political party," or

(ii) "with reference to the foreign policies of the United States," or intended

(iii) "to promote in the United States racial, religious or social dissensions" [*sic*], or

(iv) "which advocates, advises, instigates or promotes any racial, social, political or religious disorder, civil riot or other conflict involving the use of force or violence in any other American republic or the overthrow of any government or political subdivision of any other American republic by means involving the use of force or violence. . . ."

Under the governing criteria repeatedly laid down by this Court, section 4008 is invalid as impermissibly vague. The statute demonstrably falls within the class of cases which have held that a statute violates due process when it is in "terms so vague that men of common intelligence must necessarily guess at its meaning and differ as to its application."[26]

The foregoing decisions involved statutes where the individual was "required at peril of life, liberty or property to speculate as to the meaning of penal statutes," or to guess at the meaning of vague oaths required of employees "at the risk of subsequent prosecution for perjury or . . . immediate dismissal from public service."[27]

In the present case it is a government official who must reckon with the vague words of section 4008. Accordingly, the statute here is invalid under the rulings of this Court that prohibit an overbroad and imprecise delegation of legislative power to officials of the executive branch. Section 9(c) of title I of the National Industrial Recovery Act, which authorized the President "to prohibit the transportation in interstate and foreign commerce of petroleum and the products thereof," was struck down because it provided no precise guidelines.[28] And section 3 of the NIRA was likewise invalidated because it gave the President unbounded discretion to approve binding "Codes of Fair Competition" in certain industries without clarifying just what "fair competition" was or how it was to be determined.[29]

The loose standards set out in section 1(j) of the Foreign Agents Registration Act, which defines "Communist political propaganda," are equally inadequate as criteria for official action. Indeed, they are more clearly invalid than the statutes in either the *Panama Refining* or the *Schechter Poultry* case because the latter presented no threat to the preferred freedoms guaranteed by the First Amendment. In the instant case, the danger to First Amendment liberties is intense because a member of the bureaucracy is given the authority to determine, on the basis of his view of the fluid terms of section 1(j), whether mail will be delivered to the person to whom it is addressed.

The four clauses of section 1(j) noted above are impermissibly vague. Taking the clauses we have numbered (iii) and (iv) first, what are the bounds, in these days of social ferment, of propaganda that promotes "racial, religious or social" dissension or disorder? Virtually every statement on a public issue has the tendency to arouse one group or another that may feel its interests are threatened. Any comment about conflicts between Greeks and Turks, Arabs and Jews, unions and management, tends to stimulate, and indeed has stimulated, "dissension" or "disorder." It would be difficult to imagine terms more expansive in meaning or so prone to overgenerous application.

It might be said that clause (iv) above and perhaps even clause (iii) are qualified by the condition in clause (iv) that the propaganda advocates "the use of force or violence in any other American republic or the overthrow of any government." Such a reading, particularly with respect to clause (iii), seems unjustified by the plain language of the statute. Moreover, even these terms of condition are hardly precise, and it is difficult to understand how a vague condition can cure the vice of an even vaguer statutory definition.

But assuming that clauses (iv) and (iii) are made sufficiently precise by a strained reading, it seems inconceivable that clauses (i) and (ii) are valid as providing adequate guidelines to officials entrusted with the statutory responsibility of screening and holding up mail addressed to persons within the United States.

What exactly does it mean to influence the public "with reference to the political or public interests, policies or relations" of a foreign government or foreign political party? And what could be a more fluid concept than influencing the public "with reference to the foreign policies of the United States"? There would seem to be little or nothing that is published by anyone that does not arguably fall within these categories, and yet they are the criteria by which officials are to decide what persons in the United States are to be permitted to read without restraint.

Accordingly, the term "Communist political propaganda" is in violation of the due process clause of the Fifth Amendment because it provides no valid standards to guide the administrative officials charged with its enforcement.

III / The classifications of those entitled to an exemption under section 4008 are arbitrary and thereby deny appellant due process.

In *Bolling v. Sharpe*[30] this Court recognized that "the concepts of equal protection and due process, both stemming from our American ideal of fairness, are not mutually exclusive" and ruled that under the Fifth Amendment "discrimination may be so unjustifiable as to be violative of due process." The classifications established by section 4008, which determine the categories of readers who are exempt from the screening and listing provisions, are so arbitrary and unjustifiable that they deprive appellant and other members of the public of due process of law.

Section 4008 provides for unrestricted access to all literature from abroad for "any United States government agency, or any public library, or . . . any college, university, graduate school or scientific or professional institution for advanced studies, or any official thereof." On the other hand, all other persons, including publishers, writers, independent scholars and just plain citizens with lively curiosity, are required to submit themselves to the statutory mechanism.

There is no possible justification for this discrimination. The citizen's right to be informed is as great and perhaps greater than that of impersonal institutions and libraries. This Court has recognized that the individual's "right to receive" literature is constitutionally protected,[31] and that rights safeguarded by the First Amendment are "at the foundation of a government based upon the consent of an informed citizenry."[32] In short, the First Amendment is grounded, not upon the prerogative of a government agency to secure information or the ability of a university to collect data, but upon the right of the individual citizen to have unrestricted access to information of every kind in order to exercise his public responsibilities.

Section 4008 flies in the face of this high constitutional policy. Not only does it interfere with the individual's legitimate quest for information, but it subordinates the citizen's right to receive literature as compared to the right of governments, universities and other institutional recipients. The only possible reason for such a patent discrimination is that "Communist political propaganda" is too hot for the average American to handle and therefore should be kept out of his grasp as much as possible. But this is not a valid basis for discriminating either against the ordinary citizen or against writers, publishers and editors, who all may have good reasons for reading material from all sources. The Constitution does not authorize the government to protect the more timid or susceptible American citizens against material deemed harmful to them.[33]

On May 24, 1965, in a precedent-making decision, the Supreme Court in Lamont v. Postmaster General[34] *struck down the contested legislation as unconstitutional. The Court adopted the reasoning of point I in the brief and held that the statute imposed a "limitation on [the addressee's] unfettered exercise of . . . First Amendment rights." The Court declared that Congress could not control the flow of ideas to the public; that the statute had a significant deterrent effect upon those in sensitive and unprotected positions, such as government officials without tenure; and that the public at large was very likely to "feel some inhibition in sending for literature which federal officials have condemned as 'communist political propaganda.'"*

The special significance of this case lies in the fact that it is the first and only time in our constitutional history that the United States Supreme Court has flatly declared a federal statute invalid under the First Amendment. The uniqueness of the decision points up the wisdom of a dictum of Justice Oliver Wendell Holmes, Jr.: "I do not think the United States would come to an end if we lost our power to declare an Act of Congress void. I do think the Union would be imperiled if we could not make that declaration as to the laws of the several States."[35]

NOTES

Leonard B. Boudin and Henry Winestine participated in the preparation of the brief.

1. 319 U.S. 141, 143 (1943).
2. Emerson, "Toward a General Theory of the First Amendment," 72 *Yale L.J.* 877, 881–84 (1963).
3. Bates v. Little Rock, 361 U.S. 516, 522–23 (1960).
4. Thornhill v. Alabama, 310 U.S. 88, 101–2 (1940).
5. NAACP v. Button, 371 U.S. 415, 444–45 (1963).

6. New York Times v. Sullivan, 376 U.S. 254, 270 (1964).

7. Speiser v. Randall, 357 U.S. 513, 518 (1958). See also Hannegan v. Esquire, Inc., 327 U.S. 146, 155–56 (1946).

8. Lovell v. Griffin, 303 U.S. 444, 451 (1938) (emphasis in original).

9. Thomas v. Collins, 323 U.S. 516 (1945); Grosjean v. American Press Co., 297 U.S. 233 (1936).

10. New York Times v. Sullivan, 376 U.S. 254, 270 (1964).

11. 357 U.S. 449 (1958); 361 U.S. 516 (1960).

12. 362 U.S. 60, 64 (1960).

13. See generally "Note, The Constitutional Right to Anonymity," 70 *Yale L.J.* 1084 (1961).

14. 354 U.S. 234, 266 (1957).

15. Schwartz & Paul, "Foreign Communist Propaganda in the Mails," 107 *U. Pa. L. Rev.* 621, 631 (1959).

16. *Investigation of Communist Propaganda in the United States—Part I*, Hearings Before the House Committee on Un-American Activities, 84th Cong., 2d Sess., June 13, 1956, p. 4714.

17. See Joint Anti-Fascist Refugee Committee v. McGrath, 341 U.S. 123 (1951).

18. See Report of the Special Committee on the Federal Loyalty-Security Program of the Association of the Bar of the City of New York (1956).

19. See, e.g., Communist Party v. Subversive Activities Control Board, 367 U.S. 1 (1961).

20. Bates v. Little Rock, 361 U.S. 516, 528 (1960) (Justices Black and Douglas, concurring).

21. Sherbert v. Verner, 374 U.S. 398, 406 (1963), quoting Thomas v. Collins, 323 U.S. 516, 530 (1945). See also Barenblatt v. United States, 360 U.S. 109, 134 (1959) (Black, J., dissenting); Konigsberg v. State Bar of California, 366 U.S. 36, 56 (1961) (Black, J., dissenting).

22. 364 U.S. 479, 488 (1960).

23. 378 U.S. 500, 512–14 (1964).

24. See also Freund, "Competing Freedoms in American Constitutional Law," 13 *University of Chicago Conference Series* 26, 32–33; Richardson, "Freedom of Expression and the Function of Courts," 65 *Harv. L. Rev.* 1, 6, 23–24 (1951).

25. Shelton v. Tucker, 364 U.S. 479, 488 (1960).

26. Connally v. General Construction Co., 269 U.S. 385, 391 (1926). See also Lanzetta v. New Jersey, 306 U.S. 451, 453 (1939); United States v. Cardiff, 344 U.S. 174, 176 (1952). Cramp v. Board of Public Instruction, 368 U.S. 278, 285 (1961).

27. Lanzetta v. New Jersey, *supra* note 26.

28. Panama Refining Co. v. Ryan, 293 U.S. 388 (1935).

29. Schechter Poultry Corp. v. United States, 295 U.S. 495 (1935).

30. 347 U.S. 497, 499 (1954).
31. Martin v. Struthers, 319 U.S. 141, 143 (1943).
32. Bates v. Little Rock, 361 U.S. 516, 522–23 (1960).
33. *Cf.* Butler v. Michigan, 352 U.S. 380 (1957).
34. 381 U.S. 301 (1965).
35. Holmes, *Collected Legal Papers* 295 (1920).

8

Military Censorship

The power of the military establishment to censor newspapers and periodicals which offer independent views to armed forces personnel stationed overseas poses a continuing threat to First Amendment freedoms. The turbulent history of one newspaper illustrates the significance of this issue.

The Overseas Weekly was established in 1950 to provide "a free, independent, uncensored newspaper" for those soldiers whose normal sources of information had, by reason of their location, been constricted. It soon developed the largest circulation of any privately owned paper distributed by the Army. As early as 1964, certain Army officials complained that its news policies—including the use of "pornography"—engendered lack of respect among United States troops for military authority.

In 1961, an Army investigating committee concluded that The Overseas Weekly was "detrimental to the morals, morale and combat effectiveness of command," and it recommended that distribution through Army newsstands be terminated. No immediate official action was taken, and in early 1962 the Army concluded, after further investigation, that there was insufficient justification to bar the publication.

In view of the strong possibility of official censorship which these investigations represented, the ACLU requested the author to pre-

pare a letter (which appears below) presenting the Union's general policy and its particular objections to the method and purpose of the Army's inquiry in this instance.

April 24, 1962

THE HON. ROBERT J. MCNAMARA
Secretary of Defense
Department of Defense
Washington 25, D.C.

DEAR SECRETARY MCNAMARA:

For some time the American Civil Liberties Union has been deeply concerned with actions of the Department of Defense and the Department of the Army in connection with *The Overseas Weekly*, a privately published newspaper distributed largely to members of our overseas armed forces through the facilities of *Stars and Stripes*. Although we have been informed that General Lauris Norstad, Commander in Chief of the European Command, has decided not to remove the publication from *Stars and Stripes* newsstands, or to take any other action against it, we do not believe the matter should be treated as closed. Instead, we wish to direct your attention to official practices which seem to us to conflict with the American heritage of freedom of the press and of due process of law.

Since *The Overseas Weekly* and *Stars and Stripes* entered into the existing distribution agreement on August 13, 1953, there has apparently been a certain amount of displeasure with the publication on the part of military commanders in the European Theater. Recently, the Senate Armed Services Committee expressed interest and questioned you and Assistant Secretary of Defense Runge on the subject at hearings held on September 6, 1961, and March 8, 1962, respectively. Although Senator Beall said at the September 6 hearing that the Committee had received "numerous communications" about *The Overseas Weekly*, the only specific complaints brought to light had been made by General Edwin A. Walker, who on at least two occasions recommended that distribution through *Stars and Stripes* facilities be terminated.

The Department of Defense agreed to make a study of *The*

Overseas Weekly and to report to the Armed Services Committee what action, if any, was to be taken. Subsequently, the Commander in Chief of the United States Army in Europe convened a committee to investigate the publication. The committee recommended that distribution through *Stars and Stripes* channels be discontinued, but was overruled by General Norstad. This decision and the reasons supporting it are contained in a letter dated March 16, 1962, from the General Counsel of the Department of Defense, Cyrus R. Vance, to the Chairman of the Senate Armed Services Committee, Senator John C. Stennis.

As an organization committed to defense of freedom of expression, the ACLU does not make value judgments about the content of any publication, and the comment we make herein in no way concerns the editorial policies of *The Overseas Weekly*. Our purpose is to express the view that in its handling of this matter the government in two respects has abridged fundamental rights of the newspaper.

In the first place, we believe that the entire investigation into the content of *The Overseas Weekly* smacks of official censorship that has no place in an open and free society. Although we recognize that persons serving in the armed forces are in a different status from civilians, we do not believe that this difference justifies the dictation to soldiers of the material they may or may not read. These young men represent a democracy founded on the concept of free discussion, which means the right to select reading matter of one's own choice from the wide variety of material available in a democracy. For the Defense Department or the Army to inquire into the content of a particular publication with a view to deciding whether or not it is "suitable" for members of the armed services is to disregard a cornerstone of our democratic faith.

The letter of Mr. Vance to Senator Stennis provides dramatic evidence of the worst features of censorship. It discloses that first an unnamed committee and then General Norstad concerned themselves with whether the newspaper content was "acceptable," whether it encouraged "lack of respect for military authority," whether or not there was "a general improvement" during the past few months. In our opinion, these matters cannot properly be made the subject of official scrutiny. In evaluating any publication according to these vague and wholly subjective standards, the government invests officials with an almost untrammeled discretion to approve or disapprove reading matter. This it cannot do without contravening one of the basic principles of this nation. In this connection we refer you to a statement of General Dwight D. Eisenhower on March 11, 1945, to Brigadier General O. N. Solbert commenting on reports that the staff of *Stars and Stripes* felt it was being subjected to pressures by individuals and officers who sought to dictate the newspaper's policy.

Within the bounds of decent newspaper practices, "The Stars and Stripes" must enjoy the same privileges and rights as any commercial newspaper, and is not subject to censorship that does not apply to all other publications.

Mr. Vance's letter is disturbing for another reason. It implies that General Norstad might take action against *The Overseas Weekly* if in the future its standards fall to "objectionable levels." This plainly subjects the newspaper to all the inhibitions that the threat of censorship presents. We urge you to disclaim any intention by the Department of Defense to act against *The Overseas Weekly* for any reason connected with its content and to make it clear that such action taken in the field will not be approved. We seek for that publication only what it and all others are entitled to—the opportunity to compete for readers freely in the marketplace without interference or threat of interference by the government.

Although it is not the function of the ACLU to defend the content of *The Overseas Weekly,* we are puzzled by criticism of the newspaper in view of the fact that it has recently been nominated for several national citations and awards for journalistic enterprise and public service, has been lavishly praised by the Rev. Herbert Lee Stout, pastor of Bethel Baptist Church of Frankfurt am Main, Germany, and has consistently received the advertising support of twenty-one churches. It is of course understandable why military commanders should be displeased with *The Overseas Weekly,* which on occasion has subjected them to criticism. On the other hand, it does not seem unreasonable to expect military leaders to recognize the potential value of such criticism. But whatever the benefits or disabilities of particular newspaper comment, we believe that no reason exists for the Department of Defense to consider action that would impair the freedom to read: one of the basic freedoms of all Americans, whether or not in the armed services.

The second disturbing aspect of this matter is the decision by the Army to conduct an investigation of *The Overseas Weekly* and to hold hearings which could have resulted in termination of the newspaper's valuable distribution rights without granting it the most elementary forms of procedural due process such as notice of the hearing and the right to submit evidence.

As we have already said, it is the position of the ACLU that the entire investigation into the content of *The Overseas Weekly* was improper. If such an inquiry was to be held, however, it is startling to us that the publication was not given the right to be represented by counsel, and was not provided the opportunity to present evidence to refute the charges or to attempt to discredit whatever evidence was introduced against it. Moreover, it was given no chance to question the qualifications and impartiality of the members of the *ad hoc* committee convened by the Army military commander in Europe to investigate and judge the newspaper.

Likewise, *The Overseas Weekly* was denied all procedural rights after the committee completed its report and recommended that distribution through *Stars and Stripes* be terminated. It was not granted the opportunity to submit objections to the committee's factual conclusions or to present its case to General Norstad. According to its publisher, it was never even informed that an official investigation was under way.

It is well known that procedural protections are vital to the preservation of all other rights. At two separate points in our Constitution the right is guaranteed not to be "deprived of life, liberty, or property without due process of law." This right extends not only to judicial but also to administrative decisions that could result in the deprivation of "life, liberty, or property."

It is beyond dispute that *The Overseas Weekly* had a valuable asset in its arrangement for distribution through *Stars and Stripes* channels. We are informed by the publisher of *The Overseas Weekly* that Secretary Runge, upon being advised of the failure to accord the newspaper any procedural protection, fell back on the contention that *The Overseas Weekly* possessed only a "contractual" and not a "property" right. We do not believe that this type of legalistic distinction, which incidentally seems erroneous as a matter of law, is relevant to the obligation of the government to secure to all the fundamental procedural guarantees that the Constitution requires. Far less valuable properties than the newspaper's right to distribute to its readership are protected by the Constitution and such statutes as the Administrative Procedure Act. Especially when action by the government threatens to cut off an asset intimately bound up with a First Amendment right, such as freedom of the press, should all possible steps be taken to assure that a fair and adversary hearing is provided. We are disturbed that these protections were not granted to *The Overseas Weekly* in this instance.

In conclusion, permit us to say once again that we recognize the peculiar responsibilities associated with operating a military command. Nevertheless, neither the nature nor the gravity of these responsibilities justifies action by the Department of Defense or the military departments inconsistent with the requirements of the Constitution. We respectfully submit that in the present case two deviations from our fundamental law have occurred. First, by carrying out an investigation into the content of *The Overseas Weekly* with a view to possible suppression, the government abridged the freedom of the press possessed by all publications. Secondly, by conducting this investigation without prior notice and without giving *The Overseas Weekly* the right to defend itself through counsel at a fair hearing, the government denied it that procedural due process to which it was entitled before it could be deprived of a valuable property right.

We urge you to take the necessary action to relieve *The Overseas Weekly* and all other publications distributed through *Stars and Stripes* and other military channels from the threat of future censorship. This could most easily be done through a clear-cut directive reaffirming one of the basic principles of the First Amendment—the right of all men to select what they wish to read. At the same time, we hope that the Department of Defense and the military departments will make what changes are necessary in their regulations to conform them to the requirements of procedural due process insofar as they apply to investigations of the type conducted in the present instance.

Sincerely yours,
JOHN DE J. PEMBERTON, JR.
Executive Director

The Department of Defense offered the following response to the letter quoted above:

June 19, 1962

Dear Mr. Pemberton:

The Secretary of Defense has asked me to reply directly to your letter with regard to *The Overseas Weekly*.

As Secretary McNamara testified before the Senate Armed Services Committee on September 6, 1961, he is concerned with anything that suggests a limitation on the freedom of the press. The Department of Defense fully subscribes to the principle that all publications, including *The Overseas Weekly*, have the right to publish without interference or threat of interference by the government.

The constitutional principle of freedom of the press, however, is not involved in action which the Department of Defense has taken, or might take in the future, with respect to the distribution of any publication through the *Stars and Stripes* distribution system. No reasonable interpretation of this principle would place an affirmative requirement upon the government to distribute any private publication through its distribution system to military personnel. No periodical has an affirmative right to be distributed through that system.

I am sure you realize that *Stars and Stripes* cannot place on its newsstands all newspapers, periodicals and books offered to it for distribution. This would be a physical impossibility. Judgment must be exercised in determining what publications are sold on *Stars and Stripes* newsstands. The legitimate question arises, what factors should be taken into consideration in making this determination.

As you recognize in your letter, there are "peculiar responsibilities associated with operating a military command." Commanding officers are responsible for the morale and combat effectiveness of the troops entrusted to their commands. It is logical and appropriate that commanding officers consider these factors in determining which of the almost unlimited number of publications should be selected for sale on newsstands within their commands.

In discharging its responsibilities in this area, the Department of Defense does not act in an arbitrary fashion and it has not done so in regard to *The Overseas Weekly*.

Sincerely yours,
Cyrus R. Vance
General Counsel

The issues dividing the Defense Department and the ACLU came to a head in 1967, when The Overseas Weekly again locked horns with the military. The new dispute was precipitated when the Department of Defense rejected the paper's application for access to Post Exchange distribution facilities in the Pacific theater of operations. The Weekly had demonstrated its popularity in the Far East when a trial edition in Saigon sold out within twenty-four hours. Nevertheless, newsstand space was denied on the ground that the Army's "overtaxed logistic system should not be additionally burdened by new publications when there is already a well-balanced selection of printed material for sale."

The Overseas Weekly then filed suit charging arbitrary and capricious prohibition of newspaper distribution in the Far East in violation of the rights of freedom of the press and due process of law. On October 3, 1967, the United States Court of Appeals for the District of Columbia ruled in Overseas Media Corp. v. McNamara that the Secretary of Defense lacked the power "insulated from judicial review, to deny to appellants access to post exchange newsstands in the Far East when it is alleged that he has granted such access to similarly situated publishers."

The ACLU supported the newspaper in this suit. It contended in an amicus curiae brief filed with the court that the Army's failure to establish fair and impartial criteria for selection of publications has resulted in a "chilling effect" on First Amendment freedoms, and that if this unfettered discretion remains unchecked, no periodical will be safe from similar arbitrary treatment.

Earlier, in a policy statement apparently unrelated to The Overseas Weekly, Secretary McNamara in May 1967 had scored "news management" and "military meddling" that impeded the free flow of news to members of the armed forces. He ordered his civilian and military subordinates to observe a policy of "maximum disclosure" of news, except information judged to be of "material assistance to potential enemies," and he said that members of the armed forces "are entitled to the same unrestricted access to news as are all other citizens."

9

Blacklisting

Blacklisting, the organized practice of denying employment to persons because of their real or alleged political attitudes, reached its zenith in this country during the McCarthy days of the late 1940s and early 1950s. With Senator McCarthy's successful exploitation of the nation's fear of Communism, blacklisting became a national institution, particularly in the radio, TV and movie industries.

The damage to the lives, families and careers of scores of persons caused by this practice, while vast, is difficult to measure. Apart from its economic impact, the blacklist required thousands to resort to the demeaning process of rebutting vague innuendoes and of erasing the stigma of "disloyalty" which attached merely as a result of the "patriot's" favorite question: "Are you or have you ever been . . . ?" On a less personal level, but of equal importance in the long view, is the chilling effect the blacklist has had upon the exercise of free expression and association, and the role it has played in the creation of an atmosphere of sterility and conformity in political dialogue.

Protests by several groups, including the ACLU, in the early 1950s had no immediate effect. But as McCarthyism began to lose its hold on the nation's psyche, the use of classic blacklisting methods became less frequent. Nevertheless, important vestiges persisted. One was the exclusion of radio and TV performers who were un-

willing to sign affidavits concerning their political beliefs. Several famous entertainers, including folk singer Pete Seeger and the singing group The Weavers, were denied access to national networks when they refused to comply with this requirement. Efforts by the ACLU to encourage voluntary recission of these restrictions were largely futile. Further attempts by the ACLU and Congressmen William Fitts Ryan and John V. Lindsay to persuade the Federal Communications Commission to declare that continued use of political affidavit requirements is contrary to the public interest were similarly unsuccessful.

The ACLU also was concerned by an important collateral issue: the networks' policy of excluding members of the Communist Party or those espousing its viewpoint. In the letter to the networks that follows, which was prepared by the author, the ACLU deplores the consequences of this policy for freedom of political discussion.

February 21, 1964

Mr. Robert Kintner, President
National Broadcasting Company
30 Rockefeller Plaza
New York, New York

Dear Mr. Kintner:

As you are probably aware, the American Civil Liberties Union has a continuing interest in assuring the public's access to widely diverse opinions through the media of radio and television. At present, while maintaining its general interest in this question, the Union is especially concerned with the apparently per se denial of network time for the presentation of the Communist viewpoint. That this is the case is borne out by a letter to Mr. Arnold Johnson of the Communist Party from Mr. John O. Gilbert, Vice President and General Manager of the American Broadcasting Company (ABC), dated July 25, 1963, in reply to a request from the Communist Party that it be allowed to present its view on the racial crisis. Mr. Gilbert explicitly stated that as a general proposition ABC "does not make its facilities available to any known member of the Communist Party for the dissemination of the Communist viewpoint."

On October 18, 1963, the American Civil Liberties Union, in letters to the three major networks, inquired into network policies with respect to the airing of minority opinion in general and Communist opinion in particular. In response to that query, Mr. Alfred Schneider, Vice President and Assistant to Executive Vice President of ABC, affirmed the substance of Mr. Gilbert's letter and added that ABC also maintained a "firm policy" against use of its facilities by entertainers "identified" with the Communist Party. Mr. Thomas K. Fisher, Vice President and General Counsel of the Columbia Broadcasting System (CBS), in answer to the same letter, declined to furnish information as to the network's policy because he felt CBS and the Union basically disagreed on the nature of the Communist Party. Mr. Fisher said that various statutes and court decisions made it clear that the Communist Party was not to be treated in the same manner as other political parties, nor could it be considered a legitimate party at all. Although the attitude of CBS toward the airing of Communist opinion was thus not explicitly stated, we think it can be fairly said that Mr. Fisher's letter indicates that requests for presentation of a Communist viewpoint will not be favorably received by CBS. On the other hand, the tenor of a letter to us from William R. McAndrew, Executive Vice President, News Division, of the National Broadcasting Company (NBC), dated October 30, 1963, suggests that NBC does not exclude Communist speakers as a matter of policy.

At the outset, we should reiterate that the Union does not maintain that the Communist Party or speakers in its behalf are entitled to a particular stand. Indeed, the Union has explicitly rejected that position. However, the Communist Party reflects a point of view that Americans consider important in their concern about the world political scene, and the time it receives should be commensurate with its size and importance. Accordingly, whether or not a network honors a request for air time by any Communist organization should depend on its fair discretion, taking into consideration the importance of the issue sought to be discussed, programming problems, and the fairness criteria established by the Federal Communications Commission.

Furthermore, the Union maintains that refusal to allow access to radio and television under *any* circumstances violates an important obligation of the networks to the public. The airwaves are public property, and permission to use such property exists only so long as the public interest, necessity and convenience are served. This fundamental doctrine is illustrated, for example, by the long-standing obligation of networks to give candidates for public office equal time on broadcasting media.

The Federal Communications Commission early recognized the obligation of a licensee, in the public interest, to present opposing views on current controversial issues:

The criterion of the public interest in the field of broadcasting clearly precludes a policy of making radio wholly unavailable as a medium for the expression of any view which falls within the constitutional guarantee of freedom of speech. (*Robert H. Scott*, 3 *P & F Radio Reg.* 259, 264 [1946])

On July 26, 1963, the FCC clarified the scope of this fairness doctrine, declaring that an individual or group must be given time to respond to an attack explicitly directed at him or it, and that responsible groups in the community must be given time to present contrasting views on issues of importance when network facilities are used to propagate one side of the issue.

Nowhere has the FCC either explicitly stated or implied that the Communist Party is somehow excluded from the purview of the fairness requirement. While the networks have not specifically enumerated the reasons for the claim that the above provisions do not prohibit a per se exclusion of Communist opinion from their facilities, it seems clear that the position must rest on two grounds: first, the notion that any pronouncement by any Communist speaker falls outside the constitutional protection of free speech, and second, as stated by Mr. Fisher, that the Communist Party is not to be treated the same as other political parties because it is not in fact a legitimate political party. We respectfully suggest that neither reason is valid.

The first ground is based on a failure to recognize the ambivalent nature of the Communist Party. In one sense, the party is an agent of an international conspiracy. In another sense, however, the party is a political party, proffering candidates for public office, expressing views on issues it considers to be of importance, and arguing in favor of or against various legislation. Only when the Communist Party acts in the former sense may it incur any legal liabilities. The Union has continually recognized this distinction as applied to the Communist Party, as well as to other organizations such as the Ku Klux Klan or the American

Nazi Party. Certainly the ACLU does not maintain that any organization is entitled to time for the purpose of advocating violent overthrow of the government; on the other hand, it would seem that the Communist Party's views on, for example, international affairs or the problem of unemployment are fully within the protection of the First Amendment, regardless of the party's position on any other matter.

The second ground for the networks' position is that the Communist Party is not a legitimate political party. This presumably is based on the 1954 Communist Control Act (50 U.S.C. §§ 841–42), sometimes taken to mean that the Communist Party is outlawed, and the Smith Act (18 U.S.C. § 2385), which makes it a crime for an individual to be a member of any organization advocating violent overthrow of the government. As to the former statute, the Supreme Court has pointed out that "there is no legislative history which in any way serves to give content to the vague terminology" of 50 U.S.C. § 842 (Communist Party v. Catherwood, 367 U.S. 389, 392 [1961]). If the Supreme Court is incapable of determining the content of section 842, certainly it is presumptuous of the networks to interpret it as authorizing the exclusion of the Communist Party (or any other political organization) from the airwaves.

Nor does the Smith Act afford a valid basis for refusing air time to an individual who is admitted or thought to be a member of the Communist Party. The ACLU would not contend that any person *convicted* of violating this provision is entitled to a grant of air time. As a matter of fact, however, only a single individual has yet been convicted under the membership clause of the act. Therefore, a network's refusal to permit an appearance on radio or television on this basis is tantamount to an assertion of guilt of a very serious crime. That finding must remain in the sole province of the courts, and until such a finding is made every individual is protected through the presumption of innocence. We think the networks are bound to honor this presumption.

There is, accordingly, no legislation which could authorize the position of the networks on this matter. This conclusion is reinforced by the provision of section 10 of the Subversive Activities Control Act, 50 U.S.C. § 789, making it unlawful for *an organization* registered under other provisions of the act to broadcast any matter over a radio or television station within the United States unless such matter is preceded by the statement, "The following program is sponsored by ———, a Communist organization." Thus the act, while placing this requirement on such broadcasts, clearly contemplates their existence and hence by implication their legality.

Since the FCC has never excepted Communists from the scope of the fairness requirement, and since there is no other basis for excluding Communists from the air, we think the networks fail to meet their commitment to the public under their present policy.

Even assuming that the networks are not *legally* required to renounce their present practices, there are compelling reasons of policy for their so doing, derived from the fundamental fact that we live in and seek to strengthen a free and open society. We cannot afford to limit the realm of discussion within "safe" or "approved" confines; if we do, we run the risk, fatal to a free society, that every possible viewpoint may not be carefully and exhaustively explored. Furthermore, no matter what one's attitude toward the Communist Party or any other organization, all will agree that an attempt to fasten legal liabilities on speech conflicts with the basic premises of a free society. The measure of such a society, to paraphrase Mr. Justice Holmes, is its treatment of "the idea we hate," rather than of the idea we agree with or at least do not strongly disagree with. In any event, as you are probably aware, the Communist Party and many of its members have not yet been convicted of a crime. Accordingly, it is premature for private groups to determine that the party or its members are to be deprived of fundamental rights.

We therefore urge the networks, as we urge all private organizations, to leave the issue of the Communist Party to the Congress and courts, where it properly belongs. The communications media, in particular, ought to be highly sensitive to the danger of extrajudicial determinations that a particular form of speech is undesirable. The sad history of the blacklist should serve as a vivid reminder of this danger. It will serve both the immediate and ultimate self-interest of the communications media to preserve and extend the range of free speech. In so doing, they will be fulfilling their highest responsibilities to the public.

Sincerely Yours,
JOHN DE J. PEMBERTON, JR.
Executive Director

The General Counsel of the Columbia Broadcasting System replied to the ACLU's letter on February 27, 1964, as follows:

DEAR MR. PEMBERTON:

I am responding to your letter of February 19, 1964, to Dr. Frank Stanton.

In your letter you state: "In one sense, the [Communist] Party is an agent of an international conspiracy." This is the distinction between the Communist Party and the minority political parties in this country that was noted by Mr. Fisher in his letter to you of October 30, 1963. It is a distinction that cannot be ignored in the operation of any responsible communication medium.

We appreciate the elaboration of your views on this matter and we wish to assure you that CBS regards its responsibilities as a communication medium with utmost seriousness.

Sincerely,
RICHARD FORSLING

On May 14, 1964, Mr. Pemberton replied in the following way to Mr. Forsling's letter:

DEAR MR. FORSLING:

Your letter of February 27 said:

"In your letter you state: 'In one sense the [Communist] Party is an agent of an international conspiracy. This is the distinction between the Communist Party and the minority political parties in this country that was noted by Mr. Fisher in his letter to you of October 30, 1963. It is a distinction that cannot be ignored in the operation of any responsible communication medium."

However, our letter went on to say that the Communist Party carries on open, legal political activities in this country, and that so long as this was done these activities deserved the protection of the First Amendment. It seems clear that CBS chose to disregard the second part of our statement, which in our view does raise an important civil liberties question affecting the use of the radio-television medium for the dissemination of information and ideas, a significant aspect of public service.

CBS did not respond to the second letter, and neither NBC nor ABC answered the original ACLU letter of February 19.

Since the foregoing correspondence there has been some indication that the worst excesses of the blacklisting era may be over. Several important court decisions have contributed to a more tolerant public attitude, and some local and noncommercial programs have given hearings to artists formerly unable to obtain bookings. In addition, Pete Seeger, a leading figure in the modern cultural scene and a prime exhibit of the injustices of the blacklist, gained access in 1967 to a network show—on CBS—for the first time in almost two decades.

But this slight change of direction should not be overvalued. Major artists such as Paul Draper, Larry Adler and Joan Baez are still effectively excluded from the national networks—the true test of commercial acceptability and financial success. Other less prominent figures have had their careers smashed irretrievably. And in an ironic twist, when Seeger was finally scheduled to appear on CBS, the network checked out his material and refused to allow him to perform a controversial song.

Thus, although the blacklist may no longer exist as a vicious piece of paper, commercial considerations continue to elevate the art of politics above the principles of art. The result is expediency, hypocrisy, and all too often, mediocrity.

10

Academic Freedom

The concept of academic freedom has received increasing judicial recognition and approval over the past decade. Recent United States Supreme Court cases have discussed in rather broad terms the close relationship of academic freedom to the First Amendment. But the Court to date has refused to delineate the precise boundaries of academic freedom and has been reluctant to clothe the concept in explicit constitutional protections. Accordingly, both substantive and procedural rights of teachers are at present in an ambiguous state. Advocacy of unpopular theories, which in contemporary society include anti-Vietnam war policies, permissive use of drugs and stimulants, and premarital sexual freedom, has caused disputes over tenure and promotion of the faculty member involved.

In response to attempts by educational institutions to condition faculty employment upon their acceptance of "proper" subjects of controversy, there have been incidents at such universities as Cornell, Yale, Rutgers, Howard, Catholic and St. Johns. Moreover, the American Association of University Professors has initiated several investigations into discriminatory hiring and firing policies based upon political or social views. Few of these disputes have reached the courts. Some were settled by the parties involved; others, while resulting in dismissals or denials of promotions, have not been litigated. In still other instances, student unrest and protest over the schools' policies have caused administrative reconsideration and eventual re-employment of the individuals involved.

An example of a dispute over academic freedom which did receive judicial scrutiny is provided by a 1963 case which arose over the dismissal, by the University of Illinois, of Leo F. Koch, an assistant professor of biology, who in a campus newspaper published the following letter:

To the Editor:

You have made a great show of liberalism in racial problems whose center of physical and emotional disturbance is a safe, 1,000 miles away. I will be interested to see how your social conscience operates with a problem which strikes very close to home, here on campus.

The problem is broached by Dick Hutchison and Dan Bures in their article, "Sex Ritualized" (16 March) under the heading, "Off the Cuff" on your editorial page.

Hutchison and Bures are to be commended for their courage in candidly discussing the sexual problems of college students, even if only with narrow-minded, if not entirely ignorant, perspective.

Their discussion omits entirely any reference to the social milieu which compels healthy, sexually mature human animals into such addictions (of which masturbation is likely the least objectionable) to unhealthy and degenerative practices.

The first hazard encountered by the frank discussion in public of sexual problems is the widespread moralistic attitude that where there is smoke, there is fire. Anyone who insists on speaking about sex in public, say the orthodox moralists, (unless it is condemned soundly) must be a sexual deviate (a queer) in their orthodox view.

The second, and by far the more important, hazard is that a public discussion of sex will offend the religious feelings of the leaders of our religious institutions. These people feel that youngsters should remain ignorant of sex for fear that knowledge of it will lead to temptation and sin.

Hence we have the widespread crusades against obscenity which are so popular among prudes and puritanical old maids.

Bachelors are known to be immune to this disease inasmuch as they are the favored sex in a double standard of morality which accepts as respectable premarital sexual experience for men but not for women. This occasions some difficulty as most men are heterosexually inclined.

Thus we come to the crux of the problem, which is not even hinted at by Hutchison and Bures. Their article would lead a casual reader to believe that the evils portrayed by them are due only to the depravity of the individuals they observed, whereas, in fact, the heavy load of blame should fall on the depraved society which reared them.

I submit that the events described by Hutchison and Bures are merely symptoms of a serious social malaise which is caused primarily by the hypocritical and downright inhumane moral standards engendered by a Christian code of ethics which was already decrepit in the days of Queen Victoria.

College students, when faced with this outrageously ignorant code of morality, would seem to me to be acting with remarkable decorum, and surprising meekness, if they do no more than neck at their social functions.

Perhaps it would be nearer to the truth to say that such meek and very frustrating, no doubt, behavior indicates an extreme degree of brainwashing by our religious and civil authorities in the name of virtue and purity, to the point where the students have become psychologically inhibited from satisfying their needs in more obvious and healthy ways.

With modern contraceptives and medical advice readily available at the nearest drugstore, or at least from a family physician, there is no valid reason why sexual intercourse should not be condoned among those sufficiently mature to engage in it without social consequences and without violating their own codes of morality and ethics.

A mutually satisfactory sexual experience would eliminate the need for many hours of frustrating petting and lead to much happier and longer-lasting marriages among our younger men and women.

Leo F. Koch
Assistant Professor of Biology

About three weeks after publication of his letter, Koch was informed by the president of the university that his contract would be terminated at the end of that academic year. The reason given for this was that the views expressed in the letter were "offensive and repugnant [and] contrary to the commonly accepted standards of morality." Their public espousal, the president stated, "may be interpreted as encouragement of immoral behavior. It is clear that [this] conduct has been prejudicial to the best interests of the University."

Despite a recommendation by the University Senate Committee on Academic Freedom that Koch merely be reprimanded, the board of trustees ordered his dismissal.

Koch then instituted suit in an Illinois state court seeking damages for breach of his employment contract on the ground that his discharge violated the due process, equal protection, and privileges and immunities clauses of the Fourteenth Amendment and deprived him of freedom of speech. After losing in the state courts, Koch requested the author and Leonard B. Boudin to prepare a Petition for Certiorari to the United States Supreme Court. The petition follows. The reader should recall that this type of brief is intended merely to persuade the Supreme Court that the issues in the case are worthy of full review and not to present a comprehensive argument. The reader should also observe how closely related to the free-speech issues are the questions of vagueness and procedural due process, which are dealt with more fully in Section III of this book.

I / Freedom of Expression

This case presents for decision an important constitutional question that has never been decided by this Court but which was decided by the courts below inconsistently with principles that have been enunciated by this Court. That question is whether a state, consistently with the protection accorded free speech by the due process clause of the Fourteenth Amendment, can discharge a university professor on the ground that "the tone, language and content" of a letter he wrote that was published in a campus periodical was contrary to "commonly accepted standards of morality in the [university] community."

In other terms, this case presents in clear-cut fashion the question whether a state can circumvent the constitutional protection of free speech through the expedient of imposing a vague standard of correct expression on its academic personnel. If the decision below stands, and Illinois can validly terminate petitioner's employment for expressing his views on the issue of sexual relations among university students, there would seem little to restrain Illinois or any other state from discharging a professor (or teacher or other public employee) whenever he expresses a controversial opinion that does not jibe with the prevailing view in the office of the university's president or board of trustees.

The action of a publicly financed school or university, such as the respondent here, is certainly "state action" within the meaning of the Fourteenth Amendment.[1] It is settled, too, that the "liberty" of the Fourteenth Amendment embraces freedom of expression.[2]

This Court has recognized that protection of free expression is especially important when government attempts to restrain those whose lives are devoted to the pursuit and imparting of knowledge. In *Shelton v. Tucker*,[3] the Court said: "The vigilant protection of constitutional freedoms is nowhere more vital than in the community of American schools." Similarly, the Chief Justice, in the plurality opinion in *Sweezy v. New Hampshire*,[4] joined by Justices Black, Douglas and Brennan, declared:

> *The essentiality of freedom in the community of American universities is almost self-evident. No one should underestimate the vital role in a democracy that is played by those who guide and train our youth. To impose any straitjacket upon the intellectual leaders in our colleges and universities would imperil the future of our nation.*

The tenor of the "findings" by the board of trustees suggests the full implications of the decision below and its patent inconsistency with the principles expressed above. It was found that petitioner did "encourage and espouse . . . immoral conduct upon the part of . . . students" and "condemned as inhumane and obsolete the widely accepted moral standards derived from the Christian code of ethics," and that the "language of petitioner's letter was not in keeping with those standards of temperateness, dignity, and respect for the opinions of others which should characterize public expression by members of the faculty."

The letter that led to these findings, and that was concededly written to be read by the Illinois University community, is reproduced above. There would seem, at first blush, nothing particularly novel or shocking in petitioner's conclusion that "there is no valid reason why sexual intercourse should not be condoned among those sufficiently mature to engage in it without social consequences and without violating their own codes of morality and ethics." In today's world one may doubt that petitioner's opinion actually differs from the "commonly accepted standards of morality."[5] Certainly there is nothing in the record to demonstrate that it differs. But assuming that it does so differ, the critical question is presented whether Illinois can uproot petitioner from his professorial position because his expressed views—in "tone, language and content"—are found to be inconsistent with the vague standard employed by university officials.

Of course, the letter dealt with a controversial subject, but such subjects are the stuff of serious discourse. The views expressed by the petitioner may not have been conventional, but the responsibility of a scholar and teacher is to eschew the conventional when it no longer represents his best judgment. A distinguished investigating committee of the American Association of University Professors concluded that the letter was only "a comment and expression of views upon a broad problem under discussion on the campus" and that there was "nothing in the letter which constituted encouragement or espousal beyond what naturally adheres to a vigorous presentation of the ideas that Professor Koch was endeavoring to put forward."[6] As Mr. Justice Frankfurter said in *Wieman v. Updegraff*, "Education is a kind of continuing dialogue, *and a dialogue assumes, in the nature of the case, different points of view*."[7] (Emphasis supplied)

It seems plain that if petitioner's discharge is upheld, based on the subjective standards employed by respondent's president and board of trustees, there will be few, if any, independent-thinking professors or teachers who will venture into public discussion of controversial subjects. It is difficult to imagine a more disastrous consequence for institutions dedicated to the pursuit of truth and, ostensibly, to free discussion. This Court should review the decision below to decide whether "freedom in the community of American universities" need sustain this crippling consequence.

II / Vague University Regulations

This case presents the question, never decided by this Court, whether a professor at a state university can be discharged consistently with the due process clause of the Fourteenth Amendment if the standards of the university regulations pursuant to which he is discharged are so vague that they drastically inhibit freedom of expression.

Sections 38(c) and (d) of the University of Illinois Statutes provide for discharge "for cause" and define "cause" as conduct that infringes "commonly accepted standards of morality" or conduct that is "clearly prejudicial to the best interests of the University."

It is well settled that "a statute which either forbids or requires the doing of an act in terms so vague that men of common intelligence must necessarily guess at its meaning and differ as to its application, violates the first essential of due process of law."[8]

The regulation here in issue is in effect a state statute and must be judged according to the same standards, since it was passed pursuant to authority delegated by state statute and has the same regulating effect.

It is difficult to imagine a vaguer set of standards by which to guide the conduct of university personnel than the standards contained in section 38. Initially, there is serious question as to whether, fairly read, a statute directed at immoral "conduct" was ever intended to refer to expressions of opinion, however extreme. Even assuming that the regulations would be understood by a conscientious faculty member as applying to speech, it is difficult to imagine a regulation which would have a more pernicious effect on free expression. It is simply not possible to estimate when an opinion expressed on another controversial issue will be considered inconsistent with "commonly accepted standards of morality" or "prejudicial to the interests of the University."

The net effect of the regulation is to keep members of the faculty in constant jeopardy and uncertainty about their right to express opinions on matters of public interest. By giving university officials a virtual carte blanche to dismiss professors for their speech, the regulations make a mockery of the university's statement on academic freedom.

The excessive generality of the Illinois regulation must be considered in light of the established rule that vague statutes will be scrutinized with particular care when a question of free speech is involved. For example, in *Smith v. California* the Court said:

> *. . . stricter standards of permissible statutory vagueness may be applied to a statute having a potentially inhibiting effect on speech; a man may the less be required to act at his peril here, because the free dissemination of ideas may be the loser.*[9]

The committee of the American Association of University Professors considered application of the regulation to Professor Koch in the name of academic responsibility to be "little more than, through a back-door route, foreclosing expression of the idea themselves." In these circumstances, it is plain from a "mere inspection that these general words and phrases are so vague and indefinite that any penalty prescribed for their violation constitutes a denial of due process of law."[10]

There is no doubt that the vague provisions of the regulation in the instant case present a substantial question under the Fourteenth Amendment, as applied in earlier decisions of this Court.

III / Procedural Due Process

The hearing afforded petitioner when he was dismissed failed to satisfy the requirements of the due process clause of the Fourteenth

Amendment because he was found guilty of a charge that was never formally made and of which he was not informed until the conclusion of the hearing. This is so because of the allegations contained in the memorandum of the president of the university. The president's letter stated:

. . . I consider Professor Koch's letter a grave breach of academic responsibility. The views expressed are offensive and repugnant, contrary to commonly accepted standards of morality, and their public espousal may be interpreted as encouragement of immoral behavior. It is clear that Mr. Koch's conduct was prejudicial to the best interests of the University.

The board ruled that the charges contained in the president's letter were established. But its conclusion, in contrast to the charges contained in the president's letter, was as follows:

We do not condemn Assistant Professor Koch's actions in issue here merely because he expressed in his letter views contrary to commonly accepted beliefs and standards. We condemn it because of the manner in which he expressed those views in his letter. We do not consider that letter as a "responsible" and proper expression of the views stated in it.

That previous notice of the issue to be decided in an administrative hearing is an essential element of due process was squarely held in *Morgan v. United States:*[11] "The right to a hearing embraces not only the right to present evidence, but also a reasonable opportunity to know the claims of the opposing party and to meet them."[12]

While the exact basis of the board's determination is far from clear, it is certain that the board's dismissal of petitioner was based, at least in part, upon the manner in which his letter was written. The president's memorandum gave no indication that the manner of the letter would be a charge against petitioner at the board hearing. Nor did any other communication from the board indicate that petitioner's discharge might be based upon the manner.

This Court has never ruled upon the scope of a fair hearing in the present context of a hearing before the board of trustees of a state university. The importance of the issue is evident from the large number of university faculty subject to discharge in a similar manner who will be adversely affected if the decision below is permitted to stand.

The board of trustees submitted a brief in opposition to Koch's petition in which it was asserted that the Supreme Court should deny the writ because the case followed an erroneous procedural route in the Illinois courts. In making this contention, the board invoked the doctrine of the "adequate and independent non-constitutional ground" under which the Court habitually declines to consider constitutional claims if the appealing party has not complied with a state's fair procedural rules. In due course, on January 13, 1964, the Supreme Court denied the writ of certiorari.[13] *Because it is not the practice of the Court to give its reasons for refusing to hear cases, it is uncertain whether the Court relied on the "adequate state ground" theory or whether there were not four Justices that wished to decide the issues relating to academic freedom.*

The importance to the development of academic freedom of the questions presented in the Koch *case, and the increased incidence of disputes on the nation's campuses, suggest that it will be increasingly difficult for the Supreme Court to abstain from a decision on the type of question presented by the* Koch *case.*

NOTES

Leonard B. Boudin and Civil Liberties Fellow Bernard Evans Harvith participated in the preparation of the petition.

1. Brown v. Board of Education, 347 U.S. 483 (1954).
2. Gitlow v. New York, 268 U.S. 652, 666 (1925); NAACP v. Alabama, 357 U.S. 449, 460 (1958).
3. 364 U.S. 479, 487 (1960).
4. 354 U.S. 234, 250 (1957).
5. See, e.g., Judge Learned Hand's observations in Schmidt v. United States, 177 F.2d 450 (2d Cir. 1949).
6. "Academic Freedom and Tenure: The University of Illinois," 49 *Bul-*

letin of American Association of University Professors No. 1 at 1, 38.

7. 344 U.S. 183, 197–98 (1952). See also West Virginia State Board of Education v. Barnette, 319 U.S. 624, 637–38 (1943).

8. Connally v. General Construction Co., 269 U.S. 385, 391 (1926). See also Lanzetta v. New Jersey, 306 U.S. 451 (1939); Champlin Refining Co. v. Corporation Commission of Oklahoma, 285 U.S. 210 (1932); Cramp v. Board of Public Instruction, 368 U.S. 278 (1961).

9. 361 U.S. 147, 151 (1959).

10. Champlin Refining Co. v. Corporation Commission of Oklahoma, 286 U.S. 210, 243 (1932).

11. 304 U.S. 1, 18–20 (1938).

12. *Id.* at 18. See also Thornhill v. Alabama, 310 U.S. 88, 96 (1940); Thompson v. City of Louisville, 362 U.S. 199, 206 (1960); Inbau, "The Concept of 'Fair Hearing' in Anglo-American Law," 31 *Tulane L. Rev.* 67, 73 (1956).

13. Koch v. Board of Trustees of the University of Illinois, 375 U.S. 989 (1964).

11

Demonstrations and Sit-ins

In 1961 a small group of Negro college students began the historic sit-in movement, which ushered in a new era of civil rights activity in the United States. Demonstrations against all forms of segregation and discrimination were an integral part of the protest, and the legal problems raised by these events were both novel and complex. Although the underlying issues that led to civil rights demonstrations involved racial discrimination in housing, schools and public accommodations, which are considered in Section IV of this book, the question from the standpoint of lawyers and courts is one of freedom of expression: To what degree are the various forms of protest protected under the First Amendment?

In the fall of 1963, the Legal Defense and Educational Fund of the NAACP asked the author to prepare a manual for its field workers outlining in nontechnical language their rights and duties while engaging in demonstrations. The following statement was prepared in response to this request, with the title "Demonstrations: How to Protest Within the Law."

1. *Parades and Public Assemblies*

Public protest, discussion and debate have a long and honored history, and a cherished place, in American society and American politics.[1] The right to express your beliefs to the public in a public place is part of your right to free speech.[2] In exercising this right you are entitled to the protection of law enforcement officials from those who would interfere with your parade or meeting; the rowdyism of others cannot properly be the basis for denying you the right to speak openly in public.[3] Only your own actual disorder, or threat of disorder, is the proper basis for dispersing your meeting or parade or arresting any of the participants in such a meeting or parade.[4]

A parade, of course, may disrupt traffic and a public meeting compete with others in their use of parks and streets. Thus many communities require a permit or a license before allowing such demonstrations to take place. If a license is required, you should apply for one before you act. But the only proper purpose for a licensing requirement is to give notice to those officials responsible for maintaining safety and order so that they may make whatever plans are necessary to maintain safety and order. This means that the authorities cannot deny you a permit on a whim; they cannot deny you a permit because the meeting may cause some inconvenience,[5] or because some people find what you have to say objectionable,[6] or because there were disturbances at some prior meeting or parade.[7]

If the law involved says something like this: "The chief of police may issue parade or public meeting permits at his discretion," you could probably ignore the law altogether, but to be on the safe side you should still apply for your permit. If the police chief refuses to give you the permit, then go out and hold your meeting anyway.[8] On the other hand, if the law says something like this: "The chief of police must issue permits for parades or public meetings when requested to do so, but may consider the time and place of the meeting or parade," then you must make an initial request, and if that is denied, the denial may have to be challenged before you demonstrate.[9] In the first example given, the police chief's authority is too broad; it permits him to give or withhold a permit whenever he sees fit. Thus, once he denies the permit you need do nothing more. But in the second example, the police chief is not given the power to deny a permit whenever he sees fit; the law itself is valid, but his actions under it may not be. Thus, his denial must first be brought before the courts before you act.

If there is no law at all, then you need not apply for a permit, even though it is thought customary to do so.[10]

2. *Sound Amplifiers*

Because the amplified voice may disturb as well as attract, there is no absolute right to use sound equipment at any time, in any place, at any volume. And just as with parades and public meetings, a permit can be required.[11] But the issuance of such a permit may not properly rest in the discretion of the issuing authority.[12] About the only permissible regulation would relate to sound (in a business area, louder; in a residential area, softer) and time (louder at mid-day than at midnight).

3. *Leaflet Distribution*

You may want to distribute leaflets or flyers as part of a larger demonstration (e.g., a protest meeting in a park) or as an independent enterprise. You may want to distribute them to private homes and in apartment buildings as well as on the streets. And just as in the cases already discussed, your community may have a law which requires you to obtain a permit before you distribute anything. Apply. But note, you are entitled to get that permit. The authorities are not permitted to give or withhold a permit at their discretion, nor may they absolutely ban distribution of any kind.[13] This is true even though there is a "worthy" motive behind the ban.[14] Similarly, you may not be prevented, by law, from distributing material to private homeowners, although the owner of an apartment building could himself refuse you access to the premises.[15]

Some communities have tried to curtail the publication and distribution of protest literature by requiring the names of sponsoring people to be printed on the leaflets. The result, of course, is to end such distribution where the ideas expressed do not find favor with many people in the community (e.g., a demand for nondiscriminatory treatment in various aspects of daily life, when made in a Deep South town, can result in reprisals when the names of specific people become known). It is not legal to have such a requirement, and you may properly ignore it.[16] Anonymity is often important to the free expression of ideas, and you are entitled to that protection which anonymity brings.

4. *Picketing*

The following procedure should be followed when picketing to protest refusals to serve or hire Negroes: (1) you should picket only the place which is practicing discrimination; (2) you should not block access to the picketed site; (3) if you carry signs they should be informational (e.g., they should simply state the kind of discrimination practiced in this particular place); (4) your own activity should always be orderly, but you are entitled to protection from the disorderly conduct of others, and it would not be proper to halt your picketing because of the actions of others.

Picketing to force a violation of a valid state policy or law is illegal.[17] Of course, what is a "valid" state policy or law is sometimes hard to determine in advance. However, a state law or policy requiring segregation or discrimination is not valid, and picketing directed against discriminatory practices exercised under the legal or customary authority of the state is not illegal. A boycott directed toward a justifiable social goal is legal. Putting an end to discrimination and to segregation is a justifiable social goal.

In both the picketing and boycott areas *Hughes v. Superior Court*[18] raises a difficult problem. In that case it was held that a state may properly enjoin picketing directed at obtaining preferential hiring treatment for Negroes, in opposition to a state policy barring considerations of race. However, for a different and persuasive view that could one day be accepted by the Supreme Court, see the dissent of Judge Traynor in the lower court.[19]

The following points should be remembered when you do organize a boycott: (1) boycott only the place which is practicing discrimination; (2) do not attempt to enforce the boycott by physically preventing others from using or going onto the boycotted premises; (3) as in picketing, a boycott organized to force a violation of a valid state law or policy is not legal, but the maintenance of segregation or discrimination is not a valid goal of any state.

5. *Sit-ins*

The more the owner of private property (e.g., a store, restaurant, amusement park, movie house, theater) opens his establishment to the public, for his own benefit, the more he is subject to the rights of the public.[20] Contrary to the claim often made that an owner of private property can do anything with it he wants, there is a long history of public control of private property. Although the extent of this control is not a settled question, certain things are clear: (1) merely sitting down at a segregated lunch counter or at a table in a segregated restaurant cannot, in itself, be disorderly conduct, and any arrest based on that theory is unconstitutional;[21] (2) where segregation is required by state or local law it may not be enforced by a private owner of a place of public accommodation (even if he approves of the rule), and any arrest based on charge of trespass is unconstitutional;[22] (3) even if there are no written laws, if the law enforcement authorities (e.g., a major or chief of police, or governor, for that matter) make it clear that they will not tolerate attempts to desegregate, then the situation is no different than if there actually were written laws—an arrest for trespass would be illegal.[23]

But, you may ask, what if there are no laws and no statements by public officials, could we then be prevented from sitting at a lunch counter or in a restaurant, or entering an amusement park? Would a sit-in demonstration then be illegal? The Supreme Court has not finally settled this issue, but there is a strong argument that the demonstration would be lawful. First, it is consistent with prior cases to maintain that when a man operates a business and extends an invitation to the public to make use of his premises for his own gain, he may not open his business to only part of the public. This is clearest in the situation where all of a store but the lunch counter is open to

Negro customers, but it seems no less true in the situation where Negroes are not permitted to enter the premises at all. In addition, there is authority that for a state to permit its courts to be used to further this kind of discrimination is a denial of equal protection.[24]

You should know that a sit-in in a governmental facility is legal because the government may not permit its facilities to be used in a discriminatory manner. The question raised, however, is, What is a governmental facility?

There are, typically, four kinds of governmental facilities: (1) an owned facility (e.g., a courthouse, a municipally owned parking lot, a public library); (2) a facility in which the government has some kind of business interest (e.g., the government collects the rent from the private owner, the private businessman performs duties for the government); (3) a facility which is licensed or regulated by the government; (4) a facility which is financed in some degree by the government.

A facility actually owned by the government (a park, a golf course, a publicly owned restaurant in a public building, a public beach or pool, a public library) may not discriminate.[25] Furthermore, facilities which fall into this class may not even "go slow" in ending their discrimination (as public schools have been allowed to do) but must be integrated now and all at once.[26]

A facility in which the government has some business interest (a restaurant located in a public building though privately owned) may not discriminate,[27] nor may the government avoid its responsibility to provide the entire population with equal services by handing public functions to a private businessman (thus a public golf course cannot be turned into a private one merely by turning it over to a private businessman).[28]

Facilities which are licensed, regulated or financed by the government fall into an in-between area. But restaurants or amusement parks or stores or theaters or similar establishments in some way affected by government activity may still not discriminate, because of their public nature, whether or not they are considered governmental facilities. Thus, sit-in demonstrations carried on in such places are lawful.

Sit-ins are also legal when directed against private businessmen who are in some way closely connected with interstate travel,[29] or if the facility is owned directly by a carrier in interstate or intrastate commerce.[30] This rule applies to purely private facilities (e.g., a privately owned restaurant in a privately owned bus terminal) as well as to mixed publicly owned and privately owned facilities (e.g., a privately owned restaurant in a municipally owned airlines terminal).[31]

6. *Injunctions*

All demonstrations—parades, marches, picketing, boycotts, sit-ins—are affected by the power of state (and federal) courts to issue injunctions.

Essentially, an injunction issued by a court with jurisdiction over the subject matter and the parties must be obeyed even though it is erroneous. The proper way to challenge this erroneous order is to obtain judicial relief from it. If you simply ignore the injunction, you are in contempt of court.[32] As you can see, it becomes important to determine whether the court does have jurisdiction. This will vary from state to state and is not a decision you should make without legal advice.

If you wish to argue that the court is enforcing an unconstitutional law by issuing its injunction, or that the injunction itself is unconstitutional, the proper way to do this is in an action to set aside the injunction.

7. *Conclusion*

We have tried to outline the major types of demonstrations and to show that they are all legal if certain guides are followed. Of course, state and local officials may still harass you as you try to exercise your rights. But if you act in the manner suggested in each of the discussed areas, you will certainly overcome such tactics in the end.

New situations may arise which will call for means of public protest not yet tried or even thought of. The success of these new methods will depend on a wide range of facts, but your chances of success will be greatly increased if you remember the following points: (1) always maintain order and discipline in your own ranks; (2) never physically hinder others from going about their peaceful business; (3) obey the procedural requirements of the state or local government (e.g., obtaining a license when required) until it is invalidated.

Since the pamphlet was prepared, there have been many developments of major importance affecting the right to demonstrate, only some of which can be briefly covered here. Probably the single most significant event was the passage of the Civil Rights Act of 1964, which established the statutory right of equal access to public accommodations. Previously, three Justices had expressed the view that the Fourteenth Amendment by its own force prohibited state prosecutions for "trespass" in cases involving property which is used to serve the public.

The course of constitutional decision since 1964 has been irregular. In 1965 the Court reversed convictions for breach of the peace, obstructing public passages and picketing before a courthouse, growing out of a Baton Rouge demonstration.[33] But in 1966 a sharply divided Court (5–4) for the first time upheld state trespass convictions resulting from a civil rights demonstration.[34] The protest was conducted on jailhouse grounds in Florida, and the majority seemed to rely upon the need for additional security near jails. Then, in June 1967 the Supreme Court held, again by a 5–4 vote, that civil rights demonstrators were barred from violating a state court injunction which prohibited protest marches without first testing the constitutionality of that injunction in the courts.[35] And in April 1968 the Court again sustained a conviction against civil rights demonstrators.

There has been some speculation that the change in direction by the Supreme Court is a response to the new and more militant "Black Power" orientation of the civil rights movement. Others believe that the critical factor is the increased concern among some members of the Court and large segments of the public over the consequences to public order of carrying controversial issues, such as civil rights and the peace movement, into the streets. In any event, the demonstrations that took place throughout the summer of 1967 suggest that the Supreme Court will continue to be preoccupied by the problem of accommodating the right of individuals and groups to protest and the general community interest in maintaining law and order.

NOTES

Civil Liberties Fellow Paul Strok Adler participated in the preparation of the manual.

1. See American Civil Liberties Union, *How Americans Protest: A Statement on the Civil Rights Demonstrations* (1963).
2. De Jonge v. Oregon, 229 U.S. 352 (1937).
3. Sellers v. Johnson, 163 F.2d 877 (8th Cir. 1947), *cert. denied,* 332 U.S. 851 (1948).
4. Edwards v. South Carolina, 373 U.S. 229 (1962); Terminiello v. Chicago, 337 U.S. 1 (1949); *cf.* Wright v. Georgia, 373 U.S. 284 (1963).
5. Terminiello v. Chicago, *supra* note 4.
6. *Ibid.;* Edwards v. South Carolina, 373 U.S. 229 (1963). *Contra,* Feiner v. New York, 340 U.S. 315 (1951).
7. Kunz v. New York, 340 U.S. 290 (1951).
8. *Cf.* Lovell v. City of Griffin, 303 U.S. 444 (1938).
9. Poulos v. New Hampshire, 345 U.S. 395 (1953).
10. Niemotko v. Maryland, 340 U.S. 268 (1951).
11. Kovacs v. Cooper, 336 U.S. 77 (1949).
12. Saia v. New York, 334 U.S. 558 (1948).
13. Lovell v. City of Griffin, 303 U.S. 444 (1938); see also Jamison v. Texas, 318 U.S. 413 (1943), and Largent v. Texas, 318 U.S. 413 (1943).
14. See cases decided *sub nom* Schneider v. State, 208 U.S. 147, 162–65 (1939).
15. Martin v. City of Struthers, 319 U.S. 141 (1944) (distribution to private homeowners); *compare,* Watchtower Bible and Tract Society, Inc. v. Metropolitan Life Insurance Co., 297 N.Y. 339, 79 N.E.2d 433 (1948), *cert. denied,* 335 U.S. 886 (1949) (landlord may exclude from apartment house).
16. Talley v. California, 362 U.S. 360 (1960).
17. Building Service Employees Union v. Gazzam, 339 U.S. 532 (1950); Hughes v. Superior Court, 339 U.S. 460 (1950).
18. 339 U.S. 460 (1950).

19. 32 Cal.2d 850, 871, 198 P.2d 885, 897–98 (1948).

20. Marsh v. Alabama, 326 U.S. 501 (1946).

21. Garner v. Louisiana, 368 U.S. 157 (1962).

22. Peterson v. City of Greenville, 373 U.S. 244 (1963).

23. Lombard v. Louisiana, 373 U.S. 267 (1963) (criminal mischief statute which encompassed acts of trespass).

24. This argument is simply an extension of Shelley v. Kraemer, 334 U.S. 1 (1948), and Barrows v. Jackson, 346 U.S. 249 (1953). For other discussions taking this position see Hyman, "Segregation and the Fourteenth Amendment," 4 *Vand. L. Rev.* 555 (1950), and Schwelb, "The Sit-In Demonstration: Criminal Trespass or Constitutional Right?" 36 *N.Y.U.L. Rev.* 779 (1961).

25. E.g., Mayor, etc. of Baltimore v. Dawson, 350 U.S. 877 (1956) (parks); Turner v. Memphis, 369 U.S. 350 (1961) (airports); Giles v. Library Advisory Committee, 5 *Race Rel. L. Rep.* 1140 (1960) (libraries); Johnson v. Virginia, 373 U.S. 61 (1963) (courtrooms).

26. Watson v. City of Memphis, 373 U.S. 526 (1963).

27. Burton v. Wilmington Parking Authority, 365 U.S. 715 (1961).

28. Wolfe v. North Carolina, 364 U.S. 177 (1960).

29. Boynton v. Virginia, 364 U.S. 454 (1960).

30. Bailey v. Patterson, 369 U.S. 350 (1961).

31. Turner v. Memphis, 369 U.S. 350 (1961).

32. See Howat v. Kansas, 258 U.S. 181 (1922); United States v. United Mine Workers, 230 U.S. 259 (1947); *In re* Green, 369 U.S. 689 (1962).

33. Cox v. Louisiana, 379 U.S. 559 (1965).

34. Adderly v. Florida, 385 U.S. 39 (1966).

35. Walker v. City of Birmingham, 388 U.S. 307 (1967).

12

Separation of Church and State

A Conference

In 1961 the voters of New York State were asked to authorize, through a proposed constitutional amendment, certain types of aid to all institutions of higher learning within the state, including religious institutions. The Hays Program decided to hold a conference of experts to consider the complex issues involved in a program of the kind contemplated by New York and, presumably, other states. Plans for the conference were well under way when on Election Day the voters handily rejected the amendment. Despite this result, a poll of the conferees disclosed the general conviction that the issues were of such importance that there was every reason to proceed. Accordingly, in March 1962 a conference was held to consider: (1) the constitutionality of public assistance to church-related schools, and (2) the problem of obtaining legal standing, in either the federal or state courts, to assert a constitutional challenge to any program of public assistance.

The discussion of the second, more technical issue is not reproduced here. The conferees whose remarks follow are Professor Leo Pfeffer, Chairman of the Department of Political Science, Long Island University, and Special Counsel to the American Jewish Congress; Professor Louis Jaffe of the Harvard Law School; Mr. Ken-

neth Greenawalt, Director of the National Council on Higher Education; and Professor Gerald Gunther, then of Columbia Law School and now of Stanford Law School.

I / Introduction (Norman Dorsen)

The thorny problems concerning the constitutionality and desirability of aiding religious institutions with public funds have vexed the nation since its inception. There has always been ample dispute over the proper spheres for church and state, on this question as on others, but the proposals to help finance parochial schools now before the people and their political representatives have raised the debate, in the words of Professor Philip Kurland, to an "unprecedented crescendo."[1]

In this brief introduction I shall first make a few general observations and then comment on certain implications of the most recent authoritative decision bearing upon the constitutionality of public aid to church-related schools—*Engel v. Vitale,*[2] the school prayer case.

The debate about public aid to parochial schools is part of the broader and pressing question of federal aid in general. It is this possibility—that the central government will, for the first time, provide substantial amounts of financial assistance to local education untied to considerations of national security—that has focused attention sharply on whether such aid should or must be confined to public schools.

In resolving this issue, it is important, as we were often reminded during the conference, to try to distinguish between constitutional and political issues. The political issues are complex, involving not only traditional battle lines over the ideal relationship between church and state and the proper role of the federal government in an area traditionally within exclusive state jurisdiction, but also newer conflicts, notably over the potential effect of grants to nonpublic schools on the future of segregated education.

I am less confident than some that the constitutional debate can be conducted, by spokesmen for either side, free from a heavy influence of "political" views. I am even less confident that the public can participate in either legal or political debate without succumbing to the easy conclusion that those opposed to public assistance to parochial schools are antireligious, or more specifically, anti-Catholic. This conclusion ignores much history as well as the complexities of what is involved, but nonetheless will probably persist to polarize debate along unfortunate lines. Strong statements from unassailably devout sources that public aid is unwise or unconstitutional may help to moderate feelings and words. A recent example is a report of a special committee of the United Presbyterian Church in the United States, which recommended that "grants from federal, state, or local taxes for nonpublic elementary and secondary schools, including payment for tuition or scholarships of children attending such schools, grants to their parents for this purpose, or tax credits, tax forgiveness or exemption from school taxes or other taxes for such parents be opposed."[3] Nevertheless, the deeply rooted interests at stake suggest that all will not be sweetness and light as decision days approach in Congress or the Supreme Court.

These pessimistic views seem amply borne out by the response to *Engel v. Vitale*, in which the Supreme Court held that a nondenominational prayer composed by the Board of Regents could not constitutionally be made part of the daily routine in New York public schools. The prayer read: "Almighty God, we acknowledge our dependence upon Thee, and we beg Thy blessings upon us, our parents, our teachers, and our country." In certain quarters the reaction was bitter. The Court and its supporters were treated with scorn, frequently by those who had previously been critical of recent judicial rulings in favor of civil rights. In an editorial discussing *Engel v. Vitale*, the writer for one magazine that has been highly critical of the Court first said, "to try to bring [racial integration in schools] by a sudden decree by nine men directly contradicting an understanding of 65 years' duration was, in reality, a revolutionary, not a constitutional act." The editorial then went on to discuss the *Engel* case in these terms: "[S]ince June 25, 1962, we have a new Constitution, which has annulled and suppressed the old," and "There is a petty, niggling, nasty quality about this school prayer decision."[4]

Perhaps the most dismaying consequence was the bald assertion by some local officials that the decision would not be obeyed—not because of honest disagreement over the scope of the Court's ruling (for example, whether it outlaws the devotional reading of the Lord's Prayer), but as an act of outright defiance. This is not to condemn individual protests designed to alter the edict of a court (or any other law) which one cannot conscientiously obey. The point is that public officials, charged with responsibility for enforcing judicial rulings, are not free to interpose personal opinions about their correctness; the choice of officials is to comply or resign.

A clue to the reasons for the fierce outcry over *Engel v. Vitale* may lie in its implications for the constitutionality of public aid to religious schools. Superficially, of course, the "wall of separation" between church and state that *McCollum v. Board of Education*[5] preserved (or erected, depending on one's point of view) has received some repair after the erosions of *Zorach v. Clauson.*[6] In *McCollum* the Court struck down a state law providing for "released-time" religious instruction which took place in the public school, while in *Zorach* the Court upheld a similar program which involved religious instruction during school hours, but outside the public schools. Yet those seeking federal funds for parochial schools may try to use *Engel v. Vitale,* at least in the political arena, to support their position. It could be argued that since the decision makes it unlawful to engage in religious practices in the public schools, the only fair alternative in a pluralistic and nominally religious society is to establish a private school system where parents can send their children to receive a religiously oriented education, and that the only way to achieve this is through public support. This line of argument would flow naturally from the respected views of Father John Courtney Murray, who is widely regarded as a spokesman on this issue for the official Roman Catholic position.[7] If such contentions should prevail in the legislatures, the courts undoubtedly will be asked to rule on the constitutional question under the establishment clause, and this will ultimately present the Supreme Court with one of its most trying cases.

II / (Leo Pfeffer)

My feelings are pretty definite. I believe, as does President Kennedy, on the basis of the memorandum of law prepared by the Department of Health, Education and Welfare (HEW), that government assistance in the form of funds to church-related schools is a violation of the First Amendment if done by the federal government and the Fourteenth Amendment if done by a state government.[8]

I do not think this was seriously controverted until rather recently. At least I had not seen until the past several years any serious effort to justify the constitutionality of the use of government funds for parochial schools. Recently, there have been several articles, including William Ball's paper for the National Catholic Welfare Conference,[9] Paul Kauper's article in the *Michigan Law Review*,[10] and Philip Kurland's article in the *Chicago Law Review*.[11] The recent constitutional debate is, I think, to a large extent a political rather than a legal controversy.

In the past, federal or state aid to parochial schools in the form of textbooks or bus transportation has been justified on the basis that no aid to the school was involved, but rather aid to the child which was only of indirect benefit to the school. It was always tacitly recognized that direct aid would be unconstitutional. If this is wrong, I don't understand what all the fighting and arguing in the *Everson* case [12] was about—the great debate whether the legislature had gone to the "very verge"[13] of constitutional power or beyond it in upholding the use of public funds to transport children to parochial schools, whether what was involved was really or only fictionally an aid to the child rather than to the school. All this was mere shadowboxing if with one sentence the Court could have said: "There is nothing in the Constitution which prohibits the State of New Jersey from giving this money directly to the school; what are we wasting our time about?" The *Everson* case makes no sense to me except on the assumption that the state could not have given the money directly to the parochial school.

Once it is settled, as it was in *Torcaso v. Watkins*,[14] which held that a public notary could not be denied a state commission because he was an atheist, that the First Amendment means the government may aid religion neither on a nonpreferential nor a preferential basis, that it may not give money to all churches any more than it may give it to one church, then I have no real doubts about the parochial school question.

There is, however, one point which does have to be recognized. The Supreme Court assumed that the rationale of the *Everson* decision was that the purpose of this expenditure was to protect the children from getting run over by automobiles. With respect to the argument concerning taxation for private purposes, there is language in the case which goes further than that, language which says that since this is an accredited school, it is in the public interest to transport children to it.[15] It is too late, the Court said, to argue that it is not in the public interest to transport children to any school where they can satisfy the requirements of the compulsory school attendance law.[16]

And so, it could be said that if it is in the public interest to get children to school, for which public funds can be used, then it is also in the public interest to see that they get an accredited education in the schools. So it can be argued also, as William Ball does in his paper,[17] that the religious teachings can be separated from the secular teachings in the parochial school and that public funds can be used to finance the secular aspects of the school on a pro rata basis.

I think this is artificial and unreal and, notwithstanding one or two sentences, contrary to the whole tenor of *Everson*. And I think that neither the *McCollum* case nor *Zorach v. Clauson* permits this. I also suggest that the decisions of the state courts are uniformly opposed. *Almond v. Day* in Virginia,[18] the *Alaska Bus Case*,[19] the *Oregon Textbook Case*[20]—practically all state courts are agreed, I think, that public funds cannot be used for parochial schools. A few of them, a minority even after *Everson*, have allowed bus transportation, but have gone no further. And no state statute permits direct aid to parochial schools.

The evidence against direct grants is overwhelming, and I believe that were it not for the fact that this was made a political issue, we might not have the present constitutional debate. I do not know how many of you know that before the Federal Aid Bill was presented, it was debated within the Catholic Church what position the Church should take. There was a long dispute between two wings in the Church. The position of the more liberal wing—liberal according to my views—led by the Jesuits and the law school faculties, was not to demand all-out aid to parochial schools, but at most fringe benefits, i.e., those that could be justified under the child-benefit theory.[21] The bishops, who have the financial responsibility for parochial education in the United States at the elementary and secondary levels, argued for full participation by parochial schools in any program for federal aid to education. The bishops ultimately prevailed. As a result, the position of the Catholic Church for the past two years is that the parochial schools are entitled to federal funds, not tangentially, not indirectly, but as a pattern in the educational system.[22] Once that decision was made, then, of course, the next job was to justify the position legally, and I think that is why the National Catholic Welfare Conference brief was written.

But for my part, I believe that to the extent that definiteness in constitutional law is possible, it is definite, on the basis of the decisions of the Supreme Court and of the state courts, that direct grants of government funds to parochial schools would violate the Constitution.

III / (Louis Jaffe)

I hold an opposite point of view; so I think it is appropriate that I make a statement along those lines.

First, I think what might be called the dialectical framework of Mr. Pfeffer's presentation, which is a good lawyer's one, is not acceptable across the board as what Herbert Wechsler would call a neutral principle. Even if the overtones of *Everson* are fairly clear, and I suppose they are fairly clear, they are, however, fairly recent. This is not a proposition that has been standing very long. It only occurred to somebody rather recently that the First Amendment, for example, was incorporated in the Fourteenth. A number of people still wonder how the establishment clause ever became part of the Fourteenth and how Mr. Justice Frankfurter, for example, convinced himself that it was.

But I am taking the larger point. I think, to mention an instance which will occur to all of you, that the desegregation decision[23] came as quite a shock to a lot of people in certain parts of the country who thought that the thing had been settled since 1896 in *Plessy v. Ferguson.*[24] They found that they were not right after all, and so we have some new law, namely, that segregation violates the Fourteenth Amendment. Now, that is brand new, and this is just as new in the other way.

So I do not think that the fact that everybody is taking it for granted, or some people have taken it for granted, and that the overtones of *Everson* are fairly clear is the end-all and be-all for scholars who are looking to see what the merits are.

McCollum was thought to settle something which then turned out in *Zorach* not to be so clearly settled. Now there are two ways in which people can approach *Zorach*. Mr. Pfeffer can say it is wrong, in which case he is admitting that these things change pretty quickly and are not so settled, or he can say it is distinguishable. But I think he is apt to say, if I understand him, that it is wrong. So you are presented with a lot of wrong decisions and a few right ones.

It consequently seems to me that it is necessary to approach this question somewhat more broadly than precisely as it stands today.

By the way, I was reading Mr. Pfeffer's book[25] the other night, and I observed that in most places Mr. Pfeffer is remarkably precise and discriminating in the way he presents things, but when he got around to state aid to schools and federal aid to schools, he did not, as far as I could see, distinguish very much between cases that arise under a constitution which forbids aid to parochial schools, as some of the state constitutions seem to do, and cases which deal with aid to schools as being an establishment of the church.[26]

Those things are to me entirely different. I think he is absolutely right that, if you have a prohibition against state aid to schools, the kind of thing that is being suggested here is highly doubtful. There is no escape unless you can say you are aiding the child rather than the school. But if you are proceeding on the basis of the First Amendment as incorporated into the Fourteenth, then it seems to me you have an entirely different proposition. There is the proposition stated by Justice Black that you can't give aid of any sort to religion under the First Amendment and the one suggested by Justice Douglas, which is more in line with the actual way in which this whole situation has been interpreted over the years, that you can give some aid. It is unfortunately like about 99.44 percent of the propositions in the law—a matter of degree.

Now, among the things I read in Mr. Pfeffer's book, was a statement flat, out and out, without any qualification, and I think he is right, too, that tax benefits to a church are aid to religion.[27] Therefore, under the test that you cannot give any aid to religion, if that is the test, they are unconstitutional.

But it seems to me that this example proves that it is not the test. After all, something that has been in existence for 150 years or more is just as much a part of the doctrine as what was done yesterday in *Everson*. It seems to me, indeed, that it is a more significant part; it is much more significant that you can give tax benefits to churches—and you have been giving them for 150 years—than some little refined decision this way or that.

Consequently, it seems to me that Justice Douglas is absolutely right in saying that you can give some kind of aid to religion, but it cannot be too much; nor can it be too direct. The question is therefore whether any aid to education which indirectly helps religious organizations in terms of their prestige or their other activities, in terms of a whole lot of things, is so extreme or so direct that it passes the boundary of what the courts will permit.

I find it impossible to decide these issues by a completely doctrinaire method of absolutely exclusive categories. We are dealing with general phrases that do not have any precise meaning. Consequently, to apply them we must take into account why those things were and with what problems they were meant to deal.

Now, if you read Mr. Pfeffer's book, you will find that these guarantees grew out of all kinds of drastic and extreme church institutional devices, out of a great background of coercion of the conscience, of undue control of religion by the state, out of a situation in which religion had a destructive, distorted and violent effect. This is the history against which, it seems to me, one must interpret these general phrases.

I suppose Mr. Pfeffer will deny this, but I think we are in a very different position today. In the first place, the influence of the churches qua religious organizations is terribly diluted as compared to their influence in the days of their establishment. Secondly, religion as a force has ceased to have the effect on us that it had. In this country, the religious institutions are as much social organizations as they are religious organizations. There are varying degrees of religious affiliation, but for the most part affiliation does not mean the same thing. Consequently, a penny here and a penny there—let alone the large benefit of tax exemption—is not world-shaking. Nor is the fact that it may help the churches a little bit to have the city shut down on Sunday. I am suggesting that this question throughout our entire history has been treated as a question of degree, and that there are institutions which obviously exist, which can't be explained away, which do add up to aid to religion.

It is easy, of course, to avoid the political question if you say that every proposal is unconstitutional. If you take my position, you must face up to the political question.

I haven't thought too much about it, but I have a kind of vague feeling that I am for aid to the Catholic colleges for various specialized activities, but against aid to the parochial schools, partly for a reason that really has nothing to do with parochial schools. I cannot get rid of the feeling that if we aid parochial and private schools, we sabotage the whole desegregation effort in the South, because all the private schools will be eligible to get funds. That bothers me a great deal.

There are other things that bother me. I have never been able to work out to my own satisfaction whether all-out aid to the parochial schools would weaken or strengthen the public schools, whether it would release the public schools from certain kinds of tasks, make them stronger or weaker. I just do not know.

On the other hand, I am much less bothered about the college situation. It seems too that we are in a situation where we need all the strong colleges that we can get. The Catholic colleges are very respectable colleges. We get fine students from them in the law schools—very well trained and in no sense bigoted. We need all the good colleges we can get, and to be good, they need aid, at least in certain ways.

If Harvard College is going to get aid, I cannot see any reason on earth why Notre Dame should not. This particular device does not raise the same problems as does aid to the secondary schools. We already have the private colleges down South. I should add that I think Mr. Pfeffer is right, that the implication of *Everson* is that aid of this sort to parochial colleges would not be constitutional, but I don't know how solid *Everson* is.

So I come out with the conclusion that it is highly questionable whether a carefully tailored form of aid to the schools would be unconstitutional, and that it would be appropriate to give carefully tailored aid to the colleges, and not appropriate to give it to the secondary and primary schools.

IV / (Kenneth Greenawalt)

Having written the briefs for the American Civil Liberties Union in *Everson, McCollum* and *Doremus,*[28] and having argued the *Zorach* case, I am disturbed by several scholars whom I have heard talk on this subject in recent months. They are less apt to view these things in sharp outline, and are always trying to rationalize and find something new and different about these decisions so that they can make their articles interesting. The thing that disturbs me in listening to this argument is that there is an effort now to change and modify principles and to find compromises—"policy" they call it, "public policy." I think it is about time that somebody spread the alarm that what we need today in this country are more Jeffersons and Madisons. It seems to me that the First Amendment was put into the Constitution as a matter of basic principle. The Preamble to the Constitution says that it is for the general welfare. This is a matter of "policy." This is a matter of primary public policy.

It would alarm me greatly if we should abandon the basic principles of the First Amendment and allow people who want public money used in aid of religious schools and who want religion taught in the public schools to break down the principles which were fought for so hard by Madison and Jefferson. Jefferson said it was the "severest contest" of his life that resulted in the First Amendment;[29] and when you read the early debates on the subject you understand why. After all, Patrick Henry was a formidable opponent, and he is the one that Madison had in the Virginia debates.

I was interested just the other day in reading again about the Mrs. Roosevelt–Cardinal Spellman controversy, and I was struck by the rather modest suggestions that Cardinal Spellman made back when the Barden Bill was pending. About all he sought then were "minor fringe benefits," maybe medical aid, maybe free lunches, possibly transportation. But where have these demands grown today? Today he wants "full equal treatment." Their parochial school children, he asserts, are entitled to the same treatment that every public school child is entitled to. Everything is said to be for the benefit of the child today; nothing is said to be for the benefit of the institution.

I think the rule that prohibits all public financial aid which, directly or indirectly, benefits a religious school or institution must be sustained. I think that people who are interested in the separation of church and state—and with that I include religious freedom, because the two in my mind are inextricably associated—had better hold that line tight.

I happen to be on a school board in Westchester County where the recently enacted Speno Bill[30] has caused all sorts of transportation problems. Under that bill transportation at public expense must be furnished for children attending parochial schools. In our own public school the school transportation budget has gone up about five times in the past year because we are being called upon to transport parochial school children to every part of the county.

Aside from the public expense, it seems to me that we have to try to draw the line, which we tried to draw in *Everson*, and hold that such transportation is an aid to the institution and not merely to the child. Likewise, books are benefits to the institution; tuition, libraries, all sorts of facilities are benefits to the institution. Without these things the institution could not function.

It is quite a different thing to request certain medical benefits for all schoolchildren. I wouldn't take that away from any child, of course. But these aids or benefits that go to the educational process itself—"public welfare" benefits and "benefits to the child and not the institution"—must be nipped in the bud. If you ever made a study of how the concept of "aid to the child" got started, you will see that it is growing and growing; and you will realize why it was important to try to stop that concept as soon as it got started, because it is still being used to justify all sorts of public aid to church institutions.

While I do not know precisely where Leo Pfeffer and I stand today, I am sure we are not far apart on most of the basic principles relating to a real separation of church and state. I think it would be a tragic thing if people interested in the religious colleges and parochial schools were allowed to break down the basic principles which are stated in the *Everson* case and which have been reiterated by the United States Supreme Court in subsequent cases. I realize that in the *Zorach* case there was a slight suggestion that the rule of *Everson* might be modified. Yet in that case Justice Douglas said there could be no public support of religious institutions.

V / (Gerald Gunther)

I am glad to see that Mr. Greenawalt, who apparently sides with Mr. Pfeffer, does get a bit away from the conception that the Court has decided everything. I take it that Mr. Greenawalt supports Justice Black's opinion in *Everson* although he considers this result contrary to Justice Black's principle of no aid or no direct aid.

It seems to me that we cannot hope to discuss this problem very usefully by saying that the Court has decided it all, because surely no one reading the small handful of Supreme Court opinions can avoid noting the ambiguity in what the Court has done so far. Nor can our discussion be very useful if we do not try to separate the question of where the constitutional limitations properly belong from the question of where, as a matter of our views of desirable policy, the limits to aid to parochial schools properly belong.

The basis for the views about holding the line against the smallest amount of aid is one of policy, not constitutional interpretation. Certainly you cannot support the absolute-barrier view from the

Court's results; and I have difficulty finding support for it in starting afresh and looking at the Constitution and at what little I know about its history.

May I suggest this: Mr. Pfeffer, in saying that the discussion has been pretty well closed off by what had happened in the Court in the late forties and early fifties until some recent difficulties arose in the law journals and elsewhere, brushed aside what I thought was a fairly thorough, reasonable, non-axe-grinding effort by Professor Kurland at Chicago to look at these cases again.

Professor Kurland, as a matter of constitutional interpretation, suggests that you must look not only at the establishment-of-religion provision, but also at the freedom-of-religion provision, that they are intertwined; that in carrying the logic of some of the establishment principles to the extreme you do run into some difficulties with the freedom problem and with the problem of discrimination on religious grounds.

I am not buying all of what Kurland concludes, but I would be interested to hear from Mr. Pfeffer why this is so clearly untenable as not to warrant discussion. Kurland's conclusion is a very simple one—namely, that looking at the freedom and separation clauses together yields this single precept: that government cannot use religion as a standard for action or inaction, because these clauses read together prohibit classification in terms of religion, whether to confer a benefit or to impose a burden.

Is it clear that this is contrary to what the Court has done so far? Is it clear that this is contrary to the defensible conclusions that may be drawn from the Constitution as it stands, assuming that both religion provisions of the First Amendment are to be given effect?

The questions discussed at the 1962 Hays Conference have become increasingly topical. For example, the 1967 Constitutional Convention in New York State divided sharply, on both legal and political grounds, on whether the so-called Blaine Amendment should be repealed. That amendment, which was article XI, section 3 of the State Constitution, explicitly prohibited the state or any of its subdivisions from using public money to maintain a parochial school or to transport a child to and from a parochial school. After considerable debate the convention decided to repeal the amendment, and this decision became the focal point of the public debate when the proposed new constitution was submitted to the voters of New York in November 1967. As already noted in Chapter 5, the new constitution was overwhelmingly defeated.

Another important controversy was precipitated by the Federal Elementary and Secondary Education Act of 1965, which for the first time authorized large-scale federal aid to nonpublic schools, including schools run by religious groups. The stated ground for the federal aid was to assist "educationally deprived" children in each school district; it is, in short, an adjunct of the poverty program. The American Civil Liberties Union, the American Jewish Congress, and Americans United for Separation of Church and State filed suit in New York, Ohio and Pennsylvania to declare the federal program invalid. The two chief issues that developed in litigation were those discussed at the Hays Conference—establishment of religion and standing to sue. In June 1967 the New York Court of Appeals interpreted both the Federal Constitution and the New York State constitutional provision noted above to permit the use of public funds to support the cost of textbook loans to church-related schools. The United States Supreme Court on June 10, 1968, affirmed the decision of the New York court, resting on the conclusion that "no funds or books are furnished to parochial schools, and the financial benefit is to parents and children, not to schools."[31]

Another program established by the Education Act of 1965 that is being challenged in the courts is known as "shared time"; children divide their school day by taking such "neutral" subjects as languages, mathematics and gymnasium in the public school and subjects with some religious orientation—such as literature and history —in the parochial school.

All in all, it is clear that the nation can look forward to continued controversy over the scope of the establishment clause.

NOTES

The complete Conference proceedings were published in 12 *Buffalo Law Review* 35 (1962) with the title "The Arthur Garfield Hays Civil Liberties Conference: Public Aid to Parochial Schools and Standing to Bring Suit."

1. Kurland, *Religion and the Law* 7 (1962).
2. 370 U.S. 421 (1962).
3. See *Current*, Sept. 1962, pp. 60, 61.
4. *National Review*, July 17, 1962, pp. 10, 11.
5. 333 U.S. 203 (1948).
6. 343 U.S. 306 (1952).
7. See Murray, *We Hold These Truths* (1960), especially Ch. 6.
8. The Department's memorandum is printed in 50 *Geo. L.J.* 349 (1961).
9. *The Constitutionality of Church-Related Schools in Federal Aid to Education*, a study prepared for the Legal Department of the National Catholic Welfare Conference; reprinted in 50 *Geo. L.J.* 397 (1961).
10. Kauper, "Church and State, Cooperative Separatism," 60 *Mich. L. Rev.* 1 (1961).
11. Kurland, "Of Church and State and the Supreme Court," 29 *U. Chi. L. Rev.* 1 (1961), an earlier version of Kurland, *Religion and the Law*, *supra* note 1.
12. Everson v. Board of Education, 330 U.S. 1 (1947).
13. *Id.* at 18.
14. 367 U.S. 488 (1961).
15. 330 U.S. 1 at 6.
16. *Id.* at 7, citing Cochran v. Louisiana State Board of Education, 281 U.S. 370 (1930); Holmes, J., in Interstate Ry. v. Massachusetts, 207 U.S. 79, 87 (1907); Cooley, J., in Stuart v. School District No. 1 of Kalamazoo, 30 Mich. 69 (1874).
17. See note 9 *supra.*
18. Almond v. Day, 197 Va. 419, 89 S.E.2d 851 (1955).
19. Matthews v. Quinton, 362 P.2d 932 (Alaska, 1961).
20. Dickman v. School District No. 62C, 223 Ore. 347, 366 P.2d 533 (1961).
21. See Statement by Rev. Neil G. McCluskey, S.J., Editor of *America*, quoted in *N.Y. Times*, March 12, 1961, p. 9. See also Weclew, "Church and State: How Much Separation?" 10 *De Paul L. Rev.* 1 (1960).
22. See, e.g., Henle, "American Principles and Religious Schools," 3 *St. Louis U.L.J.* 237 (1955).
23. Brown v. Board of Education, 347 U.S. 483 (1954).
24. 163 U.S. 537 (1896).

25. Pfeffer, *Church, State and Freedom* (1953).
26. *Id.* at 603.
27. *Id.* at 424–83.
28. Doremus v. Board of Education, 342 U.S. 429 (1952).
29. 19 *Writings of Thomas Jefferson* 414 (Memorial ed. 1904).
30. See N.Y. Educ. Law §3635 (as amended 1961).
31. Board of Education of Central School District No. 1 v. Allen.

SECTION III

DUE PROCESS

Justice Felix Frankfurter was fond of remarking that the best test of a civilization was the fairness of its procedures in criminal trials. This idea, which can be traced to Magna Carta's insistence that no man should be convicted except under the "law of the land," is carried forward in two general clauses in the American Constitution that prohibit the federal and state governments from depriving a person of "life, liberty or property" without "due process of law."

The protection against the federal government is contained in the Fifth Amendment, which was ratified as part of the original Bill of Rights, while the similar provision forbidding arbitrary action by the states was ratified in 1868 as part of the Fourteenth Amendment. For many decades these constitutional provisions were virtually useless as guarantors of procedural fairness, and indeed were employed by the Supreme Court to insulate property rights from the effect of social and economic legislation, such as minimum-wage and maximum-hours laws. "Due process" became a dirty phrase—signifying obstruction by the Supreme Court—to those who were seeking to improve the rugged conditions endured by millions of American men and their families.

Then a judicial revolution occurred. In the 1930s the Court buried the old notion of "due process" and began to use the constitutional provisions to assure fair procedures in state and federal trials. This change in direction has been explained in various ways. Some attribute it to the evident futility felt by pivotal members of the "Old Court"—Chief Justice Charles Evans Hughes and Justice Owen Roberts—in trying to stem the New Deal and state social and economic legislation through judicial invalidation of many key statutes. This attitude was accompanied by corresponding sensitivity of the Court to the failure of many states and localities to provide fair procedures in criminal cases, particularly to Negroes and poor people. Other observers of the Supreme Court believe that the vast mandate accorded President Franklin D. Roosevelt and the New Deal in the 1936 election was a decisive event, and still others hold that not until the resignation and death of many conservative Justices from 1937 to 1941 was the judicial revolution of the 1930s a fact.

And then in the middle and late 1950s, the "Warren Court" wrought a second doctrinal revolution involving the due process clause. Once again a majority of the Court began to use the clause aggressively, but this time to protect the procedural rights of defendants in criminal cases. The Supreme Court, with accelerating momentum, has laid down rules of minimum fairness in a wide variety of cases. This new willingness to intervene in what had formerly been the virtually exclusive province of the state and lower federal courts has precipitated bitter controversies among members of the bar and the public as to whether the Court has acted wisely in interpreting the vague "due process" language. In particular, many lawyers, laymen and even judges have deplored decisions which have expanded the protections of the Bill of Rights at the expense of what they conceive to be the necessary and valid procedures of law enforcement officials.

An important aspect of the battle over the meaning of "due process" which the reader should bear in mind is the extent to which the due process clause of the Fourteenth Amendment "incorporates" the specific provisions of the Bill of Rights and thereby applies them against the States. The Bill of Rights was initially ratified in 1791 as a protection solely against the federal government, and it guaranteed all persons the privilege against self-incrimination, the right to bail and to a jury trial, and many other protections. Beginning in 1925, when the Supreme Court held the First Amendment's free speech clause to be part of Fourteenth Amendment due process, it has incorporated one after another of the provisions of the first eight amendments. These extensions of Supreme Court authority have been accompanied by considerable internal conflict within the Court, as evidenced by the long dispute, culminating in the *Gideon* case, over whether the Sixth Amendment's guarantee of a right to counsel applied to state criminal trials.

Although the chapters that follow present a cross section of recent due process issues—including some that the Supreme Court has yet to confront—earlier chapters (such as 2 and 10) have dealt with closely related questions.

In this section, Chapter 13 concerns the well-known *Gideon* case, which set off vast constitutional changes by requiring the provision of counsel in all criminal trials of a serious character and by recognizing in principle at least a minimal state responsibility for the poor. Chapter 14 deals with another seminal decision: the *Gault* case, which extended due process principles to the long-neglected category of juvenile delinquency proceedings involving half a million youngsters each year. Chapters 15 and 16 are concerned with one very old controversy—the right to a jury trial in cases of criminal contempt—and one new dispute—whether a defendant is prejudiced by the introduction of television in the courtroom. Chapter 17 involves due process outside the courtroom—as a means of protecting persons against invasions of their privacy. And Chapters 18 and 19 deal with capital punishment, the former with the general question whether it presents a civil liberties issue, and the latter with the very hard issue of the execution of a man who has become insane while in prison awaiting his death. These two chapters illustrate problems that are still beyond the frontier of due process and civil liberty.

13

The Gideon Case

Among the specific guarantees enumerated in the Bill of Rights is the Sixth Amendment's provision that "In all criminal prosecutions, the accused shall enjoy the right . . . to have the Assistance of Counsel for his defense." Under traditional principles of constitutional law, these specific commands of the Bill of Rights are addressed only to the federal government. Individual rights are protected against the states by the Fourteenth Amendment, which prohibits states from depriving persons of life, liberty or property "without due process of law." Thus, in a federal case involving denial of counsel, the issue would be whether there had been compliance with the Sixth Amendment, while in a state case involving identical facts, the issue would be whether the aggrieved party had been denied "due process of law."

To determine whether a specific claim constitutes a deprivation of "due process," a majority of the Court has employed a test of "fundamental fairness." In applying this test the Court has three basic choices. It may decide that the asserted right is so fundamental that the states should be subjected to the precise requirements of the Bill of Rights, as, for example, the First Amendment guarantee of freedom of expression; it may decide that the asserted right was not protected; or it may decide that fundamental fairness requires only a partial application of the Bill of Rights.

In 1942, when confronted with the right-to-counsel issue, the Court in Betts v. Brady *chose the third approach. Rejecting the Sixth Amendment rule entitling poor persons to the appointment of counsel in all felony cases in federal proceedings, the Court adopted a "special circumstances" rule for state cases. Under this doctrine, an indigent defendant was not entitled to counsel unless he was accused of a capital crime or could show that he would be particularly disadvantaged by the lack of a lawyer.*

Nearly two decades after the Betts *decision, Clarence Earl Gideon was accused of burglary by the State of Florida. Unable to afford a lawyer, Gideon asked the trial judge to appoint one. The judge refused; Gideon was tried and convicted, and he eventually appealed to the United States Supreme Court.*

The Court was asked to reconsider Betts v. Brady. *The American Civil Liberties Union submitted an* amicus curiae *brief, in which the author and J. Lee Rankin, former Solicitor General of the United States, were co-counsel, urging the Court to overrule* Betts *and subject the states to the requirements of the Sixth Amendment. Portions of that brief appear below.*

While reading the excerpted passages, one should consider the obstacles facing a litigant seeking to convince the Court to overrule a relatively recent decision. Three lines of argument are available. It may be asserted that the original decision was erroneous when decided; but the Court, even when it chooses to overrule one of its decisions, rarely concedes error explicitly. It is usually wiser to try to demonstrate that the original decision failed from a practical standpoint—that the rule set down was too complex, impossible to apply, too vague to be workable, or produced results inconsistent with its express purpose. It is also valuable to be able to point to subsequent decisions inconsistent with the original case, or to new doctrines that have undermined the reasoning and validity of the earlier ruling.

Introduction

Due process is a standard of basic fairness which does not admit of precise definition. In *Palko v. Connecticut,*[1] Justice Cardozo described it as including all that is "implicit in the concept of ordered liberty." Or, as the Court said in *Powell v. Alabama,* with specific reference to the right to counsel, the question is whether "the right involved is of such a character that it cannot be denied without violating those 'fundamental principles of liberty and justice which lie at the base of all our civil and political institutions.' "[2]

Applying this broad language, the Court has employed various methods of analysis for determining whether any particular practice violates the due process clause. One way of analyzing "due process" is to examine the effect upon the individual defendant to determine whether the practice is fundamentally unfair or shocking to the conscience. Another is to measure the challenged practice against contemporary community standards. Finally, "due process" may be viewed as incorporating a set of specific guarantees, including the right to a hearing and the right to be free from invidious discriminations between classes of persons. By any of these standards, as this brief will demonstrate, every criminal defendant has a right to counsel in every case.

I / Denial of counsel to criminal defendants is fundamentally unfair.

The fundamental unfairness of a rule which permits a state to deny counsel to criminal defendants can best be illustrated by considering how the rule operates in practice from the commencement of the trial to the period after trial when the defendant tries to avail himself of postconviction remedies. The unfairness is compounded in practice by the inequities and uncertainties of the "special circumstances" rule. These inequities and uncertainties can be eliminated only by an objective rule requiring appointment of counsel in every case.

A. *The cases decided since* Betts v. Brady *demonstrate that legal assistance is improperly denied to many defendants entitled to counsel under the "special circumstances" rule.*

The cases decided in this Court since *Betts v. Brady* that have dealt with a state court's application of the "special circumstances" rule reveal that even though governing decisions of this Court clearly indicated the defendant's right to legal assistance, a defendant may not be informed of his right to counsel, never request counsel and never have one appointed.[3]

Other cases disclose that even where the defendant requests appointment of counsel, the trial judge may deny the request without further inquiry. Thus, in the instant case the following colloquy took place:

> *The Defendant: Your Honor, I said: I request this Court to appoint Counsel to represent me in this trial.*
>
> *The Court: Mr. Gideon, I am sorry, but I cannot appoint Counsel to represent you in this case. Under the laws of the State of Florida, the only time the Court can appoint Counsel to represent a Defendant is when that person is charged with a capital offense. I am sorry, but I will have to deny your request to appoint Counsel to defend you in this case.*

Assistance of counsel has also been denied even though it was clear that appointment was necessary in view of the defendant's age, mental condition and education, the complex nature of the charge, and the likelihood that the trial would be unfair under all circumstances. Thus, in *Moore v. Michigan,*[4] the petitioner, a seventeen-year-old Negro with a seventh-grade education and possible mental defects, was arrested for the murder of an elderly lady. The petitioner was questioned for two days until he orally confessed. The next morning he was arraigned. Without counsel to assist him, he pleaded guilty, was adjudged guilty of murder in the first degree, sentenced to life imprisonment and transferred to prison immediately.

Among the state court cases in which no special circumstances were found and which were not reviewed here are many which run counter to prior decisions of this Court. Thus, in *Shaffer v. Warden, Maryland House of Correction,*[5] it was held that a nineteen-year-old defendant, of below-average mental capacity and with a congenital speech defect, was not deprived of due process in being required to plead to an indictment for burglary. His claim that he had in fact pleaded "not guilty" but was misunderstood by the trial court was rejected by the state appellate courts. In *Commonwealth ex rel. Ringer v. Maroney*,[6] an illiterate moron with only a third-grade education was convicted of arson without benefit of counsel.

The unwillingness of state courts to appoint counsel can often lead to the conviction of apparently innocent defendants. Thus, in *Parker v. Ellis*,[7] a sixty-seven-year-old man was convicted of forgery in a Texas court without the assistance of counsel and was sentenced to seven years imprisonment. His repeated attempts to obtain release through collateral proceedings were unsuccessful. Finally, a petition for certiorari was granted by this Court. It was subsequently dismissed as moot when it appeared that the petitioner had been released from prison after serving five years. The critical facts are contained in the dissenting opinion of the Chief Justice:

[His] trial was a sham. Although the testimony directly bearing on the issue of forgery was not strong [since the woman on whose account the check was drawn was never called as a witness], petitioner's conviction is hardly surprising, for the prosecution's case consisted in large part of a potent melange of assorted types of inadmissible evidence—introduced without objection by petitioner. But petitioner suffered as much from errors of omission as he did from errors of commission. Petitioner now alleges—and respondent does not deny—that the victim of the alleged forgery was petitioner's mother-in-law and that the principal prosecution witness was his brother-in-law, a "bitter enemy"; but petitioner introduced no evidence to this effect at the trial. Nor is this strange, for petitioner's halting attempts to defend himself disclosed utter ineptness in the courtroom.

Similarly, in *Pennsylvania ex rel. Herman v. Claudy*,[8] the petitioner, twenty-one years of age with only six years of schooling, pleaded guilty without assistance of counsel to eight charges of burglary, twelve charges of larceny, eight of forgery and two of false pretense. He was sentenced to seventeen and a half to thirty-five years. This Court ordered hearings on a petition for habeas corpus which alleged that after his arrest the petitioner had been held incommunicado for three days, during which time a "state trooper grabbed him by the neck and threatened to choke him if he did not confess." It was also claimed that "there were threats against the safety of his wife and daughter," and that when the assisting prosecuting attorney demanded that he sign a plea of guilty to all charges, and the petitioner asked what he was signing, he was told "sign your name and forget it."

B. *The "special circumstances" rule has developed such contradictions and inconsistencies that it provides no proper guidance to lower courts attempting to apply it fairly.*

Even if a trial judge in a state criminal case attempts in good faith to ascertain whether counsel should be appointed because of "special circumstances," he will find the criteria for decision laid down by this Court are confusing and contradictory and do not permit evenhanded and fair application of the rule.

The "capriciousness" of the standard for appointment of counsel may be seen in "the records of the right-to-counsel cases since *Betts v. Brady* in both state and federal courts."[9] Thus, although in *DeMeerleer v. Michigan,*[10] and in *Uveges v. Pennsylvania, supra,* the Court noted that a defendant's age was a crucial criterion, in *Gayes v. New York,*[11] and in *Canizio v. New York,*[12] the failure to appoint counsel at trial was upheld even though the defendants were sixteen and nineteen years old, respectively.

Similarly, in *Foster v. Illinois,*[13] the defendants, without benefit of counsel, were arraigned and sentenced after a plea of guilty all on the same day. This Court found that the defendants understood the effect of their plea and thus waived their right to counsel. Yet in the same year, in *DeMeerleer v. Michigan,* virtually the same fact situation produced a reversal and new trial.

The very factors to be considered often seem contradictory. Thus in *Gryger v. Burke* and also in *Quicksall v. Michigan,*[14] the prior experience of the defendants in the criminal courts was weighed *against* their right to have counsel appointed. However, this Court has recently indicated that prior convictions are to be considered *in support of* a claim to be represented by counsel because a defendant is placed in a quandary whether to testify on his own behalf and thereby risk the possibility that his criminal record will be brought out on cross-examination, or on the other hand, to remain silent and thereby risk a negative inference of guilt.[15]

Counsel is necessary to assist him in making this decision.

If the same factor has been weighed both for and against a defendant's right to counsel by this Court, surely the difficulties experienced by the lower state and federal courts in attempting to decide whether the appointment of counsel is required are understandable.[16]

C. *The complex and unpredictable course of criminal trials further demonstrates the unfairness of denying any defendant the assistance of counsel.*

Even if trial judges scrupulously attempted to apply the "special circumstances" rule, and even if the criteria for the application of that rule were not contradictory, the rule would in many cases operate unfairly to indigent defendants. It is not possible to predict the actual course of a criminal trial or the defendant's response to a novel, confusing and harrowing experience—acting as his own lawyer in defense of his liberty against the efforts of an experienced prosecutor to convict him.

Some idea of the burden on the defendant unaided by counsel can be obtained by following him through a trial and considering the enormous number of difficult legal decisions he has to make.

After an indictment is returned, should the indigent defendant challenge the indictment because it does not allege the essential elements of the crime or because if contains prejudicial material or because the grand jury was not properly impaneled? Should he request a bill of particulars or a list of witnesses from the prosecution? Should he object to the venue of trial because of inflammatory feeling in the community or because the crime was not committed within the jurisdiction? Should he attack the impaneling of the petit jury because of exclusion of certain racial groups from the lists, or if not, which jurors should he challenge for cause or peremptorily?

At trial many other difficult decisions must be made. When the prosecution presents its case, should the defendant move to exclude any evidence because it was illegally seized or obtained by wiretapping or eavesdropping? Should he object to hearsay evidence or protest the competency of any prosecution witnesses? Which of these witnesses should he cross-examine or try to impeach and on what basis? Should he take the stand himself and risk exposure of a prior criminal record or remain silent and run the risk that a jury will infer guilt from his failure to testify? Should he raise a defense of insanity, and if so, what must he prove? Should he object to the judge's instructions to the jury? If he is found guilty, how can he reverse the jury's verdict? How should he perfect his appeal and what papers must be filed or exceptions taken to preserve legal points on appeal?

The difficulties imposed on the defendant in making each of the foregoing decisions, any one of which could spell the difference between conviction and acquittal, are compounded by the increasing complexity of substantive and procedural criminal law. The common-law crimes are giving way to modern codifications; new crimes unheard of in a less advanced technological setting have been enacted; the impact of science on crime detection has revolutionized the law of evidence; and the protections of the accused against improper police methods, which were still embryonic in 1942 when *Betts v. Brady* was decided, have become one of the principal and most complex features of the criminal process.

The obstacles placed before a man without a lawyer are accentuated by recently recognized defenses based upon the Constitution. Thus, convictions unsupported by evidence are invalid under the due process clause of the Fourteenth Amendment.[17] The cruel and unusual punishment clause has been infused with new vigor.[18] The defendant's right to testify and be cross-examined has been reaffirmed.[19] And defenses relating to double jeopardy and "immunity" statutes are in uncertain flux.[20]

Increasingly intricate evidentiary rules—many being outgrowths of judicial attempts to control police conduct—illustrate further the need for a lawyer. For example, *Mapp v. Ohio*[21] requires illegally seized evidence to be excluded from state trials. Every practitioner in the criminal courts knows that the law of search and seizure is of the utmost variety and subtlety. It is complicated by the use of evidence obtained by scientific methods of crime detection, such as wiretapping, electronic eavesdropping and lie detectors. The scope of the *Mapp* rule is uncertain. Can it reasonably be expected that the unassisted layman will be able to protect his right under the

Fourteenth Amendment to have unlawfully seized evidence excluded? We submit that the answer is obviously no.

The foregoing should make it plain that the modern trial is of such complexity that any defendant is at a hopeless disadvantage in coping with the problem of defending himself without the aid of a lawyer. It is unfair and a violation of the due process clause to permit a state to require him to do so.

D. *The ineffectiveness of postconviction remedies demonstrates the need for the appointment of counsel initially at trial.*

As seen above, "special circumstances" requiring the appointment of counsel may arise only after the trial has begun. Hence, the rights of defendants under the "special circumstances" rule can be protected only if, once such circumstances become apparent, a new trial is immediately ordered at which the defendant is represented by counsel. But no case has been found in which a court, seeing the possibility of unfairness during trial, has halted the proceeding so that counsel could be appointed. Instead, courts permit the unfair trial to run its course and leave to an appellate tribunal or to a court exercising habeas corpus jurisdiction the question whether constitutional or other error occurred at the trial.

But these postconviction remedies are unsatisfactory. They do not provide due process—at most they give the defendant a second chance for a fair trial if he can prove the first unfair. They do not grant him the right to a fair trial initially. More often, they do not even permit the possibility of a second trial. This is so because of the overriding handicaps which a defendant must surmount if he attempts to rectify error committed at trial.

If conviction follows after a trial with no defense counsel, it is rare that counsel can be obtained to prosecute an appeal. Of the 139 state decisions on the issue whether "special circumstances" existed, only 34 were presented to a state court on direct appeal from the conviction. And since an effective appeal is unlikely without a lawyer, errors occurring at trial are never brought to the attention of an appellate court in many cases. The vast number of habeas corpus petitions filed in state and federal courts which raise new and substantial legal contentions demonstrate the frequency with which this unfortunate pattern occurs.

If the defendant desires relief after the time for appeal has run, he must educate himself sufficiently in the law (or somehow acquire a lawyer) so as to be able to press his claims through one of the state postconviction remedies. But state courts rarely grant relief on the ground that a trial was unfair because of lack of counsel. Of the 139 state decisions, in only 11 did the court rule that the trial judge had committed error in failing to appoint counsel.

The next step is to petition this Court for certiorari, which is usually denied, often because there was no hearing granted in the state courts that would have revealed the possible validity of a constitutional claim. If the defendant is denied relief in the state courts, he will next try to vindicate his rights by applying for habeas corpus in a federal district court. There, again ordinarily without counsel, he will often be denied a hearing on his allegations, or if a hearing is granted, he may be denied relief on the merits. The defendant then will seek review in a federal appellate court, carrying the heavy burden of first obtaining a certificate of probable cause and then persuading this tribunal that his claims are meritorious and that a new trial should be ordered.

The interplay of procedural rules with the denial of counsel under *Betts v. Brady* is especially unfair. In most states the defendant must file timely exceptions to rulings made at the trial, and failure to do so results in loss of appellate review or state postconviction remedies.[22] A procedural slip by the unassisted defendant in the state courts may also preclude the federal courts from considering the merits of a constitutional claim.[23]

No exception is made to any of these procedural rules with respect to a defendant who is denied counsel under *Betts v. Brady*. The result is that the unrepresented defendant, who cannot be expected to know about these rules, is very likely to lose the only chance of obtaining review of his conviction. Indeed, if the defendant is improperly denied counsel, he may find the doors to both state and federal courts entirely closed to him because of a procedural flaw which is the direct result of the absence of a lawyer—the precise deprivation for which he seeks review.

It is of course possible that at one stage or another an unassisted defendant will be able to overcome the procedural pitfalls and the vast obstacles of proof and satisfy some court that he was convicted without a fair trial. But if this ever occurs, it is generally years after his conviction that the defendant obtains a new trial or, in rare cases, his freedom—debasing years which he has spent in confinement resulting from an unjust trial. Thus, in *Moore v. Michigan,*[24] nineteen years elapsed between the petitioner's unconstitutional trial and vindication of his claim in this Court; in *DeMeerleer v. Michigan, supra,* fifteen years elapsed; in *Uveges v. Pennsylvania, supra,* ten years elapsed; and in *Massey v. Moore,*[25] fourteen years elapsed before the original trial was invalidated because of the lack of counsel.[26]

That the ultimate result of a new trial may prove that the defendant was guilty is, of course, of no consequence. As Judge (now Mr. Justice) Stewart has observed, in approving the dissenting opinion in an earlier case: "When a defendant has been denied due process, his guilt or innocence is irrelevant. He has not been tried by civilized standards, and cannot be punished until he has been."[27]

The practical result of the "special circumstances" rule is to place an intolerable burden on a criminal defendant who comes into court without the assistance of counsel.

II / Denial of counsel to criminal defendants contravenes the other standards embodied in the Fourteenth Amendment.

A. *Denial of counsel abridges the right to a hearing.*

In *Powell v. Alabama, supra,* the Court said that "notice and hearing . . . constitute basic elements of the constitutional requirement of due process of law." This principle has often been reaffirmed by this Court. A criminal trial without a defense lawyer, however, is not a "hearing." It is a mockery and a sham, designed to obtain the speediest possible conviction for the state, whose full power is arrayed against the defendant. As the Court stated in

Powell, "the right to be heard would be, in many cases, of little avail if it did not comprehend the right to be heard by counsel."

Any attempt to probe the issue of guilt or innocence is not meaningful in the absence of a defense lawyer, and the chances of acquittal for the lawyerless defendant are negligible.

That a trial without a defense lawyer does not constitute a "hearing" in the due process sense is further evidenced by the fact that a court itself cannot act in the role of counsel for the accused. "[A] judge, whose functions are purely judicial," the Court stated in *Powell v. Alabama*, cannot "effectively discharge the obligations for the accused"; although the judge may see to it that the accused "be dealt with justly and fairly," he cannot "investigate the facts, advise and direct the defense, or participate in those necessary conferences between counsel and accused which sometimes partake of the inviolable character of the confessional."

B. *The distinction between capital and noncapital cases with respect to a defendant's right to counsel has no proper constitutional basis.*

The distinction drawn in *Betts v. Brady* between the appointment of counsel in capital cases and that in noncapital cases has no warrant in the language of the Constitution. As Mr. Justice Black said in his concurring opinion in *Carnley v. Cochran*:[28] "[The] Fourteenth Amendment protects life, liberty, and property" and "defendants prosecuted for crime are entitled to counsel whether it is their life, their liberty, or their property which is at stake in a criminal prosecution."

Apart from the language of the Fourteenth Amendment, there is no logical reason to draw a constitutional line between capital and noncapital cases with respect to the right of defendants to be represented by counsel. This is not to overlook the finality of a sentence to death. It is merely to recognize what is well known—that a life sentence for a fixed number of years can have the same ultimate effect as a death sentence. The defendant may never emerge from prison a free man, and even if he does, he may be a broken relic of the person who entered years before. This explains the persistent speculation about the relative severity of the death penalty and a long prison sentence, particularly when the latter is meted out to a defendant of advanced years or to one who is ineligible for parole.

This Court in other contexts has refused to countenance a distinction between capital and noncapital criminal cases. In *Reid v. Covert*,[29] the Court ruled that civilian dependents of members of the armed forces overseas could not constitutionally be tried by a court-martial in time of peace for capital offenses committed abroad. Three years later, when a noncapital criminal case arose involving a civilian dependent of a member of the armed forces serving abroad, the government vigorously contended that *Reid v. Covert* should be limited to capital cases. That contention was rejected. The Court held that there was no warrant in the language of the Fifth or Sixth Amendment, in constitutional history, or in the probable consequences for military discipline to draw the proposed line.[30]

In *Griffin v. Illinois*,[31] the Court refused to accept a distinction between capital and noncapital criminal cases. Illinois provided free trial transcripts for purposes of appellate review to all indigent defendants sentenced to death, but required all other convicted defendants to purchase the transcripts themselves. The Court held that the Fourteenth Amendment required the state to provide some manner of effective review to indigent defendants whether or not they had been sentenced to death. And in *Ferguson v. Georgia*,[32] the Court explicitly stated that its decision "[did] not turn" on the fact that the appellant was tried for a capital offense, thus recognizing again that fundamental constitutional protections are applicable in all criminal cases.

C. *The net effect of* Betts v. Brady *is to discriminate unfairly against criminal defendants who are poor.*

In *Edwards v. California*, Mr. Justice Jackson observed in a concurring opinion:

> *"Indigence" in itself is neither a source of rights nor a basis for denying them. The mere state of being without funds is a neutral fact—constitutionally an irrelevance, like race, creed, or color.*[33]

The Justice considered it necessary to make this statement because in the early history of the Court the poor were stepchildren of the law, with limited rights and privileges. Although *City of New York v. Miln*[34] was subsequently overruled, the infamous reference in that case to "the moral pestilence of paupers" was to project its influence well into the twentieth century.

Although poverty is no longer equated with viciousness or with inferior status, the rule of *Betts v. Brady* persists as a grim reminder of the inequities of the past and as the law we are required to live by. The individuals in the state courts who are unable to secure counsel are ordinarily poor and without family. They are people who are least able to protect their personal liberty even when life imprisonment may be at stake.

That the size of a man's purse has no constitutional relevance in the administration of the criminal law is made strikingly evident by *Griffin v. Illinois, supra.* Although Illinois afforded every defendant convicted in a criminal trial a right of review, it allowed full appellate review only when its appellate court was furnished with a report of the trial proceedings. It was sometimes impossible to fulfill this requirement without a stenographic record of the trial, which was furnished free only to indigent defendants sentenced to death. The petitioners, who had been sentenced to prison for armed robbery, contended that they were denied rights under the Fourteenth Amendment because the state would not provide them with a transcript of the trial, and they could not therefore take an appeal. This Court agreed, ruling that the state that grants appellate review cannot do so in a way that "discriminates against some convicted defendants on account of their poverty."

Smith v. Bennett is a further and more recent example of the determination of this Court not to permit an individual's means to prescribe the quality of justice he receives. Iowa law required the payment of statutory filing fees by state prisoners before an application for a writ of habeas corpus could be made or an appeal docketed in such cases. This test was struck down as violative of the Fourteenth Amendment, the Court saying that "to interpose any financial consideration between an indigent prisoner of the state and his exercise of a state right to sue for his liberty is to deny that prisoner the equal protection of the laws."

The foregoing decisions, as well as the obvious inequities of any distinction based on means, require the demise of the rule of *Betts v. Brady*. If "the Fourteenth Amendment weighs the interest of rich and poor criminals in equal scale,"[36] surely it does so whether it is appellate review that is sought or whether it is a fair trial that is sought in the first instance.

III / The appointment of counsel for indigent defendants in criminal cases in a state court would not place an undue burden on local communities or on the bar.

In the court-martial cases decided in 1960, the government contended that the lack of practical alternatives to military jurisdiction over civilians was an important factor which the Court had to consider in deciding the petitioners' constitutional claims.[37] Although the Court recognized that the cost to the government to pursue alternatives to court-martial jursidiction must be large, it stated that this cost "is the price the government must pay in order to comply with constitutional requirements."

The situation presently before this Court is comparable; whatever cost is to be placed upon the state courts, local communities and the bar must be borne as a result of the clear constitutional requirement that all indigent defendants in state criminal cases have a right to be furnished with counsel. In point of fact, however, a system of legal representation for indigent defendants can result in a social and even a financial cost saving.

In the first place, the lack of effective representation of indigent defendants in criminal cases creates a social cost of largely indeterminable but nevertheless real and serious proportions. No state can long afford to provide one standard of justice for the rich and another for the poor. Such a situation can only create a sense that the benefits of our judicial system can be enjoyed only by those who can pay for them. As the Attorney General recently stated, "If justice is priced in the market place, individual liberty will be curtailed and respect for law diminished."[38]

Over and above the questions of social cost, a system of legal representation for indigent defendants may save a community more than it costs. Such a system reduces the burdens on the judiciary and prosecution from the flood of collateral postconviction proceedings based on real or fancied trial injustices resulting from lack of trial counsel. And by helping to eliminate delays in the administration of justice, the prompt assignment of counsel sharply reduces detention and other costs presently borne by the state.

The states that now require appointment of counsel are located in every geographic area of the country. The four basic systems that have been developed, and their success in the states employing them, suggest strongly that the practical implementation of at least one of these plans is well within the power of the fifteen or fewer states that do not currently provide legal assistance to indigents.[39] The four systems are as follows:

1. *The assigned counsel.* Under this system, when a defendant appears at arraignment without counsel, the judge assigns a lawyer to represent him. In capital cases, the assigned counsel is generally experienced, and reasonable compensation is provided. The cost has not been high because of the relative infrequency of such cases. In noncapital cases most states do not provide a fee for assigned counsel. Thus, the cost to the community is kept to a minimum and the burden is placed upon the local bar.

2. *The voluntary defender.* Voluntary defender offices are generally privately controlled and supported by charity. A voluntary defender system may use salaried investigators or it may be aided by volunteers from private law offices or local law schools. Such a system is typical of the large urban centers in the East. Its cost to the community and the bar is minimal.

3. *The public defender.* Since a public defender is a public official, public funds are necessary to finance this means of providing counsel to indigent defendants. In some communities, particularly in the West, it has been found that a public defender system is more economical than an assigned counsel system and only 15 to 25 percent as expensive as the office of the public prosecutor.[40] This is an expense which the large urban communities could easily bear.

4. *The mixed private-public system.* This plan involves the use of charitable funds as in the voluntary defender system, and the use of public funds, as in the public defender system. Since part of the cost

is borne by voluntary contributions, the direct cost to the public is smaller than that of the public defender system. A defender is employed by the Legal Aid organization of the community and thus relieves the bar of its obligation. Although private participation may be limited to furnishing full-time counsel as in Rochester and Buffalo, New York, a system may be provided, as in Puerto Rico, which receives direct appropriations from the legislature, funds and facilities from the Bar Association, and contributions from the public.

There is, therefore, no basis for the claim that it would be an intolerable burden for states to satisfy the demands of fairness implicit in the due process clause by appointing counsel for indigent defendants in criminal cases.

In a memorable decision the Court on March 18, 1963, overruled Betts v. Brady *in* Gideon v. Wainwright,[41] *holding that the Sixth Amendment right to counsel is a fundamental right made obligatory on the states by the Fourteenth Amendment. The majority opinion of Justice Black, who had dissented in* Betts, *is unusual in that he condemns the* Betts *decision as having been erroneous when decided.*

While the technique of overruling may be of interest to legal scholars, the practical impact of Gideon *is of far greater significance, not only because of what was decided but also because of the vast implications of the case. In subsequent decisions, building on* Gideon, *the Supreme Court has held that the right to counsel extends backward in time to preliminary hearings, arraignments, in-custody interrogations, and most recently, to police "lineups," and forward in time to appellate proceedings. With regard to the types of offenses to which the right extends, it seems clear that at least all felonies are included, and although some lower courts have extended the right to misdemeanor cases, the Supreme Court has not yet resolved this question.*

Another area of growing concern is noncriminal proceedings. Should an indigent who may very well suffer serious injury from an unfavorable decision be entitled to appointed counsel in administra-

tive proceedings, such as a hearing on whether to suspend his driver's license, or even in civil cases, where a defeated litigant may incur great pecuniary liability? Furthermore, if the rationale of Gideon is that indigent defendants must be enabled to defend themselves as effectively as their more fortunate fellow citizens, it may be necessary to provide them additional assistance—for example, expert witnesses or investigative services.

The questions raised by Gideon are fundamental to our notions of law and justice. Justice Black regarded the Gideon decision as a means of ensuring that "every defendant stands equal before the law." Many years may pass and many cases may be argued before that goal is realized, but Gideon and its progeny have certainly produced a change in our attitudes toward public responsibility for the less fortunate members of our society.

NOTES

J. Lee Rankin, former Solicitor General of the United States, James M. Edwards, John Dwight Evans, Jr., Leon Friedman, Richard J. Medalie and Melvin L. Wulf participated in the preparation of the brief.

1. 302 U.S. 319, 325 (1937).
2. 287 U.S. 45, 67 (1932).
3. See Uveges v. Pennsylvania, 335 U.S. 437 (1948).
4. 355 U.S. 155 (1957).
5. 211 Md. 635, 126 A.2d 573 (1956).
6. 177 Pa. Super. 509, 110 A.2d 801 (1955), *cert. denied*, 350 U.S. 916 (1956).
7. 362 U.S. 574, 578–79 (1960).
8. 350 U.S. 116, 119 (1956).
9. Carnley v. Cochran, 369 U.S. 506, 519 (1962) (Black, J., concurring).
10. 329 U.S. 663 (1947).
11. 332 U.S. 145 (1947).
12. 327 U.S. 82 (1946).
13. 332 U.S. 134 (1947).
14. 334 U.S. 728 (1948); 339 U.S. 660 (1950).
15. See Carnley v. Cochran, 369 U.S. at 511.
16. See Beaney, *The Right to Counsel in American Courts* 194–95 (1955).

17. Thompson v. City of Louisville, 362 U.S. 199 (1960).
18. Robinson v. California, 370 U.S. 660 (1962).
19. Ferguson v. Georgia, 365 U.S. 570 (1961).
20. See Bartkus v. Illinois, 359 U.S. 121 (1959); Ullmann v. United States, 350 U.S. 422 (1956); Knapp v. Schweitzer, 357 U.S. 371 (1958).
21. 367 U.S. 643 (1961).
22. See Irvin v. Dowd, 359 U.S. 394 (1959).
23. See generally Reitz, "Federal Habeas Corpus: Impact of an Abortive State Proceeding," 74 *Harv. L. Rev.* 1315 (1961).
24. 355 U.S. 155 (1957).
25. 348 U.S. 105 (1954).
26. See 133 F. Supp. 31 (S.D. Tex. 1955).
27. Henderson v. Bannan, 256 F.2d 363, 388 (6th Cir. 1958) (dissenting opinion).
28. 369 U.S. 506, 519–20 (1962).
29. 354 U.S. 1 (1957).
30. Kinsella v. United States *ex rel.* Singleton, 361 U.S. 234 (1960).
31. 351 U.S. 12 (1956).
32. 365 U.S. 570, 596 (1961).
33. 314 U.S. 160, 184–85 (1941).
34. 11 Pet. 102, 142 (1837).
35. 365 U.S. 708 (1961).
36. Smith v. Bennett, 365 U.S. 708, 714 (1961).
37. See Kinsella v. United States *ex rel.* Singleton, 361 U.S. at 243–44; McElroy v. United States *ex rel.* Guagliardo, 361 U.S. 281, 287 (1960).
38. Address by R. F. Kennedy before the House of Delegates, American Bar Association, Aug. 6, 1962.
39. See, generally, Special Committee of the Association of the Bar of the City of New York and the National Legal Aid and Defender Association, *Equal Justice for the Accused* 47–52 (1959).
40. *Id.* at 81, 137.
41. 372 U.S. 335 (1963).

14

Justice in the Juvenile Courts

Although there are more than half a million delinquency hearings each year in the United States, until very recently the Supreme Court had never considered the validity of the rules under which juveniles are accorded justice in different court systems throughout the country. Then in 1966, in Kent v. United States, the Court construed the law of the District of Columbia to require its juvenile court, before relinquishing jurisdiction to the regular criminal courts over a minor accused of wrongdoing, to grant him a fair hearing. The Court said it need "go no further" and explicitly left open the larger question whether the "constitutional guarantees which would be applicable to adults charged with the serious offenses for which Kent was tried must be applied in juvenile court proceedings."

Soon thereafter a case arose in Arizona which raised the fundamental and far-reaching question left undecided in Kent. Gerald Gault, a fifteen-year-old boy, was committed to the State Industrial School for up to six years for allegedly making an obscene telephone call with another boy to a woman in town. He was tried without a written statement of the charge, without the right to cross-examine the complaining woman, without the benefit of the privi-

lege against self-incrimination, and perhaps most important, without the right to a lawyer. Moreover, no transcript was kept of the proceeding and no appeal was allowed.

After Gerald Gault's petition for habeas corpus was denied by the Arizona courts, his Arizona counsel, Mrs. Amelia Lewis, brought the case to the author, who on behalf of the American Civil Liberties Union briefed and argued the case before the United States Supreme Court. Excerpts from the brief follow.

I / Historical Background of Procedural Deficiencies in Juvenile Courts

The history of juvenile courts in this country reveals the high purposes of the movement that led to juvenile courts and how these purposes came to be perverted in the form of proceedings—as exemplified by this case from Arizona—that lack the most elemental protections of due process.

Before the enactment of juvenile court acts, criminal prosecutions against juveniles and adults were handled identically and included the same procedural safeguards.[1] At the turn of the century, insights acquired through the development of the behavioral sciences—penology, psychiatry, psychology and social work—led to popular and professional dissatisfaction with prosecutions against children. This led to the establishment of the first juvenile court in 1899 in Cook County, Illinois. Since then, all states have provided by statute that children who are accused of acts which violate the criminal law or who are alleged to be beyond the control of their parents—"incorrigible," "wayward" or "ungovernable"—are subject to proceedings in a juvenile or family court.

Underlying all juvenile law is the concept of the state as the guardian of the child, or *parens patriae*. The principle is that the child who has acted wrongly should be treated by a court as a prudent parent treats his erring child, not as a criminal. The early juvenile courts emphasized the individuality of the child, the causes of his act and the means to help him become a useful citizen. "The problem for determination by the judge is not, Has this boy or girl committed a specific wrong, but What is he, how has he become what he is, and what had best be done in his interest and in the interest of the state to save him from a downward career."[2]

It was a short step from the concept of individualized justice in the treatment or rehabilitative phase of a proceeding to a greater informality in the trial itself. It was feared that the fact-finding procedures of our accusatory, adversary system of criminal trials were inimical to the establishment of the relationship between court and child which was thought necessary to his proper treatment and rehabilitation.

The consequence of this "swapping" of due process for *parens patriae* was that many traditional legal safeguards of criminal proceedings were dispensed with, to the inevitable detriment of individual rights.[3] Some courts even went so far as to insist flatly that constitutional safeguards of criminal procedure were not applicable to juvenile proceedings.[4] In other courts the result was a host of questionable decisions. Vague allegations of antisocial behavior were sufficient to bring a child before some juvenile courts,[5] and the informality of the juvenile procedure often allowed acceptance of uncorroborated admissions, hearsay testimony and the untested reports of social investigations.[6] The right to counsel and the right to notice of charges were sometimes dispensed with.[7] The protections against self-incrimination and double jeopardy also were rejected in some courts on the ground that the juvenile proceeding is a civil rehabilitative procedure and not a criminal proceeding.[8]

The disturbing state of affairs regarding the quality of justice meted out to young people recently received the attention of this Court in *Kent v. United States.*[9] There, with specific reference to the gap between ideal and reality, Mr. Justice Fortas said:

> *While there can be no doubt of the original laudable purpose of juvenile courts, studies and critiques in recent years raised serious questions as to whether actual performance measures well enough against theoretical purpose to make tolerable the immunity of the process from the reach of constitutional guarantees applicable to adults. . . . There is evidence, in fact, that there may be grounds for concern that the child receives the worst of both worlds: that he gets neither the protections accorded to adults nor the solicitous care and regenerative treatment postulated for children.*

The remainder of this brief will try to demonstrate that the petitioner in this case, like countless other juveniles in Arizona and other jurisdictions, has in fact been receiving the "worst of both worlds" in plain derogation of the requirements of the due process clause of the Fourteenth Amendment.

II / The Failure of the Arizona Juvenile Proceedings to Provide Gerald Gault with Fundamental Procedural Protections

In the instant case Gerald Gault was "tried" and committed to the State Industrial School in a proceeding conducted under the Arizona Code that sharply illustrates the "procedural arbitrariness" that often characterizes juvenile courts.

In attempting to justify this handling of Gerald Gault, the Supreme Court of Arizona adhered closely to the usual formulation:

> *. . . juvenile courts do not exist to punish children for their transgressions against society. The juvenile court stands in the position of a protecting parent rather than a prosecutor. It is an effort to substitute protection and guidance for punishment, to withdraw the child from criminal jurisdiction and use social sciences regarding the study of human behavior which permit flexibilities within the procedures. The aim of the court is to provide individualized justice for children. Whatever the formulation, the purpose is to provide authoritative treatment for those who are no longer responding to the normal restraints the child should receive at the hands of his parents. The delinquent is the child of rather than the enemy of society and their interests coincide. . . .*

This statement reduces to two overlapping theories. The first is the *parens patriae* notion already alluded to under point I. The second is that the child is not involved in a criminal proceeding and is not receiving punishment but treatment. Neither of these arguments, nor any other possible theory, can justify the refusal to accord Gerald Gault and other juveniles the protection of the Bill of Rights.

It has already been pointed out that although *parens patriae* has roots in a genuine attempt to rehabilitate juvenile delinquents, what "a child charged with crime is entitled to, is *justice*, not a *parens patriae*."[10] The failure to provide appellants with due process—i.e. "justice"—is the basis for the claim in this case, and it is submitted that the theoretical comforts of a surrogate parent are barren in the face of the hard realities of a proceeding in which the vital interests of a child are engaged.

These interests of the child are equally compelling in rejecting the mischievous notion that what is being meted out in juvenile proceedings is "treatment" and not "punishment." In the first place, modern criminology accords a high place to "rehabilitation" of criminals, thereby invalidating any purported distinction between juvenile and adult proceedings on this score. This Court has said:

Retribution is no longer the dominant objective of the criminal law. Reformation and rehabilitation of offenders have become important goals of criminal jurisprudence.[11]

Even apart from the failure of the "rehabilitation" theory to justify a refusal to provide juveniles with procedural protection, the plain fact is that in this case and in countless others the juvenile is forcibly removed from his home and family through the power of the state. He is confined, perhaps until his majority, to a building with whitewashed walls, regimented routine and institutional hours.[12] That he is sent to a "home" or a "training school" rather than a prison does not in the least detract from the coerced loss of freedom. The child stands to lose every bit as much as an adult in a comparable situation. In fact, the child's situation may be drastically worse, as this very case demonstrates. While an adult accused of the "crime" of using obscene language over the telephone could be convicted in Arizona of a misdemeanor and sentenced to a maximum of two months imprisonment, Gerald Gault was deprived of his liberty for up to six years for the very same act, even though he was not convicted of a "crime" and technically was not "punished."

In these circumstances, it is idle to suggest that the lax Arizona juvenile procedures relating to notice of charges, right to counsel, confrontation of witnesses and the rest can be justified on the ground that juvenile court actions are not "criminal." As stated by a California court, the fact that delinquency involves the possible deprivation of liberty makes the differentiation between adult criminal proceedings and juvenile civil proceedings "for all practical purposes . . . a legal fiction presenting a challenge to credulity and doing violence to reason."[13]

The underlying basis for this holding has been set forth in *Trimble v. Stone:*

The fact that the proceedings are to be classified as civil instead of criminal does not, however, necessarily lead to the conclusion that constitutional safeguards do not apply. It is often dangerous to carry any proposition to its logical extreme. These proceedings have many ramifications which cannot be disposed of by denominating the proceedings as civil. Basic human rights do not depend on nomenclature. What if the jurisdiction of the Juvenile Court were to be extended by an Act of Congress to the age of twenty-one or even twenty-five, or what if it were to be reduced to sixteen? Could it be properly said that the constitutional safeguards would be increased or diminished accordingly?

Manifestly the Bill of Rights applies to every individual within the territorial jurisdiction of the United States, irrespective of age. The Constitution contains no age limits.[14]

Due process for juveniles is particularly necessary in a time of an increasing juvenile population. With full appreciation of the high stakes in these proceedings both from the standpoint of the child himself and from that of society in preventing the permanent loss of a law-abiding citizen, Judge Midonick of the New York Family Court said in *In re Ronny:*

I can think of few worse examples to set for our children than to visit upon children what would be, if they were older, unreasonable and unconstitutional invasions of their all-too-limited privacy and rights, merely because they are young. . . . We would do well to stand solidly in behalf of children before us to avoid contamination of the fact sources and to see to it that we brook no shabby practices in fact-finding which do not comport with fair play. We must not only be fair; we must convince the child . . . that the judge, a parent image, is careful to ensure those civilized standards of conduct toward the child which we expect of the child toward organized society.[15]

Modern juvenile and family court acts have also been responsive to the fundamental unfairness of subjecting young people to proceedings in which their liberty is at stake without the procedural protections accorded adults in criminal trials. The Standard Juvenile Court Act, as well as the California Juvenile Court Law and the New York Family Court Act, incorporates basic due process requirements, such as the rights to counsel, a record of the proceeding and appeal.

There are, in sum, compelling reasons of fairness and authority to provide young people with fundamental procedural protections in juvenile court. Accordingly, this Court should rule that appellants were denied due process of law by the failure of Arizona to provide the basic elements of procedural fairness in this juvenile proceeding. The specific guarantees of the Bill of Rights denied appellants will now be considered with particularity.

A. *Notice of Charges and Hearing*

The first essential of due process, where an individual's liberty is in jeopardy, is that he be clearly informed of the nature of the charge against him so that he can prepare his defense. Further, he must be given adequate time and opportunity after notice of charges to decide on his course of action and to prepare that defense.[16]

Notice, to be fully effective, must contain at least three ingredients: (1) it must state what acts are complained of; (2) it must state what statute or applicable rule of law such acts violate; and (3) it must give some indication of the consequences of a finding against the accused. All of these were absent in the proceedings below.

No official notice of the nature of the iminent hearings was given to appellants. In the most casual fashion, and only after she requested the information, was Mrs. Gault orally informed by Officer Flagg on the night of June 8 that Gerald had been detained that afternoon and that a hearing would be held the very next day. The only written notice of any kind appellants ever received was contained in a handwritten note on blank paper addressed to Mrs. Gault and received from Probation Officer Flagg on Friday, June 12. It merely stated that Judge McGhee had set Monday, June 15, as the time "for further hearings on Gerald's delinquency."

No effective notice of the underlying basis for the charge of delinquency was given to appellants. This worked severely to appellants' prejudice. Judge McGhee testified that he based his adjudication of delinquency in part on a finding that Gerald had violated Arizona Revised Statutes, section 13-377, the obscene-language provision of the Arizona Criminal Code. Yet this statute was never cited to appellants.

Thus appellants' attention was never called to any statute or statutory language which might have given them some guidance as to what the charge of delinquency was based on, or how to prepare a legal defense to it, or even how to decide intelligently whether to contest it at all. Nothing brought home to them the advisability of consulting with or retaining counsel, or impressed on them the potential seriousness of the proceedings for their son as evidenced by the drastic sanction later imposed by the court.

Even the minimal standards required by the Arizona statute with regard to notice of delinquency charges as interpreted by the Arizona court, i.e., that it is sufficient if the court advises the parents no later than the hearing itself about "the facts involved in the case," were not satisfied in this case. As stated by Judge McGhee, his finding of juvenile delinquency was based not only on the boy's use of lewd language but also on his "habitual involvement in immoral matters," based on a referral report in the probation file which had never led to an accusation or hearing. The parents never had notice of this report, even at the hearings held in this case, and had no opportunity to deny those charges or defend against them. As to this basis for the adjudication of delinquency, there was simply no notice and no opportunity to be heard at all.

Finally, the time allowed to appellants to prepare their case was extremely short: for the first hearing, from eight o'clock at night until three o'clock the next day; for the second hearing, from Friday afternoon until Monday morning at eleven o'clock. The Arizona court contented itself with adopting the rule that "If the charges are denied, they [the child and his parents] must be given a reasonable time to prepare." The court failed to recognize that reasonable time is necessary not merely to prepare denials and defenses but to decide whether to deny or defend at all. It was unfair in this case, in the scanty time afforded appellants before the hearings, to make an intelligent decision on how best to proceed in their son's interest, especially in the absence of the advice of counsel.

B. *The Right to Counsel*

In both juvenile hearings appellants and their son appeared without counsel. Neither appellants nor their son were informed that they had a right to counsel or that they would be provided with counsel in case of need. The Arizona court stated that "parents of an infant cannot be denied representation by counsel of their choosing," but nevertheless went on to hold that due process does not require "that an infant have a right to counsel."

The denial of the right of counsel in this case is inconsistent with minimal standards of procedural fairness. It denies the most basic procedural right, without which all other procedures in juvenile courts and all other rights ostensibly given in such proceedings are unsubstantial and incapable of effective implementation.

The decision below on this point also flies in the face of principles painstakingly and deliberately elaborated by this Court over many years. *Powell v. Alabama*[17] and *Gideon v. Wainwright*[18] have established that the right to counsel in criminal proceedings is an essential part of the Fourteenth Amendment's due process clause. Together they also establish that no distinction may constitutionally be drawn between the right to appear by retained counsel and the right to have counsel appointed in criminal proceedings. "In our adversary system of criminal justice," the Court said in *Gideon*, "any person hailed into court, who is too poor to hire a lawyer, cannot be assured a fair trial unless counsel is provided for him."[19]

Even if juvenile proceedings are denominated "civil" in nature, the fact that a juvenile may be deprived of his liberty through an adjudicatory process in which the aid of counsel would be indispensable to him requires the application of the *Powell* and *Gideon* principles in such proceedings.

Just last term in *Kent v. United States*,[20] the Court held that assistance of counsel in the "critically important" determination of waiver of jurisdiction by a juvenile court is essential to the proper administration of justice. Indeed, this Court in *Kent* explicitly approved *Black v. United States*,[21] and *Shioutakon v. District of Columbia*,[22] which had gone further and "held that effective assistance of counsel in juvenile court proceedings is essential."[23] Although these cases did not involve the Fourteenth Amendment directly, since they all arose in the District of Columbia, the considerations upon which they are based apply as well to juvenile proceedings in state courts.

A juvenile proceeding involving a determination of delinquency carries with it sufficient social stigma and danger of deprivation of liberty for it to be considered a "critical stage" in the same sense as that term was used not only in *Kent* but also in *Hamilton v. Alabama*[24] and *White v. Maryland*,[25] which required appointment of counsel in adult criminal proceedings prior to the trial itself.

By contrast to these cases, the issue in the instant case is whether due process requires the assistance of counsel at the trial itself, a stage of the juvenile process, needless to say, which is not merely "critical" but its very essence. It is the central fact-finding inquiry, where the determination is made whether the accused juvenile committed the acts charged. The resolution of this inquiry determines whether the juvenile will be denominated a juvenile delinquent and possibly deprived of his liberty.

To say that the juvenile judge can fully protect the accused juvenile's interests is no more true in juvenile than in adult proceedings, no matter how deliberately the judge may discharge his duty as the embodiment of the *parens patriae*. As this Court said in *Powell v. Alabama*, *supra*, although the judge may see to it that the accused "be dealt with justly and fairly," he cannot "investigate the facts, advise and direct the defense, or participate in those necessary conferences between counsel and accused which sometimes partake of the inviolable character of the confessional." Indeed, there is far less warrant to rely on a judiciary one fifth of whose members are not even lawyers and more than half of whom devote less than one fourth of their time to juvenile and family matters.

The majority of legal writers, federal and state court decisions, and modern juvenile codes, such as in California and New York, have taken the position that the right of a child and his parents to the assistance of counsel in a juvenile proceeding is founded in due process. Following this trend, the Supreme Court of Mississippi, in *Interest of Long*,[26] recently ruled:

Where a minor is charged with being a delinquent and is subject to being deprived of his liberty, minor and parent should be advised by the court in delinquency proceedings that they are entitled to legal representation.

To the argument made by some judges, social workers and lawyers that the introduction of lawyers into juvenile proceedings would make the proceedings legalistic, overtechnical and argumentative, would prolong the hearings, create a chaos of crowded dockets and introduce dilatory tactics with dismissal of the charges uppermost in the defense lawyer's mind, Mr. Charles Schinitsky of the New York Legal Aid Society has replied:

The desire for a smoothly operating court should not be used as an argument to deprive those accused of the right to determine for themselves their need for counsel. An essential function of the court is to establish an atmosphere of fairness in its dealings with those persons appearing before it. Vital to the creation of this atmosphere is that an accused parent or child, without funds, know they may have counsel to guide them through their difficulty.[27]

Finally, it goes almost without saying that if we are correct in our contention that other traditional safeguards of the criminal law should be applicable in juvenile court proceedings, such as fair notice of charges and the rights of confrontation and cross-examination, the aid of counsel is also indispensable to effectuate those rights. Only an attorney can enable an accused juvenile to assert such other procedural rights as he may have. Conversely, even if it is held that juvenile court proceedings can constitutionally be conducted with a procedural informality impermissible in adult criminal proceedings, the assistance of counsel becomes all the more essential. It then may be the only way to keep the adjudicatory hearing in the juvenile court from becoming a sham and a mere rubber stamp for the charges made against the juvenile.

C. *Confrontation and Cross-examination*

In *Pointer v. Texas*,[28] this Court unanimously held that the Sixth Amendment guarantee of confrontaton and cross-examination applies in state prosecutions under the due process clause of the Fourteenth Amendment. In reaching that result, the Court recognized the indispensable role played by confrontation and cross-examination "in exposing falsehood and bringing out the truth."

The requirement of confrontation and cross-examination is one of the most vital and lasting contributions of Anglo-American law to the attainment of a reliable fact-finding proceeding. In Dean Wigmore's famous statement:

For two centuries past, the policy of the Anglo-American system of Evidence has been to regard the necessity of testing by cross-examination as a vital feature of the law. The belief that no safeguard for testing the value of human statements is comparable to that furnished by cross-examination, and the conviction that no statement (except by special exception) should be used as testimony until it has been probed and sublimated by that test, has found increasing strength in lengthening experience. . . . [I]t is beyond doubt the greatest legal engine ever invented for the discovery of truth.[29]

The rule is clear: absent confrontation and cross-examination, there can be no fair or reliable determination of truth sufficient to comply with the requirements of due process.

Furthermore, since the right to confront and cross-examine is essential to the fairness of any judicial proceeding, it should be available even in a proceeding deemed to be civil in nature. Surely a judicial order which causes the deprivation of personal liberty results in harm at least as grievous as termination of employment by the government, where cross-examination must be allowed.

The facts of this case demonstrate that the determination of delinquency in a juvenile court proceeding is of critical consequence.

The adjudication of Gerald Gault's delinquency on the basis of his alleged participation in an allegedly obscene telephone call was made without any consideration of the testimony of the recipient of the call, the complaining witness Mrs. Cook. The request of appellants for Mrs. Cook's appearance at the hearings was denied by

Judge McGhee because he "didn't feel it was necessary." Indeed, Judge McGhee, the trier of fact in this case, did not even elicit Mrs. Cook's version of what had happened either in or out of the presence of appellants. It is an extraordinary procedural notion that an adjudication can be made and that a person can be deprived of his liberty without the trier of fact even hearing the testimony of the alleged victim, especially when the victim is readily amenable to the processes of the court.[30] Furthermore, in the light of the testimony of Probation Officer Flagg to the effect that Gerald Gault had not admitted to him making any lewd or indecent remarks over the telephone but said the other boy engaged in the conversation, the testimony of the complaining witness Mrs. Cook became even more essential. Had she been called as a witness, appellants could have attempted to show that Gerald had not used any offensive language toward her. Indeed, the court would have had a proper basis for ascertaining the exact nature of the entire incident, what in fact was said and who said it.

The Arizona court took the curious view that "the relevancy of confrontation only arises where the charges are denied." Similarly, Judge McGhee explained that no adult witnesses were heard or sworn and he did not talk to Mrs. Cook personally, since he had the "admissions" of the boys to go on.

This attitude turns topsy-turvy the concept of the juvenile hearing as an adjudicatory proceeding to determine the facts based on evidence. It in effect treats the hearing as an inquisition of the accused to determine whether, without hearing any of the evidence against him and without the advice of counsel, he will relieve the persons who made the charges against him of any obligation to support them by testimony. The purposes served by the right of confrontation and cross-examination—so important to the proper performance of the court's fact-finding functions—are thereby thwarted.

As we show in the next section of this brief, this attitude also resulted in this case in the violation of Gerald Gault's privilege against self-incrimination.

D. *The Privilege Against Self-Incrimination*

Gerald Gault was found to have committed a crime under the law of Arizona, a violation of section 13-377 of the Arizona Statutes, and his commitment by the court rested in part on that finding.

There can be no dispute that admissions of the elements of this offense were elicited from him under questioning by the court at the hearings of June 9 and June 15. Indeed, his own statements were decisive in the court's decision to commit him. Judge McGhee described in detail his questioning of Gerald Gault at these hearings. He further testified: "Q. Were any adult witnesses sworn and/or heard against the boy Gerald Gault? A. No. It was all, in my mind, done upon the admissions of Gerald Gault."

No advice was given by the court to Gerald that he did not have to testify or make a statement unless he chose to do so. The Supreme Court of Arizona upheld this procedure, holding that the juvenile court is not required to advise a juvenile of the privilege against self-incrimination.

Under familiar principles, this course of proceedings violated Gerald Gault's Fourteenth Amendment rights. With respect to the privilege, it is entirely immaterial whether a juvenile court proceeding is labeled criminal, civil, in the nature of *parens patriae*, or anything else. The law has long been settled that:

> *The privilege can be claimed in* any proceeding, *be it criminal or civil, administrative or judicial, investigatory or adjudicatory . . . it protects* any disclosures *which the witness may reasonably apprehend* could be used in a criminal prosecution or which could lead to other evidence that might be so used.[31]

The relevant inquiry in determining the applicability of the privilege, therefore, is not the nature of the proceeding, but whether the witness may in any way incriminate himself by testifying or making a statement. Under the law of Arizona, the interrelationship between juvenile proceedings and criminal prosecution is such that at the time he made his statements to the juvenile court, Gerald Gault ran the risk of furnishing evidence which could be used against him in a criminal prosecution for violation of section 13-377.

It is apparent that the Arizona system for handling juveniles does not exempt them from the criminal law or divest them of legal capacity to commit crimes. The criminal law remains in full force and effect in its application to their conduct. The constitutional and statutory scheme simply provides that judges of the superior courts, sitting as juvenile court judges, shall consider cases involving juveniles accused of crime in the first instance, to decide whether to "suspend criminal prosecution" or to allow criminal prosecution to proceed. And the Arizona courts have so held.[32]

It is therefore clear that Gerald Gault ran the risk of self-incrimination when he was questioned at the hearings of June 9 and June 15. He was accused of conduct constituting a crime, the statements elicited from him could have led to his conviction of that crime, and he had no assurance that he was safe from criminal prosecution based on his statements.

Under these circumstances and the applicable decisions of this Court, the state was required either to afford him the privilege or grant him immunity commensurate with the risk. It did neither. Furthermore, Gerald Gault's failure to claim the privilege specifically at his hearings cannot be a basis for depriving him of it, since he was without counsel throughout the proceedings. Nor can he be held to have waived his privilege, since he was never advised that he had it.

State courts have divided on the applicability of the privilege in juvenile court proceedings.[33] Cases denying the applicability of the privilege, however, have almost invariably followed the theory that the juvenile proceeding is not criminal in nature, without consideration of the crucial question of the interrelationship of the juvenile and criminal proceedings.

Contrary to the reasoning of the court below, recognition of the privilege does not impair "the necessary flexibility for individualized treatment." There is ample scope for individualized treatment when the court comes to decide the proper disposition of a juvenile it has adjudged delinquent. But the adjudicatory process in juvenile court cannot be allowed to serve, however inadvertently, as a means of compelled self-incrimination.

E. *Right to Appellate Review and to a Transcript of the Proceedings*

The Arizona statute's failure to provide a right to appellate review of juvenile court orders or a right to a transcript of the proceedings in the juvenile court constitutes a departure from the requirements of due process of law.

Although it has been said that "a State is not required by the Federal Constitution to provide appellate courts or a right to appellate review at all,"[34] this fact does not "authorize the imposition of conditions that offend the deepest presuppositions of our society."[35] It can hardly be doubted that one of the "deepest presuppositions" of American law is that unbridled and absolute discretion shall rest in no judicial official. Yet the State of Arizona lodges practically unlimited discretion in the juvenile court judge, and permits him to conduct his proceedings with virtually total informality. Thus the right to review by appeal the decisions of such a juvenile court becomes extremely important.

Just last term, this Court emphasized that the special concerns and interests sought to be furthered by juvenile court statutes do not justify placing the procedures employed by these courts beyond the scope of appellate scrutiny:

> *But this latitude* [*to determine waiver of jurisdiction*] *is not complete. At the outset, it assumes procedural regularity sufficient in the particular circumstances to satisfy the basic requirements of due process and fairness, as well as compliance with the statutory requirement. . . .*[36]

Moreover, although a statute may confer on a juvenile court a "substantial degree of discretion," it cannot grant "a license for arbitrary procedure."[37] The fact that the juvenile court functions as *parens patriae* is in no way "an invitation to procedural arbitrariness." Yet how can such prohibited exercises of discretion in the juvenile courts be corrected when the state makes no provision for appellate review? Forcing appellant to resort to the ancillary procedure afforded by habeas corpus, as in this case, is an inadequate method of meeting the problems posed by the power vested in the juvenile court.

The absence of an official transcript of the original hearings, one of the basic shortcomings of this case which confronted appellants in obtaining judicial review, would also be remedied by allowing review by appeal. This is apparent from the fact that the Supreme Court of Arizona in this case justified the failure to provide for a transcript mainly by the absence of a right to appeal, reasoning that one of the main purposes of a transcript is to support an appeal.

Whether review of juvenile court proceedings is by appeal or habeas corpus, a transcript is indispensable. Even if this Court rules that due process does not require the right to appellate review of juvenile court proceedings as a method of controlling unchecked discretion, parties in juvenile court proceedings will nevertheless continue to be able to resort to the habeas corpus method, as did appellants here, to test the legality of the deprivation of liberty. Without an official transcript or record of the proceedings in the juvenile court, even the questionable efficacy of the habeas corpus remedy will be minimal. For example, there was sharp dispute at the habeas corpus hearing about whether Gerald Gault, at either of the two delinquency hearings, had admitted speaking any of the allegedly lewd words over the telephone. Mrs. Gault said that her son, at the first hearing, said he had only dialed, but Probation Officer Flagg and the judge testified that Gerald admitted saying some of the words. On the other hand, Mrs. Gault and Mr. Flagg agreed that at the second hearing Gerald had admitted only having dialed, but the judge insisted that Gerald had admitted making some of the allegedly obscene remarks.

The net effect of the failure of the state to transcribe juvenile proceedings is the unseemly spectacle of the juvenile court judge testifying in the habeas corpus hearings to what transpired before him in the delinquency hearing.

In sum, orderly and fair procedure requires both a transcript of proceedings and a right to appellate review.

In a historic decision handed down in May 1967, the Supreme Court reversed the Arizona tribunals and ruled[38] *that Gerald Gault was deprived of due process of law in four respects: he was not* afforded a written notice of charges sufficiently in advance of court proceedings to permit him to prepare a defense; he was not allowed to cross-examine the complainant; he was not afforded the privilege against self-incrimination; and neither he nor his parents were notified of the right to retain counsel, or, if he was without funds, to have a lawyer assigned to defend him. It did not rule on whether due process required an appeal or a transcript of the proceedings.

Although the Supreme Court has now established the basic rule that due process must be given juveniles accused of delinquency, one can only speculate about the full ramifications of the decision. For example, does the ruling mean that juvenile courts must provide all elements of due process generally provided in a criminal trial? If so, then the role of the juvenile judge, who has traditionally operated without a jury and in relative privacy, will be vastly changed. In addition, the Supreme Court left open the applicability of the decision to the period before a hearing, when the juvenile is first taken into custody, and to the period after a hearing, when the question is the proper sentence or other disposition. Only case-by-case litigation over many years will reveal the full implications of the Gault decision for juvenile justice.[39]

NOTES

Amelia D. Lewis, Gertrud Mainzer, Daniel A. Rezneck, Melvin L. Wulf and Joel Gora participated in the preparation of the brief. Subsequently, the author and Mr. Rezneck wrote an article discussing the meaning and ramifications of the *Gault* decision, "In re Gault and the Future of Juvenile Law," 1 *Family Law Quarterly* No. 4 at 1 (December 1967).

1. See Welch, "Delinquency Proceedings—Fundamental Fairness for the Accused in a Quasi-Criminal Forum," 50 *Minn. L. Rev.* 653, 654–55 (1966); *In re* Poff, 135 F. Supp. 224, 225 (D.D.C. 1955). See, generally, Antieau, "Constitutional Rights in Juvenile Courts," 46 *Cornell L.Q.* 387 (1961).

2. Mack, "The Juvenile Court," 23 *Harv. L. Rev.* 104, 119 (1909), quoted in People v. Lewis, 260 N.Y. 171, 177, 183 N.E. 353, 355 (1932).

3. Glueck, "Some 'Unfinished Business' in the Management of Juvenile Delinquency," 15 *Syracuse L. Rev.* 628, 629 (1964). See also Note, "Juve-

nile Courts: Applicability of Constitutional Safeguards and Rules of Evidence to Proceedings," 41 *Cornell L.Q.* 147 (1955); Paulsen, "Fairness to the Juvenile Offender," 41 *Minn. L. Rev.* 547 (1957).

4. *In re* Holmes, 379 Pa. 599, 603, 109 A.2d 523, 525 (1954), *cert. denied,* 348 U.S. 973 (1955).

5. *In re* Bentley (Harry v. State), 246 Wisc. 69, 16 N.W.2d 390 (1944); State *ex rel.* Raddue v. Superior Court, 106 Wash. 619, 180 P. 875 (1919).

6. Uncorroborated admissions: In the Matter of Gonzalez, 328 S.W.2d 475 (Tex. Ct. App. 1959); Matter of McDonald, 153 A.2d 651 (D.C. Munic. Ct. App. 1959). Hearsay: *In re* Holmes, 379 Pa. 599, 109 A.2d 523 (1954), *cert. denied,* 348 U.S. 973 (1955); State *ex rel.* Christensen v. Christensen, 119 Utah 361, 227 P.2d 760 (1951); Sylvester v. Commonwealth, 253 Mass. 244, 148 N.E. 449 (1925).

7. Notice of charges: *In re* Duncan, 107 N.E.2d 256 (1951); *In re* Bentley, 246 Wis. 69, 16 N.W.2d 390 (1944). Right to counsel: People v. Dotson, 46 Cal.2d 891, 299 P.2d 875 (1956); Akers v. State, 114 Ind. App. 195, 51 N.E.2d 91 (1943); In Interest of T.W.P., 184 So.2d 507 (Fla. Ct. of App. 1966).

8. Self-incrimination: *In re* Holmes, *supra* note 6; People v. Lewis, 260 N.Y. 171, 183 N.E. 353 (1932); *In re* Santillanes, 47 N.M. 140, 138 P.2d 503 (1943). Double jeopardy: People v. Silverstein, 121 Cal. App.2d 140, 262 P.2d 656 (1953). *In re* Santillanes, *supra.* See, generally, Sussman, *Juvenile Delinquency* 11–16 (1955).

9. Kent v. United States, 383 U.S. 541, 555–56 (1966).

10. *In re* Holmes, 379 Pa. at 615, 109 A.2d at 530 (dissenting opinion).

11. Williams v. New York, 337 U.S. 241, 248 (1959). See also Benson v. United States, 332 F.2d 288, 292 (5th Cir. 1964); Radzinowicz and Turner, "A Study of Punishment I: Introductory Essay," 21 *Canadian Bar Rev.* 91–97 (1943); and Allen, "Criminal Justice, Legal Values and the Rehabilitative Ideal," 50 *J. Crim. L.,C. & P.S.* 226 (1959).

12. *In re* Holmes, 379 Pa. at 616, 109 A. 2d at 530 (dissenting opinion).

13. *In re* Contreras, 109 Cal. App.2d 787, 789, 241 P.2d 631, 633 (1952).

14. 187 F. Supp. 483, 485–86 (D.D.C. 1960).

15. 40 Misc.2d 194, 210; 242 N.Y.S.2d 844, 860–61 (Family Ct. 1963).

16. Cole v. Arkansas, 333 U.S. 196 (1948). See also Hovey v. Elliott, 167 U.S. 409 (1897); Powell v. Alabama, 287 U.S. 45 (1932); *In re* Oliver, 333 U.S. 257 (1948); *In re* Murchison, 349 U.S. 133 (1955); Williams v. New York, 337 U.S. 241 (1949).

17. 287 U.S. 45 (1932).

18. 372 U.S. 335 (1963).

19. *Id.* at 344.

20. 383 U.S. 541 (1966).

21. 355 F.2d 104 (D.C. Cir. 1965).

22. 236 F.2d 666 (D.C. Cir. 1956).

23. 383 U.S. at 558.

24. 368 U.S. 52 (1961).

25. 373 U.S. 59 (1963).

26. 184 So.2d 861, 862 (1966).

27. Schinitsky, "The Role of the Lawyer in Children's Court," 17 *The Record* (The Association of the Bar of the City of New York) No. 1 at 24 (Jan. 1962).

28. 380 U.S. 400, 404 (1965).

29. 5 Wigmore, *Evidence* §1367 at 28–29 (3d ed. 1940). Emphasis added.

30. Cf. Pointer v. Texas, 380 U.S. 400 (1965).

31. Murphy v. Waterfront Commission, *supra,* 378 U.S. at 94 (concurring opinion of Mr. Justice White). Emphasis supplied. See also Malloy v. Hogan, *supra,* 378 U.S. at 11; McCarthy v. Arndstein, 266 U.S. 34, 40 (1924).

32. Application of Gault, 99 Ariz. 181, 407 P.2d 760 (1965); Application of Vigileos, 84 Ariz. 404, 330 P.2d 116 (1958). As the Supreme Court of Arizona has said, the Arizona juvenile court act "affects the *treatment* and not the capacity of the offender." Burrows v. State, 38 Ariz. 99, 110, 297 Pac. 1029, 1034 (1931). Emphasis in original.

33. *Compare* Dendy v. Wilson, *supra; Ex parte* Tahbel, *supra; In re* Sadleir, 97 Utah 291, 85 P.2d 810 (1938), on rehearing, 97 Utah 313, 94 P.2d 161 (1939) (allowing privilege), *with In re* Santillanes, 47 N.M. 140, 138 P.2d 503 (1943); *In re* Holmes, 379 P. 599, 109 A.2d 523 (1954); State v. Shardell, 107 Ohio App. 338, 153 N.E.2d 510 (1958) (disallowing privilege).

34. Griffin v. Illinois, 351 U.S. 12, 18 (1956).

35. *Id.* at 22 (Frankfurter, J., concurring).

36. Kent v. United States, 383 U.S. at 553.

37. *Ibid.*

38. *In re* Gault, 387 U.S. 1 (1967).

39. See generally Dorsen & Rezneck, "In re Gault and the Future of Juvenile Law," 1 *Family Law Quarterly,* No. 4 at 1 (Dec. 1967).

15

The Right to Trial by Jury in Contempt Cases

In the fall of 1962, after James Meredith's efforts to register at the University of Mississippi had been thwarted by state officials, the United States Court of Appeals for the Fifth Circuit issued a temporary restraining order against Mississippi, its governor, its lieutenant governor and other state officials to prevent their interference with Meredith's registration. Governor Barnett and Lieutenant Governor Johnson refused to obey the order and were consequently held in criminal contempt for their willful disobedience. They appealed, contending that they were entitled to trial by jury on the criminal contempt issue.

To understand the question raised by this appeal, one must recognize the distinction between civil and criminal contempts. A civil contempt is merely a means of securing compliance with a court order. Its sole purpose is to coerce compliance, through the imposition of fines or imprisonment. Once compliance occurs, the penalties cease. In addition, one can ordinarily remove oneself from civil contempt by demonstrating inability to comply. Criminal contempts are far more serious, and virtually identical to other crimes in purpose and effect. Usually imposed upon persons behaving "contumaciously" toward a court, criminal contempts are designed to *punish, to vindicate the honor of the courts, and do so through the imposition of fixed penalties, including fines and imprisonment.*

At this point, one might wonder why Barnett and Johnson needed to appeal, since the Constitution clearly guarantees trial by jury in all criminal cases. It is because a historical quirk led the Supreme Court to hold that criminal contempts are triable by a judge alone, sitting without a jury. The Supreme Court had reaffirmed this doctrine as recently as 1958 in Green v. United States. *The Barnett case reached the Supreme Court solely on the jury-trial issue, and Barnett and Johnson sought to overrule* Green. *The ACLU submitted an amicus brief, prepared by the author, urging the abolition of the anomalous* Green *doctrine. Of particular significance is the use of legal history, a valuable tool for a lawyer seeking to contest a doctrine whose validity rests primarily on its supposed historical origins.*

A feature of this case that attracted wide public attention was the suggestion heard in some quarters that a jury trial, in the race-conscious climate of Mississippi, would not only assure the acquittal of these locally popular defendants but severely impair the movement for Negro civil rights. As the brief that follows states, the American Civil Liberties Union rejected these reasons for denying anyone a jury trial in a criminal case.

I / A jury trial is an indispensable component of a fair trial; this is especially so in criminal contempt actions.

The jury system has long been recognized as one of the fundamental procedural safeguards of our system of jurisprudence. Its history dates back at least to Magna Carta, where it was provided:

> *No freeman shall be taken or imprisoned, or disseised, or outlawed, or banished, or any ways destroyed, nor will we pass upon him, nor will we send upon him, unless by the lawful judgment of his peers, or by the law of the land.*

The importance of trial by jury in America was recognized even before the Revolution. The Declaration of Rights issued in 1765 by nine of the thirteen original colonies stated: "That trial by jury, is the inherent and invaluable right of every British subject of these colonies."[1]

One of the enumerated grievances mentioned in the Declaration of Independence was that laws had been adopted, "For depriving us in many cases, of the benefits of Trial by Jury."

The importance of jury trial in our system of justice derives from the fact that in a very real sense the tribunal of last resort in questions of fact is the people themselves. De Tocqueville expressed this fact with his usual insight:

> *The institution of the jury . . . places the real direction of society in the hands of the governed, or of a portion of the governed, and not in that of the government. . . . He who punishes the criminal is . . . the real master of society. . . . All the sovereigns who have chosen to govern by their own authority, and to direct society instead of obeying its directions, have destroyed or enfeebled the institution of the jury.*[2]

This Court has often been called upon to reaffirm the vital place which the right to jury trial has in our constitutional framework. Only recently, the Court has stated that, "This right of trial by jury ranks very high in our catalogue of constitutional safeguards."[3] And in a judgment striking down a court-martial conviction obtained against a civilian dependent of a member of the armed forces, an opinion joined in by four of the Justices of this Court stated:

> *Trial by jury in a court of law and in accordance with traditional modes of procedure after an indictment by grand jury has served and remains one of our most vital barriers to governmental arbitrariness. These elemental procedural safeguards were embedded in our Constitution to secure their inviolateness and sanctity against the passing demands of expediency or conveniences.*[4]

That the right to jury trial has proved to be a crucial safeguard against the abuse of criminal process in a wide variety of contexts needs no elaborate citation of authority. But this right is even more important in the case of criminal contempt because of the novelty of the method of prosecution. There is an obvious built-in unfairness in permitting a judge, in order to "vindicate his authority" and on the grounds that he is the aggrieved party, to act as prosecutor, witness, jury and judge. It is elementary that no man can be judge in his own case and that no man is permitted to try cases where he has an interest in the outcome.[5] Yet in criminal contempts, the judge, with the full panoply of his power, is an unequal match for the defendant. The judge's power to punish contempt is virtually limitless as to the scope of the offense, the means of punishment and the procedure employed. The only effective restraint upon him is the often ineffectual right of judicial review, where the sole question is whether the judge has abused his discretion. The judiciary, as the final bastion against oppression, must be free of even the slightest suggestion of unfair practices.

It has been argued that because of the favored position of these defendants in the eyes of Mississippians, no jury will be found to convict them. But the administration of impartial justice, and not the rendering of swift and easy convictions, is the business of the courts. Every procedural safeguard in the Constitution makes it more difficult to secure convictions, just as every other provision in the Bill of Rights affords an added measure of protection against the coercive power of the government, whether existing or potential. That a particular constitutional liberty may in some cases make it possible for the guilty to escape punishment has never been a reason for not invoking it. Experience has taught us that such a sacrifice is necessary to the vindication of a critical constitutional principle. In the oft-quoted words of Mr. Justice Holmes: "We have to choose, and for my part I think it a less evil that some criminals should escape than that the Government should play an ignoble part."[6]

Finally, it may be argued that these defendants do not deserve a jury trial because of the flagrant nature of the contempts charged against them. But this Court has often rejected the proposition that because a particular defendant is a "bad man" his constitutional rights are not worth protecting. Unsavory characters may occasionally be benefitted in order to affirm an important liberty.

II / Summary trial of criminal contempts is not "necessary" to vindicate the authority of the court or for any other reason.

As Mr. Justice Black observed in *Green v. United States,*[7] those who defend summary trial of the crime of contempt attempt to justify this procedure as a "necessity" if judicial orders are to be obeyed and the authority of courts maintained. Even if there were such a "necessity," it is doubtful that it would permit a deviation from the Bill of Rights. But in fact, no "necessity" exists that conceivably warrants this extraordinary method of trial.

In the first place, criminal proceedings are unnecessary to assure compliance with lawful court orders. Civil contempt has always been the appropriate remedy to assure such compliance. As long as a defendant faces imprisonment for refusal to comply, a court's order will eventually be satisfied. Long ago, this Court described the limits of the power to punish for contempt as "the least possible power adequate to the end proposed."[8] The remedy of criminal contempt is a power in excess of the end proposed, compliance with court orders.

Related to the claim that compliance with court orders necessitates a summary trial is the assertion that a judge is able to dispose of a criminal contempt faster and cheaper, and thus more swiftly vindicate his authority. This idea misconceives the purposes of both the criminal law and the Bill of Rights. Whatever speed and economies might result can hardly justify abandonment of a basic constitutional protection. As Mr. Justice Black stated:

Cheap, easy convictions were not the primary concern of those who adopted the Constitution and the Bill of Rights. Every procedural safeguard they established purposely made it more difficult for the Government to convict those it accused of crimes. On their scale of values justice occupied at least as high a position as economy.[9]

Even more important, once there is no longer any question of compelling compliance with a court order—the province of civil contempt—there can be no justification for swift disposition. In such cases, there is ample time to provide the defendant the full benefit of all constitutional safeguards. This was recognized by Justices Holmes and Brandeis when they declared that "when there is no need for immediate action contempts are like any other breach of law and should be dealt with as the law deals with other illegal acts."[10] The instant case provides a dramatic example of the absence of any need for haste. It is now almost a year since the incident involving James H. Meredith's admission to the University of Mississippi that led to the citation of these defendants for contempt of the Court of Appeals. Meredith has been graduated, and there is no present violence or any other reason which would justify a hasty trial for criminal contempt.

Equally unavailing is the contention that jury trial for criminal contempt, especially where racist sympathies exceed respect for federal courts, will subject judges to personal abuse and to courtroom disturbances because no jury will be likely to convict the miscreants. But the present lawsuit does not involve a contempt in the presence of the court or so near to it as to disrupt proceedings. That category of contempts is not pertinent to the disposition of the present case.

The claim of "necessity," so clearly unpersuasive in the general run of cases, takes on a peculiar coloration in the present context. Lurking in the background of this case is the unarticulated premise that unless these defendants are criminally punished for violation of the order of the Court of Appeals, irreparable damage may befall the movement to secure civil rights for Negroes in the South and elsewhere. The idea is, no doubt, that only punitive action will prevent certain Southern officials from intervening with the authority and power of their office to head off attempts to comply with judicial orders entered on behalf of Negroes. This claim lacks any validity and reflects a misunderstanding of the purposes of criminal contempt as well as of the struggle of the Negro for equality. The resources of the law, including civil contempt, are sufficient to coerce governors and private citizens into compliance with lawful orders of federal courts. The subsequent invocation of the criminal process can have little or no added effect on the government's ability to assure that such edicts are obeyed. The only purpose of such process is to *punish* violators for past acts, a punishment that surely need not be hasty or expeditious.

It should be obvious from recent events that the Negro civil rights movement does not depend on the criminal law. Within recent years, indeed recent months, the Negro has made historic gains in hundreds of communities in more than a score of states with the assistance, as far as we have been able to determine, of federal criminal contempt in only one episode.[11]

The paucity of such cases involving criminal contempt is particularly significant in light of the varied circumstances under which Negroes have sought vindication of their rights and the numerous court orders entered for this purpose. This strongly indicates that the availability of criminal contempt is unimportant to the success of the civil rights movement and that the just claims of the Negro can be achieved without subverting the constitutional rights of any criminal defendant.

Finally, it may be suggested that a jury trial will virtually assure the acquittal of these defendants because a white Mississippi jury would not hold them in contempt for flouting an order to admit a Negro to the University of Mississippi. This may be so, but it is irrelevant to the present issue. Securing convictions is not the only goal of the criminal law. The means by which convictions are obtained has a claim of equal stature. This faith remains the cornerstone of our system of criminal law.[12]

III / The power to punish contempt without a jury trial rests upon a historical error which should not be perpetuated as a constitutional principle.

The constitutionality of the power to punish contempt summarily and without trial by jury has been bottomed on the assertion that it derives from the earliest origins of the common law, antedating the adoption of the Constitution. Blackstone asserts that the power derives from "long and immemorial usage."[13] However, modern scholarship has discovered that this historical interpretation is at best dubious. In a notable series of essays, Sir John Charles Fox, Senior Master of the Chancery Division, has revealed that until the early part of the eighteenth century contempt was regarded as an ordinary proceeding attended with all of the procedural safeguards of a criminal trial. He details many instances where such cases were punished only upon indictment and after trial.[14] Fox's researches included an examination of the original rolls of the English courts, and it was his conclusion that the power to punish contempt summarily is without historical basis.[15]

Ancient historical error, in this case the fiction of "immemorial usage," should not furnish the precedent for a limitation of the right to jury trial, perhaps the most important single liberty guaranteed by the Constitution. But even assuming that the English common-law courts did possess the power to punish contempt summarily, our Constitution represented a radical departure from past practice. The founders rejected many prevalent political and legal institutions and determined upon a new experiment in democratic government. The very concept of a written constitution, alien to the English system, is reason enough for rejection of a *sub silentio* transplanting of summary punishment for contempt into American law.

Article III, section 2, of the Constitution provides: "The Trial of all Crimes, except in Cases of Impeachment, shall be by Jury. . . ." The Sixth Amendment provides: "In all criminal prosecutions, the accused shall enjoy the right to a speedy and public trial, by an impartial jury. . . ." There is no implicit exception regarding contempt anywhere in the Constitution. Can it be denied that criminal contempt, carrying as it does a fixed sentence of imprisonment, as opposed to the indeterminate sentence of civil contempt, is within the meaning of the terms "all Crimes" and "all criminal prosecutions"? This Court has rejected any semantic distinction between the crime of contempt and other crimes. For instance, it has been held that a criminal contempt is within the federal statute of limitations.[16] Similarly, it has been held that criminal contempt is an "offense against the United States" within the presidential power of pardon.[17]

This Court has often stated that the words of the Constitution are to be interpreted in their ordinary meaning:

The constitution was written to be understood by the voters; its words and phrases were used in their normal and ordinary meaning as distinguished from technical meaning; where the intention is clear there is no room for construction and no excuse for interpolation or addition.[18]

In "normal and ordinary" as distinguished from "technical" usage, there can be no difference between criminal contempt and any other crime. The Seventh Amendment, which guarantees a jury trial in all suits at common law where the amount in controversy exceeds twenty dollars, presents a *reductio ad absurdum* of a construction which asserts that the Constitution excepted criminal contempt, punishable by a definite term of imprisonment, from the right of jury trial. Surely such a strained and unwarranted interpretation, based upon erroneous history, is incompatible with constitutional principles and should be rejected by this Court.

IV / The doctrine of *stare decisis* does not impede a ruling that the Constitution bars a summary trial for criminal contempt.

Although criminal contempts have been tried summarily in the United States from the beginning, no substantial obstacle flowing from the doctrine of *stare decisis* bars this Court from returning to the correct constitutional principle.

Mr. Justice Brandeis, in a famous passage, defined the extent of the Court's obligation to adhere to prior rulings:

Stare decisis *is usually the wise policy because in most matters it is more important that the applicable rule of law be settled than that it be settled right. . . . But in cases involving the Federal Constitution, where correction through legislative action is practically impossible, this Court has often overruled its earlier decisions. The Court bows to the lessons of experience and the force of better reasoning, recognizing that the process of trial and error, so fruitful in the physical sciences, is appropriate also in the judicial function.*[19]

Bowing before "the lessons of experience and the force of better reasoning," this Court has altered long-standing rules in order to rectify its own errors even to the present day.[20]

The principles underlying *stare decisis* are particularly attenuated here. The issue presented is of constitutional dimensions and therefore is primarily for this Court. Moreover, no arguable questions of social and economic policy need be debated; as shown above, demonstrable historical error has for almost two centuries prevented defendants in criminal contempt actions from receiving the benefit of the Bill of Rights. In this setting, this Court certainly need not fear that it is exceeding its authority by acting as a "third branch of the legislature." This Court's obligation is undiluted by any of the other policies associated with *stare decisis*. In urging this result, Mr. Justice Black has stated:

> *No justified expectations would be destroyed by the course I propose. There has been no heavy investment in reliance on the earlier cases; they do not remotely lay down rules to guide men in their commercial or property affairs. Instead they concern the manner in which persons are to be tried by the Government for their alleged crimes. Certainly in this area there is no excuse for the perpetuation of past errors, particularly errors of great continuing importance with ominous potentialities.*[21]

The unbroken line of cases permitting summary trials in cases of criminal contempt are a monument to the ease with which historical error can be perpetuated, even in matters of the utmost gravity. This Court should recognize that error has been committed and that the error can be cured with no substantial infringement of the policies supporting continuity of decision. By rejecting the device of summary trial in criminal contempt actions, it will reaffirm the vitality of the "scheme of ordered liberty" that must at all costs be preserved.

In early 1964, in United States v. Barnett,[22] *the Supreme Court by a 5–4 majority reaffirmed the Green doctrine, denying Barnett and Johnson the right to a jury trial. The majority opinion suggests, however, that the judge's power to punish for criminal contempt may not be so broad as it was held to be in the Green case. In fact, the Barnett opinion, while refusing to grant a jury trial on its own facts, indicates in a footnote that in criminal contempt cases involving* severe *penalties* (Green *involved a three-year prison sentence*) *a jury trial might be required, and this was the conclusion reached by the Supreme Court in* Bloom *v.* Illinois *on May 20, 1968.*

Thus, the Barnett *opinion, rather than reaffirming settled doctrine, created a distinction that may signal a gradual decay of the* Green *doctrine, by the slow process of distinguishing rather than by the rapid device of overruling.*

NOTES

Alfred Lawrence Toombs participated in the preparation of the brief.

1. 43 *Harvard Classics* 147, 148.
2. 1 De Tocqueville, *Democracy in America* 282–83 (Reeve trans. 1948 ed.).
3. United States *ex rel.* Toth v. Quarles, 350 U.S. 11, 16 (1955).
4. Reid v. Covert, 354 U.S. 1, 10 (1957) (opinion of Black, J.).
5. *In re* Murchison, 349 U.S. 133, 136 (1955).
6. Olmstead v. United States, 277 U.S. 438, 470 (1928) (dissenting opinion).
7. 356 U.S. 165, 213 (1958).
8. Anderson v. Dunn, 6 Wheat. (19 U.S.) 204, 231 (1821). See also *In re* Michael, 326 U.S. 224, 227 (1945); *In re* Oliver, 333 U.S. 257, 274 (1948).
9. Green v. United States, 356 U.S. 165, 216 (1958) (dissenting opinion).
10. Toledo Newspaper Co. v. United States, 247 U.S. 402, 425–26 (1918) (dissenting opinion).
11. See Kasper v. Brittain, 245 F.2d 92, 97 (6th Cir.), *cert. denied,* 355 U.S. 834 (1957); Bullock v. United States, 265 F.2d 683 (6th Cir.), *cert. denied,* 360 U.S. 909, 932 (1959).
12. Mapp v. Ohio, 367 U.S. 643 (1961); Gideon v. Wainwright, 372 U.S. 335 (1963).
13. 4 Blackstone, *Commentaries,* *288.
14. Fox, "The King v. Almon," 24 *L.Q. Rev.* 184, 191; 266, 270 (1908); Fox, "Eccentricities of the Law of Contempt of Court," 36 *L.Q. Rev.* 394, 396 (1920).
15. Fox, "The Summary Process to Punish Contempt," 25 *L.Q. Rev.* 238, 242–44 (1909).

16. Gompers v. United States, 233 U.S. 604 (1914).

17. *Ex parte* Grossman, 267 U.S. 87 (1925).

18. United States v. Sprague, 282 U.S. 716, 731 (1931).

19. Burnet v. Coronado Oil & Gas Co., 285 U.S. 393, 406–8 (1932) (dissenting opinion).

20. Erie R.R. v. Tompkins, 304 U.S. 64 (1938), overruling Swift v. Tyson, 16 Pet. (41 U.S.) 1 (1842); West Virginia State Board of Education v. Barnette, 319 U.S. 624 (1943), overruling Minersville School District v. Gobitis, 310 U.S. 586 (1940); Brown v. Board of Education, 347 U.S. 483 (1954), overruling Plessy v. Ferguson, 163 U.S. 537 (1896); Mapp v. Ohio, 367 U.S. 643 (1961), overruling Wolf v. Colorado, 338 U.S. 25 (1949); Gideon v. Wainwright, 372 U.S. 335 (1963), overruling Betts v. Brady, 316 U.S. 455 (1942), are only a few of the many cases in which this Court has revised constitutional decisions of the first magnitude.

21. Green v. United States, 356 U.S. 165, 197 (1958).

22. 376 U.S. 681 (1964).

16

Trial by Television

Nearly all American jurisdictions, as well as the American Bar Association in rule 35 of its Canons of Judicial Ethics, condemn the televising or broadcasting of court proceedings. Texas, however, does not prohibit such practices, but merely relegates the question of television coverage to the discretion of the trial judge. The Texas rule recently provided the Supreme Court with its first opportunity to decide on the propriety of television in the courtroom. The issue reached the Court as a result of the trial and conviction of Billie Sol Estes for swindling. Prior to the commencement of Estes' trial, the trial judge, over the defendant's objection, authorized live television coverage of the proceedings.

The Estes case required the Court to resolve an apparent conflict between basic constitutional rights. Freedom of the press, traditionally placed in a "preferred position" relative to other constitutional rights, logically includes a right of access to information. One might therefore conclude that this right of access should be applied to permit communications media to broadcast from the courtroom. Equally basic to our constitutional system, however, is the notion that every defendant is entitled to a fair and impartial trial, one in which the verdict is based on the evidence introduced in the courtroom rather than the prejudice of the community. Another relevant constitutional principle is the ambiguous right to a "public" trial embodied in the Sixth Amendment. May a defendant waive this right, thereby denying the public access to the proceedings, or does the public have a right to a public trial, to ensure, through its scrutiny, the proper administration of justice? If the public has such a right, must it be exercised by physical presence in the courtroom, or can the public assert its right through a demand for live television coverage?

The ACLU took the position that a televised trial is inherently prejudicial and therefore deprives a defendant of his due process right to a fair trial. Excerpts from the ACLU brief, which was prepared by the author, appear below. With respect to the techniques of constitutional litigation, the Estes brief illustrates two significant and recurring problems.

The first, alluded to above, is the problem of defining constitutional rights so precisely as to prevent apparent conflict from becoming actual conflict. The second, which was of crucial significance in Estes, is how one demonstrates that a particular set of circumstances is "inherently prejudicial." This type of argument should be distinguished from an argument that there has been actual prejudice in a given case, the goal of the latter being merely to show that the given defendant was prejudiced by the peculiar circumstances of his case. The argument based on inherent prejudice seeks to establish that the challenged circumstances are necessarily prejudicial and therefore must be prohibited under an absolute constitutional rule. In Estes, therefore, it was necessary to demonstrate that television coverage would always produce a dangerous probability of prejudice. To sustain this burden, the author thought it essential to analyze thoroughly the ways in which the various parties to a criminal case—judge, jurors, witnesses, attorneys and defendant—might be affected by the presence of television.

Introduction

Strict compliance with the basic elements of a fair trial is essential to due process. Indeed, as Mr. Justice Black stated in *In re Murchi-*

son,[1] "our system of law has always endeavored to prevent even the *probability* of unfairness."

This insistence upon a fair trial was reaffirmed in a recent series of cases revealing the Court's deep concern with the inherently prejudicial effects of widespread news publicity on the outcome of a trial. In *Rideau v. Louisiana*,[2] the defendant's out-of-court "confession" had been telecast three times to the community in which he was tried. The Court reversed the conviction without reviewing the *voir dire* examination of the jurors, holding that "any subsequent court proceedings in a community so pervasively exposed to such a spectacle could be but a hollow formality."[3] *Rideau* thus departed from the approach of the earlier cases of *Stroble v. California*,[4] and *Irvin v. Dowd*,[5] where the Court carefully examined the record to determine whether the pretrial newspaper releases had in fact influenced the outcome of the trial, so finding in *Irvin* but not in *Stroble*. In *Rideau* it was properly recognized that prejudice was inherent in the widespread nature of the television publicity.

In this case it is even clearer that a fair trial was out of the question because the extensive live telecasting impeded a purposive, solemn search for the truth and injected into petitioner's trial matter not properly before the court. Its effect was far more subtle and insidious than that involved in the earlier cases. For here the publicity was felt at the time of maximum sensitivity, during the trial itself, and was far more pervasive, since not limited to particular prejudicial items.

Moreover, the earlier cases dealt with the significantly different problem of pretrial publicity *outside* the control of the court. Because such publicity is inevitable and cannot be effectively curtailed by the court short of holding the news media in contempt, the efficient administration of justice demands that a petitioner demonstrate with some certainty that the publicity affected the outcome of the trial. But where a court can eliminate this substantial threat to a fair trial simply by barring telecasting of the proceedings, it is unconscionable for a defendant to be exposed to such intensive publicity.

The federal courts have adopted the policy of canon 35 of the American Bar Association and absolutely barred television from the courtroom, and most states have arrived at a similar conclusion. These decisions reflect a mature awareness that a telecast trial cannot be fair. The Court should now apply the due process clause of the Fourteenth Amendment to invalidate all convictions obtained in the inherently prejudicial atmosphere created by television.

I / The presence of television in the courtroom created an atmosphere that made it impossible to conduct a fair trial.

In allowing the proceedings to be televised, the trial judge lost sight of the admonition that "a courtroom is a place for ascertaining the truth in controversies among men, and has no other legitimate function."[6] The record makes clear that the presence of television diverted the participants from their sole function of presenting, weighing and passing upon the evidence pertaining to petitioner's guilt or innocence.

The New York Times described the courtroom on the opening day of trial:

> *A television motor van, big as an intercontinental bus, was parked outside the courthouse and the second floor courtroom was a forest of equipment. Two television cameras had been set up inside the bar and four marked cameras were aligned just outside the gates.*
>
> *A microphone stuck its 12 inch snout inside the jury box, now occupied by an overflow of reporters from the press table, and three microphones confronted Judge Dunagan on his bench. Cables and wires snaked over the floor.*[7]

There is plainly nothing to the argument that telecasting techniques are so far perfected that coverage of a trial can go unnoticed.

Both petitioner, who arrived in court the first day of the proceedings, and the jurors, who were sworn in the second day, were exposed to this chaos in the courtroom. Although conditions were substantially improved when the hearing resumed on October 22, the point had already been driven home that the proceedings would be on the air. For the following reasons the net effect was to interfere completely with the sober search for truth that characterizes a fair trial.

1. The trial judge was forced to devote an unduly large portion of his time and attention to keeping the situation within manageable bounds. Accordingly, he announced no less than ten separate rulings on television coverage during the trial. Many of these determinations were quite extensive, occupying over a full page in the record, and were of considerable difficulty. The judge's rulings are the best testimonial to the demands imposed on him: no newsmen behind the bar, control camera noise, no photographing on second floor, officers to enforce these orders, identifying badges to be carried but not worn, "working area" off bounds to television personnel, remove cameras to booth, no flashbulbs or floods, no cameras in anteroom, cease sound coverage, no tape of interrogation of jury or taking of testimony, no photographing of defendant's attorneys.

2. Television in the courtroom makes difficult, if not impossible, an effective presentation of evidence. Not only is the paraphernalia in the courtroom bound to divert the witness, but the prospect of a vast audience observing him is likely to heighten his discomfort. These factors convinced one court not to hold in contempt a witness who refused to appear before televised hearings of the Kefauver committee: "The concentration of all these elements seems . . . necessarily so to disturb and distract any witness to the point that he might say today something that next week he will realize was erroneous."[8]

Some witnesses may be deterred from giving a complete presentation of testimony by the fear of embarrassment by widespread telecasting of their statements.[9] Others may allow their theatrical flair to come to the fore and "ham it up" for the television viewers. The argument often made in support of television coverage of trials, that there is no way of determining just what effect the camera will have on a particular witness,[10] merely reinforces the need to bar all television from the courtroom.

The television camera may inhibit testimony which offends prevailing public sentiment. Consider, for example, the reluctance of a witness in a case involving an explosive racial issue to testify for the "wrong" side before an entire community of television viewers. Indeed, in the present case a considerable amount of public opinion had already formed that could affect the testimony of a less than courageous witness. For similar reasons, this Court has always been careful to insulate judicial trials from the pressure of public opinion.[11]

3. If the defendant takes the stand, the unnecessary added burden of exposure to a television audience will undoubtedly affect his testimony adversely. Even if he does not take the stand, he is in constant view of the jurors, who may take his discomfort for an indication of guilt rather than the result of inordinate publicity.

It is essential to the fair conduct of a trial that the participants approach their tasks with an appreciation of the serious and important nature of the hearing. The dignity and austerity of the courtroom and the solemnity of the proceedings should drive this home to them. In a "circus atmosphere" this is impossible.

During the trial petitioner's attorney protested to the judge:

> *. . . this courtroom doesn't look like a courtroom to me; it looks like a moving picture theater . . . and this trial has assumed to me a character of proceedings to entertain and instruct the public. . . . The cameras . . . shine out of the booth just as cameras do at a moving picture show. . . . It is like the defendants of Perry Mason's.*

Mr. Justice Douglas has been a severe critic of televised trials from this perspective: "The trial is as much of a spectacle as if it were held in the Yankee Stadium or the Roman Coliseum. When televised, it is held in every home across the land. No civilization has ever witnessed such a spectacle."[12]

This loss of dignity may not only affect the outcome of the trial; it also goes against "deep-rooted feelings" expressed by this Court that elementary standards of decency and civilization must attend all criminal proceedings.[13]

II / Television coverage of the trial denied petitioner due process of law because the jury could not render a verdict based solely upon the evidence introduced at the trial.

Mr. Justice Holmes stated that "the theory of our [judicial] system is that the conclusions to be reached in a case will be induced only by evidence and argument in open court, and not by any outside influence, whether of private talk or public print."[14] This admonition becomes meaningless when a trial is allowed to be televised.

It is difficult to believe that some jurors will not turn on their television sets when they return home from the trial, in spite of the judge's instruction, if only to see how they appeared on the screen. Since the telecast will be edited to fit a limited time period, it is likely that the portions of the trial replayed will be those of the greatest audience interest. This distortion of the evidence, based on commercial considerations, serves to emphasize in the juror's mind selected portions of the case, and the impact of the television evidence accordingly will be greater than that of testimony observed at the trial. This danger of distortion cannot be risked if the defendant is to have a fair trial.

Further, evidence may be ruled inadmissible at the trial without any assurance that the television director will follow the judge's order to "disregard the testimony." Similarly, there is no guarantee that bench conferences, supposedly outside the jury's hearing, will not reach the juror at his home. Again, preliminary examinations held on an issue such as the voluntariness of a confession may be witnessed improperly by the jurors via television.

In order to prevent such situations, a judge could perhaps exercise control over television content, but this would saddle him with one more distraction from the main job of conducting the trial. There is no feasible way (short of locking up the jury, which is impractical in a trial of any length) of ensuring that the jurors will not watch television, nor is it likely that a juror would admit that he violated the judge's admonition.

Because television coverage generates added interest in a trial and identifies the participants, members of the jury may be approached by friends and strangers who want to volunteer evidence or just talk the issues over. It has been recognized, however, in federal trials at least, that receipt of otherwise inadmissible extraneous evidence from third persons can result in a mistrial.[15]

If a prevailing community attitude, fanned by television publicity, is sensed by the jurors, they may be reluctant to hand down a verdict contrary to public opinion. A juror need only recall the nationwide television coverage of the polling of the jurors in the Jack Ruby trial to be deterred from rendering what he believes to be a just verdict.

Questioning individual jurors as to whether they have been influenced by public opinion would not necessarily prevent this evil. First, a juror might be reluctant, in the face of strong public sentiment, to be the cause of a mistrial by such a declaration. Second, it is not at all clear that the juror is consciously aware of the pressures that bear upon his verdict:

> *One cannot assume that the average juror is so endowed with a sense of attachment, so clear in his introspective perception of his own mental processes, that he may confidently exclude even the unconscious influence of his preconceptions as to probable guilt, engendered by a pervasive pretrial publicity.*[16]

III / Television coverage of the trial denied petitioner the right to effective counsel.

In order to protect their client's right to be free from the interference of the television camera, petitioner's attorneys were forced to divert their attention from the merits of the case. They made eight separate and often elaborate motions to eliminate or limit television coverage.

Early in the trial Estes' attorney protested to the judge that "motion pictures and the grinding of cameras while I am interrogating or cross-examining witnesses makes it almost impossible for me to give my attention to the case and to properly represent my client."

A television technician admitted on examination that one of the cameras was positioned so that an accurate picture could be taken of all papers and documents on the counsel table, as well as of the actions of defendant and his attorney. The possibility of a microphone picking up conferences at the table was also conceded.

In spite of the judge's attempt at corrective measures, the petitioner's attorney was faced with a moral dilemma in conducting the trial:

To me it is highly distasteful to be forced to defend a man in a criminal case where cameras are trained on me during the trial or any part of the trial. I believe sincerely in Canon 35 of the American Bar Association which prohibits photography or cameras in the court room.

Telecasting not only hinders attorneys in the conduct of the case, but raises serious possibilities of unethical conduct. As a leading commentator has pointed out:[17]

The bar has always been regarded as the nursery of political careers. The temptation offered to the elected prosecutor by television coverage is a great one. . . . his conduct in the televised trial may be dictated by what the public thinks he should do rather than what he knows is proper. The defense counsel who appreciates that the interests of his client require that he lay back and avoid forensics may be affected by the fact that television viewers who do not understand his strategy may never seek his services.

In the face of these obstacles to effective representation, it is difficult to see how televised trials comport with the demands of due process.

IV / Exclusion of television from the courtroom does not conflict with other constitutionally protected interests.

Neither the freedom of communication assured by the First Amendment nor the right to a public trial guaranteed by the Sixth Amendment offers any protection to televised trials. First, this Court "has not yet decided that the fair administration of criminal justice must be subordinated to another safeguard of our constitutional system—freedom of the press."[18] Second, the right to a public trial is not infringed by the mere exclusion of technical equipment from the courtroom; the general public, including press and television personnel, is free to attend. This is all that the Sixth Amendment requires.[19]

It has been argued, however, that a decision to bar television from the courtroom will curtail freedom of communication because television educates the public and guards against abuses of the judicial process.[20] But the press serves both these purposes and does so without the impediments to a fair trial necessarily associated with live telecasts.

Most abuses of the judicial process, such as illegal searches, coerced confession and deprivation of counsel, take place before trial, and television coverage would have no effect on them. At the trial itself, the court, counsel and the press ensure a fair hearing to both sides. The presence of television personnel and a home audience could hardly provide further safeguards; indeed, only those trials which are heavily attended and carefully observed would receive television publicity.

Press coverage, it should be pointed out, presents none of the threats of televised trials. The physical presence of newsmen cannot affect the course of the proceedings, as must a battery of television equipment. Nor does a newspaper have the deep psychological effect that television has on a juror who sees a telecast afterwards.[21] The abuses of press coverage generally arise before the trial and can be corrected by inquiry on the *voir dire,* a change of venue or a postponement of the trial. The effects are not as severe since, unlike those of the telecast, they are not felt during the trial, the time of greatest sensitivity. And since press coverage is generally not as pervasive as a network telecast, there is not nearly the same risk that it will taint a new trial if one should become necessary.

In Estes v. Texas,[22] *the Supreme Court, by a 5–4 majority, decided in early 1965 that Estes had been denied a fair trial because of the presence of television in the courtroom. The decision, however, fails to resolve the question whether television coverage of a trial is in-*

herently prejudicial. Four justices, in two opinions containing many of the arguments from the author's brief, expressed the view that television coverage is inherently prejudicial. The four dissenting justices, however, would not reverse absent actual prejudice, which they did not find. Justice Harlan, who cast the deciding vote, agreed that television should be barred from the trial of one so notorious as Estes, but suggested that "non-notorious" cases might be treated differently.

Although the Court has not yet had another opportunity to rule on the television issue, it did confront the publicity problem again in the celebrated Sheppard murder case.[23] The Court once again found a "probability of prejudice," and clarified the underlying principle of Estes, at least to the extent where it seems clear that a trial judge has the duty to prevent prejudicial publicity where he can do so through his inherent powers to control the conduct of the trial. In Sheppard, the Court, by an 8–1 decision, held that the trial judge should have prevented the creation of a "carnival atmosphere" in the courtroom by members of the press, should have insulated witnesses and jurors from the press, and should have controlled disclosure of information to the press by witnesses and counsel during the course of the trial.

Thus, given the Estes and Sheppard cases, the law is hardly settled beyond the single rule stated above. Aside from the problem of television in "non-notorious" cases, it is unclear what standard is to be applied by the trial judge in a given case. Under Sheppard, the judge must exercise control when he finds a dangerous probability of prejudice. If he exercises this control when the facts do not warrant it, however, it is likely that he will infringe the other constitutional rights mentioned earlier. It seems certain that the Supreme Court will be called upon to offer further guidance to these trial judges in order to ensure protection of the rights of the press, the public and the defendant.

NOTES

Civil Liberties Fellows Robert J. Rabin and Lawrence D. Ross participated in the preparation of the brief.

1. 349 U.S. 133, 136 (1955).
2. 373 U.S. 723 (1963).
3. *Id.* at 726.
4. 343 U.S. 181 (1952).
5. 366 U.S. 717 (1961).
6. Griswold, "The Standards of the Legal Profession: Canon 35 Should Not Be Surrendered," 48 *A.B.A.J.* 615 (1962).
7. *N.Y. Times,* Sept. 25, 1962.
8. United States v. Kleinman, 107 F. Supp. 407, 408 (1952).
9. See Pye, "The Lessons of Dallas—Threats to Fair Trial and Free Press," in National Civil Liberties Clearing House, Report of the 16th Annual Conference, March 19–20, 1964, p. 11.
10. See, e.g., Wiggins, "Should Canon 35 Be Amended? A Newspaperman Speaks for the News Media," 42 *A.B.A.J.* 838, 841, 842 (1956).
11. See Frank v. Mangum, 237 U.S. 309 (1915); Moore v. Dempsey, 261 U.S. 86 (1923); Shepherd v. Florida, 341 U.S. 50 (1951) (concurring opinion).
12. Douglas, "The Public Trial and the Free Press," 33 *Rocky Mt. L. Rev.* 1, 5 (1960).
13. See Jackson v. Denno, 378 U.S. 369, 385, 386 (1964); Spano v. New York, 360 U.S. 315, 320, 321 (1959); Rochin v. California, 342 U.S. 165, 172, 173 (1952).
14. Patterson v. Colorado, 205 U.S. 454, 462 (1907). See also Irvin v. Dowd, 366 U.S. 717, 722 (1961).
15. Coppedge v. United States, 272 F.2d 504, 508 (D.C. Cir. 1959).
16. Delaney v. United States, 199 F.2d 107, 112–13 (1st Cir. 1952) (Magruder, C.J.).
17. Pye, *supra* note 9 at 11.
18. Irvin v. Dowd, 366 U.S. 717, 729 (1961) (concurring opinion).
19. See Radin, "The Right to a Public Trial," 4 *Temp. L.Q.* 381, 391 (1932); 1 Cooley, *Constitutional Limitations* 647 (8th ed. 1927).
20. See, e.g., Monroe, Remarks, Conference of the National Civil Liberties Clearing House, Washington, D.C., March 20, 1964. Wiggins, *supra* note 10 at 839.
21. See Committee on Civil Rights, New York County Lawyers Association, *Television and the Accused* 3.
22. 381 U.S. 532 (1965).
23. Sheppard v. Maxwell, 384 U.S. 333 (1966).

17

Official Intrusions on Private Property

The rapid urbanization, industrialization and population expansion of the twentieth century have caused a proliferation of municipal codes aimed at preventing urban decay and protecting the public from health, fire and safety hazards. Few would argue with the purposes of these laws; but many have voiced strong objection to the potentially destructive effect which unchecked modes of enforcement may have on the individual's right of privacy. This is a problem that affects the owner and even the occupants of every building in the United States.

In 1959, in the case of Frank v. Maryland,[1] the Supreme Court upheld the constitutionality of a city ordinance which permitted searches of dwellings without a search warrant if there was cause to suspect the existence of a danger to public health. According to the majority, the Fourth Amendment protected the homeowner only against searches for evidence of crime and not against searches for evidence of health, fire or other civil violations.

In 1966, the Supreme Court agreed to review two cases which presented once again the issues decided in Frank. One of these involved a health inspector who sought entry without a search warrant although he had no evidence of a violation or a danger to *health. The other case,* See v. Seattle, *involved an owner of a private commercial building who was convicted for refusing to permit fire officials on a routine inspection to enter because they lacked a warrant. When the case was set down for review by the Supreme Court, the ACLU requested the author to prepare the brief, segments of which appear below, to support the proposition that* Frank v. Maryland *should be overruled, or at least limited to its particular facts.*

I / Frank v. Maryland is distinguishable.

In *Frank v. Maryland,* the Court by a 5–4 vote sustained the constitutionality of a city ordinance which authorized daylight inspection of buildings and premises, without a warrant, by health department officers who had cause to suspect the existence of a nuisance that was a hazard to health.

Not only was probable cause explicitly required by the ordinance, it was clearly present in the case. A health department officer's inspection, made pursuant to a complaint concerning the presence of rats in the area, revealed that Frank's house was in an "extreme state of decay" and that a substantial amount of rodent feces and debris had collected in the rear of the house.

Mr. Justice Frankfurter, speaking for the Court, said:

> *The power of inspection granted by the Baltimore City Code is strictly limited, more exacting than the analogous provisions of many other municipal codes.* Valid grounds for suspicion of the existence of a nuisance must exist. Certainly the presence of a pile of filth in the back yard combined with the run-down condition of the house gave adequate grounds for such suspicion.[2]

The Seattle ordinance is devoid of any of the safeguards which the *Frank* Court found so significant. It dispenses with the need for even a mere suspicion of the existence of an unwholesome or dangerous condition and establishes no restrictions as to place or duration of search. Presumably no room, alcove, closet or drawer is free from inspection. In addition, it authorizes searches to be conducted at any time, and as often as may be said to be necessary. An ordinance could scarcely be broader, or more susceptible to abuse of discretion.

If allowed to stand, the Seattle ordinance and thousands like it across the country open the door to unreasonable, arbitrary or politically motivated searches. As Mr. Justice Brennan remarked in *Eaton v. Price:*

> *It hardly contradicts experience to suggest that the practical administration of local government in this country can be infected with such [political and personal] motives. Building inspection ordinances can lend themselves to such abuse. We do not at all say this to be the case here . . . but that simply points up the issue.*[3]

Nor is it only the ordinance which distinguishes this case from *Frank*. The relevant facts here differ markedly as well. The Frank house was in a disreputable condition; appellant's premises evinced no suspicion of danger. Rats infested the Frank neighborhood; apparently no fire hazards were discernible in the area contiguous to appellant's warehouse. In short, while probable cause existed in *Frank*, the instant search was neither part of a routinized, regular inspection nor was it made pursuant to even a suspicion or complaint of a proscribed condition.

In light of the substantial distinctions between *Frank* and the instant case, *Frank* cannot be considered as controlling on this appeal.

II / The Court below applied an erroneous standard of reasonableness to searches of commercial premises.

The reliance of the Supreme Court of Washington upon the distinction between searches in dwellings as contrasted with commercial premises is wholly misplaced.

In finding the inspection authorized by the Washington ordinance to be within constitutional limits, the Court below stated in *Davis v. United States:* "The United States Supreme Court has applied different standards of reasonableness to searches of dwellings than to places of business."[4]

This statement is without foundation. In the first place, *Davis* turned not on the purported distinction between the nature of commercial premises and dwelling places, but on the fact that the case dealt "not with *private* papers or documents but with *public* property in the custody of a citizen."[5] The other factors stressed by the Court were the "public character of the property, the fact that the demand was made during business hours at the place of business where the coupons were required to be kept . . . the fact that the initial refusal to turn the coupons over was soon followed by acquiescence in the demand," and the "ocular evidence that a misdemeanor had been committed."[6] The case at bar is plainly distinguishable from *Davis* by the absence of these controlling factors.

Secondly, as the dissenting opinion in the case recognized, it would "constitute a sudden and drastic break with the whole history of the Fourth Amendment and its application by this Court" if the decision were to be construed as suggesting that the Fourth Amendment protects homes and not places of business. Finally, to interpret *Davis* as did the Court below is to ignore the essential purpose of the constitutional protection. The Fourth Amendment was designed to protect private papers and personal effects which may be found as readily on business premises as in a home or on the person. Therefore, the premises here should stand in the same constitutional posture as any other private place where such personal effects could reasonably be stored. It has been recognized that these premises are within the purview of Fourth Amendment protections: in *Lanza v. New York*,[7] it was stated that a "business office is a protected area, and so may be a store."

III / A search conducted without probable cause is unreasonable and violative of the Fourth Amendment.

No case has been found in which this Court sanctioned a search, whether labeled "criminal" or "civil," under circumstances evidencing no probable cause for its undertaking. Likewise, the Court has never upheld a law such as the Seattle ordinance, which permits searches without a prior demonstration of probable cause. For the Court to sanction this major step beyond *Frank* would "reduce the protection of the householder 'against unreasonable searches' to the vanishing point."[8]

Probable cause is specifically required by the second clause of the Fourth Amendment. Exceptions which have been grafted on that amendment in regard to the requirement of search warrants are strictly limited. None sanctions or contemplates action without probable cause. Thus a search and seizure may be effected without a warrant if incident to a legal arrest,[9] if an officer has reasonable or probable cause to believe that an automobile which he has stopped contains contraband,[10] or if the exigencies of a particular situation compel immediate action.[11] These exceptional circumstances, by hypothesis, imply a strong element of probable cause.

The constitutional protections against unreasonable searches have their origin and justification in the preservation of the sanctity of one's premises and the privacy of one's personal effects. This proposition has long been recognized.

> *It is not the breaking of his doors, and the rummaging of his drawers, that constitutes the essence of the offence; but it is the invasion of his indefeasible right of personal security, personal liberty and private property. . . .*[12]

To be sure, the *Boyd, Go-Bart, Johnson, McDonald, Carroll* and *Rabinowitz* cases involved "criminal" searches. Even assuming that the validity of the decision in *Frank* that a warrant is not needed in "civil" searches, there is no basis in that case or in principle to vitiate the requirement of probable cause. This is not to say that the standards which must be met in establishing probable cause must necessarily be identical for "criminal" and "administrative" searches. What is necessary, however, is some degree of factual need for the search. Constitutional precedent and the preservation of privacy mandate this conclusion.

Health, housing and fire inspectors are not all benign, forbearing public servants. They too can be corrupt and arbitrary. The potential for abuse of discretion, by those who are not dedicated public servants, is enormous. Moreover, as Judge Prettyman noted in *District of Columbia v. Little,*[13] "the constitutional guarantee [of personal privacy] is not restricted to unimportant statutes and regulations or to malevolent or arrogant agents." And in his historic dissent in *Olmstead v. United States*, Justice Brandeis cautioned:

> *Experience should teach us to be most on our guard to protect liberty when the Government's purposes are beneficent. Men born to freedom are naturally alert to repel invasion of their liberty by evil-minded rulers. The greatest dangers to liberty lurk in insidious encroachment by men of zeal, well-meaning but without understanding.*[14]

IV / *Frank v. Maryland* was incorrectly decided and should be overruled.

The decision in *Frank v. Maryland* is based upon an artificial division of the Fourth Amendment into the right of privacy and the right of self-protection. Although both are barriers against unreasonable searches and seizures, *Frank* finds that only the latter, concerned with criminal and forfeiture proceedings exclusively, requires issuance of a warrant.

This artificial distinction and resulting limitation upon the necessity for a search warrant is based on a misunderstanding of the history of the Fourth Amendment, including the old English case of *Entick v. Carrington.*[15]

The Fourth Amendment has its roots in the hostility to the arbitrary government intrusions associated with the infamous general warrants and writs of assistance which, as pointed out in the Court's opinion in *Frank*, were generally aimed at the seizure of criminal evidence, and toward forfeitures. But they were not so limited. They had other—"civil"—uses such as the collection of debts and the granting of preferences between creditors.

Surely a fire inspection which has as its object that persons inspected conform their premises to certain norms, the failure of which can result in criminal penalties, is an application of "the coercive power of the state against the individual." Equally, if a violation is revealed and not remedied, the initial inspection has resulted in "information which may be used to effect a further deprivation of life or liberty or property."

The view that privacy from government intrusion of any kind, either criminal or civil, is at the crux of the matter is further supported by the fact that these general warrants were often used to penalize so-called seditious libel and to suppress freedom of the press.[16] Thus searches and seizures were, and continue to be, intimately related to freedom of expression. *Entick v. Carrington* itself arose out of a search for evidence of seditious libel. It was this to which Mr. Justice Douglas referred when he said, dissenting in *Frank*, that "The Court misreads history when it relates the Fourth Amendment primarily to searches for evidence to be used in criminal prosecutions," and that "the Fourth Amendment thus has a much wider frame of reference than mere criminal prosecutions." The roots of the Fourth Amendment go far deeper than the Court acknowledged in *Frank*.

Once the history of the Fourth Amendment is seen to reflect a major concern for freedom of expression and human dignity, it becomes evident that the motivating force behind the Fourth Amendment was not merely the fear of the arbitrary search for criminal evidence but the general animosity toward governmental intrusions of any kind.

This Court, in cases subsequent to *Frank*, has enlarged the concept of privacy both in the Fourth Amendment area and as a general constitutional right. The emphasis in Fourth Amendment cases is not merely on "privacy" but on its expanded concept, a concept in accord with concerns broader than, though sometimes couched in terms of, abhorrence of the search for criminal evidence. As indicated earlier, *Stanford v. Texas*[17] spoke in terms of "human dignity." In *Silverman v. United States*,[18] the Court said, "The Fourth Amendment, and the personal rights which it secures, have a long history. At the very core stands the right of a man to retreat into his own home and there be free from unreasonable governmental intrusion." Again, in *Schmerber v. California*,[19] the Court said, "The overriding function of the Fourth Amendment is to protect personal privacy and dignity against unwarranted intrusion by the State." Surely these sentiments give "privacy" a far more important place in the scheme of the Fourth Amendment than acknowledged by the majority opinion in *Frank*. And in *Griswold v. Connecticut*,[20] privacy was elevated to the status of a self-contained right not dependent upon any single clause or amendment in the Constitution, but rather on a "penumbra" of freedoms and rights surrounding various amendments to the Constitution.

V / Administrative procedures are available which will protect the right of privacy without unduly restricting the power of inspection.

A. If this Court accepts appellee's insistence that private property must be subject to inspection on the mere say-so of an official, an important facet of the right to privacy will be abrogated just at a time when the important personal and social values it protects have been subject to redefinition and expansion by this Court. This is not to deny the obvious need for administrative power of inspection and enforcement in an increasingly urbanized society. Rather it is to assert that this power of inspection is not an absolute, but is qualified by individual rights protected by the Constitution, and that it cannot be permitted to vitiate the individual's interest in the sanctity of his private premises. In short, if an inspector—or a person claiming to be an inspector—automatically can gain entry to private property over the objection of the owner, privacy is reduced to the vanishing point and the right to be free from "unreasonable searches" is read out of the Fourth Amendment.

Consider this very case. There is nothing to show that the inspection was for the purpose of fire prevention, that it was part of a spot check or an area search of general applicability, and certainly nothing to show that appellant's property posed a fire risk. Indeed, there may have been no valid motive whatever for the inspection. Appellee made no effort to demonstrate the reasonableness of the search conducted in this case. In fact, it concedes that "no facts are in the record before this Court to indicate whether the public officials were reasonable in their approach." In effect, appellee asserts an absolute right to search appellant's premises at any time, "as often as may be necessary" in the judgment of the searching officials.

The ordinance from which appellee derives its claim of right to search contains no limitations on the time or frequency of searches, and it specifically authorizes a search for the purpose, *inter alia,* of uncovering evidence of violation of the ordinances of the city. The prevention of general exploratory searches for evidence of crimes is of course the central purpose of the Fourth Amendment.[21]

The essence of appellant's claim is that there must be *some* recognition of Fourth Amendment limitations and the right of privacy in the administration of fire prevention programs. There must be *some* judicial barrier to the exercise of unchecked discretion by administrative officials seeking to gain admission to private premises. There must be *some* rational means of assuring the private citizen that his property is being opened as part of a rational inquiry of authorized representatives of local government and not for frivolous or even venal motives of inspectors or impostors. And as pointed out in the opinion of Mr. Justice Brennan in *Eaton v. Price,* the time for an official seeking entry to make an independent justification is not in a criminal proceeding—by which time the individual has acted at his peril—but in advance of prosecution before a magistrate empowered to issue warrants. This is the practice in England, and it reflects an approach that will protect the right of privacy without stultifying regulation of the public health and safety.

B. Appellee has made numerous references to the supposed dire consequences that will follow reversal of the decision below. For example, appellee states: "The upholding of Appellant's claim means the complete nullification of Seattle's fire prevention program as to Appellant's warehouse. Under the stipulated facts no Fourth Amendment warrant can issue. Thus no inspection can be made."

This incendiary claim is without substance. In the first place, available empirical data reveals that very few persons object to official searches.[22] Thus the requirement of a warrant in a rare instance can hardly be said to be disruptive of the administrative program. The enforcement of health and safety codes will not be frustrated. Where considerations of health and safety are involved, there will surely be a different standard of "probable cause" than in the case of criminal investigations. The two situations are simply not comparable, and should be distinguished for constitutional purposes, particularly in view of the fact that the Constitution, by prohibiting "*unreasonable* searches and seizures" (emphasis added), rejects a mechanical approach indiscriminately applying the concept of probable cause.

Accordingly, a program of area-by-area searches, spot checks or periodic inspections can be justified without requiring proof of the probable existence of illegal or dangerous conditions.[23] Certainly, if there is such proof, or especially an emergency warranting immediate action, a search can properly be made. "The test of 'probable cause' required by the Fourth Amendment can take into account the nature of the search that is being sought." The critical constitutional requirement is that an unwilling door should not be opened without a showing of some valid administrative need and some regulation of the time and manner of the search. This is a far cry from justifying the conclusion, which permeates appellee's brief, that probable cause will be inflexibly adopted from the different setting of the criminal law.

A sensible application of the Fourth Amendment along the lines suggested above should dispose of any fears that tragedy will inevitably follow if this Court provides some procedural protection for the individual right to privacy. Considerations of administrative convenience have never proved the definitive test of a reasonable search under the Fourth Amendment. It is always more convenient for administrative officials to proceed *ex parte*, without having to justify their actions before a neutral and detached official. Frequently, there have been attempts to limit constitutional rights on these grounds, and just as frequently these have been rejected.[24]

Similarly, it is surely off the mark to claim, as does the appellee here, that an administrative search is "aimed at the saving of life and property" and that the criteria for determining the propriety of such searches "are matters for administrative judgment and such inquiries are not peculiarly judicial in nature." These contentions have forcibly been rejected, again and again, with respect to the criminal law. And certainly it is indefensible to suggest that somehow the Constitution is less solicitous of privacy when the purpose of the search is "administrative." The terse language of Chief Judge Prettyman in *District of Columbia v. Little*,[25] puts the matter in proper perspective:

To say that a man suspected of crime has a right to protection against search of his home without a warrant, but that a man not suspected of crime has no such protection, is a fantastic absurdity.

On June 5, 1967, the United States Supreme Court, in the related cases of Camara v. Municipal Court of San Francisco[26] and See v. Seattle,[27] overruled Frank v. Maryland in holding that property owners and occupants may refuse, except in emergency cases, to admit health, fire or other inspectors onto their premises unless they have search warrants.

In Camara, the Court adopted the suggestion included in the See brief that the "probable cause" requirement upon which a warrant may issue could be satisfied by showing that the premises had not been inspected in a certain number of years, or that the buildings in the area are old, or that the neighborhood is run-down. In See this new rule was extended to cover private commercial premises as well as private dwellings and residences. While the opinions provide a measure of protection to privacy, they do not clearly state that individuals may present their reasons for resisting a search to the magistrate empowered to issue the warrant. This right to a hearing is essential to safeguard the interests of owners and occupiers of property.

These decisions have significant implications outside their immediate province. For example, for many years state and local welfare departments used "midnight raids" on the homes of female welfare recipients to discover whether a man was sleeping with the woman. If he was, welfare payments would be cut off on the ground that "a man in the house" means that the woman is receiving support and needs no public assistance. The extraordinary intrusions on privacy that these midnight raids represented were widely criticized, and the California Supreme Court eventually held in early 1967 that they violated the Constitution. The decisions in the Camara and See cases lend powerful support to this conclusion, and when the welfare cases eventually reach the Supreme Court it is likely that warrantless midnight searches will be held invalid.

NOTES

Melvin L. Wulf, Paul D. Jackson, and Civil Liberties Fellows Michael D. Kaufman and David Rudovsky participated in the preparation of the brief.

1. 359 U.S. 360 (1959).
2. *Id.* at 366. Emphasis added.
3. 364 U.S. 263, 271 (1960) (dissenting opinion).
4. 328 U.S. 582 (1946).
5. *Id.* at 589. Emphasis in original. See also *id.* at 587–91.
6. *Id.* at 592–93.
7. 370 U.S. 139, 143 (1962).
8. Eaton v. Price, 364 U.S. at 269.
9. United States v. Rabinowitz, 339 U.S. 56 (1950).
10. Carroll v. United States, 267 U.S. 132 (1925).
11. See McDonald v. United States, 335 U.S. 451 (1948); Johnson v. United States, 333 U.S. 10 (1948).
12. Boyd v. United States, 116 U.S. 616, 630 (1886).
13. 178 F.2d 13, 17 (D.C. Cir. 1949), *aff'd on other grounds,* 339 U.S. 1 (1950).
14. 277 U.S. 438, 479 (1928).
15. 19 Howell, *State Trials,* col. 1029 (1765).
16. See Lasson, *The History and Development of the Fourth Amendment to the United States Constitution,* in The Johns Hopkins University Studies in Historical and Political Science, Ser. 55, No. 2 (1937); Boyd v. United States, 116 U.S. 616 (1886); Marcus v. Search Warrant, 367 U.S. 717 (1961); Stanford v. Texas, 379 U.S. 476, 482–85 (1965).
17. 379 U.S. 476 (1965).
18. 365 U.S. 505, 511 (1961).
19. 384 U.S. 757, 767 (1966).
20. 381 U.S. 479 (1965).
21. See, e.g., Go-Bart Importing Co. v. United States, 282 U.S. 344 (1931).
22. Frank v. Maryland, 359 U.S. at 372, 383–84.
23. Cf. Frank v. Maryland, *id.* at 383 (dissenting opinion).
24. See, e.g., Weeks v. United States, 232 U.S. 384 (1914); Mapp v. Ohio, 367 U.S. 643 (1961).
25. 178 F.2d 13, 17 (1949), *aff'd on other grounds,* 339 U.S. 1 (1950).
26. 387 U.S. 523 (1967).
27. 387 U.S. 541 (1967).

18

Capital Punishment

Proponents and opponents of capital punishment have devoted considerable time and energy to debating the question whether the death penalty infringes constitutionally protected civil liberties. Many persons—including some who oppose the death penalty—believe that no civil liberties issues are involved and that the proper method of eliminating or restricting capital punishment is solely through the legislative process, where ethical and other policy considerations can best be vindicated.

The United States Supreme Court, in an early decision, ruled that "the punishment of death is not cruel, within the meaning of that word as used in the Constitution." For many years organizations like the American Civil Liberties Union accepted the Court's position, concurring in the conclusion that capital punishment does not raise a civil liberties issue. In 1963, however, the ACLU undertook to re-evaluate the relation of the death penalty to civil liberties. The author was requested to prepare a memorandum, set out below, presenting both sides of the argument, along with a recommendation to the Union on the question of abolition.

There is some difficulty in presenting both sides of the argument on capital punishment because past discussions of the death penalty have frequently taken place in a rather uncertain context—whether capital punishment "raises a civil liberties issue." I suggest that this formulation is confusing and that the ACLU instead should consider the question in two parts, as follows:

1. Whether capital punishment, per se, is unconstitutional as violating a provision of the Bill of Rights.

2. Even if capital punishment does not of itself violate the Constitution, whether the practice should be opposed by the ACLU, and if so, how.

This two-part formulation is consistent with prior issues in which the Union has taken stands that did not relate to an alleged violation of the Constitution. For example, in 1954 the Union protested a vigilante program by a Connecticut branch of Veterans of Foreign Wars under which the names of local residents considered "Communistic" were reported to the FBI. In 1956, the Union condemned the cancellation of an overseas art exhibit by the United States Information Agency after four of the exhibiting artists had been charged with sympathy for Communism. In the same year, the Union urged the New Jersey State Senate to reconsider its rejection of Judge John O. Bigelow as a member of the Board of Governors of Rutgers University because he had represented a schoolteacher who had invoked the Fifth Amendment before the House Committee on Un-American Activities.

In all these cases, the Union's action was predicated, not on an alleged constitutional violation, but rather on its belief that the criticized activities were inconsistent with the "spirit of the American concept of justice" or "foreign to the American concept of due process." A similar approach would seem indicated now.

A. The Competing Contentions

We can obtain assistance from a recent debate on capital punishment with particular reference to the proper role of the Civil Liberties Union.[1] The participants were Emanuel Redfield, Esq., Counsel to the New York Civil Liberties Union, and Professor Norman

Redlich, Counsel to the New York Committee to Abolish Capital Punishment. Mr. Redfield made the following statement:

"In its legal posture, the Constitution of the United States as interpreted by the Supreme Court does not forbid capital punishment, nor is such punishment deemed 'cruel and unusual.'

"What punishment should be meted out for violation of law is society's search for a means to deter transgressions. It may be that no punishment adequately fulfills the needs of society, and there will be many persons with scruples against any quantum of punishment whatsoever. Perhaps other means, such as social and psychiatric treatment, may be more efficient for the objective sought. This implies that the problem is one to be solved not by the civil libertarian but with the tools of the sociologist, the social worker, the psychiatrist and others who are equipped to determine what means will serve the state best for the solution of the problem.

"If one weighs the question of whether a life sentence or a twenty-year sentence or a ten-year sentence should be imposed for a crime, the thinking will not be along civil liberties lines. The thoughts will turn toward the appropriateness of the punishment in attaining the goal of deterring antisocial behavior. Consistently, there should be no distinction in thinking when the punishment is death.

"Arguments [to the contrary] do not go to the heart of the question whether capital punishment in itself raises a civil liberties issue. Those arguments dwell on procedural abuses which are to be found in the trial of criminal cases generally. Likewise, argument that a greater proportion of a certain race is convicted of a capital crime does not by itself call for its abolition, for logically, this argument would call equally for the abolition of any other penalty, when it can be shown that a higher percentage of a certain race is punished. Nor is lack of counsel an adequate ground. Abolition of capital punishment can be justified on many grounds, but not because of procedural problems arising in the administration of the criminal law. The errors and abuses found in a capital case should be corrected, as should those in trials for other crimes. It weakens the argument for abolition of capital punishment to rest it on grounds equally applicable to other penalties.

"It is preferable that the opponents of capital punishment place their case on a more solid basis, even if in doing so they eschew the support of the Civil Liberties Union for their cause. They should bear in mind that the Union's effectiveness in its field derives in no small part from its singleness of purpose.

"This brief note was not intended to present the writer's views on the desirability of the abolition of capital punishment. They are omitted solely to help focus the point that capital punishment does not raise a civil liberties issue."

Several comments may be made on this statement. First, although the view that capital punishment violates the Constitution is not widely held, there is a contrary view, which was reflected in the dissenting opinion of Justice Goldberg (joined by Justices Douglas and Brennan) from a denial of certiorari in *Rudolph v. Alabama.*[2] Justice Goldberg maintained that the lower court decision should have been reversed as a violation of the cruel and unusual punishment clause of the Bill of Rights because it involved a death sentence for rape, a crime that did not result in loss of life. Accordingly, there is now substantial room to argue that the Constitution, at least in some cases, prohibits capital punishment.

Second, the statement does not come to grips with the question whether in the absence of a constitutional issue the ACLU should nevertheless take a position against the death penalty; in other words, it assumes that the Union has no interest if there is no infringement of the Bill of Rights. As already pointed out, this assumption seems unwarranted in view of the long history of intervention by the Union in cases where the "spirit of civil liberties" is infringed by public or private action, and in view of the position already taken against capital punishment by several ACLU affiliates. In addition, Mr. Redfield makes no serious attempt to refute the contention, expressed below, that the death penalty operates in practice to deprive defendants in capital cases of civil liberties, even if these do not rise to the stature of a constitutional deprivation.

I turn now to the argument in favor of an ACLU policy stand against capital punishment. This breaks down into two separate lines of analysis. The first suggests ways in which the death penalty adversely affects the fair administration of criminal justice or, because of its capricious quality, discriminates against one or more classes of defendants. The second line of analysis is broader in nature; it suggests that capital punishment is inconsistent with the spirit that underlies and animates civil liberties.

1. In presenting the ways in which the death penalty discriminates against certain groups and impairs the rights of all defendants forced to stand trial for a capital offense, I shall draw on Professor Redlich's statement in *Civil Liberties in New York* as well as on the comprehensive brief he prepared for the New York Committee to Abolish Capital Punishment that was submitted to the Temporary State Commission on Revision of the Penal Law and Criminal Code.

a. The death penalty discriminates against the poor and underprivileged. As stated by the former warden of San Quentin Prison, "I hate the death penalty because it always hits the little man, who is not only poor in material possessions but in background, education and mental capacity as well. . . . The defendant of wealth and position never goes to the electric chair or to the gallows."[3] There is considerable evidence to buttress this conclusion of arbitrariness in the selection of those persons committing homicides who are sentenced to death. Thus, a recent study conducted by the Ohio Legislative Service found that

> *Persons sentenced to death are seen to have had relatively less formal education than either other prison inmates or persons in the general population. . . . Nearly all of the persons sentenced to death came from family backgrounds at the lower socio-economic levels. . . . In only six death sentence cases (all six of which were later commuted) did available information describe conditions which might be considered "middle class."*[4]

b. The reasons for discrimination against the poor in the application of the death penalty are intertwined with other important civil liberties issues. For example, a poor person will not have counsel at the time of his arrest and will generally not be able to obtain counsel until at least the time of arraignment. This explains why practically every inhabitant of the death house is prejudiced by an early confession and why the overwhelming majority of coerced confession cases reaching the Supreme Court are capital cases.

c. As a concomitant to its discrimination against the poor, the death penalty discriminates against nonwhites. This is not to say that judges and juries harbor outright prejudice against Negroes and other nonwhites—although it is not far-fetched to suppose that some prejudice does exist, at least in the South. It is rather to suggest that whatever group is at the bottom of the economic ladder will have a disproportionally higher representation in the death house. Nonwhites, being at the bottom of the ladder, pay the penalty. Thus, more than half of those executed in the United States since 1930 have been Negroes. In New York during the last five years, 80 percent of the persons sentenced to death were Negroes or Puerto Ricans, and all but two of the thirteen men actually executed were either Negro or Puerto Rican. The same pattern exists in other states. Such statistics led Professor C. Ray Jeffery to comment as follows upon the practice of executing very few of the persons who commit intentional homicide:

> *There is a certain injustice in this system since whether a man is executed or not becomes a capricious and arbitrary matter. Of those executed, most are poor, ignorant and from minority groups, especially from the Negro population.*[5]

d. The fact that murder and rape (i.e. capital offenses) are the crimes which receive the most lurid press coverage results in a climate of opinion least conducive to the selection of an impartial jury. It is not surprising, therefore, that virtually every Supreme Court case dealing with the effect of newspaper publicity on a state trial has involved a capital offense. This problem impelled Justice Frankfurter to ask whether "fallible men and women [can] reach a disinterested verdict based exclusively on what they heard in court when, before they entered the jury box, their minds were saturated by press and radio."[6]

e. Jury selection also operates unfairly in capital cases because panels are chosen partly on the basis of a belief in the death penalty. For example, the New York Code of Criminal Procedure allows a challenge for cause upon a showing that a juror has "such conscientious opinion as would preclude his finding the defendant guilty."[7] Under this provision a juror can be challenged even though he states that, despite his personal objection to capital punishment, he could find the defendants guilty of a capital crime. The result seems to be that the state is protected against a jury biased against a capital conviction, but the defendant is not protected against a jury biased in favor of it.

f. Following trial and appeal, the death penalty operates to limit postappellate review in the class of cases where it is needed most. For example, when the Supreme Court retroactively applied the holding in *Griffin v. Illinois*[8] that states must provide free transcripts on appeal to poor defendants, the ones who could never take advantage of this constitutional rule were those who had been executed. A second example derives from the fact that a defendant in a capital case has no right to the assignment of counsel after his appeal. The failure of states to assign counsel during the postappellate stage of a capital case frequently precludes indigent prisoners under sentence of death from pursuing those remedies available to prisoners convicted of less serious crimes.

2. My second point here is that capital punishment is inconsistent with the spirit of civil liberties, and therefore should be opposed by the ACLU even if it does not transgress any provision of the Bill of Rights. Capital punishment, in other words, represents a challenge to civil liberty at least as serious as the cases of the VFW vigilante program, the unwarranted cancellation of the USIA overseas art exhibit, and the rejection of Judge Bigelow as a Rutgers trustee, all discussed above.

In substantiating this assertion, it is necessary to refer again to the numerous ways, described immediately above, in which capital punishment diminishes rights protected by the Constitution—the right to nondiscriminatory treatment by the law, the right to an unbiased jury of one's peers and the right to postconviction remedies not aborted by the conclusiveness of death. The impact of capital punishment casts a dark shadow on the claim that justice is meted out evenhandedly and according to appropriate standards of due process.

More important for the present point is the recognition of the peculiar qualities of the death penalty that render it so shocking to many who possess the finest sensibilities. This is not the occasion to review the many arguments that have been presented by Albert Camus,[9] among others, to demonstrate the inhumanity and ineffectiveness of capital punishment as well as its devastating effect on the citizenry in terms of its conception of the value of human life. "Official murder," in the words of Camus, "adds a second defilement to the first, and does so for no useful ends that have ever been demonstrated."[10]

The only "useful end" that is seriously suggested as vindicating capital punishment is deterrence. Space is too limited to review the ever mounting evidence that this is a myth. A recent report prepared for the model Penal Code Project of the American Law Institute by Professor Thorsten Sellin of the University of Pennsylvania, on the effect of the death penalty on rates of homicide, presents a wide range of statistics to this effect.[11] Professor Sellin's conclusion is consistent with the available data:

The important thing to be noticed is that whether the death penalty is used or not and whether executions are frequent or not, both death penalty states and abolition states show rates which suggest that these rates are conditioned by other factors than the death penalty.[12]

In fact, the American states with the highest homicide rates all have capital punishment and the homicide rate has not increased in the various states as the execution rate has decreased.

But, it is asked, is not the death penalty merely one mode of punishment for crime, and is it not clear that the ACLU is not concerned with the particular form criminal punishment may take absent a challenge to constitutionality? The answer lies in facts that uniquely exist in the case of capital punishment: the finality of the penalty and the sanctity of every human life.

It would not be necessary to say even a word about finality except that it is sometimes maintained that death is not more final than any other punishment—that, for example, a twenty-year sentence, once served, is as irrevocable as execution. But this contention misses the point. During the twenty-year period of confinement the prisoner is free to try to obtain release by proving his innocence through new evidence or by showing that his trial was infected with constitutional error. This, of course, is often done successfully. But these remedies are obviously not available for the man—including the innocent man—who goes to Death Row. This is the "finality" of the capital sentence.

The second set of facts relate to the sanctity of the individual life. This philosophical assumption has, as such, been a cornerstone of liberal and humanistic thinking from the beginning, and as the indispensable condition for all other rights, it has been the *raison d'être* of the ACLU. Those who would snuff out a life thus carry a heavy burden. Some believe that the state can carry this burden in the case of murderers and rapists duly convicted. However, there are others who think, once again to quote Albert Camus, that capital punishment "is a disgrace to our society which its partisans cannot reasonably justify."[13]

B. Conclusion and Recommendations

My belief that the ACLU should take a position against the death penalty will come as no surprise to readers of this memorandum. This conclusion is not based on the opinion that the courts are ready to declare capital punishment, per se, a violation of the Bill of Rights. Rather it is a response to the persuasiveness of the arguments, reviewed above, that the death penalty both impairs individual liberty (even if not in the constitutional sense) and dehumanizes the society which employs it.

Accordingly, I submit the following recommendations:

1. The Due Process Committee and, subsequently, the National Board of Directors should issue a policy statement against capital punishment.

2. This policy statement should be implemented:

a. Through determined efforts to secure the legislative repeal of laws authorizing the death penalty or to limit the class of crimes for which the death penalty is imposed.

b. Through appropriate legal assistance to defendants accused, or in particular, convicted of a capital offense and sentenced to death. This legal assistance could be patterned on efforts of the New York Committee to Abolish Capital Punishment, which raises on behalf of all persons sentenced to death any substantial constitutional issue that could save the convicted person from execution.

In 1965, after much internal debate, the Board of Directors of the ACLU adopted a revised policy statement accepting the recommendation of the author's memorandum. It asserted that "capital punishment is so inconsistent with the underlying values of a democratic system that the imposition of the death penalty for any crime is a denial of civil liberties."

Since then empirical evidence has been compiled as to the discriminatory application of the death penalty and its nondeterrent effect on crime. The NAACP Legal Defense Fund has completed an exhaustive study demonstrating the discriminatory use of the death penalty against Negroes. Accordingly, what might be called the second-round judicial attack has now been initiated, complementing the increased activity on the legislative level.

Leading this attack is Professor Anthony G. Amsterdam of the University of Pennsylvania Law School, who heads a battery of lawyers affiliated with the NAACP Legal Defense and Educational Fund and the ACLU. Their efforts have met with initial success. In Florida and California, for example, federal courts in 1967 enjoined all scheduled executions pending the outcome of suits which present the "new" constitutional arguments against capital punishment. In addition, the Supreme Court has held recently that a jury from which persons opposed to capital punishment have been excluded can not constitutionally impose a sentence of death.[14]

On the legislative front thirteen states, including New York, have abolished the death penalty. And even where it has not been outlawed, the penalty has fallen into comparative disuse—in 1930 there were 155 executions, and in 1966 and 1967, only one and two respectively.

NOTES

1. See the publication of the New York Civil Liberties Union, *Civil Liberties in New York* 2 (May 1963).
2. 375 U.S. 889 (1963).
3. Duffy, 88 *Men and 2 Women* 256 (1962).
4. Ohio Legislative Service Commission, *Capital Punishment* 76–79 (Staff Report No. 46, 1961).

5. Davis *et al.*, *Society and the Law* 281 (1962).
6. Irvin v. Dowd, 366 U.S. 717, 729–30 (1961).
7. N.Y. Code of Criminal Procedure, § 337.
8. 351 U.S. 12 (1956).
9. See Camus, *Reflections on the Guillotine* (1959).
10. *Ibid.*
11. Sellin, *The Death Penalty* (American Law Institute, 1959). See also Bedau, *The Death Penalty in America* (1964).
12. Sellin, *op. cit. supra* note 11 at 24.
13. Camus, *op. cit. supra* note 9.
14. Witherspoon v. Illinois, 36 U. S. L. W. 4504 (1968).

19

Execution of the Insane

On December 7, 1961, Frederick Charles Wood was convicted of murder and sentenced to death. The New York Court of Appeals affirmed the conviction, rejecting defense counsel's contention that Wood had been insane at the time the offense was committed. New York law, however, explicitly requires that a murderer be sane not only when he commits the crime but also when he is executed. To determine the latter question of sanity, three psychiatrists examined Wood on December 18, 1962, subsequent to affirmance of the conviction, and concluded that he was sufficiently sane to be executed. Subsequent legal attempts to delay the execution failed, and Wood was sentenced to die on March 21, 1963.

The author, acting for the New York branch of the ACLU, entered the case about a week prior to the date set for execution. Appearing voluntarily, and in fact contrary to Wood's express desire to be executed, the author contended that the determination of Wood's mental capacity to be executed had been constitutionally invalid because counsel for Wood had not been present at the examination. Asserting that the facts cast considerable doubt on Wood's sanity, the author petitioned the United States District Court for the Southern District of New York for a writ of habeas corpus and a stay of execution so that Wood could assert his constitutional claim.

Excerpts from the author's memorandum submitted to the district court on Wood's behalf appear below. While reading the excerpted passages, one should consider the implications of the Wood case for a legal system such as ours, which desires maximum protection of basic constitutional rights but nevertheless tolerates capital punishment. Does a convicted murderer who desires to be executed have a right to die, even where such an execution might be tantamount to "state-sponsored suicide"? The author obviously felt that compliance with the Constitution was more important than the death-wish of the individual, especially because there was much evidence that the individual involved lacked the capacity to make a voluntary waiver of his constitutional rights.

In addition to its philosophical implications, the Wood case exemplifies the practical obstacles facing an attorney confronted with the impending finality of capital punishment. Presumably, the state must comply strictly with the Constitution before it executes a man; however, a particular constitutional violation, such as the absence of counsel at one of the proceedings prior to execution, may not become apparent until it is too late. Having discovered a proceeding of doubtful validity, the attorney must then secure a stay of execution. This presents a difficult problem when only a short period of time remains before the date fixed for execution.

UNITED STATES DISTRICT COURT

SOUTHERN DISTRICT OF NEW YORK

IN THE MATTER OF THE APPLICATION

FOR WRIT OF HABEAS CORPUS

BY

FREDERICK CHARLES WOOD, PETITIONER

v.

WILFRED L. DENNO, AS WARDEN OF SING SING

MEMORANDUM OF LAW IN SUPPORT

OF PETITION FOR WRIT OF HABEAS CORPUS

The petitioner respectfully submits that his petition for writ of habeas corpus and stay of execution should be granted for the reasons stated below.

1. Decisions of the United States District Court for the Southern District of New York provide ample and controlling precedent for the authority and the duty of the Court to grant a stay of execution of a condemned prisoner so that state remedies can be exhausted when a substantial constitutional question exists that could result in the release of the prisoner or the vacation of a sentence of execution.[1]

2. The earlier habeas corpus proceeding brought on behalf of Wood in no way bars the present proceeding. The issue in that case was whether Wood had a general constitutional right to appointment of postappellate counsel. No such claim is now being made. The only issue presented is whether the lunacy proceeding held by New York under section 495(a) on December 18, 1962, was consistent with the requirements of the Fourteenth Amendment to the United States Constitution. The earlier petition did not raise this question; indeed, that petition, which was dated January 21, 1963, did not even take cognizance that a section 495(a) proceeding had taken place on the preceding December 18.

3. The existence of a substantial claim under the due process clause of the Fourteenth Amendment is plainly established by *Caritativo v. California*.[2] In that case petitioner raised before the Supreme Court the validity of the California procedure for determining the sanity of prisoners scheduled to be executed. A five-man majority of the Court, in a brief *per curiam* order, affirmed the judgment of the Supreme Court of California sustaining the contested procedure. Three Justices of the Supreme Court dissented, arguing that the Constitution required some procedure for hearing the prisoner on the question of sanity. In the words of Mr. Justice Felix Frankfurter:

> *There can hardly be a comparable situation under our constitutional scheme of things in which an interest so great, that an insane man not be executed, is given such flimsy procedural protection, and where one asserting a claim is denied the rudimentary right of having his side submitted to the one who sits in judgment.*[3]

A fourth Justice, Mr. Justice Harlan concurred in the Court's judgment, but declined to join in its order. He based his opinion on the ground that the *particular* California procedure in issue fulfilled the requirements of the Fourteenth Amendment. He made it abundantly clear that in a case involving the procedure of another state his conclusion might be different.[4]

There is, accordingly, no doubt about the substantiality of the issue raised in this case concerning the validity of a proceeding under section 495(a) which permits the sanity of a condemned man to be determined without a voice raised on his behalf. The precise form of the procedure employed by the state in satisfying the demands of due process is not pertinent. The critical issue is the requirement that the prisoner have counsel so that his claim can be heard.

4. The final point concerns the objections to the presence in the case of the New York Civil Liberties Union, which is acting as volunteer attorney for Wood. Or, to put it another way, the question is the legal effectiveness of Wood's expressed wish to be executed without the intervention of any counsel on his behalf. The contention of the respondents, of course, is that the New York Civil Liberties Union has no standing and that Wood, if he chooses, can go to his death without legal assistance. It is respectfully submitted that this contention is not only specious, but that it is wholly inconsistent with the governing legal principles as set down by the United States Supreme Court.

a. It is perfectly plain that if the State of New York has deprived Wood of constitutional rights by holding an invalid insanity hearing, he is entitled to habeas corpus unless he has waived his rights. It is recognized that a state prisoner may waive constitutional rights, but it is clear that such a waiver cannot be based merely on the statements of a person of doubtful sanity without determining whether he has the capacity to make the "intelligent" and "understanding" waiver which the Supreme Court requires before a constitutional right can be relinquished.

The Court has ruled that a prisoner must have the "mental capacity to make an intelligent, understanding waiver of constitutional rights of supreme importance."[5] In the same case the Court said:

"This conclusion against an intelligent waiver is fortified by the inferences which may be drawn from the . . . evidence of emotional disturbance. . . ."[6] Wood's statements, by themselves, cannot support a claim of waiver in the light of the extensive psychiatric and other evidence pointing toward his lack of capacity to make a knowing and intelligent choice.

b. The evidence of record in this case compels the conclusion that Wood is without capacity to make an effective waiver of constitutional rights.

The factual basis underlying the claim that Wood lacks mental capacity includes the following matters of record: Wood spent four months in a mental institution at the age of seventeen "for observation"; he spent seven years in Dannemora State Hospital for the criminally insane; four psychiatrists testified that on the day of the homicides he did not know the nature and quality of his acts or that his acts were wrong; psychiatrists from Bellevue Hospital ruled that Wood was mentally unfit to stand trial, a determination that was set aside by the trial judge after a hearing. But only the record of the insanity hearing conveys the full flavor and evidence of Wood's chronic mental disturbance.

Finally, the fact that the Governor convened a commission under the provisions of section 495(a), which depends on a finding that "a defendant . . . appears to be insane," is evidence that a substantial question as to Wood's sanity exists. The only way to refute the inference of insanity is to *assume* that the commission made a proper determination of Wood's mental capacity. But the validity of the commission's action is the very matter in issue, and to assume that it reached a proper decision in the absence of counsel representing Wood's interests is to make an unwarranted leap from conjecture to conclusion.

Two critical points should be re-emphasized:

First, the fact that Wood was found sane under the McNaughten rules is not dispositive of the claim that he is presently insane, which represents an entirely distinct constitutional issue.

Second, no claim is being made that Wood is *in fact* insane. The petitioner is obviously not qualified to make such a suggestion. What is being claimed is that Wood's record creates such grave doubts concerning his present mental state that a district court is not authorized to withhold habeas corpus solely on the basis of Wood's expressed wishes.

c. The petitioner in this proceeding fully appreciates the serious problem of federal-state relations created by the habeas corpus jurisdiction of federal courts over state criminal proceedings. The petitioner also fully recognizes the possible effects on the administration of justice in the state courts if volunteer lawyers could generally invoke federal habeas corpus despite the opposition of a state prisoner to the assertion of federal constitutional rights on his behalf.

But these considerations do not go to the merits of the present petition. The petition in this case is squarely based on the unusual and particular circumstances surrounding Wood's threatened execution—the presence of a substantial constitutional question plus the prisoner's lack of "mental capacity" to make the "intelligent" and "understanding" waiver that the Supreme Court requires before a constitutional right can be relinquished.

In this connection, it should be made clear that no claim is being made that the defendant is entitled to repetitive hearings on his sanity up to the time of execution. The only claim is that the proceeding held by the State of New York on December 18, 1962, was fatally defective for the reasons stated above and that the defendant is entitled to a proceeding which affords him the protections of the Fourteenth Amendment.

On March 19, 1963, the district court denied the petition for habeas corpus; on March 20, the Second Circuit Court of Appeals affirmed this decision. These decisions apparently pleased Wood, who stated on March 19, "I really want to ride the lightning sans further delay," and, commenting on the author's efforts, "I do not welcome any intrusion into this stinking case of mine." The author nevertheless pursued the case to the only tribunal remaining available—the United States Supreme Court. On March 21, the day set for execution, the author submitted a memorandum to the Court, excerpts from which are reprinted below, in order to obtain a stay of execution.

SUPREME COURT OF THE UNITED STATES
October Term, 1962
Docket No.———
UNITED STATES OF AMERICA EX REL.
FREDERICK CHARLES WOOD, RELATOR,
v.
WILFRED L. DENNO, RESPONDENT

MEMORANDUM IN SUPPORT OF APPLICATION FOR AN ORDER STAYING WILFRED L. DENNO, WARDEN OF SING SING, FROM EXECUTING THE SENTENCE OF DEATH UPON FREDERICK CHARLES WOOD

Frederick Charles Wood, having been found guilty of murder in the first degree, is scheduled to be executed this evening, March 21, 1963, at 10:00 P.M.

The proceedings leading up to the present action were as follows:

1. Wood was convicted of murder in the first degree on December 7, 1961, and sentenced to death. . . .

5. Evidence was introduced before Judge Tyler that, on December 18, 1962, three psychiatrists examined Wood in connection with his possible insanity for purposes of execution.

Uncontradicted evidence introduced at the hearing before Judge Tyler established that counsel for Wood, who had been assigned to represent him, were not present at the hearing of December 18, 1962, and never received notice of such hearing. . . .

8. On March 15, 1963, Norman Dorsen, Esq., retained by the New York Civil Liberties Union, simultaneously filed two proceedings on behalf of Wood.

a. A petition for writ of error *coram nobis* was filed in the New York State Supreme Court, Queens County. On March 18, 1963, the petition was denied by Judge Bosch in an opinion annexed hereto as exhibit I. It is the intention of petitioner to appeal this order.

b. The instant proceeding was commenced by the filing of a petition for writ of habeas corpus and stay of execution in the District Court for the Southern District of New York, alleging that the procedures employed by New York State to determine Wood's present sanity deprived him of due process under the Fourteenth Amendment.

Following a hearing, Judge Tyler denied the petition for writ of habeas corpus in an opinion annexed hereto as exhibit II.

The application for a stay of execution in this Court is based on the fact that this record presents important constitutional questions which should be heard in accordance with petitioner's right to full appellate review under 28 U.S.C. § 2253.

This Court on two prior occasions has ruled on the power of a state to execute an insane man without providing him with the right to be heard by counsel.[7] The seriousness of the constitutional question presented here is evident from a comparison of the abundant record of insanity in this case with the absence in the earlier Supreme Court cases of evidence that the petitioners there lacked the requisite mental capacity to be executed.

In the *Solesbee* case, as far as appears in the opinions in this Court or the opinion of the Supreme Court of Georgia,[8] there were merely general allegations of mental illness. In the *Caritativo* case this was likewise true. In the *Rupp* case, which came to this Court as a companion to *Caritativo,* there were allegations of past mental illness contained in Rupp's petition for habeas corpus, but these say-so allegations are a far cry from the fully documented record of insanity that is found in the present record.

The full flavor of the extensive and lifelong record of Wood's mental illness can be fully appreciated by reading the record of the insanity hearing held in this case on April 19, 1961, which is annexed hereto as exhibit III, and from the opinion of the Court of Appeals.[9]

Although this Court divided in both the *Solesbee* and *Caritativo* cases, recognizing the gravity of the constitutional issue raised in those cases, there was nothing in either record comparable to the facts of insanity contained in this case. In these circumstances, it is difficult to justify foreclosing for all time the substantial constitutional issue of Wood's right to a proceeding, at which he is represented by counsel, to determine insanity for purposes of execution.

Important questions of federal-state relationships also dictate that the stay be granted so that the state *coram nobis* proceeding referred to above can be appealed to the Court of Appeals of New York

State. The confusion concerning the nature of the hearing held on December 18, 1962, raises the possibility that the hearing was not in accordance with the statutory requirements of section 495(a) of the New York Code of Criminal Procedure. There has never been a statutory interpretation of section 495(a) by the highest court of New York State. Such a decision might result in an interpretation which satisfies the constitutional claims set forth in the petition for writ of habeas corpus. Since no New York State judge has authority to grant a stay of execution in this case, see section 495 of the New York Code of Criminal Procedure, only if a federal judge grants a stay of execution will the New York courts have the opportunity to rule on an important and hitherto undecided question of state law.

WHEREFORE, the applicant respectfully prays for oral argument on the issues presented herein and prays further for an order staying the execution of Frederick Charles Wood scheduled for Thursday evening, March 21, 1963, at 10:00 P.M. pending disposition of his appeal.

The Supreme Court refused to stay the execution. All efforts having failed, the State of New York granted Wood his death-wish shortly after 10:00 P.M. *on March 21, 1963.*

Ironically, the New York Legislature, perhaps motivated by cases such as Wood's, soon acted to abolish capital punishment for murder as of June 1, 1965.[10]

NOTES

Leon Friedman and Martin Garbus participated in the preparation of the papers in this case.

1. See LaMarca v. Denno, 159 F. Supp. 486 (1958) (Dimock, Ch. J.); Correa v. Denno, Order of July 25, 1962 (MacMahon, J.).
2. 357 U.S. 549 (1958).
3. *Id.* at 552–53 (dissenting opinion).
4. *Id.* at 551–52 (concurring opinion).
5. Moore v. Michigan, 355 U.S. 155, 164 (1957).

6. *Id.* at 164–65.

7. Solesbee v. Balkcom, 339 U.S. 9 (1950); Caritativo v. California, 357 U.S. 549 (1958).

8. 205 Ga. 122, 52 S.E.2d 433 (1949).

9. 12 N.Y.2d 69 (1962).

10. Under the new law, capital punishment is only available when a peace officer is murdered in the line of duty, or when a murder is committed by a person serving a life sentence, and in those cases only by special recommendation of the jury.

SECTION IV

DISCRIMINATION

The most important clause of the Constitution concerning discrimination is found in the Fourteenth Amendment. There it is provided, "nor shall any state . . . deny to any person within its jurisdiction the equal protection of the laws." The genesis of this clause, as well as the rest of the amendment, was in the desire of the post-Civil War Reconstruction Congress and the Northern states to assure equality for the recently emancipated black man. Indeed, in an 1883 decision Mr. Justice Miller, speaking for a majority of the Supreme Court, expressed doubt whether the equal protection clause would ever be employed except to bar discrimination against the Negro. This prophecy proved incorrect, however, and over the years other types of "invidious" discrimination by the states have been invalidated.

At one point in American constitutional history the Supreme Court was relatively free in striking down state legislation, including tax laws and regulatory statutes, that it found "unequal" in application. But it soon became clear that almost all legislation of an economic character is, strictly speaking, discriminatory; there are, for example, different taxes for different types of taxpayers and different sorts of regulation depending on the business affected. It likewise became clear that if all such statutes were declared invalid the state legislatures could not function. Accordingly, the Supreme Court eventually developed the rule that the equal protection clause permits the states a "wide scope of discretion" and only voids laws that are "without any reasonable basis" and "purely arbitrary." In practice, the laws considered arbitrary are those that classify individuals to their disadvantage because of race, religion or (more recently) poverty, and those laws discriminating against the free exercise of constitutionally protected rights. All other laws, and the distinctions they embody, are accorded a heavy presumption of validity.

Thus, during the last thirty years, in only one maverick case has the Supreme Court held that a statute involving economic or social regulation denied a person the equal protection of the laws. On numerous occasions, however, the Court has invalidated laws discriminating against the poor, the Negro, and other minority groups.

Two chapters in Section III (14 and 19), while primarily concerned with due process as it affects poor persons, also raised issues pertinent to this section. One such theme—the close relationship between discrimination based on race and that based on poverty—is carried forward in the opening chapter of this section, "Poverty, Civil Liberties and Civil Rights."

The next four chapters deal with different aspects of racial discrimination. The reader should recall that until 1954, when the Supreme Court decided in *Brown v. Board of Education* that public school segregation was invalid, the equal protection clause was of little use in securing a more egalitarian society. In fact, the provision was virtually emasculated in 1893, when the Court ruled that it was consistent with the Constitution to afford Negroes "separate but equal" facilities. In ensuing decades, although Negroes often received inferior facilities for traveling, learning and eating, the Court rarely intervened. Since 1954, as the selections in this section reveal, this has radically changed.

Chapter 21 involves a case brought by the federal government to eliminate arbitrary voting practices in Mississippi. In addition to the equal protection clause, the case invoked the Fifteenth Amendment, which specifically prohibits racial discrimination in voting. The next two chapters concern segregated education, but in contexts which require an extension of the principles of the *Brown* case. Chapter 22 involves *de facto* segregation, where the evil occurs not through overt discrimination against the Negro but as a product of long-standing housing patterns and other indirect causes, and Chapter 23 examines several facets of a problem that until recently has not received the attention it merits: segregation in nonpublic schools.

The final two chapters in this section illustrate other aspects of discrimination. Chapter 24 explores the possibility of a novel anti-trust remedy for racial or religious discrimination in private housing; this idea emerged in reaction to the failure of legislatures and administrative agencies to end such practices. It presents an example of the lawyer's traditional technique of casting about for original means of solving a problem that has not yielded to more conventional solutions. Chapter 25 presents an issue at the frontier of civil liberties—discrimination against persons of illegitimate birth. Although this group has suffered legal prejudice for centuries in fields such as inheritance, welfare and support, solely because of the acts of others over which they have no control, there have been few constitutional challenges to the discriminatory laws and almost no successful ones.

An interesting constitutional issue that runs through this section occurs when activity that is ostensibly private in character becomes "state action" as a result of financial support by the government or other evidence of governmental responsibility. The equal protection clause prohibits only discrimination carried on by the "state," and it is therefore necessary to determine the degree of governmental involvement in considering whether "private" discrimination is constitutionally forbidden. Chapters 22 and 23, in particular, explore the ramifications of this problem.

20

Poverty, Civil Liberties and Civil Rights

A Conference

The accelerating interest in the applicability of general legal doctrines to poor persons, the development of certain new legal concepts, and the incorporation into the Economic Opportunity Act of 1964 of legal services as an integral part of the antipoverty program led the Hays Program to hold its 1965 conference on the relation of poverty to civil liberties and civil rights. Conference participants were Elizabeth Wickenden, Consultant, National Social Welfare Assembly; Marvin E. Frankel, then Professor of Law at Columbia University School of Law, now United States District Judge; Stephen J. Pollak, then Deputy General Counsel, Office of Economic Opportunity, now Assistant Attorney General for Civil Rights; and Charles E. Ares, then Professor of Law at New York University School of Law, and now Dean of the Arizona Law School. Although it presents an excellent short summary of the federal government's approach, Mr. Pollak's statement is not reproduced because of changes in the poverty program since the date of the conference.

I / Introduction (Norman Dorsen)

The historic role of the lawyer was to counsel and represent the wealthier groups in society. Even today an overwhelming percentage of lawyers serve corporations and individuals earning more than $10,000 per year. Legal services are needed at that level, and practitioners engaged in the law of trusts, taxes and indentures are both performing an important public function and assisting a class. This would be admirable and harmless were it not that poor persons also require legal assistance. The welfare society as well as private wealth creates legal problems, and these have largely been ignored. As this conference hopefully will suggest, the organized bar has finally come to appreciate the difficulties faced by those who cannot afford fancy retainers but whose futures may be at the mercy of the law. There are, it must be remembered, some 35,000,000 persons in families with annual incomes under $3,000.

The remedies that must be tried, the resources that must be invested, and the intellectual inquiries that must be undertaken are explored in the pages that follow and need no comment. What may be of use, however, is a brief underscoring of two salient points: first, the intimate relation between the legal needs of the poor and civil liberties and civil rights, and second, the paradoxical fact that much of the new law is not a special "law of the poor," but has solid roots in wider legal doctrine.

Miss Wickenden highlights the fact that a prime characteristic of poverty is that it is a minority problem; in the United States, for perhaps the first time anywhere, the comfortable classes form the majority. Poverty is a minority problem in another sense. Negroes and other nonwhites constitute a large and disproportionate percentage of those who suffer from the absence of entitlement to public benefits. Dark skin invites disaster in two distinct ways: as the passkey to the poverty group and as an invitation to discrimination both before and after that sad status is achieved. Title VI of the Civil Rights Act of 1964, which conditions federal aid on nondiscriminatory administration of program benefits,[1] is a testimonial to these facts.

The relation between poverty and civil liberties is equally striking. The basic issues of welfare law are now familiar: the right to privacy and protection from illegal search; the right to freedom of movement and choice of residence; the right to competent legal assistance and due process at all stages of proceedings vitally affecting the individual; and the right to benefits untied to loyalty oaths or other political tests. It is odd and disturbing to me that procedures that would be regarded as outrageous when applied to traditional legal contacts between citizen and government, as in the economic regulatory field, somehow become tolerable in the context of public benefits. It is worth emphasizing in this connection that many deprivations of individual liberties have been at the instance of welfare departments and other agencies devoted to aiding the impoverished. In the words of Harold Rothwax, Legal Director of Mobilization for Youth, "a beneficent purpose is no guarantee against arbitrariness and sloth."[2]

It is at this juncture that the second point I wish to stress emerges. The law being developed in the course of establishing the rights of poor persons is not in any sense peculiar, but instead involves principles basic to common-law and statutory rights, and ultimately, constitutional rights. For example, the question whether a welfare recipient can be denied further benefits without a due process hearing bears obvious relation to the question whether a lawyer can be disbarred or whether a restaurant owner's license can be revoked without such protections. Similarly, the validity of conditioning Medicare or welfare rights on a loyalty oath has been litigated, in different guise, by teachers and other public employees.

The participants in the conference would agree, I think, that the legal profession has only begun to understand these complex and important matters. It has lately been argued that if poorer persons are truly to be admitted to full equality they, as well as wealthy clients, should enjoy the services of lawyers for consultation and planning. The suggestion of this possibility in the past has evoked a fierce reaction—because of the cost that would have to be borne by the entire society and because of the uncertain implications for the economic health of the legal profession. These are not chimerical or carping objections. They must be confronted before full progress can be made in securing for all persons the legal rights to which the law theoretically entitles them. Happily, this confrontation has begun.

II / Elizabeth Wickenden

This is the first meeting in which I have participated where the true situation of poor people in this affluent society is being defined as basically a civil liberties and a civil rights problem. The Fourteenth Amendment provides that "No state may deprive any person of life . . . without due process of law." Yet a few years ago, an infant in Arlington, Virginia, froze to death because his parents had recently arrived in Virginia and he, therefore, was not entitled to aid under the residence laws of that state. Last year a child died in Wilmington because the state legislature decided to reduce the amount of welfare money available. The family's grant was cut and the whole family was undernourished; the child, close to the margin of starvation, died. I do not think that it is altogether improper to say that our society is depriving people of life itself because of the restrictive and discriminatory nature of our public benefits.

Why has a nonlawyer like myself come so desperately to seek the help of lawyers in this area? At the end of 1959 or the beginning of 1960 the Louisiana Legislature insisted on retroactive enforcement of a law that effectively cut off from public assistance, and consequently deprived of their only means of livelihood, the families of 23,000 children, because their parents were not married at the time the children were born.[3] Since other states had been doing this on a piecemeal basis, we were indebted to the Legislature of Louisiana for doing it in a dramatic manner, arousing the good people of the country. Borrowing from the civil rights movement, some of us said, "Well, let's see what the law says. Let us see what lawyers can do for us in this situation of injustice and hardship to innocent children." We did, and found that there was a very good reason to maintain that this enactment was contrary to the Social Security Act, if not the Constitution itself. We succeeded in persuading the Social Security Commissioner to call a hearing, at which the State of Louisiana was obliged to defend its legislation. As a result the regulations of the department were changed, and Louisiana and all other states were informed that it was not within the terms of the law to deprive children of aid solely because of the circumstances of their birth.

After this dramatic victory, I and many others asked: Why have we failed to draw on this marvelous potential for righting the imbalance imposed by adverse public opinion? We began to search for other ways in which people dependent on public benefits, the people who cannot survive without some help from the public, were in effect the objects of discrimination.

One kind of infringement, perhaps the most important, occurs when people do not receive equal or full access to public programs or are subjected to discriminatory treatment so that the public benefit that has been set up by Congress or the states to meet their needs is not fairly applied to all applicants.

The Social Security Act[4] contains the most clear-cut effort to protect the entitlements of the beneficiary because its authors had a very clear concept of the importance of entitlement, i.e., the right of the beneficiary. Unfortunately, the potential recipients have often been unaware of these protections and lawyers have not been available to assist them. Even in the case of public assistance, which is given on the basis of need, every individual has a right, equal to that of all people in similar circumstances, to apply for and to receive assistance. A private agency, or some public agencies, can say, "I am sorry, our money is all used up; you'll have to go over to the Public Welfare Department"; but the Public Welfare Department can't say, "Our money is all gone," because they must treat equally everyone in the same situation within the terms of the law. Moreover, there is a legal right to appeal within the agency and a right, under certain circumstances, to go into the courts. Appeal is infrequent, however, because there are no lawyers to help these people and their rights are not understood.

There are a variety of other forms of public benefits, public housing for example, in which this factor of entitlement is less clear-cut. It is difficult for me to know precisely who is or is not entitled to public housing. The other day I read of the complaint of a lady who was not permitted in public housing because she had two children and her husband had left her. She was told, "You are unmarried, so you might have gentlemen callers and you might have wild parties." Nobody said she did these things; she just might do them. Is this an equitable, fair classification under the terms of the Housing Act? Somebody should test it. There are many other programs, including all the programs under the new Poverty Act,[5] in which the factor of entitlement is highly discretionary and needs clarification.

Poor people are subject to highly discriminatory actions in another way. The people who are paying the bills, particularly in public welfare, tend to think that if somebody seeks public aid he really does not have precisely the same rights as the rest of us. This involves an invasion of civil liberties guaranteed under our Constitution. For instance, the Supreme Court in *Edwards v. California*[6] determined that we have freedom of movement in this country. Yet there are several ways in which the threat of withholding a person's source of livelihood is used to prevent him from moving from one place to another.

Then, through the articles of Professor Reich and others, we have learned that the practice of sending an investigator in the middle of the night to pounce upon a welfare family to see if there is an unreported man in the house, who is therefore a possible source of income, is an invasion of the guaranteed right of privacy, the right against illegal search and seizure.[7]

We have many kinds of interference with people's personal relationships. A woman on assistance in many states is expected to lead a life of such celibacy—indeed of total isolation from the opposite sex—that only the most rigid nunnery would impose upon its self-elected members. In California, if a woman is charged with spending the grant that is given her for a needy child "in behalf of a man in the role of a spouse," she is subject to criminal penalties.[8] But what does the vague phrase "in the role of a spouse" mean? A man visiting a woman on assistance in the District of Columbia may discover that he is presumed to be the father of her children and therefore presumed to be responsible for their care. The result is that she is immediately taken off welfare. These are terrible interferences with what we regard as private rights.

There are also requirements that impose political restraints on public beneficiaries. For example, a member of the Communist Party is deprived of his earned rights under the Social Security Act,[9] of his earned pension under the Hiss Act,[10] and in some states of his right to survival assistance. Under the recent Economic Opportunity Act, we say to poor youngsters and others going into the poverty program, "You must take an affidavit of loyalty to the government, not other people but you, a public beneficiary."

We have ways in which we coerce the labor of people dependent upon public benefits. A recent case in New York involved five men who had been put in jail because they refused to work out their relief on a work project.[11] They said, among other things, that there was too much snow. When their lawyer was asked by the judge under which principle of law he was arguing the case he said, "Under the Thirteenth Amendment." It was a shock to a New York judge that the antislavery amendment might be invoked in New York State.

There is another series of discriminatory actions in which people who are obliged to seek public aid are subject to discriminatory applications of other laws. New Jersey and other states have adultery and fornication laws, which are never enforced. In some counties of New Jersey, however, when a woman with illegitimate children applies for assistance, someone in the welfare office telephones the district attorney and says, "Here's a woman who has several illegitimate children," and immediately a morals charge is placed against her.

In an even worse type of case, a woman with illegitimate children, typically a Negro in the South, applies for assistance and is told: "Yes, you are entitled to assistance for your children under the laws of the federal government and this state, but we have to warn you that if you go on assistance we are going to look into your situation to see if those children are getting adequate care, whether they're not possibly subject to neglect, and whether we should not take these children away and put them in an institution." When this was done in Florida, they had "voluntary" withdrawals of 45 percent of all recipients because those women chose to starve rather than risk losing their children.

This is what I mean when I say that poverty itself is a civil liberties risk. It seems that, to complete a very cursory treatment of a large subject, we could state a series of simple propositions:

First, this is a very rich country. Poverty is not a necessity; poverty is something we tolerate but could rectify.

Second, poverty is a social problem. This is no longer a personal matter or a family matter. We have to take social measures to remedy it, to prevent it and to ameliorate it.

Third, if we are going to have to change provisions in our social system to deal with poverty, this is obviously a considerable threat to the comfortable majority, who are not too happy about the prospect of bearing additional taxes.

In order to relieve our consciences we have a public welfare system. I think public welfare is the essence of the problem because it is the measure of our failure to deal with social problems through social change in more preventive, better adapted ways. In a public welfare program we have at once a sop to our conscience and a measure of our failure.

People look at the mounting welfare rolls—eight million at the present time, half a million in New York City—and they say, "This is terrible." They do not say, "What is wrong with us?" they say, "What is wrong with them? What is wrong with those poor people that they cannot manage better?" Naturally, if one believes that poor people are poor because of their own inadequacies and their own failures, then any punitive or repressive or controlling measure you put upon them is absolutely all right.

Finally, I would say that we who are comfortable have no business talking about "the poor" as "they," as if they were a group apart. It is an easy next step to subdivide "the poor" into two groups and thus distinguish between them: the worthy or deserving poor who are managing, and the poor-poor who are living on public benefits. I consider this a dangerous classification because in a sense the security of our society, the health of our society, the conscience and morality of our society can be measured by what we do for those who have fallen on hard times. I do not believe that any of us is immune. If any one of us happened to have the wrong set of circumstances, the wrong age, the wrong location, the wrong color, the wrong skill or the wrong set of catastrophic personal or social disasters, there is not one of us who could escape dependence on others.

Therefore, what we do for all of us, what we guarantee by rule of law for all of us, is protection for each of us.

III / (Marvin E. Frankel)

The poor, as Miss Wickenden points out, have various legal problems. There is, of course, the standard kind of legal business—the consumer problems, the domestic problems, the contract problems —that is common to the whole community. In addition, there is a host of problems peculiar to the poor. Among them are the problem of the poor man and the slum landlord, a special kind of problem with which our law copes feebly at best; the problem of the poor with the government landlord, who unfortunately is not always a benign and considerate landlord; and the problem of the poor man with arbitrary rules of how you get into housing, and how you may occasionally, and perhaps unfairly, be thrown out of government housing. There is also a great range of welfare problems.

To solve these problems, we need more than the kind of voluntary fireman-lawyer previously thought to be sufficient for the poor. We need lawyers who are specialists in the problems of poverty. We need lawyers who are advocates, counselors, advisors, partisans for poor people; lawyers who make that their daily, not intermittent, concern not simply in courts but before legislatures and before administrative agencies in all the situations where people who can afford lawyers use them.

The problem I want to discuss primarily is how to supply these legal services. It appears that substantial amounts of money will be available under the poverty legislation and the Economic Opportunity Act of 1964 and undoubtedly from other sources. The problem is how to use it.[12] One quick answer—and some people are giving it—is to expand the existing Legal Aid services. Legal Aid is in the business, and has been for a long time, of serving the poor. It is established, it is respectable, and in many ways it has been successful. Some people, not surprisingly among them the National Legal Aid and Defender Association, have tended to take the view that this new money, these new resources for legal services for the poor, ought to go into expanding Legal Aid; that new and untried methods of serving the poor will be duplication, will very probably fail, and will possibly raise ethical problems that should be avoided by using the traditional form of service.

My thesis is that it would be a disaster if the Legal Aid approach were adopted. Although Legal Aid has been a useful, important instrument in helping the poor in the past, it has traditionally been insufficient and is almost inevitably destined to be insufficient under the approaches that we now deem necessary for dealing with poverty and, specifically, the legal problems of the poor. This is not to detract from the services a great many unknown people have given over many years at low pay, when poverty was less fashionable. Nevertheless, if the Legal Aid institutions were to become the monopolists of poverty law today, my suggestion—and it is by no means unique—is that this would be a grave misfortune and would undercut in advance the rendering of effective legal services to the poor.

Legal Aid is old, established, reputable, acceptable and safe. These things are themselves arguments against entrusting this whole new business to that kind of organization—steeped in tradition, bureaucratized, committed to relatively fixed views about how the poor can best be served.[13] All these attributes are, in some measure at least, out of step with the spirit of the new legislation, the experimental spirit, the notion that under the new legislation the poor themselves must participate, that new devices must be sought.[14]

Related to this factor of tradition and settled habit is the character of Legal Aid as a philanthropic service. It is a benevolent and charitable grant from the rich to the poor. Illustrious men sit on the boards of the Legal Aid societies. The next problem is what is usually called the attitude of paternalism that, in general terms, has characterized Legal Aid societies and Legal Aid people. A statement from a recent publication of a Legal Aid society by a top attorney running a Legal Aid office in a large nearby city illustrates this point. He said: "People may say that poverty prevents . . . [the poor] from having the same rights to get a divorce as a person with money, yet we must remember that obtaining a divorce is not a right but a privilege. For most Legal Aid clients, a separation is just as useful and practical as a divorce."[15]

If there is any notion in the law that is a plague to poor people, it is the distinction between a right and a privilege. Whatever merit the distinction still may have for some people, the least we can say is that a lawyer who is committed to representing poor people ought utterly to reject any suggestion that what is, in effect, a right for an affluent man somehow changes and becomes a mere privilege when a poor man reaches for it.

There are other things wrong with Legal Aid, but I want to abbreviate this apparent indictment. It has been noted that Legal Aid offices tend to be centrally located, frequently unknown, and inaccessible to the poor people.[16] Writers with some claim to knowing tell us that the urban poor tend to be bound by the most straitened physical horizons—the block or the slightly larger neighborhood; a journey "downtown" or to a distant neighborhood is likely to be a rare and perilous enterprise. Legal Aid people are discreet, they worry about charges of unlawful practice, they content themselves with very modest telephone listings.

It has also been charged that Legal Aid has failed to give meaningful education to the poor about the law and about their legal problems. Moreover, it is charged that, in the critical area that Miss Wickenden discussed, the problems of the poor confronting the government agency, the Legal Aid societies have been hesitant, weak, timid and ineffectual. They have not pressed the claims of the welfare applicant the way many people think they could be pressed.

What other possibilities are there? There are some that are familiar, some that are speculative, and undoubtedly others that imaginative lawyers and social scientists may develop.

One new kind of legal service for the poor is the now considerably discussed neighborhood law office. Such an office is typified by the effort here on the East Side of the legal unit in Mobilization for Youth. This law office should be a part of, or closely integrated with, a general community service program, an office of lawyers who work closely with social workers and other community service people in giving a unified or at least collaborative service to the poor. It should be an office that—and this is always touchy to say in front of lawyers—in some measure reaches out for legal business that exists among clients who are frequently ignorant of the law or unaware that it may be a friend as well as an enemy.[17]

The neighborhood law office is becoming fashionable in the literature, although it is still not widespread. It may be too fashionable.

It may tend to divert thinking from other possibilities that we ought to be considering. I mention, for instance, the possibility of publicly financed, nonorganizational, private lawyers receiving fees for service to the poor, a kind of legal counterpart to Medicare which would have some of the advantages of allowing the poor man to select his lawyer as the affluent man does. If we could encourage the proper attitude in the bar, this perhaps would introduce the affluent lawyer to the poor client in a way that might be interesting and beneficial to both. England has been doing something like this for over fifteen years with its Legal Aid and Advice Act.[18]

Another possibility is public counsel. Most lawyers are familiar with the public defender for criminal cases and with the quarrels about whether a government-paid lawyer can fairly, adequately and wholeheartedly represent the poor against the government.[19] That argument is not resolved. I think it is entirely possible that public defenders, paid by the government and given a sufficient staff, can fight the "government" vigorously in the proper social and political environment.[20] I think also that we ought to consider the possibility of public counsel committed to the interests of the individual citizen in dealing with government and governmental agencies through criticism, attacks, and where necessary, suit.

Finally, I think the poverty legislation presents us with an opportunity to stop writing about, and start working with, a concept that Sweden gave us, the concept of the ombudsman. As I think most people know, the ombudsman is an arm of the Swedish government over 150 years old. To describe him too briefly, he is a kind of inspector general of official agencies and people. He is a receiver of complaints, he is a snooper, he is an inspector, he is a watchdog, and judging by the literature, he evidently worked very effectively in Sweden—so effectively that all of Scandinavia has adopted this institution, as have West Germany and New Zealand. Recognizing that so many of the problems of the poor relate to bureaucracy, there is no reason, I suggest, why the ombudsman could not be tried in some communities.

I think it is obvious, although we have no statistics, that poverty is going to be a volume business. Problems are going to be repetitive and simple, and there is a question whether lawyers are really needed for all of these problems. The same question, put a different way, is, If lawyers are going to be needed, are the resources of the bar going to be adequate?

One interesting line of inquiry is the possibility of creating a new class of legal technicians, something short of lawyers, who can learn about these routine, standardized problems and deal with them under the supervision of lawyers. This has already begun to happen. A couple of weeks ago I read about something that has been going on for some time. I refer to the legal aid organization of the Hotel Trades Council, where hotel workers come to an office and receive legal aid and advice, often from people who are not lawyers. Should not the bar and the law schools turn serious attention to the question of training people for this kind of technical, perhaps "subprofessional" (but we will think of a better name for it) work in these problems that are repetitive and manageable by people who have not received full-scale legal training?

When we pick up a newspaper and read about nonlawyers giving what we would ordinarily regard as legal advice, we have one of two reactions. The first is to pull down the unauthorized-practice guns and start shooting. This is a common reaction of the bar. The second is the one I have suggested—a sympathetic, cooperative, inquiring look at the actual situation to see whether we can constructively contribute to the handling of these problems, problems that are likely to be flooding us.

I have tried to say that the problems in the law relating to this area of poverty are enormous and still largely unknown. Handling them is a subject on which we have hardly enough questions, let alone sufficient answers. I am suggesting that we need new rules of law, because the old rules do not fit the situation for the poor. We need new ways of reaching the poor consumer of law. We need new rules of practice; we need newer views of our ethical prohibitions against solicitation and other kinds of barriers that were suited to the lawyer and the middle-class client but are unsuited to this new kind of problem. In short, we need a new look at the law in all its parts.

IV / (Charles E. Ares)

Astonishing changes in patterns of thought are emerging as a result of the urban explosion. In religion, the Ecumenical Council as well as developments in Protestant theology reflect the new condition of urban man. In economics, we have become accustomed to the idea that unbalanced budgets are not always sinful and may sometimes be good things. We passed an education bill without really even arguing about whether federal aid to education is an evil. This was once an emotionally charged issue, as was Medicare, which went whistling through the Congress in the face of minimal opposition. If concepts such as these can change, then there is no reason why civil liberties cannot be regarded as encompassing the problems of poverty. In fact, without minimizing familiar problems of civil rights and civil liberties, I would venture the assertion that the achievement of procedural and substantive due process for the poor will be our principal challenge in the next few decades. In this respect, I should like to make four points concerning the relation of poverty and the law.

First, in important respects the *substantive* law is biased against the poor in ways quite distinct from the procedural or structural bias that naturally confronts those who are without means to hire advocates.

Second, in order to alert lawyers to the need to remove that bias, legal education must undergo some fundamental changes.

Third, as a result of re-examination of the law and of fundamental changes in legal education, a new kind of lawyer must be produced.

Finally, this new lawyer must be *of* the people and not simply *for* the people whom he will represent.

As Mr. Frankel has described it, the role of the lawyer with respect to the problems of poverty, although unfamiliar to him because he has not been performing it, is at least a traditional one in the profession. He represents clients. Where the law is clear or can be clarified, he seeks clarification and compliance. Where the law is uncertain, he tries to see that it is turned to the benefit of his clients.

The basic premise of Mr. Frankel's discussion, it seems to me, is that the *structure* of the legal profession is middle class in its assumptions. We assume that the lawyer can sit quietly in his office awaiting the knock on the door by a client who has discovered that he has a legal problem and has found the way to the lawyer's office. He suggests, moreover, that this assumption is not valid for the great mass of people who live in poverty in the United States.

It is equally important to recognize that the substantive law is in many vital respects as much based upon middle-class assumptions as is the structure of the legal profession; this aspect of the law must be re-examined if the law is to be bent to the uses or the protection of the poor.

Often, when one speaks in this way, the proposition is immediately rejected because it seems to imply that there has been some malevolent purpose in structuring the law so that it serves the purpose of the "haves" against the interests of the "have-nots." This is, of course, simply not the case. The fact that the law is middle class is merely a reflection of the historical allocation of power in society. But if we are to make law available to the poor, then we may have to readjust that allocation somewhat where we determine that the law operates unfairly with respect to the poor.[21]

What are some examples of the way in which the law in its assumptions and its structure operates unfairly against the poor? The easiest, of course, lie in the criminal area, and I think it is significant that tonight we have talked practically not at all about criminal problems. *Griffin v. Illinois*,[22] *Douglas v. California*[23] and *Gideon v. Wainwright*,[24] have sparked a fundamental re-examination of the criminal process. There is some evidence, for example, that the conscience of the country has been awakened to such questions as the discriminatory nature of the bail system.[25] We seem finally to be recognizing that bail is simply an irrelevance insofar as the poor are concerned. This is a simple but dramatic example of how the law, without malevolent purpose, has developed so as to prejudice the poor.

Although examples of discrimination in civil cases are more difficult to discern, if one puts his mind to it a good many occur. Historically, for instance, the law of negligence developed to protect those who had from those who had not. The law of contributory negligence, the defense of assumption of risk and the fellow-servant rule were then devised to protect enterprises whose operations were thought important to a developing country.[26] They operated to protect those who had wealth against those who would take it from them by the processes of the law.

Our litigation system, it seems to me, has served to discourage litigation, to make litigation too difficult, too expensive, too time-consuming for the man who has little money. In recent years, we have ameliorated this to a good degree by more liberalized procedural rules, but lawsuits are still expensive. One of the finest improvements in our procedural system has been the development of discovery devices, the method by which one obtains facts from his opponent before trial. It is a wonderful aid in preparing for trial, but expensive, and very often beyond the reach of the poor.

I suppose the most glaring example of the way in which our civil law operates unfairly against the poor is the divorce laws. Although not by design, a law such as New York's, which restricts the grounds for divorce to adultery, makes it impossible for a poor person, short of perjury, to secure a divorce. A man with means can go to some other part of the country where the laws are not nearly so stringent.

In the field of landlord and tenant, it seems to me that the law is most clearly designed for the benefit of the "haves," or those with power. For example, eviction proceedings brought by a landlord are summary in nature,[27] designed to enable landlords to evict nonpaying tenants quickly and easily; this clearly illustrates solicitude for the interests of one powerful segment of the community.

Substantively, the law in this area is loaded against the tenant. One defense available to the tenant is that the landlord is guilty of recorded violations of the building code. If the tenant gets a stay of proceedings on this basis, he may then pay his rent to the court until the violations are corrected.[28] The system is defective in that the tenant must show a violation of record, which means he must have made a complaint to the appropriate agency, gotten an inspection and secured a finding of a violation before he is really able to take advantage of this defense. Furthermore, despite the fact that the landlord's violations might have deprived the tenant of vital services such as heat or water, he still must continue to pay the full amount of the rent. Yet he obviously is not getting what he bargained for in the lease. He may pay a part of the rent to the court to abide the correction of the violations, but he is nevertheless paying the full amount of the rent.

Another important area of the law where substantive rules seem to operate unfairly is installment buying and credit practices. David Caplowitz, in a book called *The Poor Pay More,* has endlessly documented the fact that those protections for the consumer that seem to exist in the statutes governing credit buying are simply not available to the poor because of their lack of legal services and their lack of know-how in protecting themselves and in taking advantage of these rules. It may also be true that the substantive rules themselves are not adequate to the situation of the poor. I have in mind such things as bait advertising and overselling by a merchant to a person who he knows very well will not be able to meet all the payments. Why should this kind of conduct on the part of the merchant not play some part in determining his rights when the inevitable occurs and the purchaser defaults on his contract? Why should the merchant's knowledge of the situation when he knowingly oversold not be taken into account in adjusting those rights?[29]

I suppose one area of the law which strikes a responsive chord with most of us is taxation. Our policies as to the income tax and sales taxes, if you examine them, will reflect the lack of power on the part of the people we are here concerned with. The result is that many of these laws produce effects which are unfairly disadvantageous to the poor.[30]

We know far too little about this bias in the law and thus need an occasion to examine the law from the perspective of the poor. A new look at the law by the law schools is essential to any correction of this bias. Law schools must adopt what my late good friend Edmond Cahn called "the consumer perspective." This will require the development of new courses, difficult as that may be, and, as has been suggested several times this evening, it will require new lines of research. It is easy enough to preach this, but it is immensely difficult to practice it. In order to examine the law as it operates you have to see the law in action, and if one thing has been characteristic of legal education, it is that we do not see the law in action; we see the law in the books. Therefore, we have to devise new methods by which we, as teachers and students, can get into the world to see how the law operates. This suggests much greater use of clinical experience in law schools.

In addition to a re-examination of the law stimulated by new teaching methods, I think the law schools have to produce a new kind of lawyer. The lawyer has traditionally been the generalist. He has been the one person in the community uniquely qualified to take the overview. Perhaps this is a romantic image of the general practitioner who has disappeared forever and cannot be recaptured. In any event, we have moved a long way from him. Many things, I suppose, have contributed. As our society becomes more complex, the lawyer cannot possibly know it all and must become a specialist.

I think our educational system also contributes to the trend; our legal educational system produces a fairly narrow product. Many are beginning to worry about this and to wonder how we can broaden the scope of legal education and teach law grandly and, to an extent, in an interdisciplinary fashion.[31] "Interdisciplinary" is a bad word in legal education. Efforts to teach law this way have been notoriously unsuccessful in the hands of most of us, and as one who has made a modest effort in that direction, I can speak with some authority. We are not very good in disciplines other than our own narrow one. Teachers in other disciplines will have to learn how to help us teach law students. I have had some experience with people from other disciplines attempting to lecture to law students. The knowledge of economists and sociologists, for example, is too generalized, especially with regard to the problems of the poor. Thus, difficult as it may be and unsettling to the traditionalists among us as this kind of legal education is, we have to combine our efforts to make legal education more meaningful and realistic.

Furthermore, I think a new lawyer *of* the people, not merely *for* the people, has to emerge. This is most difficult of all. The motivation for people to go into the kind of legal practice that has been described here has to be radically different from that which motivates most of us now.

Although there is a large amount of money in poverty right now, money for lawyers' fees is not going to be plentiful over the long haul. When the bloom is off the rose and we are all down to hard work, no one is going to become wealthy representing the poor. This kind of law practice is not likely to be attractive to people who have been taught that Wall Street is the pinnacle of the profession. Somehow a different kind of prestige factor or reward system has to be developed to make up for the lack of that downtown prestige and for what will undoubtedly be a much lower rate of financial return.

Practitioners in this field will have to have the spirit that the poverty program is now showing—that is, a kind of Peace Corps spirit. The difficulty is that this is no two-year enlistment; it is a long-time pull. I do not know how durable the Peace Corps spirit will be. Gratifyingly, there seems to be among our students a new sense of dedication, a new realistic idealism, about meeting these problems. I have the haunting feeling that we are failing these students because we have not found the way to put them to work and to nurture their idealism so that it will carry them through the frustrations and deprivations of a career devoted to public service.

As Miss Wickenden remarked, so often when society responds to the needs of the "minority poor" it responds in terms of its own assumptions. This generally means, I think, that we treat symptoms. Fine as most of the programs that have been suggested are, they are treatments of symptoms, and unfortunately, this is what lawyers are so often in business to do. We sweep up the pieces. With respect to clients of great wealth, however, we are able to do quite nicely in protecting them *before* trouble occurs. This is what we must do for the poor. It is much more difficult than providing them with a lawyer after they have found themselves in trouble. The new lawyer, if he is to be truly effective, will have to provide the political leadership that the minority poor must have if they are to marshal the power necessary to make a dent in the fundamental imperfections in society that hold 34,000,000 people in poverty. This is basically a political problem, and I think the lesson of the civil rights movement is that fundamental reforms come only when the people involved exercise political power. It has been rightly said that we must develop the so-called indigenous leadership in the poor community. But I think we ought not to be naive about how much leadership they alone are going to provide. They are not trained to it, and by the nature of their situation they are inarticulate and politically unskilled. Somebody else, therefore, will have to provide the initial political leadership to organize the poor into an active political force.

This seems to me to be the task we have to undertake. We must provide lawyers who are of these people, who feel what poverty is, who understand what poverty means to individuals not simply intellectually but emotionally, and who see the solution politically. They must have the stamina to stand and fight against the greatest odds and against all the pressures that middle-class conformity can bring to bear on one who represents people of this segment of society. They must be able to inspire, to nag, to stimulate people, to articulate their needs and to organize themselves into action.

To produce that kind of lawyer, it seems to me, is the greatest challenge that a law school can face, and to be that kind of lawyer is worthy of the best of the mind and spirit of the very fine students who are now coming through our doors.

Recent events point up the significant impact which the poverty issue has had upon the American legal structure. The principal legacy of the long-delayed extension of legal services to the poor is the wide gap between the manifest need for representation of this class and the meager resources currently available to support these services.

Largely for the reasons stated by Mr. Frankel, the traditional Legal Aid approach was not considered adequate to do the job alone. The chief new technique for providing legal services to the poor is the neighborhood law office, hundreds of which are currently operating under the aegis of the Office of Economic Opportunity. These offices represent a radical break with the past by offering a comprehensive and personal approach to the legal problems of the ghetto.

Recognition of the intimate connection between poverty and the legal problems involved in civil rights and civil liberties is also exemplified by the establishment of a National Office of the Rights of the Indigent by the NAACP Legal Defense Fund, of the Project on Social Welfare Law by the Arthur Garfield Hays Civil Liberties Program at the New York University School of Law, and of the Center on Social Welfare Policy and Law by Columbia University.

Fruits of this new approach have already appeared. For example, in its 1967 term the Supreme Court considered (and postponed decision on) whether one-year residence requirements for welfare were valid; ruled in favor of illegitimate children challenging restrictions on their welfare rights; and agreed to hear a case involving the rights of tenants in public housing. In addition, there is now a steady stream of lower-court decisions concerning the legal rights of poor persons.

Nevertheless, effective redress for the arbitrariness and discrimination often prevalent in the dispensation of government "benefits" such as education, public housing and welfare, while encouraging, is still in the embryonic stage. Until legal services are readily available to all who require them, and until public welfare is no longer considered a charity that can be withheld at will but a legal entitlement, the war on poverty will not be won.

NOTES

The full transcript of the conference was published in 41 *New York University Law Review* 328 (1966) with the title "Poverty, Civil Liberties, and Civil Rights: A Symposium."

1. 78 Stat. 252, 42 U.S.C. § 2000d-1.
2. Rothwax, "The Poor, the Law and Civil Liberties," in *Civil Liberties in New York* 1, 6 (March 1966).
3. See La. Acts 1960, No. 251, § 1, at 527.
4. 49 Stat. 620 (1935) (codified in scattered sections of 42 U.S.C.).
5. Economic Opportunity Act of 1964, 78 Stat. 508, 42 U.S.C. § 2701–981.
6. 314 U.S. 160 (1941).
7. See Reich, "Midnight Welfare Searches and the Social Security Act," 72 *Yale L.J.* 1347 (1963).
8. Cal. Welfare & Inst'ns Code §§ 1508, 1575.
9. See Flemming v. Nestor, 363 U.S. 603 (1960).
10. 75 Stat. 640 (1961), 5 U.S.C. §§ 2281–88 (1964).
11. See People v. La Fountain, 21 App. Div. 2d 719 (3d Dep't 1964) (memorandum decision).
12. See "National Legal Aid and Defender Association Adopts Policy Guides for Federal Legal Services to Poor," 51 *A.B.A.J.* 275 (1965).
13. See, generally, Frankel, "Experiments in Serving the Indigent," 51 *A.B.A.J.* 460 (1965).

14. There must be "maximum feasible participation" by the poor in programs for their betterment. Economic Opportunity Act of 1964, § 202(a)(3), 78 Stat. 516, 42 U.S.C. § 2782(3).

15. Quoted, with other similar references, in Carlin & Howard, "Legal Representation and Class Justice," 12 *U.C.L.A.L. Rev.* 381, 413–15 (1965).

16. *Id.* at 427, 430.

17. For a discussion of the possibility of such an office actively searching out legal problems see Cahn & Cahn, "The War on Poverty: A Civilian Perspective," 73 *Yale L.J.* 1317 (1964).

18. See, e.g., Lord Parker, "The Development of Legal Aid in England Since 1949," 48 *A.B.A.J.* 1029 (1962).

19. *Compare* Dimock, "The Public Defender: A Step Towards a Police State?" 42 *A.B.A.J.* 219 (1956), *with* Harrington & Getty, "The Public Defender: A Progressive Step Towards Justice," 42 *A.B.A.J.* 1139 (1956).

20. See H.R. Rep. No. 864, 88th Cong., 1st Sess. 10–11, 13–14 (1963), expressing strong dissent from the elimination of the public-defender alternative from the bill that became the Criminal Justice Act of 1964, 18 U.S.C. § 3006A. See, generally, Shafroth, "The New Criminal Justice Act," 50 *A.B.A.J.* 1049 (1964).

21. See, e.g., the clash between traditional notions of the rights of property and the sit-in demonstrations in Bell v. Maryland, 378 U.S. 226 (1964).

22. 351 U.S. 12 (1956).

23. 372 U.S. 353 (1963).

24. 372 U.S. 335 (1963).

25. National Conference on Bail and Criminal Justice, *Proceedings and Interim Report* (1965). For an excellent survey of the problem of the pretrial release and detention see Freed & Wald, *Bail in the United States* (1965).

26. Malone, "The Formative Era of Contributory Negligence," 41 *Ill. L. Rev.* 151 (1946).

27. N.Y. Real Prop. Actions Law §§ 711, 721.

28. *Id.*, § 755.

29. Cf. Williams v. Walker-Thomas Furniture Co., 350 F.2d 445 (D.C. Cir. 1965).

30. See Eisenstein, *The Ideologies of Taxation* 4 (1961).

31. See Reich, "Toward the Humanistic Study of Law," 74 *Yale L.J.* 1402 (1965).

21

Voting Discrimination in the South

The struggle to ensure the Negro his constitutional right to the franchise has been furthered on many levels. Demonstrations, protests, federal legislation, attempts at mass registration and legal action in the courts all have worked to provide the Negro citizen a measure of voting equality in 1968.

The movement, particularly by way of lawsuit, has been slow and tedious. Thousands of man hours have been spent on cases which succeeded in adding only a few voters to the rolls. In the Southern states, efforts to enfranchise the Negro met with vigorous resistance, and until the mid-1960s and the passage of the historic 1965 Voting Rights Act, statistics revealed that equality of the vote was a long way off.

Yet prior to 1965 it was through the judicial process that the most significant achievements were recorded. State devices designed to circumvent the Fifteenth Amendment, including various literacy, property, residence and character qualifications, the "grandfather clause" and the poll tax, were repeatedly challenged and declared unconstitutional in the federal courts.

In the State of Mississippi the pattern of discrimination against the Negro existed in an aggravated form. In August 1962, in a case of crucial importance to the freedom of nearly one-half million eligible Negro citizens to exercise their right to vote, the United States brought suit against the state, the members of the state board of election commissioners and six county voter registrars to invalidate the state's literacy and "good moral character" requirements. By way of relief, the United States requested that the challenged provisions be declared unconstitutional; that the Court find that the implementation of the invalid legislation had deprived Negro citizens of the right to vote on account of their race, and that the deprivations had been pursuant to a pattern or practice of racial discrimination.

When the case was appealed to the Supreme Court, the author was asked by the ACLU to draft an amicus curiae brief in support of the government's position. In attacking the Mississippi poll tax, as well as the other state obstacles to an open franchise, the brief advocated an even more far-reaching decision than was requested by the United States. Relevant portions follow.

I / Historical Introduction

The constitutional invalidity of the Mississippi voting laws discussed in this brief is shown by their history and past and present effects. These laws intentionally discriminate on the grounds of race and implement Mississippi's long-standing legislative policy of disenfranchising Negroes. The state constitutional and statutory provisions attacked here might in other circumstances be defended as valid measures to protect the quality of the electorate. Any such defense by appellees is obviously a sham because of the studied effort made by Mississippi since the nineteenth century to enact laws which are innocuous on their face but invidious in operation. The following brief historical survey overcomes any presumption that Mississippi's voting laws were passed and are being administered in good faith.

During Reconstruction in Mississippi, Negro males were enfranchised for the first time and soon constituted a majority of the Mississippi electorate. By 1870, many Negroes had seats in the state legislature. White resentment led to attempts to again subjugate the Negro through the use of violence, intimidation and economic sanctions—all designed to deprive him of the vote. By 1875 this goal had been achieved. The new white-controlled legislature then provided for the appointment of voting registrars with broad discretionary powers to be used in discouraging Negro voting.

Because some white Mississippians were displeased with the extralegal tactics (often subject to corruption and use against whites) employed to keep the political structure white, a state constitutional convention was called to find permanent methods of maintaining white control. Although a majority of the registered voters were Negroes, an ugly campaign resulted in only one Negro delegate being elected to the convention.

From the outset there was complete candor that the purpose of the Convention of 1890 was to assure the ascendency of that "race whose rule has always meant prosperity and happiness to all races." (Opening address of the president of the convention, S. S. Calhoon.) The Mississippi Supreme Court later acknowledged that the intent of the convention was "to obstruct the exercise of the franchise by the Negro race."[1]

Several means were employed to effect this purpose. Timely payment of a poll tax was made a prerequisite to voting. The poll tax "was primarily intended by the framers . . . as a clog upon the franchise."[2] A voting applicant was henceforth required to read a section of the state constitution or to give a reasonable interpretation of a section read to him. The literacy requirement was chosen to take advantage of the sharp disparity between the number of illiterate Negroes (76 percent) and illiterate whites (11 percent). Moreover, the interpretation alternative, with registrars having discretion to judge answers, in effect exempted white illiterates from the literacy requirement.

The convention also adopted an apportionment system, retained to the present day, which ensured that the counties whose populations are predominantly white control the legislature and election of the executive through an electoral college.

Upon the adoption of the constitution, the president of the convention congratulated its members and noted: "[The white] race alone can now safely exercise the function of ruling." The confidence of the speaker was justified; prior to the convention, Negroes constituted a majority of the registered voters in Mississippi, but by 1892 only 8,615 Negroes were included among the 78,742 registered voters.

In 1902, whites, fearing that the Negro would overcome the literacy barrier by taking advantage of the public education system, adopted a white primary. When this device was declared unconstitutional in 1944, Mississippi responded by establishing as a qualification for primaries a vague and indefinite test (that voters be "in accord with the party's principles") and provided for its discretionary administration by white primary officers.

In 1954, partly due to specters raised by *Brown v. Board of Education*, the state constitution was amended to require a voting registrant (1) to read and write any section of the state constitution, *and* (2) to give a reasonable interpretation thereof, *and* (3) to demonstrate an understanding of "the duties and obligations of citizenship," *and*, finally, (4) to present a registration form prepared and sworn to by him.[3] These new tests were to be applied only to people registering after passage of the amendment. The brunt of this obnoxious "grandfather clause" fell, of course, on those not already registered, a group containing a vastly higher percentage of prospective Negro voters than of prospective white voters. Moreover, the requirements imposed were more burdensome generally to unregistered Negroes than to unregistered whites—even apart from the hostile registrars—because Mississippi provided Negroes with inferior educational opportunities.

The discretion of registrars was recently augmented by a statute providing that voters be of "good moral character."[4] This provision has been reinforced by requiring the names and addresses of new applicants for voter registration to be published in local newspapers so that any person having knowledge of their lack of "good moral character" may contest the registration.[5] Publication itself is an additional burden. Much worse, however, it is an open invitation to those who employ fear and force to intimidate prospective Negro registrants.

II / Mississippi's requirement that voting registrants read and write and interpret the state constitution denies Negro citizens the equal protection of the laws, due process of law, and the right to vote guaranteed by the Fourteenth and Fifteenth Amendments.

Section 244 of the Mississippi Constitution provides:

Every elector shall . . . be able to read and write any section of the Constitution of this State and give a reasonable interpretation thereof to the county registrar. He shall demonstrate to the county registrar a reasonable understanding of the duties and obligations of citizenship under a constitutional form of government.

Any new or additional qualifications herein imposed shall not be required of any person who was a duly registered and qualified elector of this state prior to January 1, 1954.

The Legislature shall have the power to enforce the provisions of this section by appropriate legislation.

The Mississippi literacy test appears egalitarian on its face, but analysis reveals that its effect is inevitably discriminatory because of the social and legislative setting in Mississippi. Accordingly, the test violates the equal protection and due process clauses of the Fourteenth Amendment and the Fifteenth Amendment. Furthermore, the literacy test and interpretation provisions, in leaving uncontrolled discretion to state officials, violate the Fourteenth and Fifteenth Amendments by permitting and, indeed, inviting racial discrimination in the application of the tests. That such discrimination has actually taken place on a wide scale is a matter of public knowledge and is demonstrated by the evidence in the record.

The early case of *Williams v. Mississippi*[6] is not in any respect inconsistent with these contentions. *Williams* decided that a Negro convicted of murder by an all-white jury was not denied equal protection of the laws. The petitioner contended that (1) the literacy test, in conjunction with certain oath requirements, was susceptible of manipulation by registrars to prevent Negroes from registering, and that (2) since the jury panel was drawn from voter registration lists, Negroes were disqualified from jury duty. In other words, the vice of the literacy test was claimed to lie in its administration. The Court, relying on a prior decision of the Supreme Court of Mississippi which found that jurors were selected without reference to voting lists, ruled that petitioner had not proven discrimination in the administration of the literacy test.

But *Williams* rests on the discredited proposition that unless a statute says *in haec verba* that Negroes cannot vote it is not void on its face. Since 1898, when that case was decided, the Supreme Court has departed from that position. In *Davis v. Schnell*,[7] it was held that merely because discrimination is subtle does not mean it is valid, and that the Fifteenth Amendment nullifies sophisticated as well as simple-minded modes of discrimination. The *Davis* court went behind the innocent words to find an impermissible purpose:

> *We cannot ignore the impact of the Boswell Amendment upon Negro citizens because it avoids mention of race or color: "To do this would be to shut our eyes to what all others than we can see and understand."*[8]

The literacy and constitutional interpretation tests in section 244 of the Mississippi Constitution do in fact, and were intended to, impede Negro voter registration, not only by inviting discrimination by the registrars who grade the essays on the meaning of the constitution, but also because Negroes, as a result of deliberate state policy, receive substantially poorer education than whites. As the Greenville, Mississippi, *Delta Democrat-Times* said editorially on October 10, 1954:

> *The proposal* [*section 244*] *was designed to slow down Negro registrations and a number of* [*legislative*] *committee members have said they felt any long-range success in keeping Whites and Negroes separated lies in keeping Whites in control of the ballot boxes.*

The 1961 report of the Mississippi State Department of Education, Division of Finance and Administration, shows that Negro pupils receive on a state-wide basis less than one fourth as much support from local school funds as do white pupils. Such local funds constitute over one half of the public school support. State-level funds are also discriminatorily allocated in favor of whites. Almost all white schools are accredited; almost all Negro schools are not.

In sum, there is the vicious cycle of (1) relatively high educational requirements for voting (and for holding public office[9]) and consequently almost no Negro voting, which allows the election of (2) an all-white legislature that purposely keeps Negroes uneducated, which therefore means that (3) Negroes cannot qualify to vote, and the cycle begins again.

Literacy tests are not inherently unconstitutional, but as Mr. Justice Douglas pointed out in *Lassiter v. Northampton Election Board*,[10] a "literacy test may be unconstitutional on its face" if the legislative setting of that test reveals that it is a "device to make racial discrimination easy."

A state which provides such unequal educational facilities for the Negro and white races may not deny the underprivileged race the opportunity to learn to read and write and to interpret its constitution, and then use this deprivation to disenfranchise that race. In such a setting, both a literacy test and a constitutional interpretation test are unconstitutional on their face. That such tests are unconstitutional also finds support in the cases invalidating the white primary.[11]

The Mississippi literacy test, which is now mandatory rather than an alternative to the constitutional interpretation test, also embodies a forbidden "grandfather clause": those persons already registered are exempted from the more stringent requirements by the device of permanent registration.

In speaking of the Oklahoma literacy test in *Guinn v. United States*,[12] the Supreme Court stated:

> *It is true it contains no express words of an exclusion from the standard [for registration] which it establishes . . . on account of race . . . but the standard itself inherently brings that result into existence. . . .*

In Oklahoma lineal descendants of those entitled to vote prior to enactment of the Fifteenth Amendment were expressly exempted from the literacy test. Thus a vast number of white citizens escaped the literacy burden and retained their franchise in spite of it, while Negro citizens felt its full burden.

In Mississippi prior to the 1954 amendment to section 244 of the Mississippi Constitution, there was no mandatory literacy test. The

1898 version of section 244 was drafted in the disjunctive, requiring registrants to be able to read *or* to understand the constitution when read to them. Under the biased eye of registrars, whites were registered and Negroes were not, as planned. In 1954 the section was rewritten in the conjunctive, making literacy an affirmative requirement. Thus the necessary effect of the new standard, as in *Guinn*, is to discriminate on grounds of race, an effect prohibited by the Fifteenth Amendment and the equal protection clause of the Fourteenth Amendment. The literacy test, a subtle "grandfather clause," is therefore unconstitutional on its face.

The requirement of section 244 that a voter registrant interpret a section of the state constitution is also void for vagueness. The state constitutional provision and its implementing statutes do not define "a reasonable interpretation." Is it to mean what the Mississippi Supreme Court has said, what the words of the constitution would seem on their face to mean, any reasonable interpretation showing intelligent comprehension of the meaning of written language, or something else? In fact, the individual registrar has unlimited discretion to determine whether an interpretation is sufficient. The test thus is void not only for vagueness, but also because it provides no uniform standard by which all voters are to be judged equally. Different registrars will have different views as to the meaning of the constitutional provisions, the provisions put to registrants and the type of interpretation which will be satisfactory.

The Court's recent ruling in *Baggett v. Bullitt*[13] reaffirmed the established rule that "a law forbidding or requiring conduct in terms so vague that men of common intelligence must necessarily guess at its meaning and differ as to its application violates due process of law." In *Baggett*, the Court invalidated loyalty oaths for state employees because their vagueness created "the hazard of being prosecuted for knowing but guiltless behavior." Certainly the solicitude for individual conscience and rights, evidenced so forcefully by that opinion, encompasses protection of Mississippi's citizens against loss of their precious voting right through application of a standard even vaguer than those contained in the invalid loyalty oaths. *Baggett* and the authorities cited therein lend conclusive support to the contention that the interpretation test for voting violates due process of law.

Obviously, opinions can and do differ, even among trained lawyers and political scientists, as to the meaning of a state constitutional provision. Where a state's highest court has interpreted a provision, even a lawyer might well be unaware of it unless he had researched the particular point. Clearly it is unreasonable to assume that a citizen is unfit to vote unless he has studied all state court opinions construing provisions of the state constitution.

This conclusion is reinforced by the fact that no valid state purpose is served, reasonably or otherwise, by the requirement that a voter registrant be able to interpret the state constitution. It is not the duty of voters to be able to determine the validity of legislation; their intelligence is not revealed by answers to questions involving technical points of law. Indeed, most members of the state bar, and most elected officials of the state, would probably be unable to interpret the state constitution satisfactorily.

III / The Mississippi voter registration provision requiring an applicant to possess "good moral character" is unconstitutionally vague on its face and has been applied in violation of the Fourteenth and Fifteenth Amendments.

The Mississippi legislature has made the judgment that only citizens of "good moral character" are suited to vote. The present case does not require the Court to decide the reasonableness of that legislative determination, because the "good moral character" requirement must fall since it contains no standards to guide the registrars who are to apply it, and is therefore unconstitutionally vague.

The legislature may not delegate authority to the registrars without enunciating some guidelines for the exercise of that authority. The United States Supreme Court has recognized this principle and has consistently applied it to legislative delegations of authority. For example, in *Panama Refining Co. v. Ryan*[14] the Court invalidated an act of Congress because it contained no ascertainable standard. True, the Supreme Court has upheld delegation of authority in which no standards were ascertainable, but these cases involved delegation to administrators in areas where long-standing customs had been established or the terms of the statute involved words susceptible of reasonably uniform interpretation. For example, the statute in the *McKinley* case[14a] authorized the Secretary of War to suppress "houses of ill fame" within reasonable distances of military camps. The term "houses of ill fame" obviously referred to houses of prostitution, and any interpretation of the words would raise only the factual issue of whether prostitution was being practiced in the given case. There is, however, considerable controversy over what constitutes "good moral character," to put it mildly.

If the Mississippi legislature had performed its duty of indicating what in its judgment constituted "good moral character," Negro registrants would have been apprised of the requirements they were obliged to meet. If they had failed to meet the explicit standards, they could have sought court review of the constitutionality of the standards as applied to them.

The difficulty of achieving a universally acceptable definition, rather than being an excuse for the abdication of legislative responsibility, indicates that the term chosen by the legislature was improper. A more precise term should have been used, if possible; if not, a series of standards should have been stated by the legislature. In the complete absence of guidelines, registrars are free to impose their individual moral views upon applicants. Indeed, in Mississippi, registrars may view Negro applicants as lacking in character by the very fact of their desire to vote, despite the constitutional mandates of the Fourteenth and Fifteenth Amendments.

The "good moral character" requirement, contained in an amendment to the Mississippi Constitution, approved by the voters in 1960, was intended as a means of maintaining segregation and perpetuating Negro disenfranchisement. The *Jackson Clarion-Ledger* said of the amendment and a companion proposal that "apparently both are aimed at maintaining segregation."

The Citizens' Council newspaper urged voters "to safeguard Mississippi from the black bloc vote" by approving the proposed amendment which would require registrants to be of good moral character. The editorial said the proposed amendment would help "protect Mississippi ballot boxes from the self-seeking forays of bloc voting pressure groups" and discourage mass registration efforts on the part of irresponsible and immoral elements.

Two implementing bills added a new dimension to the "good moral character" requirement by effectively facilitating the intimidation of would-be Negro voters.[15] The statutes provide that within ten days after receiving an application for registration, the registrar shall publish the applicant's name and address in a local newspaper once a week for two weeks. Within two weeks after the last publication, any other registered voter in the county may file an affidavit challenging the good moral character of the applicant. When such a challenge is filed, the registrar sets a date for a hearing, holds the hearing, considers the evidence and makes a finding as to the applicant's character. In effect, the burden of proving good moral character is on the applicant. Most Negroes, knowing that their names will be published, are deterred from registering. If they attempt to register, these laws increase the possibility of economic, psychological or physical coercion. The history of the "good moral character" provision and of the legislation implementing it shows that the purpose of the new laws is perpetuation of racial discrimination in regard to voting,[16] and that it has had that effect.

IV / The Mississippi poll tax violates the Fourteenth and Fifteenth Amendments since it discriminates against Negroes and imposes a privilege tax upon voting.

The passage of the Twenty-fourth Amendment to the United States Constitution makes it unnecessary to consider the constitutionality of Mississippi's poll tax as applied to federal elections.[17] However, the recent amendment does not deal with the constitutionality of a poll tax for voting in state elections. Certainly, failure to outlaw such a requirement is not to legalize it. Therefore, the constitutionality of Mississippi's poll tax, as applied to state elections, is still undecided.

The 1890 Convention was called to perpetuate white dominance over the Negro and eliminate the need for lawless action by those in positions of responsibility. These aims were clearly indicated by statements made at the convention and in contemporary newspapers. The poll tax it adopted has stood for nearly seventy-five years.

The Supreme Court of Mississippi in *Ratliff v. Beale* construed section 243 of the Constitution of 1890. The court said:

In our opinion, the clause [§ 243] *was primarily intended by the framers of the constitution as a clog upon the franchise and, secondarily and incidentally only, as a means of revenue.*[18]

The court made it plain that the poll tax provision was not an isolated instance of discrimination through voting qualifications:

Within the field of permissible action under the limitations imposed by the federal constitution, the convention swept the circle of expedients to obstruct the exercise of the franchise by the Negro race. By reason of its previous condition of servitude and dependence, this race had acquired or accentuated certain pecularities of habit, of temperament and of character, which clearly distinguishes it, as a race, from that of the whites—a patient, docile people, but careless, landless and migratory within narrow limits, without forethought and its criminal members given rather to furtive offenses than to the robust crimes of the whites. Restrained by the federal constitution from discriminating against the Negro race, the convention discriminated against its characteristics and the offenses to which its weaker members were prone.[19]

The Supreme Court of Mississippi has not changed its interpretation of the legislative intention behind the poll tax. In *Wylie v. Cade*,[20] that court adopted and approved its statement in *Ratliff* about that purpose. The conclusion is thus inescapable that the Mississippi poll tax is a privilege tax on voting and is intended to prevent Negroes from voting.

The poll tax puts an onerous burden on persons earning small amounts of money, if they wish to vote. A man earning less than $1,000 a year cannot be expected to pay two dollars in February to preserve a right which cannot be exercised until November, especially if he is uncertain about being allowed to vote even if he pays the tax. To vote in a primary he must pay almost two years in advance.[21]

The economic burden imposed by the Mississippi tax affects Negroes more than it does whites. The 1960 census showed the disparity between the earnings of Negroes and whites in the state. Of Mississippians fourteen years of age or older, about 70 percent of each race have some income. Of these, 33 percent of the whites and 69 percent of the Negroes earn less than $1,000 per year, and 50 percent of the whites and 87 percent of the Negroes earn less than $2,000 per year. The disparity is even greater when the earnings per family are compared:

	PERCENTAGE OF FAMILIES	
FAMILY INCOME	White	Negro
Under $1,000	10.1%	37.1%
$1,000–1,999	11.9%	29.1%
$2,000–2,999	12.4%	16.7%
$3,000–3,999	13.0%	8.0%
$4,000–4,999	12.2%	4.2%
$5,000–5,999	11.1%	2.0%
Above $6,000	29.3%	2.9%

The stock Southern answer to these figures is that the Negroes' economic situation and consequent inability to pay the poll tax are their own fault, that they should be more responsible and energetic in order to increase their earnings. But economic opportunity is inextricably intertwined with the ability to vote and with access to educational opportunities. Other parts of this brief demonstrate that Negroes in Mississippi are denied equal access to educational opportunities, and the poll tax coupled with other measures severely restricts Negroes' right to vote. The discriminatory practices which prevent the Mississippi Negro from earning a living wage can be erased only when the Negro can vote and thereby help to determine who will make the crucial economic decisions.

Breedlove v. Suttles[22] is the leading Supreme Court decision dealing with poll taxes. Payment of the tax discussed in that case was a prerequisite for voting (except for the blind or those over sixty years of age), but the tax was compulsory for all other males whether or not they voted. The Court in *Breedlove* dealt primarily with the contentions that the tax violated the Nineteenth Amendment and the equal protection clause of the Fourteenth Amendment.

The Court held that the tax was not a deprivation of women's rights. It found that the Georgia tax was primarily a revenue measure which was universally enforced within permissible classifications:

Payment as a prerequisite is not required for the purpose of denying or abridging the privilege of voting. It does not limit the tax to electors. Aliens are not there permitted to vote, but the tax is laid upon them if within the defined class.[23]

Therefore, the Georgia tax was not a privilege tax on voting, but was a capitation tax on certain classes of people. For this reason, the holding in *Breedlove* is not dispositive of the present case. Here we do not have a compulsory capitation tax imposed on a reasonably selected class of people, but rather a tax which has to be paid only in order to vote, and which is discriminatory in both intent and application. As previously noted, the Mississippi poll tax provision appears in the franchise, not the revenue, article of the Mississippi Constitution.

The Supreme Court has long maintained an aggressive and diligent policy of enforcing the spirit of the Fifteenth Amendment:

The [Fifteenth] Amendment nullifies sophisticated as well as simple-minded modes of discrimination. It hits onerous procedural requirements which effectively handicap exercise of the franchise by the colored race although the abstract right to vote may remain unrestricted as to race.[24]

This policy should be applied here to invalidate Mississippi's poll tax.

Because of certain procedural obstacles, the Supreme Court did not decide the case on the merits, but it did rule in March 1965 that if the allegations were proved at trial, the contested Mississippi practices were unconstitutional.[25] *In a companion case,*[26] *the Court reached the constitutional questions and struck down Louisiana's literacy statute on grounds similar to those urged in the brief.*

After the Mississippi case was remanded to the district court, the intervening enactment of the 1965 Voting Rights Act and the United States Supreme Court's 1966 decision in Harper v. Virginia

State Board of Elections *invalidating poll taxes in state elections removed any need to prove the allegations. The lower court thus proceeded immediately to fashion a decree striking down the objectionable Mississippi laws.*

NOTES

Francis Biddle, former Attorney General of the United States, and Civil Liberties Fellow Bernard Evans Harvith participated in the preparation of the brief.

1. Ratliff v. Beale, 74 Miss. 247, 266, 20 So. 865, 868 (1896).
2. *Id.* at 869.
3. Miss. Const. § 244.
4. Miss. Code, § 3235.
5. *Id.*, §§ 3212.7, 3217.01–3217.15.
6. 170 U.S. 213 (1898).
7. 81 F. Supp. 872, *aff'd per curiam* 336 U.S. 933 (1949).
8. *Id.* at 881.
9. Miss. Const. § 250.
10. 360 U.S. 45, 53 (1959).
11. Nixon v. Herndon, 272 U.S. 299 (1927); United States v. Classic, 313 U.S. 299 (1941); Smith v. Allwright, 321 U.S. 649 (1944).
12. 238 U.S. 347, 364 (1915).
13. 377 U.S. 360 (1964).
14. 293 U.S. 388 (1935).

14a. McKinley v. United States, 249 U.S. 397 (1919).

15. Miss. Code, §§ 3212.7, 3217.01–3217.15.
16. J.P. Coleman, *The Origin of the Constitution of 1890*, reprinted from the *Journal of Mississippi History* (April 1957).
17. The Twenty-fourth Amendment, ratified in 1964, outlaws poll taxes and any other tax that denies or abridges the right to vote for President, Vice-President, Senator or Representative.
18. 74 Miss. 247, 268, 20 So. 865, 869 (1896).
19. 74 Miss. at 266, 20 So. at 868.
20. 174 Miss. 426, 432–33, 164 So. 579 (1935).
21. Miss. Code, § 3160.
22. 302 U.S. 277 (1937).
23. *Id.* at 282.
24. Lane v. Wilson, 307 U.S. 268, 275 (1939).
25. United States v. Mississippi, 380 U.S. 128 (1965).
26. Louisiana v. United States, 380 U.S. 145 (1965).

22

De Facto School Segregation

A Conference

As the 1964 Hays Civil Liberties Conference convened, there was no question about the overwhelming timeliness of the subject. The air was full of the crisis generated by the apparent impregnability of Northern schools to significant integration, and numerous school boards and courts were facing up to the fact that de facto *segregation—largely a product of racial housing patterns in cities and suburbs—was undercutting the promise of the Fourteenth Amendment and of the Supreme Court's* Segregation Cases. *Discussing these issues at the conference were Will Maslow, Executive Director of the American Jewish Congress; Robert Carter, General Counsel of the NAACP; Professor John Kaplan, then of Northwestern Law School and now of Stanford Law School; and Stanley H. Lowell, then Chairman of the New York City Commission on Human Rights.*

I / Introduction (Norman Dorsen)

The sad violence of the summer just ended has only emphasized the general predicament. Governments at all levels are now trying to do something about the plight of the Northern Negro. The trouble is that nobody knows just what should be done. It is becoming more widely understood that the problem differs markedly from the traditional issue of liberating the Southern Negro. Karl E. Meyer, an American journalist writing to a British audience soon after the July riots, had this to say:

> *In the South, the Negro is sealed off from white society by custom and oppressive local government. The northern reality is in some ways more diabolical, since it is laced with pious hypocrisy. In law, the Negro has full civil rights, and his cause enlists the cautious good will of white liberals. But he remains invisible and unheard, walled into ghettoes that extinguish hope itself. This is the larger evil that lies behind the lesser evil of violence and looting that have forced whites to stare into the lower depths.*[1]

Mr. Meyer could have added that the South has a further advantage—there the two races have come to know one another well. The Negro is part of the scene and there is reason to hope that when the old political and social order finally collapses, he will play a realistic role in community life. In the North, however, because he is "invisible," he is not only excluded from the privileges of the white man, but unknown to him and therefore a questionable candidate, even when all privileges become available, for comprehensive participation in white society.

The participants in the Hays Conference recognized that the vicious circle of inferior housing, jobs and schools hemmed the Negro in, and that each of these conditions deserved study. Nevertheless, we confined our discussion to education, partly because it was the problem of *Brown* itself, and partly because the subject was so ripe, with vociferous parents' groups being formed for and against the "Princeton Plan" and for and against school busing.

Mr. Maslow pointed out at the start of the conference that there are two basic issues. First, is there any constitutional impediment to a school board's decision to recognize the racial composition of a school or neighborhood for the purpose of taking action to reduce *de facto* segregation? Second, apart from the question of whether a school board wishes to act, does a board have a *duty* to try to reduce racial imbalance which exists due to housing patterns or other factors over which the board has no control?

The first question elicited a uniform response among the participants, all agreeing that the Constitution is not "color blind" when it comes to a school board's decision to assist the Negro, the famous dictum of the first Justice Harlan notwithstanding. As chairman of the conference, I must regard this confluence of attitudes as an implied criticism, as it suggested a failure to bring together all shades of opinion. There is some support for another view, which holds that the Fourteenth Amendment absolutely forbids the use of race as a criterion for official action such as zoning of districts or assignment of pupils. In response to the argument that race can be used for the beneficial purpose of promoting integration, it is said that once government begins making decisions based on race, the end cannot be foreseen, and in the long run this will lead to invidious as well as benign distinctions. But the conferees all rejected this position, and I shall leave it to the transcript to disclose why.

It was the second major question that proved the bone of contention during our discussion. Professor Kaplan took the view, as against the others, that segregated schools are not automatically invalid under the Fourteenth Amendment and the *Brown* decision, in the absence of affirmative state action to separate the races; accordingly, he concluded that there is no duty imposed by the Constitution requiring school board action to reduce racial imbalance. It is only fair to point out that though he was a minority of one on the panel, Professor Kaplan was hewing to what seems the prevalent opinion. The three reasons for his conclusion are suggested in the transcript that follows and are set forth at length in Part II of his three-part article entitled "Segregation Litigation and the Schools."[2] First, the *Brown* decision lends little or no support to the theory of automatic invalidation of segregated schools because that case dealt with officially required segregation. Second, Professor Kaplan claims it is "at least possible" that a Negro child will appreciate the difference between attending a segregated school because authorities have ordered him there and because of the happenstance of the housing pattern in his city; it thus cannot be said with complete confidence that the child will be harmed psychologically by attending a *de facto* segregated school. Third and most important, it does not follow that geographical districting is unconstitutional merely because "the same harm is visited upon Negro children by districting on purely geographical lines as would be visited by racial segregation under forces of law."

Professor Kaplan's analysis is worth studying in its unabridged form because it represents possibly the most comprehensive and lawyerlike analysis of *de facto* segregation. I must say frankly, however, that despite its sophistication, indeed perhaps because of it, I am unpersuaded.

My view is that the cause of racial integration is entitled to a "preferred position" in the hierarchy of constitutional values. Given that position, school boards and courts must act to desegregate schools whether or not the pattern was innocently or maliciously established, and irrespective of "other values," such as the neighborhood school. These "other values" do of course exist, and they must be given weight by the school board. But they are less important constitutionally than an integrated school system. Thus, in the fashioning of school boundaries and school sites, race *must* be considered, although other factors may be considered too. The duty of the school board in the usual case would be to draw district lines to maximize racial integration. The working out of a specific school plan in the best of circumstances is not a simple task, and no pat formula will do more than provide overall direction. But that direction will often be the difference between a segregated and an integrated school.

What basis is there for the premise of the above argument—that racial integration is entitled to a "preferred position" among constitutional values? The answer lies in the words and history of the Fourteenth Amendment, the *Brown* case and its progeny, and the moral element underlying these decisions. Professor Kaplan deals in his article with the issue of preferred position, but curiously suggests that it would "fail for many of the same reasons" as the contention that the First Amendment, embodying free speech and other fundamental values, occupies a favored constitutional status.[3] A more accurate statement would be that it will "*succeed* for many of the same reasons." Granting variations in doctrinal approach among individual Justices, the fact is that the Supreme Court for a generation has accorded freedom of expression a "preferred position," and it has done so because of the language of the First

Amendment, and the Court's recognition of the moral imperative of uninhibited expression.[4] These same elements, in my judgment, apply to the problem at hand.

It does not detract from these conclusions to express the hope that other institutions—school boards, legislatures—will assume primary responsibility for diminishing segregation in the North. There are indeed some encouraging signs. Some school boards are acting boldly, and California and Illinois have enacted statutes designed to further this end. The California statute empowers its Department of Education to advise on "problems involving the ethnic distribution of pupils and school attendance areas."[5] Illinois took a further step by making it the duty of school boards, in building or acquiring schools, not to do so in a manner that promotes segregation. Perhaps more important, boards were also directed to change, as soon as practicable, existing attendance units in a way that takes into consideration the elimination of segregation.[6] Such political solutions are to be welcomed not only because they open the door to genuine integration of schools, but because they relieve the judiciary from the burden of first-line decision-making in a highly volatile area.

But there is no law dealing with *de facto* segregation, aside from the few scattered legislative and administrative actions referred to above. The 1964 Civil Rights Act is no help, for it explicitly excludes the problem of "racial imbalance" in public schools.[7] How then can boards and legislatures be encouraged to take vigorous action to end school segregation innocently caused? This is the sticking point, for few answers are in evidence, even among ordinarily optimistic men, just as there are few solutions apparent in coping with the large ghettos of the North. It may be that this is one of those problems that are just too tough, that the expenditure of resources in any likely amount will hardly make a dent, that the wheel has turned too far to save us. Indeed this is a possibility, but it would be cowardly and foolhardy to act on these assumptions. The effort must be made, not only because the specter of violence and social disintegration hovers in the background, but because it is right.

II / (Will Maslow)

Our topic is school segregation, which means that we are not going to address ourselves to the related problem of improving the quality of education in New York, although in a sense, these are the face and the reverse of the coin. Nor are we going to deal with another related matter, the recruitment, promotion and assignment of teachers.

Our task is one of examining the legal problems involved in what have come to be known as *de facto* segregated schools.

There are 592 elementary public schools in New York City, with an average population of more than a thousand. Of these 592 public elementary schools, no less than 134 have a Negro-Puerto Rican population of 90 percent or higher. And this number continues to increase.

While New York's figures may be larger than those of other cities, they are not exceptional. Detroit has 81 schools with a Negro population of 90 percent or higher. Chicago has 79; Philadelphia 76; Cleveland 47; Los Angeles 44. And in Washington, D.C., 85 percent of the school population is Negro.[8]

As a result of these massive concentrations of minority group populations, and residential discriminatory housing patterns, we have islands, black ghettos, within our metropolitan areas. They are hemmed in just as though they were hemmed in by walls. Obviously, any school within these black enclaves will very quickly become a school with a heavy racial imbalance.

These situations arise without any conscious interference or contrivance on the part of a board of education. No one charges that the New York City Board has done anything to bring about these heavy concentrations. That is, perhaps, one of the reasons that the legal problems became so complex.

Of course, when you have a situation in which there has been some contrivance, you have what we know today as *de jure* segregation, which has been illegal since 1954 and which, therefore, presents no conceptual problems, but only problems of proof. In the famous New Rochelle case, you had a town with twelve schools, one of which was the Lincoln School. New Rochelle sought to channel almost all its Negroes into this one school.[9]

This contrivance, of course, does not have to be effectuated by a statute or even by a formal resolution found in the minute books. It can be done by any policy of the board which will affect the composition of the school. It can be done, first of all, by carefully choosing the location for a new school. If you build a school in Harlem today, it is obviously going to be an all-Negro school, and if you build it in an all-white area, you will have no Negroes. District lines can be drawn to gerrymander an area, either to keep Negroes in or to allow whites to remain out. So the very first decision, the location of the school, is a crucial element in its future composition.

Another procedure which may affect the racial composition of a school is the transfer policy of a school system. In New York City, before 1960, no one was allowed to transfer out of his neighborhood into another school, with certain exceptions. Baltimore and Philadelphia, on the other hand, allowed any child to transfer to any area. Sometimes you had zones where children were compelled to go to a particular school, and in the fringes you would have optional zones where the children had their choice, the optional zones being carefully devised so that white children would not be compelled to go to a Negro school.

Lastly, you can effect segregation by a process of overutilization or underutilization of classrooms and school buildings. In Chicago we witness the spectacle of heavily crowded Negro schools. And then, perhaps right across a main highway, a few blocks away, there is a white school with empty classes. The Board of Education has refused, however, to transfer some of the children from the overcrowded Negro school to the underutilized white school, and instead has built temporary mobile classrooms which have been located in the playgrounds of the Negro school. This is another way to maintain segregation.

By and large, we are not discussing these contrivances. We are discussing the much more complex problem of the nature of the legal duties of a school board which has not been responsible in any way, by any kind of manipulation, for heavy racial imbalances. This situation is sometimes called *de facto* segregation, and sometimes "racial imbalance."

From this situation two legal questions arise. First, does a school board have a legal responsibility, aside from an educational or moral one, to do something about racial imbalance which exists due to housing patterns, or other factors, over which the school board has no control? Second, aside from the question of whether the school board must take action, is there any legal impediment to its taking such action if it wants to? That is, is it constitutionally permissible for a school board to recognize the racial composition of a school or neighborhood for the purpose of alleviating *de facto* segregation?

A new body of case law is developing with some rapidity. There have been about ten cases decided by federal courts, state courts and state commissioners of education. Some school boards, hauled before tribunals and charged with failure to do something about racial imbalance, replied that this is no concern of theirs. They argued that they have no responsibility and that, indeed, under the Constitution they are required, in the classic phrase of Justice Harlan set forth in 1896, to be "color blind."[10] They maintain that far from having a duty, they would violate the Constitution if they were to take into account, in any official action, the racial composition of a school or a neighborhood. This is the so-called "color-blind" policy. It is still the policy of Boston.

Against that is the color-conscious policy of a city like New York, where the school board has publicly recognized its educational and moral responsibility to alleviate *de facto* segregation. The question in New York, therefore, is not whether the city has some responsibility, but rather what are the most practical, the most educationally sound, methods of reducing such racial imbalance, assuming that there are such methods? It is at this point that the legal problem arises—may a school board take into account the racial composition of a neighborhood or a school building for the purpose of trying to reduce racial imbalance?

We all know that no school board may take the racial composition of a neighborhood or a building into account for the purpose of achieving segregation. Does it necessarily follow, however, that taking into account racial composition for the purpose of desegregation in the North is likewise a violation of the command of the Fourteenth Amendment?

Different courts have given different answers to these problems. The answer in the Southern courts is uniform and categorical. They simply say that the Fourteenth Amendment does not command integration; it merely forbids discrimination, and therefore, as long as the school board does nothing affirmative to bring about segregation, it is not required to do anything affirmative to reduce any racial imbalance.

In the North, the cases fall into several categories. In the Gary, Indiana, case,[11] a suit was brought to challenge *de facto* segregation in an entire city. The Court of Appeals for the Seventh Circuit said very simply, "a school system developed on the neighborhood school plan, honestly and conscientiously constructed, with no intention or purpose to segregate the races, must not be destroyed or abandoned, because the resulting effect is to have a racial imbalance in certain schools where the district is populated almost exclusively by Negroes or whites." That is what I referred to as the Southern viewpoint.

There is a contrasting viewpoint that is likewise in the process of being formed. A recent expression was that of the Appellate Division in *Balaban v. Rubin.*[12] In this case, the New York Board of Education considered the racial composition of a neighborhood in drawing district lines for a new school. The board admitted it; it took pride in the fact that it had done so. But the board had done so for the purpose of reducing the racial imbalance. The court upheld the board.

There are dicta in two recent opinions which go the whole way. The Supreme Court of California said that apart from educational responsibility, the Board of Education has a legal responsibility to desegregate *insofar as it is feasible to do so.*[13] That is a very important proviso. Then, Federal Judge Dooling in this state has held: "The central constitutional fact is the inadequacy of segregated education. That it is not coerced by direct action of an arm of the State cannot alone be decisive. How far that duty extends is not answerable perhaps in terms of an unqualified obligation, but the effort to mitigate the consequent educational inadequacy has not been made. . . ."[14]

These are perhaps straws in the wind. They indicate the way in which the courts are beginning to grapple with this problem. We see the law in a state of development. It would be rash to predict what the law will be. I can tell you, however, what I think the law ought to be, which may not be the same as what it will turn out to be. I believe that segregated education represents inferior education and a board of education therefore must, so far as it can, and within the limitations of educationally sound methods, do what it can to reduce racial imbalance. It means that it must be color conscious; it must take into account, if necessary, the racial composition of a school building or neighborhood. There is one important proviso: at no time should an individual be granted or denied a privilege because of his race. That kind of discrimination against an individual, or in behalf of an individual, because of his race, will run afoul of the Constitution, and for a variety of reasons is educationally and politically unwise.

III / (Robert Carter)

I have a great deal of difficulty in talking about a problem like this as if it were an abstract legal problem, because we really are talking about social policy.

As lawyers we will have to translate that policy into a legal format. But it seems to me that what we are really doing is attempting to formulate a basic decision: that is, whether the ban against segregation is to be a legal abstraction or a real-life bar that can deal with all the varied manifestations of segregation.

It seems to me that one of the basic deterrents to segregation rests not on some of the legal issues with which we will deal, but on a fundamental concern about caste and color differences and their consequences. For example, one of the things you hear is that if you integrate the schools you will drive all the white people from the public school system. That is one of the objections to dealing with this problem openly.

As the figures of Mr. Maslow indicate, it is clear that in the urban North there are large concentrations of Negroes, that as a matter of fact, the public school system is becoming increasingly nonwhite. It seems to me that one of the reasons for the flight of the whites out of the public school system is the vast difference between academic standards in the nonwhite schools and the white schools. As the Negro and Puerto Rican people move into the city, and their children into the city schools, there is fear that the encroachment will lower school standards and that white children will not get a decent education. This fear that white children will be driven out of the school system is similar to what the South was and is saying, that if you remove segregation you will destroy the public school system itself.

Then we are told that the problem can't be solved until residential segregation is solved. But *de facto* school segregation is not a problem of residential segregation; it is a problem of school organization. It is school organization superimposed on residential segregation that produces the segregation in the schools. It seems to me that even if we were to start a drive today to eliminate residential segregation, we would have to wait fifty years or more before we could really have, in our largest cities, any widespread residential integration.

The other objection we have is, of course, the bus ride. Busing creates a great deal of difficulty in dealing with this problem. As a matter of fact, the bus ride really does not mean anything to most people. It is what is at the end of the bus ride that concerns them. In fact, busing is one of the things that is probably more indigenous to American education than anything else. Being a frontier society, we are used to busing children. People now bus children privately to nonsectarian schools, to parochial schools and the like. As a matter of fact, I had a case recently on Long Island where there were three schools, one Negro and two white. In the two white schools the children were bused to and fro; the kindergarten and the first and second grades were bused to school, home for lunch and back to school and home again. The Negro school was within walking distance of its pupils.

When we went into court about the issue of segregation, the defense was that it would be terrible to have the Negro children bused to school, although busing, of course, was an accepted part of the school life of the community.

Before turning to the question of the "neighborhood" school, let me say that I think all these arguments against integration are myths and evasions. What we really ought to be concerned about is whether the public schools are going to be the instrumentality for the accommodation and absorption of nonwhite people into the political, economic and social life of this country, as full and equal citizens. Only then will the public schools really serve the purpose that they served for the European immigrant. If the function of the public school is to provide citizens with the essential equipment to give them upward mobility in our society, it is clear to me, and it should be clear to all of us, that the *de facto* segregated schools have failed in that purpose.

The achievement-test results show an increasing gap between the nonwhite schools and the white schools from the fourth grade on. The gap is about one half-year in the fourth grade. It increases to a year and a half at the fifth grade and gets up to about two and a half years at the sixth grade. To be facetious about it, it would appear that the Negro children are becoming less educated as they progress in school.

The neighborhood school is one of the things that we are told must be preserved. If you reorganize the school system, what's going to happen to the neighborhood school? I don't know what a neighborhood school is. A neighborhood school, it seems to me, is all shapes and contours. In one case I tried recently, the neighborhood school wasn't even in the neighborhood that it was supposed to serve. In fact, a neighborhood school is really anything that the school board says it is. I have no objection to the neighborhood schools as such. The only thing that I would want is an integrated neighborhood school, and not a *de facto* segregated neighborhood school.

What seems to be forgotten is that the neighborhood school policy, which in effect is geographical districting, filling a school up on the basis of geography, is only a form of school administration. There may be some value and there may be a great value in preserving the neighborhood school. I don't know. But we must decide that the maintenance of a common school system in which residence, race and color are not handicaps to obtaining the best education the public schools can offer outweighs the advantages of schools based on residential patterns where they result in the creation of high-status and low-status schools.

The legal argument, mentioned by Mr. Maslow, that if you affirmatively plan for integration you are making an unconstitutional racial classification, is unsound. I don't know how any school board in modern America, particularly in the urban centers, can draw school zone lines without acting on the basis of race. This is not true in the South—as a matter of fact, in the course of the argument in Prince Edward County, which involved the closing of schools in Virginia, one of the counsel for the school board said, "One of the reasons that we can't abide by the Court decision is that we don't have any segregated neighborhoods, and, therefore, if we desegregate our schools, it would really result in integrated schools. We can't rely on *de facto* school segregation."

In modern-day America, we have definite and distinct patterns of residential segregation. The school board that plots the school, places the school, draws the school zone lines, knows with a considerable amount of accuracy where these segregated neighborhoods begin and end. They know which schools are predominantly Negro and which are predominantly white. You do not need to have anything on the child's forms to realize, for example, that if you place a school at Lenox Avenue and 125th Street and zone it for 127th Street and from Eighth Avenue, say, to Fifth Avenue, you are going to have a 100 percent Negro school. I don't know by what logic or yardstick it is possible to say that a school board that does this, where the result is inevitable, is acting less on the basis of race than a school board that looks at the problem and, for example, decides to place a school at 95th Street and Madison Avenue. I don't know what the racial composition of that area is; let's assume hypothetically that it is possible to produce an integrated school in that area. The board zones the school from 86th Street to 94th Street and from the East River to Madison Avenue because if it placed the school in another place, or zoned it differently, a *de facto* segregated school would result, but to place it as indicated would produce a multiracial school. How can it be said that this school board, conscious of what it is doing, is any more guilty of illegal racial discrimination than is a school board where the results of what it does appear inevitable and the natural result of what it does is to produce discrimination?

Finally, I think that the boards of education are under a legal obligation to promote integration. The Supreme Court has ruled that segregated education is unconstitutional in theory. It stressed the impact on the Negro child in terms of lower motivation and personality hurt. It had earlier found, in *McLaurin v. Oklahoma State Regents,*[15] that the enforced separation of races in the same classrooms produced inequality in education even though the Negro litigant had the same books and was taught by the same teacher. The separation interfered with the ability to study and learn. In *Sweatt v. Painter,*[16] the Court recognized that community attitudes about the reputation and status of a school had a great deal to do with the issue of educational equality. Such equality included these and similar intangibles.

State action was stressed in the *Brown* case. But it seems to me the Negro child does not know, when he is in a 100 percent Negro school in New York, Detroit or Long Island, that he is in this school as a result of board policy, and therefore feels better about it than if he were in such a school in Georgia or Alabama as a direct result of state constitutional and statutory law. I think that this is too subtle a difference for the child to absorb, although I can see where these differences, whether it is law or board policy, can be made into a vast legal difference. In other words, the United States Supreme Court could well say that *Brown* meant only that state policy manifested by state laws or constitutional provisions which enforced separation are unconstitutional. I doubt that they would reach that conclusion because this would be a departure from what they have traditionally regarded as state action in other cases. I think that the issue is, as I said at the outset, whether we are going to have a legal abstraction, whether the constitutional mandate against discrimination is going to be merely a legal formula, or whether that prohibition is going to reach all the manifestations of segregation as they occur in real life.

IV / (John Kaplan)

It seems to me that Mr. Carter is quite right that this is a great issue of social policy. It is an issue of social policy every bit as important as, if not more important than, the issue of birth control. It is as important as many other issues not the least of which is the attack upon poverty.

The interesting thing I find about these examples is that nobody argues that the attack on poverty or solution of the other problems is compelled by the Constitution of the United States. The point is that we are not arguing, at least in the resolution of the constitutional question, what is the moral or the proper thing to do. We are arguing what the Constitution of the United States compels.

Frankly, I believe—and I am willing to state it very clearly—that Mr. Carter is going to lose his lawsuit in Gary, Indiana.[17] The Supreme Court will either deny certiorari[18] on the matter or, if it reviews, it will uphold the decision. I doubt if the plaintiffs, the petitioners in that case, will get two votes.

I believe this for a number of reasons. One is that to say *de facto* segregation is unconstitutional is at odds with all of the constitutional precepts that we learn. *Brown v. Board of Education* was clearly a correct decision. Though the Court phrased its opinion as paying lip service to the separate-but-equal rule, the decision simply means that the state cannot draw racial classifications. Now, there has been some argument, which I am sure the Supreme Court has since regretted making, that it has been demonstrated that segregated education causes harm to the Negro child. The evidence that they cited was, at best, pathetic. It was in great part the work of one psychologist who tested sixteen Negro children and found that their self-image was worse in one part of the South, Clarendon County, than it was in New York. He neglected to point out that by the test he used, the Negro self-image in Clarendon County, South Carolina, was better than it was in Springfield, Massachusetts, where you do have a reasonable degree of integration.

The basic point of the *Brown* decision is very simply that it is unconstitutional, depriving students and people of equal protection of the laws, to classify by race or to say, "You are a Negro, you must do this; you are white, you can do something else." In this day and age when the Negro is effectively denied a voice in such decisions over large areas of the nation, it should be obvious that this is not "equal protection of the laws."

Interestingly enough, the Supreme Court has held this kind of classification unconstitutional even when there is no harm of any observable kind.[19] A park or golf course being set aside for Negroes, it seems to me, cannot be said to be inferior in the same way that an educational system can be said to be inferior. It is unconstitutional because of the separateness by racial classification.

There are many reasons why this does not apply to *de facto* segregation.[20] Classification by residence in the sense of the geographical classification is a rational one, and also is one that has many values. True, integration is said to be more valuable. It may be and it may not be. I am not, however, willing to make the educational superiority of integration a matter of constitutional truth, because it involves a very serious question of educational policy. For reasons I will elaborate later, I think in most cases we are better off making positive efforts toward integration, but I do not like the idea of this being decided by a majority of the nine appointed judges of the United States Supreme Court. One solution to a problem may be better than another, but where both are reasonable I think non-elected judges should keep hands off.

Just to appreciate that the goal of integration cannot override all other values, you should realize that one thing we could do to increase integration in our schools would be to close down the parochial schools. Certainly that would do it. Also, if we wanted to increase the degree of integration in our schools, I suppose we might set aside one house on every block in the United States specifically for a Negro family. And if they did not move there, I suppose we might just pick them up and put them there whether they liked it or not. This would accomplish integration.

But there are other values in our society, too, and other values that the Court must stress. I think the Supreme Court agrees with this approach because, on February 17, they handed down a very interesting decision involving electoral districts.[21]

You can argue that a *de facto* segregated electoral district is not as bad as a *de facto* segregated school district. In some ways it is not. On the other hand, in many ways it is worse. The political power of the Negro tends to be diluted by this type of *de facto* segregation because it essentially crams all the Negro voters into one district. Political power is at the base of our whole democratic system. Certainly the Court should, and it has, taken a closer look at what might be considered tampering with the popular sovereignty than at the area of schooling where, as a practical matter, the answers to the question of just how bad segregated schooling is are not obvious. It is not at all clear to me that an all-Negro school with first-rate teachers and first-rate buildings is poorer as a school than an integrated school, or an all-white school with run-down buildings and worse teachers.

This, in some areas, is a theoretical problem. The Negro schools happen to be the ones with run-down buildings and with poorer staffs, but not always, and if it is a law of constitutional dimensions, I assume that it will have to operate all the time, regardless of what the faculty and the school are like. In New York City, for instance, considerably more money is spent per pupil on the all-Negro schools than on the all-white ones.[22] Interestingly enough, in the electoral case, where the Supreme Court held that *de facto* segregation was not unconstitutional, not only is the harm done to the Negro at least as palpable as that in the *de facto* segregated school, but also the truth is that it is vastly easier for the state to cure that harm. There is no problem about busing young children, about taking them out of their neighborhoods, about exposing children to the elements or creating traffic jams. The fact is, if you want to do away with the *de facto* segregated electoral district, all you have to do is use any other system of counting votes. Even if adults had to travel a long distance to the polling places, you could say to them that once every two years on Election Day they just had to make the journey and you could say this a great deal more easily to them than you can say to students, "You've got to go every morning of your whole school career to a place that's far away from you."

This is the constitutional issue, and I do not really think that it is a very difficult one. I think it is a red herring and that Mr. Carter is right in saying that when the problem is solved, it will be solved primarily through the political processes. No court has ordered the New York Board of Education to take any action in this sense. The New York Board of Education has done this because it feels it has a moral obligation to create some degree of, possibly even full, integration.

But there are two big obstacles even when the political processes are willing to take action. First is the cost. True, sometimes the cost of busing children is more than balanced by the better utilization of school buildings and the lessening of new construction in the Negro areas. At other times, what is represented as the cost of integration is in reality the cost of improving Negro schools to make them equal to white ones. Despite this, integration often takes up scarce resources which could be better spent on education. It often makes more difficult the concentration of remedial aids and special counseling in the schools that most need it. And insofar as busing does not result in any savings, its costs may be a most uneconomical method of allocating tax dollars.

The second problem is that even if the political processes favor it, "artificial" integration may cause many former supporters of public education to enter private schools. Even without this, in many areas there soon just won't be enough white children to integrate with, even if busing is used. If a large-scale exit from the public schools takes place, this problem will become more acute, and even more important, the problem of raising money for public-school purposes will be vastly increased.

Despite this, I think that at least in most Northern areas the public schools are strong enough to weather the blow. Moreover, in many areas, I think that the Constitution requires us to act on this principle.

For instance, I do not doubt that the gerrymandering of a school zone to keep it primarily white is unconstitutional and improper even if, in the long run, it may promote integration by allowing say, 20 percent of the Negroes to go to this school rather than having the school three quarters Negro for the first year and then all Negro for the second year, when all the white parents, as perhaps they can easily afford to in that neighborhood, just take their children out.

One might then ask why, if I worry about these problems, do I favor efforts to promote integration. There are three basic reasons —arranged in what I feel is the increasing order of importance. First, while I am very dubious about the educational value of preventing *de facto* segregation, I must admit that in some situations it does help. Though saturation education might be better, where racial integration leads either to the improvement of inadequate Negro schools or to class integration, it does have educational value. Second, elimination of *de facto* segregation is a gesture of good faith—albeit an expensive one—which the Negro has every right to ask for from a white society which in the past has treated him shamefully. Finally, right or wrong, the Negro, or at least the Negro leadership, is convinced that all-Negro schools must be inferior, and is willing to exert all kinds of devisive forces to eliminate them. Integration is therefore the price, or at least one of the prices, of peace, and I for one do not think it is too high.

It is for this reason that I personally would draw the line well short of sending children from white-school areas into Harlem for their education, not so much on the ground that this is in theory any worse, but just on the ground of practicality. I do not believe that many white parents will withdraw their children from the school system if Negroes are bused into their schools, in anything less than a majority. But I do believe that as soon as you bus white children to the schools in Harlem, then parents will withdraw them, and worse, the peace we have purchased will be gone. We must remember that in a society based in great part on consent, the government can go only so far in placating one group lest it rouse others. Now, I may be wrong, but this is my estimate of the situation.

The question then is what we can do. As to this, I think that Mr. Maslow had a very good point; we cannot solve this all at once. The idea of busing the fifty thousand Negro and Puerto Rican children out of Harlem to attend white schools in Queens or in Brooklyn would create the most monstrous traffic jam every morning that you could possibly think of, and I don't think that the results would be that good. Causing a child to lose three quarters of an hour of his day going and coming is just a very foolish thing to do. It costs a great deal of money which can be better spent on other things, and I think that there are many better ways of handling the situation. True, most of the ways will not provide complete integration. I think we might as well realize that we are not going to provide completely integrated education for everybody no matter what we do. More than token but less than complete integration will be a sufficient gesture of good faith and will, I believe, be enough to secure at least a large degree of peace on this front. I would assume that compulsory busing of children from the Negro areas could be undertaken for about 25 percent of the children and that an open enrollment plan for the rest would be sufficient.

The last area I would like to touch on tonight is that of any constitutional impediment to solving the problem of *de facto* segregation. I tend somewhat hesitantly to agree with Mr. Maslow that a school board can consider race in achieving integration, even though it cannot consider race in attempting to segregate.[23] But when I say "consider race" I mean that it can draw a district to include Negroes and whites deliberately even though the district is shaped like a salamander. I believe that it can refuse to locate schools in Negro areas if it believes this would prevent integration. I believe that it can bus those children who want to go out of primarily Negro schools or even those who do not want to go out of primarily Negro schools, provided that it uses some nonracial classification to decide which of the children get bused and which do not.

One might think that in the North, having one rule for Negro children and another for white children was so far-fetched that nobody would try it. But in New Rochelle, when they closed down their Negro school, they allowed all of the white children in the school, about 10 percent, to transfer to any school they wanted to in the city. The Negro children in the school could transfer to any school they wanted except three. The aim was to prevent those schools from becoming too heavily Negro.

I believe that if there is any one thing that causes a feeling of inferiority, if that is relevant, it is the differential treatment of people on the basis of race by the government. I think this is wrong, I think it is poor policy, and I think it is unconstitutional. Some day we will have a suit from Negro parents in New Rochelle and I think that when that suit comes up, they will be successful, at least to the extent of allowing Negroes the same rights in New Rochelle as whites have. Even if it is done for their own good, it is not a good thing for government to do.

V / (Stanley H. Lowell)

I have found out tonight that some of the people who are involved are so busy theorizing on this subject that they are not living with it. I think the first thing we have to recognize is that we are involved, as you have heard before, in a revolution in America. It is a revolution as real and intense as the one that largely changed the face of Africa in the years after 1946 and 1947. The fact that the American Negro in our society has not done what the Mau Mau in Kenya has done is only, up to this point, a difference in degree. It is not a difference in substance and content. He has not done it, because we have a society which moves with the times, I hope; a society which is prepared to make whatever changes are necessary in order for us to have the kind of image that we think we have but which, of course, we do not have.

We are involved here, very simply, in a conflict of social issues. I submit that if you are practicing law or learning to be a lawyer, the first thing you have to learn is that the courts are aware of the world in which we live. With respect to whether we are going to have segregated schools or a free, democratic society and free democratic education, we should remember that if the choice is to be made by the courts, they will do it on the basis of *what the society wants*, not because they interpret a word one way or another, or define what a "duty" is.

This is how the issue will be truly determined. When Professor Kaplan shifted from the law, where I was deeply impressed, and started to tell us about the techniques of integration, discussed busing, discussed the neighborhood schools, he left his area of specialization and was moving into another; he was moving out of the law into a completely different area, that of social forces; and that, I submit, is what is actually going to decide this legal issue.

Let us examine busing. First of all, it is not the issue. It has been made the issue over the strenuous objections of the Board of Education in New York, my own Commission on Human Rights, Mr. Carter's organization and everybody else in the civil rights field. Those who do not want integrated education in New York, in the North or in America have made busing the issue. They have done this by saying, when I debate this subject, not in a legal setting, that the Board of Education is going to take children from Riverdale and bus them to Coney Island. Anything less is not the kind of busing they are opposed to.

Incidentally, it has been three years now since the open enrollment program was begun in New York City. It is a most fascinating contrast. New York's Glendale and a few other areas in Queens and Brooklyn deluged the commission and the Board of Education with literature and pickets and what have you, saying, "Don't bus Negro children into our white areas. They are going to do things to the schools"—some of the things which Mr. Carter described. But three years later, when the possibility of cross-busing arose (the Princeton Plan, the pairing of schools, the changing of feeder patterns) and the Board of Education put in a geographical limitation of not more than a mile and a half, you would be amazed at the number of communities, who originally opposed the Negro children being bused in, who completely reversed their position and said, "Send us the Negro children. We love to have them. Just send them to us. But don't make our children go there." And of course, the reason why they did not want their children to go "there" is because they acknowledge in their inner hearts, if they have them, or in their inner minds—and I am sure they have them—the responsibility for the fact that the Negroes have so much less in every way in their schools in our society. Those who favor the "saturation" program so strongly accept the guilt of the New York school system of inferior segregated schools going back many years.

By the "saturation" program they are seeking to do something which I think the Supreme Court, in *Brown v. Board of Education*, said could not be done; the Court in essence said that "separate" education in a palace with Phi Beta Kappas as teachers (if that's good) is inferior education. Separate but equal is not equal, and the moment you divide people, that's the moment when you create inferiority and inequality.

Now, let me move to another subject—that of color consciousness versus color blindness. I have been a liberal all my adult life, and as a liberal, I was conditioned to the importance of color blindness. "No discrimination because of race, color, religion or national origin." And I lived that life. I argued cases, I helped write briefs for the American Civil Liberties Union as a volunteer, and I argued the point over many years that color blindness was truly the only basis on which the American society could proceed.

I say that this is no longer so. The argument is specious. You cannot say, in society which has discriminated for a hundred years or three hundred years because of color, that you cannot take color into account in order to equalize the situation, in order to remove the inequality. What we say is simply this: Whether it is in jobs or in housing, or in school segregation, you must take color into account in order to remedy the evils in the society. In the field of job opportunity, to give an example, if you own a bank and you never had a Negro teller, then we say, "Go out and find a Negro teller." Don't wait for him to wander haphazardly in the door. If you do make that kind of *special effort*, take that kind of *affirmative action*, you are not discriminating against anybody, because we want you to find a qualified person and we don't want you to fire any whites in order to give that Negro teller that job. You can take that example and spread it over the society, including the schools. I say that it is not possible to avoid the issue of color consciousness.

What are we talking about as far as integration is concerned? I said the question was not busing. The issue is integration and equal education. The Board of Education, the City Commission on Human Rights, the various civil rights organizations have come up with a whole list of techniques—redrawing the district lines, pairing of schools, and one that I am particularly intrigued about, the educational center. We say, "Are you going to throw down the Polo Grounds? Then use it as an educational center. We have slums all over Harlem. Knock down nine square blocks, six square blocks, whatever is the appropriate number, and build six, eight, ten elementary schools together in a beautiful complex. You save money, no duplication in gymnasium, no duplication in equipment, no duplication perhaps for lunchrooms, no duplication for social service." If we can educate in an educational center on a collegiate level and on a prep school level, why can't we do it on an elementary school level? It is an exciting thing to contemplate—children coming out of Harlem to the Polo Grounds, children coming down from Inwood and Washington Heights and going to this wonderful area for an integrated education, and meanwhile, we can knock out ten or twelve Harlem schools that are now totally segregated. Use that space to open up a few playgrounds; open up a little light into the slum area and we will see what will happen to it in terms of values all around.

I want to finish on one last point. The problem within the Board of Education in New York, within all boards of education as far as I am concerned, involves the bureaucracy. It was reflected on the front pages of *The New York Times* last week. The Association of Supervisory Personnel, representing principals and superintendents, said, "We are against all this. We are against change. You are going to harm middle-class Negro and Puerto Rican children." Do you remember that line? "Middle-class Negro and Puerto Rican children." They also added, "White parents are going to flee the school system and move to the suburbs." What middle-class Negro and Puerto Rican children are they talking about? Is this the group they are protecting against the excesses of integration? The bureaucracy is one of the Board of Education's major problems, because when those conscientious members of the board and the School Superintendent receive reports, they receive them from the bureaucracy, and it is most unfortunate to have progress dependent upon this.

My recommendation for the solution in New York is that a Commission on Integration be appointed which will consist of all responsible elements within the community, white, Negro, civil rights, parents and teachers, whatever they may be. I am confident that these together can solve this great and most important social problem, and if we do not solve it, then America is faced with the most serious, most difficult time it has ever experienced in its 180 years. An example of the potential resistance is the group now coming forth and appearing on television and radio and expressing its view about the sanctity of the "neighborhood school," which it would appear is in the Bible, or at the least in the First Amendment somewhere. The neighborhood school has become an absolute. You don't attack neighborhood schools. Even Mr. Carter was for the neighborhood school. I appreciated the way he watered it down slightly, but he was for the neighborhood school. There is no such absolute in our society. The absolute that I feel is in the Constitution, the absolute that I feel is in the Bill of Rights, the absolute that I feel is in our Bible is *equality!*

Since the 1964 Hays Conference, numerous decisions by state and federal courts have served only to accentuate the legal conflict.

Sophisticated arguments have not caused a discernible shift in judicial thinking or in the public reaction to the question of whether the school boards must consider racial factors in implementing plans to relieve imbalance in their schools. The United States Supreme Court has tenaciously refused to resolve the issue.

The basic problem has become even more serious—the United States Commission on Civil Rights in its 1967 report found that racial imbalance is increasing in Northern schools. Escalating violence stems in part from the frustration of minority groups, which is induced by their recognition that the discrimination against them will not be easily eliminated, partly because government officials have not given the issue top priority. Compensatory programs have done little to offset the terrible legacy of inferior schooling.

In the face of this situation, a number of Negro leaders, including Black Power advocates Floyd McKissick and Stokely Carmichael, have suggested that integration may be quite irrelevant to the effective education of minority groups. Rather, they propose that giving the black community control of their schools' educational programs and placing Negroes in positions of authority in these schools will do more than full integration to raise the level of learning, repair the psychological damage caused by discrimination and restore the self-respect of the community.

NOTES

The full transcript of the conference was published in 10 *Howard Law Journal* 127 (Fall 1964) with the title "Arthur Garfield Hays Conference: Northern School Segregation."

1. Meyer, "The Ghettoes Explode," *New Statesman*, July 31, 1964, pp. 141–42.

2. "Segregation Litigation and the Schools—Part II: The General Northern Problem," 58 *Nw. U.L. Rev.* 157, 170–88 (1963).

3. *Id.* at 182.

4. See, e.g., United States v. Carolene Products Co., 304 U.S. 144, 152 n. 4 (1938); Bridges v. California, 314 U.S. 252, 262 (1941). See, generally, Charles L. Black, Jr., *The People and the Court* 217–21 (1960);

McKay, "The Preference for Freedom," 34 *N.Y.U.L. Rev.* 1182 (1959).

5. Calif. Ed. Code, § 363 (Supp. 1963).

6. Ill. Stat. Ann., §§ 10–21.3, 10–22.5 (Supp. 1963).

7. Section 401(b) of Public Law 88–352, 78 Stat. 246.

8. *The Journal of Intergroup Relations* (NAIRO), special issue on public school segregation and integration in the North, November 1963, p. 15 *passim.*

9. Taylor v. Board of Education of New Rochelle, 191 F. Supp. 181 (S.D.N.Y. 1961), *aff'd,* 294 F.2d 36 (2d Cir.), *cert. denied,* 368 U.S. 940 (1961).

10. Plessy v. Ferguson, 163 U.S. 537, 559 (1896) (dissenting opinion).

11. Bell v. School Board of Gary, 213 F. Supp. 819 (N.D. Ind.), *aff'd,* 324 F.2d 209 (7th Cir. 1963), *cert. denied,* 377 U.S. 924 (1964).

12. 248 N.Y.S.2d 574 (1963), *aff'd,* 14 N.Y.2d 193, 250 N.Y.S.2d 281 (1964).

13. Jackson v. Pasadena City School District, 59 Cal. 2d 876 (1963).

14. Branche v. Board of Education, 204 F. Supp. 150 (E.D.N.Y. 1962).

15. 339 U.S. 637 (1950).

16. 339 U.S. 629 (1950).

17. Bell v. School Board of Gary, *supra* note 11.

18. This occurred some four weeks after the conference, on May 5, 1964.

19. E.g., Johnson v. Virginia, 373 U.S. 61 (1963).

20. See Kaplan, *supra* note 2 at 190–206.

21. Wright v. Rockefeller, 376 U.S. 52 (1964).

22. See Silberman, *Crisis in Black and White* 257 (1964).

23. See Kaplan, *supra* note 2 at 207–8.

23

Racial Discrimination in "Private" Schools

As the preceding chapter indicates, the controversy over segregation and racial imbalance in education has focused primarily upon the public school. By far the greater number of pupils attend such institutions, and public responsibility is direct and comparatively uncomplicated legally. Accordingly, despite their importance in American education, private schools for the most part have escaped both judicial and public scrutiny.

The material that follows examines racial discrimination in the private schools of both the North and the South from the perspective of legislatures and school administrators as well as that of courts. The growing significance of private education—in part due to the pressures to integrate public schools—is mirrored in the many varied problems concerning private schools that have been almost wholly obscured by the traditional concern over race relations in public schools.

Particularly important and difficult issues arise in connection with religiously operated schools, which educate millions of children. The goal of integration there must be tempered not only by the desirability of permitting such schools maximum autonomy, but by the provision of the First Amendment guaranteeing the "free exercise of religion." A further complication will be introduced if large-scale and direct financial aid is provided parochial schools under federal and state programs, as was discussed in Chapter 12.

It is folly, in my opinion, to try to identify a single key to racial discrimination. Equality is indivisible, and the American dilemma will not be resolved until all channels of opportunity are cleared for citizens irrespective of their origins, beliefs and color. It is not inconsistent with this unitary view to focus special attention on the blight of segregated education. This condition led to the massive legal and public effort culminating in the *Brown* case, and success in that litigation opened the modern era of race relations. Ever since, a high proportion of civil rights energy has been expended in trying to fulfill the noble promises of that decision.

The record is not uplifting. In the 1965–66 school year only 6 percent of Negro children in the South attended public school with white children, and although the record is improving, only a small percentage of black children in the South receive an integrated education.[1] In the North, too, there is a severe problem of racial isolation, and there the problem is getting worse rather than better. The figures are that 72 percent of all Negro first-graders in the North attend schools that have a majority of Negroes, and in some cities there is virtually total segregation. The evidence shows that this pattern does not vary much whether it is a large Northern city or a small one, or whether the Negro proportion of the population is large or small.[2]

It is against this background of a still unfulfilled constitutional promise that the situation of the nonpublic school must be considered. My broad thesis is that a great opportunity awaits the independent school, that these institutions have a chance to prove to the nation that the quality education for which they are known can be sustained, and indeed enhanced, with an integrated student body. If this opportunity is grasped, these schools will both improve their moral position and provide the kind of education that will be most relevant for national leaders of the next century.

I shall discuss four particular subjects. First, the role private schools have played in the general Southern resistance to *Brown v. Board of Education.* Second, the judicial power under the Constitution to force private schools to integrate racially. Third, some legal problems a private school might confront that desires to accept Negroes for the first time. And finally, the special situation of parochial schools.

I

First the South. The "massive resistance" of that region to integrated public education is well known, as is the fact that the means chosen to assure the perpetuation of lily-white schools ran the gamut from pure violence to sophisticated constitutional arguments of "interposition" and "nullification." Less well known is the fact that "private" schools were and are being used as an important instrument of state policy to avoid integration.

Most Southern states, at one time or another, provided for the closing of public schools when these were under court order to integrate, and simultaneously passed laws making state funds available to white parents who wanted to send their children to segregated private institutions. The state aid took many forms, including scholarships, tuition grants and tax credits for private donations to the schools.[3] For example, Georgia provided for suspension of state funds to closed schools and allowed the Governor to make grants to school boards in districts where schools were closed in the same amount as when the public schools were open; the state also provided for grants of state and local funds directly to parents of a child going to a private nonsectarian school.[4] The net effect, of course, was the use of public moneys for segregated and ostensibly "private" education.

These efforts to circumvent the command of the Constitution naturally found their way into court. The judicial experience of Virginia and Louisiana is most instructive.

In Virginia the controversy centered on the school system of Prince Edward County, which was brought into litigation as far back as 1951 and was one of the constituent cases handed down with

Brown v. Board of Education. The state responded promptly by enacting legislation to close any public schools where white and colored children were enrolled together, to cut off funds to such schools, and to pay tuition grants to children choosing to enter the new private schools.[5] This legislation was struck down in 1959 by the Supreme Court of Virginia as inconsistent with the state constitutional requirement of compulsory public education.[6] The General Assembly then enacted a new tuition-grant program and made school attendance a matter of local option by repealing the state's compulsory attendance laws. A federal court immediately ruled that this plan was invalid and ordered the Prince Edward County schools to open as integrated institutions.[7] But the supervisors of the county refused to levy school taxes. As a result the county's public schools did not reopen in the fall of 1959, although the public schools of every other county in Virginia continued to operate. At the same time a private group, the Prince Edward School Foundation, was formed to operate private schools for white children, who were aided by the tuition grants.

This scheme continued for five long years, during most of which the Negro children of Prince Edward County received no formal education at all. Eventually, in May 1964, the Supreme Court ruled that the schoolchildren of the county were deprived of equal protection of the laws, because they were treated differently from the schoolchildren of all other Virginia counties.[8] In ordering the reopening of public schools in the county, the Court said:

> A *State, of course, has a wide discretion in deciding whether laws shall operate state-wide or shall operate only in certain counties. . . . But the record in the present case could not be clearer that Prince Edward's public schools were closed and private schools operated in their place with state and county assistance, for one reason, and one reason only: to ensure, through measures taken by the county and the State, that white and colored children in Prince Edward County would not, under any circumstances, go to the same school. Whatever nonracial grounds might support a State's allowing a county to abandon public schools, the object must be a constitutional one, and grounds of race and opposition to desegregation do not qualify as constitutional.*[9]

The decision had a profound impact on every Southern state that had authorized the closing of public schools. But it remained for litigation arising in Louisiana to administer the *coup de grâce* to private-school programs transparently designed to avoid integration.

There are two cases. First, in 1961 a federal court invalidated a 1958 Louisiana statute which provided a way by which public schools under desegregation orders could be changed to "private" schools operated in the same way, in the same buildings, with the same furnishings, with the same money and under the same supervision as the public schools.[10] Louisiana was not through yet. Its legislature immediately enacted a simpler plan to replace the 1958 law. The new act did away with provisions for closing public schools; it provided for payments to be made to students and parents rather than directly to the "private" schools, and it transferred administration of the program from the State Board of Education to the Financial Assistance Commission.[11]

In August 1966 a federal court in the case of *Poindexter v. Louisiana Financial Assistance Commission*[12] dashed the hopes of any who thought that this version of the "private" school technique would succeed. Terming the tuition-grant program merely "a refined, sophisticated substitute" for the earlier program, the court struck it down because public payment of tuition grants was state action forbidden by the Fourteenth Amendment in that it perpetuated segregated schools and placed a stamp of official approval on Negro inferiority. Second, the funds provided a "stimulus" in the founding of the "quasi-public" segregated schools and were used to support these schools.

A vital aspect of this decision is the test used by the court to determine when a "private" school comes within the ban of the Constitution. The court referred to an earlier decision by another federal court that held segregated private schools invalid under the Fourteenth Amendment if they were "predominantly maintained" by the state.[13] The earlier ruling was based in part on section 401(c) of the Civil Rights Act of 1964, which defines "public school" as any school "operated wholly or predominantly from and through the use of governmental funds."[14] Despite this statutory language, the court in *Poindexter* rejected the test of whether private schools are "predominantly maintained" by the state. It instead held that "*any amount* of state support to help found segregated schools or to help maintain such schools is sufficient to give standing to Negro school children."[15] It said: "Any affirmative and purposeful aid promoting private discrimination violates the equal protection clause. There is no such thing as the State's legitimately being just a little bit discriminatory."

The importance of this holding should not be underestimated. If not disturbed by a higher court, it could mark the end of circumvention of the *Brown* decision by Southern states through the use of phony private schools. Second, the decision could have important ramifications for independent schools in all parts of the nation. These will be explored shortly.

II

I turn now to the general problem of civil rights in private schools: that is, to the issue uncomplicated by, or perhaps I should say unsimplified by, public payments as an inducement to maintain the races in separate institutions.

There seems to be no accurate count of the number of pupils enrolled in private schools. Apart from my own research, the National Association of Independent Schools, which has 780 member institutions with about a quarter of a million pupils, has stated that no reliable figures exist for the total national enrollment in private secondary or elementary schools. We are fortunate, however, to have available the results of a survey conducted earlier this winter by NAIS. Of the 780 member schools, 740 responded to a questionnaire, and 463 (over 62 percent) reported at least one Negro enrolled this year. Several of these schools had several Negro pupils; 239 schools reported five or more and 109 reported ten or more. All told there were 3,720 Negro students, or 1½ percent of the total student population in NAIS member schools.[16]

This figure of 1½ percent plainly means that there is some way to go before racial balance is achieved in independent schools. I do not think it unfair to add that because NAIS members include some of the most enlightened schools in the country, it would not surprise me to learn, if comprehensive figures were available, that Negro enrollment in *all* private elementary schools fell below 1½ percent. This is not racial balance.

What is to be done? At once I reject one possible answer: doing nothing. Needless to say, this conclusion reflects not only a personal preference but, more important, the fact that the nation as a whole has made a profound commitment to remedy its great and longstanding debt to the Negro people. The independent schools must do their share, along with all other public and private institutions.

We therefore must inspect potential solutions under existing law. First to be considered are the Fair Educational Practices Acts. Six states have enacted such a statute—Indiana, Massachusetts, New Jersey, New York, Pennsylvania and Washington. These laws are enforced by administrative commissioners, and each is part of omnibus state antidiscrimination legislation which also prohibits discrimination in private employment, housing and accommodations.[17] Typical provisions of such laws are found in the recently promulgated Model Anti-Discrimination Act of the Commissioners on Uniform State Laws. The Model Act provides in part that it is a discriminatory practice for a private or public education institution:

> (1) *to discriminate against an individual seeking admission as a student or an individual enrolled as a student because of race, color, religion, or national origin; or*
> (2) *to make or use a written or oral inquiry or form of application for admission that attempts to elicit information concerning the race, color, religion, or national origin of an applicant for admission, or*
> (3) *to print or publish a catalogue or other notice or advertisement indicating a preference, limitation, specification, or discrimination based on the race, color, religion, or national origin of an applicant.*[18]

Such a statute is comprehensive in its prohibitions. Further, there is little question about its constitutionality (no such act has been declared invalid)[19] or of the fact that the legislature and especially the administrative agency can be flexible in establishing and carrying out the enforcement process. Why, then, are not such laws an ideal solution to racial discrimination in private schools?

The answer is a practical one. Despite the early high hopes for antidiscrimination commissions, more than two decades of experience reveals that they promise more than they deliver. Timid administrators, niggardly budgets and insufficient statutory powers all have played a part.[20] While critics have focused on the failures of enforcement against discrimination in employment, it is also true that the six education laws have hardly been implemented at all. Whatever the reasons, and whatever their potential, the fact is that they have become something of a dead letter except to the extent that they exercise a salutary if vague influence on the policies of school administrators. Fair education laws thus do not appear to be a promising solution, at least for the present.

There is a second statutory alternative. Several states include private schools in their laws prohibiting discrimination in "public accommodations." Thus, the Pennsylvania Public Accommodations Act[21] covers "kindergartens, primary and secondary schools, high schools, academies, colleges and universities, extension courses, and all educational institutions under the supervision of this Commonwealth." There is an exception for places of public accommodation that are "in their nature distinctly private," and this provision is currently in litigation in the latest installment of the *Girard College* case, about which I shall have more to say later. The important point now is that these general public accommodations laws, which can be found in several states (for example, Illinois and Minnesota), have never proved a satisfactory vehicle for desegregation of private schools, or for that matter of anything else. They are, assuredly, not the answer here.

This brings us to the Federal Constitution. The Fourteenth Amendment in its terms prohibits arbitrary action by the "state." Can this provision be interpreted to ban racial discrimination by independent schools? In my view the Fourteenth Amendment can properly be interpreted by courts to reach this result, and I suggest that private school administrators should immediately act on the implications of this fact, *before* courts are called upon to render decision.

Two constitutional theories support this conclusion. The first has been partially developed above in the context of the Southern problem. It will be recalled that in the Louisiana *Poindexter* case Judge Wisdom stated that "any amount of state support to help found segregated schools or help maintain such schools is sufficient to give standing to Negro school children."

This line of reasoning traces back to the important *Little Rock* case, where the Supreme Court said:

State support of segregated schools through any arrangement, management, funds, or property cannot be squared with the [Fourteenth] Amendment's command that no State shall deny to any person within its jurisdiction the equal protection of the laws.[22]

The "state support" necessary to fulfill the constitutional test of the *Poindexter* case can be found in the financial aid now provided private schools through many federal programs, including the National School Lunch Act, the National Defense Education Act, the Economic Opportunity Act of 1964, and particularly the Elementary and Secondary Education Act of 1965.[23] Likewise, at least in some jurisdictions, there is much state aid to independent schools. If the constitutional test is "any support," there would seem ample basis for a judicial decision that private schools are subject to the Fourteenth Amendment.

The second route to the same result is premised on the theory, now well established in its general outline, that where private individuals are allowed to perform a function ordinarily undertaken by the state, they are to be treated as agents of the state for constitutional purposes and their discriminatory acts therefore prohibited. This theory has been applied where private bodies conducted a primary election, administered a company town or operated a park.[24] Its potential application to an elementary or secondary school is obvious. At least one federal judge, J. Skelly Wright, has made the point forcefully. In a desegregation case involving Tulane University, a "private" institution, he said:

. . . one may question whether any school or college can ever be so "private" as to escape the reach of the Fourteenth Amendment. . . . institutions of learning are not things of purely private concern. . . . Clearly the administrators of a private college are performing a public function. They do the work of the state, often in the place of the state. . . . And, if so, are they not agents of the state, subject to the constraints on governmental action, to the same extent as private persons who govern a company . . . or control a political party . . . ?[25]

Although Judge Wright's judgment in the *Tulane* case was vacated on a procedural ground,[26] this language was not disapproved;

moreover, since he spoke in 1962, additional judicial support for his views has appeared.[27]

In summary, I believe that the "law" is there and waiting under which an enterprising court could rule that private schools are subject to the constitutional command to desegregate. Whether it will be so employed is perhaps less a legal than a political question, less a matter of principle than of timing.

What lesson should be drawn from this conclusion? Should civil rights lawyers immediately repair to the nearest courthouse and begin suits to force all independent schools in the nation to admit Negroes at once? I hardly think that is the answer, although one day it could come to pass. The vicissitudes and frustrations of litigation are amply illustrated by the *Girard College* case in Philadelphia. In February 1954 two Negroes applied for admission and were rejected on the ground of race. Now, more than thirteen years and many judicial opinions later, there is still no final order requiring a nondiscriminatory admissions policy for this school. The latest episode in the courts is that a federal district court has permanently enjoined Girard College from denying admission to Negroes, and the order has been affirmed on appeal.[28]

No, the courts are not the preferable forum for integrating the nation's independent schools. The right forum, it seems to me, is one that most of you are familiar with—the offices and boardrooms of the schools themselves. In this forum administrators and directors can act without compulsion, with full regard to the particular problems of each school. They can fulfill their general obligation as citizens and their special obligation as educators by working toward the high civic goal of equal opportunity, and simultaneously they can fulfill their professional responsibilities to their institutions by achieving the goal without the embitterment or the expense or the loss of dignity that has characterized the *Girard College* litigation.

The next logical question is whether there is any legal impediment to *voluntary* integration by independent schools. A difficult issue is presented for schools that have accepted gifts whose terms specify an all-white student body. Girard College, for example, was established by a trust that specified that the school should be maintained for "poor, white, male orphans." Is there a legal means to avoid such anachronistic instruments? In the *Girard College* case the Negro plaintiffs sought to *force* the unwilling school to accept a modification of the trust and admit children irrespective of race or color, in accordance with the grantor's alleged intent to benefit all citizens of Philadelphia. It is important to see that it is a different situation from the one now being proposed, where a school administration *desires* to terminate a donor's limitation to white children.

Two recent cases suggest that success can be achieved by such a school but also that obdurate state officials can at least delay a favorable outcome. In 1964 Rice University of Houston, a private institution, brought an action in a Texas court against the Attorney General of Texas, seeking authority to ignore restrictions in its charter which prohibited it from admitting Negroes. The court impaneled a jury, which made special findings of fact that the main purpose of the benefactor of the university was to create an educational institution of the first class; that the restrictions on admitting Negroes render impracticable the development of Rice University as such an institution; and that it has now become impractical to carry out the intent of the benefactor. The court thereupon rendered a judgment authorizing the university to admit qualified applicants without regard to color or race.[29]

In this case, not only did Rice University wish to eliminate the restriction but the Texas Attorney General had no apparent objection. In our second case, involving the Sweet Briar Institute of Virginia, a more complex situation is presented, largely because the state officials opposed the petition. After the *Rice* decision, Sweet Briar, which had been set up by a trust to carry on a school "for the education of white girls and young women" and had operated in that fashion for more than sixty years, brought suit in a Virginia court against the State Attorney General and the County Attorney to eliminate the restriction. A state judge refused to grant relief, ruling that the will was unambiguous and could not be modified under Virginia law.[30] Sweet Briar then went into federal court.

The case soon became something of a labyrinth. Once the federal suit was begun, the state judge took no further action. Then the federal court also decided to abstain from further action. The federal court said that considerations of federalism required deference to the Virginia courts on an issue of Virginia law.[31] Rather than return to an unreceptive state court, counsel for Sweet Briar appealed the decision of the federal court. The Supreme Court found that abstention was inappropriate and remanded the case to the district court for consideration on the merits.[32] This is where the matter rests now.

My guess is that Sweet Briar will ultimately prevail, that the Supreme Court, if pushed to decision, will hold that it is a violation of the equal protection clause for state courts to apply rules of law to prevent a private party from disregarding a restriction in a private trust requiring it to discriminate against Negroes. This decision would be patterned on the landmark case of *Shelley v. Kraemer*,[33] in which it was held almost twenty years ago that state courts could not constitutionally enforce private racial restrictive covenants on land against an owner who wished to ignore the restriction and sell to a Negro.

However the litigation comes out, it is plain from the Rice University experience that if state officials do not obstruct willing school officials, integration can be achieved very easily. The *Sweet Briar* case disclosed some of the difficulties when state officials do stand in the way, but perhaps that case—if it is finally disposed of as I have predicted—will be the precedent that clears the path for other institutions seeking to avoid racial restrictions imposed by donors from another era.

Having tried to do justice to some of the legal problems involved in the desegregation of independent schools, I should like to underscore the point that the future will be in the hands not of the legislatures or the courts or the fair education commissions, but rather of the schools themselves. As the NAIS statistics show, many private schools have already accepted this view. Further, as recounted in a recent study, vigorous and sensitive efforts are being made in many schools to recruit and smooth the way for Negro applicants to private schools.[34] The vital ingredient is the will to achieve the end; once that is present, the practical problems—the admittedly difficult practical problems—can be solved.

III

We must now consider the integration of parochial schools, a matter of particular importance because some very difficult problems of policy and constitutional law are presented against a backdrop of a vast and increasing parochial school population. Church schools are now a formidable bloc in American education, and about 90 percent of church education is Roman Catholic. From 25 percent to 50 percent of school-age children in Northern cities attend nonpublic (mostly Catholic) schools; for example, in Philadelphia it is 40 percent and in Pittsburgh 46 percent.[35] All told about 5.7 million students are enrolled in Catholic elementary and secondary schools; this is one out of every seven students in the nation, double the proportion of twenty-five years ago.[36]

It is thus plain that if American schools are to be integrated, church-related schools have a major part to play. It is also true that many parochial schools have taken strong steps to achieve racial balance.[37] Nevertheless, the fact that such schools attract a higher proportion of white than Negro students from public school systems tends to upset an already unbalanced racial situation, particularly in the central cities of the nation. The evidence is clear that parochial as well as other schools have a serious problem of racial imbalance.[38]

I should like to raise briefly two sets of questions in this regard: first, those that might arise if it is decided to coerce unwilling church schools to integrate, and second, those that could emerge if church schools themselves wish to improve racial balance.

First, coercion. This issue could arise in two ways. Either through legislation requiring all schools, including parochial schools, to refrain from racial discrimination, or through a court action based on the Fourteenth Amendment. The first route would most likely be in the context of a fair educational practice act, and the second route would presuppose all that we have discussed earlier regarding "state action"—the possibility that church schools, like other private schools, are subject to the Fourteenth Amendment because they receive financial aid from the government or because they perform a "public function" which makes them in effect agents of the state.

The specific question that emerges is whether it is an unwarranted interference with the autonomy of church schools, and perhaps a violation of their right to free exercise of religion, to require them to integrate against their will. For example, could a statute validly provide that it was unlawful for a parochial school to prefer applicants of the same religion? While I know of no directly applicable case, it appears to me that such a statute would be gravely suspect from a constitutional standpoint, as well as unwise in policy.

But does this mean that a church school cannot be ordered to end discrimination on *racial* grounds? The Commission on Uniform State Laws recently wrestled with that problem in the preparation of its Model Anti-Discrimination Act and concluded that there was no good reason to permit such discrimination unrelated to the religious purposes of the institution.[39] On the other hand, title VII of the federal Civil Rights Act of 1964, which prohibits discrimination in employment, grants a total exemption for religious educational institutions.[40] The federal act does not deal with private school education, but the employment title reflects a policy choice different from that of the Commissioners, and I should add, different from my own.

The final question in this series will perhaps be of interest only to law professors who must strive each year to prepare imaginative examination questions. Suppose that a parochial school discriminates on the ground of race and does this because of some religious belief associated with the religion. Black Muslims might so exclude white children from their schools, and there may be white religious groups that exclude Negroes on doctrinal grounds. Should this be forbidden by the state, and if so, is it an interference with religious freedom? I must confess I have not thought the problem through, but my tentative solution is to resolve the issue in favor of prohibiting the discrimination, even if it apparently flows from a bona fide religious belief, because of the opportunity for disingenuous racial exclusion that a contrary decision would permit.

Now to the second broad question. Suppose that a parochial school desires to integrate and achieve a healthy racial balance.

What problems can be expected? For present purposes I put to one side strictly educational matters. Obviously, the church school can aggressively recruit Negro students, and indeed it can do so without problems of divided control that might plague a public institution. It can also arrange for redrawing of parochial school district lines and provide for busing between say, a predominantly white suburban school and a Negro neighborhood in the central city. It can even close some or all of the parochial schools in an area where this would lead to reduction of racial imbalance in the public schools. All these steps can be taken by the school system of a particular denomination, without difficulty, assuming the policy is accepted by the church leaders.

But these efforts may be insufficient. There just may be too few Negroes of the same religious faith to achieve more than token integration. In response to this problem, a writer in *Commonweal* magazine has recently proposed that public and parochial schools share their facilities, so that children from the two systems could attend certain classes together and thus to that extent eliminate racial isolation.[41]

Here we encounter a difficult constitutional problem. "Shared time" programs have a long history, and it is much mooted whether the establishment clause of the First Amendment forbids children to divide their school day by taking such "neutral" subjects as languages, mathematics and gymnasium in the public school and subjects with some religious orientation—such as literature and history—in the parochial school.

This is not the occasion to delve deeply into the controversy. Suffice it to say that strong arguments have been mounted on both sides. Shared-time proponents say that it will break the deadlock on federal aid to public schools; that it will help breach the wall isolating the Catholic community and give it a greater stake in the public school system; and that it is consistent with church-state separation because the program provides assistance to the child and not to the parochial school. The other side argues that shared time will not solve the federal-aid problem, nor will it in practice break down the isolation of Catholic children, for they will be a special and identifiable group within the public school. Moreover, there will be administrative havoc and added expense. Finally, it would be inconsistent with separation of church and state, first because it would involve aid to church schools, which would be saved considerable sums that would go into strictly religious aspects of education, and second, because it would involve church officials in the management of public schools, where their voices could have considerable influence.[42]

How the dispute will be resolved in the courts is yet unclear, although a leading authority has suggested that no doctrinaire answer will be forthcoming and that the result will depend on the precise form of a given shared-time program.[43]

How does this controversy bear on our problem of civil rights? Presumably not at all if a particular shared-time program is upheld under the First Amendment; in that case it would be one further useful method of achieving racial balance in public and parochial schools.

But what if a particular shared-time program ordinarily would violate the establishment clause? Might such a plan survive if its purpose is to achieve racial balance in the schools? In other words, would the command of the First Amendment be tempered in the interest of carrying out a mandate of the Fourteenth Amendment? Much would depend, of course, on the precise nature of the program. But in general my guess is that the constitutional balance is sufficiently close so that the use of shared time as a way of helping to eliminate racial isolation would be sympathetically received in the courts, especially if the Fourteenth Amendment is ever held to mean that schools have an affirmative duty to integrate.

Because I know of no precedent that would control the decision, I merely present the question as a final perplexing problem that our courts one day may have to answer.

NOTES

The complete version of this paper was delivered on March 28, 1967, at a National Invitational Conference on State Regulation of Nonpublic Schools, at the Center for Continuing Education, University of Chicago. It was subsequently published in 8 *William and Mary Law Review* 39 (1967).

1. Statistics recently released by the Southern Education Reporting Service show that 16% of the 3,000,000 Negro students in the South are now attending desegregated schools. This figure includes an additional 305,000 pupils in such schools for the first time in 1966–67. See *N.Y. Times,* April 3, 1967, p. 21, col. 2.

2. United States Commission on Civil Rights, *Racial Isolation in the Public Schools* 2–10 (1967). See also Coleman *et al., Equality of Educational Opportunity* (1966), a study conducted pursuant to title IV of the Civil Rights Act of 1964.

3. For a rundown of the pertinent statutory provisions, see 2 Emerson, Haber & Dorsen, *Political and Civil Rights in the United States* 1652–1654 and 1659–1662 (3d ed. 1967). See also Leeson, "Private Schools Continue to Increase in the South," 2 *Southern Education Report,* No. 4, at 22–25 (Nov. 1966).

4. Ga. Acts 1959, No. 8, p. 18, 4 *Race Rel. L. Rep.* 180 (1959), Ga. Acts 1961, No. 13, p. 31, 6 *Race Rel. L. Rep.* 289 (1961), Ga. Acts 1961, No. 14, p. 35, 6 *Race Rel. L. Rep.* 290 (1961).

5. Va. Code, § 22-188.3 *et seq;* §51-111.38:1.

6. Harrison v. Day, 200 Va. 439, 406 S.E. 2d 636 (1959).

7. Allen v. County School Board of Prince Edward County, 266 F.2d 507 (4th Cir. 1959).

8. Griffin v. County School Board of Prince Edward County, 377 U.S. 218 (1964).

9. *Id.* at 231.

10. Hall v. St. Helena Parish School Board, 197 F. Supp. 649 (E.D. La. 1961), *aff'd* 368 U.S. 515 (1962).

11. Act 147 of 1962, La. Rev. Stat. 17:2959.

12. 258 F. Supp. 158 (E.D. La. 1966).

13. Griffin v. State Board of Education, 239 F. Supp. 560, 565–66 (E.D. Va. 1965), *cert. denied,* 385 U.S. 960 (1966). This case is a later version of the Virginia School Closing Litigation, discussed at pages 361–62 of the text.

14. 42 U.S.C. § 2000 (c).

15. 258 F. Supp. at 164. Emphasis added.

16. National Association of Independent Schools, *Summary Report on Enrollment of Negro Students* (March 1967).

17. Citations to these statutes can be found in 2 Emerson, Haber & Dorsen, *op. cit. supra* note 3 at 1793.

18. Section 502 of the comprehensive version of the act.

19. See Fox, "Discrimination and Antidiscrimination in Massachusetts Law," 44 *B.U.L. Rev.* 30, 71 (1964). See generally "Note, Fair Educational Practices Acts: A Solution to Discrimination?" 64 *Harv. L. Rev.* 307 (1950).

20. See the criticisms contained in "Symposium, Fair Employment Practices Acts," 14 *Buffalo L. Rev.* 1 (1964).

21. Act of May 19, 1887, P.L. 130, § 1, as amended, 18 P.S. 4654.

22. Cooper v. Aaron, 358 U.S. 1, 19 (1958).

23. See Pfeffer, *Church, State and Freedom* 596–604 (rev. ed. 1967).

24. See Terry v. Adams, 345 U.S. 461 (1953); Marsh v. Alabama, 326 U.S. 501 (1946); Evans v. Newton, 382 U.S. 296 (1966).

25. See Guillory v. Administrators of Tulane University, 203 F. Supp. 855, 858–59 (E.D. La. 1962).

26. 207 F. Supp. 554 (E.D. La. 1962), *aff'd* 306 F.2d 489 (5th Cir. 1962).

27. See Evans v. Newton, *supra* note 24.

28. For a history of the case, see 11 *Race Rel. L. Rep.* 1696–98 (1966).

29. William Marsh Rice University v. Carr, 9 *Race Rel. L. Rep.* 613 (Harris Cy. Tex. Dist. Ct. 1964), *aff'd sub nom* Coffee v. William Marsh Rice University, 408 S.W.2d 269 (Tex. Civ. App. 1966).

30. Sweet Briar Institute v. McClenny, 10 *Race Rel. L. Rep.* 1005 (Amherst Cy. Cir. Ct. 1965).

31. Sweet Briar Institute v. Button, 12 *Race Rel. L. Rep.* 85 (1966) (2–1 decision).

32. 387 U.S. 423 (1967).

33. 334 U.S. 1 (1948). See also Barrows v. Jackson, 346 U.S. 249 (1953).

34. Mallery, *Negro Students in Independent Schools* (NAIS 1963).

35. Cronin, "Negroes in Catholic Schools," 85 *Commonweal* No. 1, at 13–14 (1966).

36. "The Changing World of Catholic Education," 14 *Columbia College Today* No. 1, at 19 (Fall 1966).

37. The United States Catholic Conference, comprising all American bishops, has called a nationwide conference on "racial isolation." *N.Y. Times,* March 27, 1967, p. 41, col. 1.

38. See, for example, the statistics contained in the 1964 Intercultural Survey of Roman Catholic elementary and secondary schools in Manhattan and the Bronx, New York City. See also the exchange in the *Catholic News* for Aug. 18, 1966, and Oct. 6, 1966, between Msgr. George A. Kelly and Mr. Aryeh Neier, Executive Director of the New York Civil Liberties Union.

39. Section 503(1).

40. Section 703(e), 42 U.S.C. § 2000e-2(e) (2).

41. Cronin, *supra* note 35 at 14–15.

42. See the thoughtful discussion in Pfeffer, *op. cit. supra* note 23 at 571–79.

43. *Id.* at 578–79. See also the statement of the American Civil Liberties Union on shared time, issued April 4, 1965.

24

Housing Discrimination and the Antitrust Laws

Among the prevailing forms of racial and religious discrimination in the United States are the restrictions that exist in many communities on the sale and rental of private homes and apartments. This widespread practice reflects not only a deep personal antipathy by the white majority against living near members of minority groups, but also a desire to safeguard other important local institutions, such as schools, playgrounds and churches, from an influx of unwanted neighbors.

Although the Supreme Court established in early cases that the state could play no part in housing discrimination, this had relatively little effect because by far the bulk of such action is privately inspired and implemented. One of the chief means employed has been the "restrictive covenant" in housing deeds, which the High Court held in 1947 could not be judicially enforced but which it has never held to be automatically invalid.

In 1961, deeply disturbed by reports that racial and religious barriers to open housing were prevalent in the nation's capital, and despairing of any prompt action by Congress to remedy the situation, the American Jewish Committee conceived of the possible use of the federal antitrust laws to break up combinations interfering with the free transfer of real property within the District. The Committee requested the author to analyze the prospects for this novel line of attack, and the memorandum that follows was his response.

This memorandum illustrates the desirability of including all possible approaches to a problem, including some that seem to have little chance of judicial adoption. For example, for a court to enjoin a recorder of deeds from recording a deed with a racial restrictive covenant (see pages 381–82) would require considerable extension of existing doctrine. But the argument is included here because in a volatile area of the law such an extension is often forthcoming, and also because even if it is not, it is useful for a lawyer to suggest a wide range of legal theories so that a court, in rendering a decision, can be satisfied that it is relying on the ground it deems most solid.

I / The Washington Real Estate Community (REC)

Testimony before the Civil Rights Commission in 1961 detailed fourteen areas in and near the District of Columbia in which racial and religious minority groups are excluded as owners or occupants of dwellings through the use of restrictive covenants. This testimony is consistent with apparent home occupancy in these areas. Included are homes of better quality—above the approximate value of $30,000.

The most common pattern of home-site development in the District of Columbia is for one developer (who may also function as a builder and/or real estate broker) to acquire a large tract. If his resources are sufficient he will develop the entire tract himself, marketing homes there under the popular name of the area (e.g., Berkeley, Kent or Spring Valley). In other cases, additional builders and/or real estate firms will be offered a chance to buy sites and construct homes. The pattern calls for developers to obtain construction loans from lenders, who in most cases involving better homes are also the sources of mortgage money for the individual home buyer. In Washington, at least half the home loans are made by building and loan associations. The remainder are made by banks.

Several of the large lenders apparently have ties with certain title companies. These lenders attempt to influence the title business by maintaining a list of "approved" title firms, from which alone they will accept title insurance on the property for which they are advancing mortgage money. There are also apparent ties between certain developers, real estate brokers and title companies. (For convenience, this memorandum will refer to the various firms involved in restrictive practices in the Washington, D.C., real estate community as the REC.)

In District of Columbia real estate transactions the title companies play three roles. They conduct the title search to assure that the seller has a marketable title, they offer title insurance, and they act as the agent when the transaction is completed—collecting the funds involved in the deal and paying the seller and also, on occasion, the lender its special charges. The title insurance company is commonly brought into the picture by the real estate broker (who may be the developer, if it is the first sale of the home). The title insurance company is thus in a position to aid the developer by "policing the covenants," that is, making certain that particular covenants appear in a new deed.

These cooperative arrangements are entered into because Washington does not have the multiple listing system common to most communities, under which all member firms have access to a list of homes up for sale, the agency for which is held by another member firm.

One example of how discrimination takes place involves the X Development Company, which is both a developer of large-tract home sites and a real estate broker. The X Company deeds to new homes contain the following covenants:

FOURTH. *No lot of the property hereby conveyed shall be occupied, leased, rented, conveyed, or otherwise alienated, except conveyance by Deeds of Trust, nor shall the title or possession thereof pass to another without the written consent of the X Development Company . . . except that said company may not withhold such consent, if a written request has been made to it to permit such occupation, leasing, renting, convey-*

ing, or alienation, signed by a majority of the owners of the lots which are subject to the same restrictions as the property hereby conveyed, and which adjoin or face said lot upon both sides of the street, or streets, and within a distance of five lots from the side lines thereof.

TWELFTH. *No part of the land hereby conveyed shall ever be used, or occupied by, or sold, demised, transferred, conveyed unto, or in trust for, leased, or rented, or given, to negroes, or any person or persons of negro blood or extraction, or to any person of the Semitic Race, blood, or origin, which racial description shall be deemed to include Armenians, Jews, Hebrews, Persians and Syrians, except that; this paragraph shall not be held to exclude partial occupancy of the premises by domestic servants. . . .*

FOURTEENTH. *That, in order to facilitate operation of the covenant numbered "Fourth," above, the grantee covenants for——heirs and assigns, that in the event, at any time, he or they shall desire to lease, rent or sell to another the said property hereby conveyed to——, he or they will appoint the said X Development Company, agent for such purpose.*

These provisions are designed, of course, to exclude Negroes, Jews and other minorities from the communities in which they are used. The provisions appointing the X Company as exclusive sales agent for resales of the home, unless a majority of the owners of lots in the neighborhood request an exception, are designed to assure the enforcement of the restrictive covenants by limiting the resale rights of the purchaser.

II / The Validity of the Restrictive Covenants

In *Buchanan v. Warley*,[1] the Supreme Court declared invalid municipal ordinances restricting occupancy in designated areas to persons of specific race and color. It held that such ordinances denied rights to white sellers and Negro purchasers of property that were guaranteed by the Fourteenth Amendment.

Shelley v. Kraemer[2] and *Hurd v. Hodge*[3] extended this ruling. In the *Shelley* case, the Court held that racial restrictive covenants could not be enforced in equity against Negro purchasers because enforcement by courts would constitute state action denying equal protection of the laws to the Negroes, in violation of the Fourteenth Amendment.

In the *Hurd* case, the Court applied this ruling to the District of Columbia on two distinct grounds. First, it held that enforcement of discriminatory agreements by the courts of the District of Columbia was prohibited by section 1978 of the Revised Statutes,[4] which guarantees to all citizens of the United States equal rights to inherit, purchase, lease, sell, hold and convey real and personal property. Secondly, the Court held that, even in the absence of a statute, it would not be consistent with the public policy of the United States to permit federal courts in the District of Columbia to exercise general equitable powers to compel action forbidden the state courts by the equal protection clause of the Fourteenth Amendment.

It is important to recall, however, that the Supreme Court rulings prohibiting judicial enforcement of racial restrictive covenants in cases where "state action" is found do not purport to render invalid the private agreements. In *Hurd v. Hodge,* the Court said: "We may start with the proposition that the statute does not invalidate private restrictive agreements so long as the purposes of those agreements are achieved by the parties through voluntary adherence to the terms. The action toward which the provisions of the statute under consideration are directed is governmental action."[5] Subsequent decisions have adhered to this view.[6]

One recent case, however, perhaps could be used as a basis for challenging the covenants used by the Washington REC. In *Ming v. Horgan,*[7] the Court enjoined a project developer from discriminating in the sale of properties which were privately financed on the ground that the developer's houses were approved for mortgage insurance by the Federal Housing Administration and the Veterans Administration. The Court reasoned that such FHA and VA financing provided sufficient "state action" under the Fourteenth Amendment to invoke the *Shelley* doctrine by creating for the seller a ready market that would not otherwise have been available.

The *Ming* case could possibly be extended to render ineffective all restrictive covenants. The office of the Recorder of Deeds for the District of Columbia is financed out of public funds. It is possible to argue that the recorder could be enjoined from recording a deed containing a restrictive covenant on the ground that the United

States, by making available the facilities for recording, is lending its assistance to racial discrimination in violation of the Constitution. If this contention prevailed in court, restrictive covenants would probably disappear because a title company would obviously be reluctant to insure a title in an unrecorded deed. As far as I know, this theory has never been judicially tested.

III / Concerted Refusals to Deal

It is likely that the Washington REC has violated section 3 of the Sherman Act by engaging in a "concerted refusal to deal." A concerted refusal to deal is an agreement by two or more persons not to do business with other individuals, or to do business with them only on specified terms. Diverse reasons may motivate these agreements, although they are generally grounded in the desire of the boycotters to protect or expand their economic status or power. Although not expressly governed by any particular antitrust provision, it is settled that refusals to deal may violate the Sherman Act's prohibition on contracts, conspiracies and combinations in restraint of trade and the general ban on "unfair methods of competition" in section 5 of the Federal Trade Commission Act.[8] For convenience this memorandum will discuss concerted refusals to deal under the Sherman Act provision.

In order to establish a concerted refusal to deal, it is first necessary to prove the existence of a conspiracy. If an agreement not to deal with certain individuals is proved, it probably constitutes a per se violation of the Sherman Act. Even if such an agreement is not a per se violation, it is probable that the concerted refusal by the REC to deal with minorities in certain communities in the District of Columbia violates the Sherman Act under the "rule of reason" that would be applied to determine whether the restraint of commerce was "unreasonable."[9]

Section 3 of the Sherman Act provides:

Every contract, combination in form of trust or otherwise, or conspiracy, in restraint of trade or commerce in any Territory of the United States or the District of Columbia, or in restraint of trade or commerce between any such Territory or Territories and any State or States or the District of Columbia, or with foreign nations or between the District of Columbia and any State or States or foreign nations, is hereby declared illegal.

That the business of a real estate agent is "trade" within the meaning of the Sherman Act is now established.[10]

A. *The Conspiracy*

It is frequently difficult to ascertain the existence of a conspiracy. Absent tangible proof, such as letters and memoranda of understanding, the starting point in proving an illicit agreement is uniformity of conduct among the alleged conspirators. It appears that such uniformity is present in respect of sales of homes to Negroes, Jews and other minorities within the communities mentioned above.

The doctrine of "conscious parallelism" comes into play at this point if it can be shown that the uniformity, or "parallel" conduct, occurred with the knowledge of each member of the REC that the others were pursuing the same conduct. It seems clear from the facts submitted to me that the parallel discriminatory conduct was pursued "consciously" in this case.

There has been variation in Supreme Court cases concerning the precise meaning and scope of the doctrine of "conscious parallelism." There has also been considerable confusion engendered among lower courts and commentators. In the early cases, the Court seemed to be saying that no understanding among participants in an unlawful plan was necessary. For example, in *Interstate Circuit v. United States*[11] the Court said:

It is elementary that an unlawful conspiracy may be and often is formed without simultaneous action or agreement on the part of the conspirators. . . . Acceptance by competitors, without previous agreement, of an invitation to participate in a plan, the necessary consequence of which, if carried out, is restraint of interstate commerce, is sufficient to establish an unlawful conspiracy under the Sherman Act.

On the other hand, several years after these two decisions, the Supreme Court repudiated the view that consciously parallel action is conclusive proof of a conspiracy.[12] Nevertheless, it is clear that such behavior is to be considered substantial evidence on the issue of conspiracy.[13]

Whether or not the force of "conscious parallelism" would of itself serve to sustain an inference of conspiracy from uniform conduct, it is believed that the provable facts in the present case would justify such a finding. This would clearly be true, as noted above, if evidence of an agreement among members of the Washington REC could be shown in the form of memoranda, conferences, correspondence, trade association resolutions or other means.

Even if such direct evidence could not be adduced, an illicit understanding might be established through the use of circumstantial evidence. That such evidence is sufficient to prove a conspiracy is well established.

Facts, in addition to uniform conduct pursued knowingly by the members of the REC, that would bolster the inference that a conspiracy exists to bar minorities from certain Washington communities are:

1. The close and interlocking relationships between the X Company, the keystone of the discriminatory policy, and other members of the REC. For example, as noted above, developers and brokers have common directors with (*a*) banks and lenders that provide home loans and (*b*) title companies that act as escrow and closing agent in addition to providing title insurance.

2. Meetings among members of the REC at which the restrictive policy was discussed.

3. The resale provisions in the X Company's deed and the manner in which the X Company has policed its contractual right to act as exclusive resale agent of homes that it has sold. The fact that under covenant Fourth a majority of neighbors are permitted to authorize a sale by the owner without the company's approval suggests an illicit motive for the provision. The same can be said about the fact that the company has permitted rival brokers to represent sellers covered by its resale agreement and has thereafter "cooperated" with these same brokers in other transactions. Unless a rival broker assumed that the covenant had as its purpose the exclusion of minorities, it seems unlikely that he would deal with a seller bound to the company. To do so would ordinarily invite a lawsuit

against the seller as well as jeopardize the broker's business relationship with it.

It seems likely that these facts, and perhaps others that could be shown, would warrant a jury finding of a concerted refusal to deal in violation of section 3 of the Sherman Act.

B. *Defensive Arguments*

The defendants to an action would of course claim that their uniform conduct was not the result of agreement, but instead represented independent decision-making on their part. Various lines of argument would be presented to explain the uniform conduct, but it is unlikely that these would prevail.[14]

1. Each member of the REC could argue that it acted independently to further an independent desire to keep certain communities white and Christian. This argument would not be persuasive, as a trier of fact might well infer that each participant had an interest in seeing to it that none of the others disturbed the prevailing makeup of the area and that this goal, as with a boycott based upon economic motives, could be achieved only through concerted action.[15]

2. Each participant might state that he feared the loss of customers if he aided members of minorities to enter the area, and that therefore he independently decided not to do so. The major shortcoming of this argument lies in the element of proof, for mere voicing of such fears would not have much probative value and it probably would be difficult to show actual threats of withdrawal of business. In addition, if such threats were made to a broker by other members of the REC, this would help cement their status as coconspirators.

3. It might be argued that individual minority buyers were poor credit risks or otherwise of doubtful reliability in terms of home occupancy. There is every reason to believe that this assertion is not true.

4. It might be argued that each broker and other member of the REC feared to sell to members of minority groups because in the

long run it would depress the market value of the property in the restricted communities, and that each independently had an interest in maintaining the high value of such property. Evidence would be developed of value patterns in other communities where formerly restricted neighborhoods were opened up. It is our understanding that property values have not been depressed in such cases. Indeed, there is some reason to believe that the contrary is true in view of the greater competition that would be engendered for scarce high-quality homes in these areas.

C. *Restraint of Trade*

There is little doubt that the discriminatory behavior of the Washington REC effects a restraint of trade within the meaning of the Sherman Act. This restraint occurs in at least three ways. First, brokers and other sellers of reality are restrained, by the mutual understanding, from showing homes to members of the minority groups excluded from the various sections of the city. Second, the owners of property within those areas are prevented from selling their homes to Negroes, Jews and other minorities. Third, the prospective purchasers themselves, who would wish to buy homes in the restricted communities, are restrained from doing so.

The net result is that there is a substantial impediment to the free sale of homes in numerous residential areas. This impediment undoubtedly influences the price at which homes are sold, but it is not necessary for such a showing to be made in order to establish a restraint of trade.[16] This restraint is accomplished entirely by the concerted refusal to deal.[17]

D. *Illegality of Concerted Refusals to Deal*

1. It is believed that proof of a concerted refusal by the Washington REC to deal with members of minority groups would establish a per se violation of the Sherman Act. Until recently, the question whether group refusals to deal were automatic violations of the act

was subject to doubt. For example, despite strong evidence to the contrary in Supreme Court decisions,[18] lower courts and commentators, probably influenced by earlier cases permitting certain types of group limitations, have assumed that not all group refusals to deal violate the law. The result has been a vigorous search for a standard by which to distinguish legal from illegal group boycotts. Two tests that were suggested were the direct versus the indirect effect of the restraint,[19] and whether or not the restraint fostered the economic productivity of the group.[20]

The recent case of *Klor's, Inc. v. Broadway-Hale Stores, Inc.*[21] appears to have ended the uncertainty. The Supreme Court held that the "nature" and "character" of a group boycott in that case was such as to bring it within the class of restraints which Congress and the common law condemned without regard to the presence of public injury. In so doing it relied on cases classifying group refusals to deal as per se illegal, thereby indicating that good motive or business necessity would no more justify the restriction than would the lack of effect upon the public.

The *Klor's* decision applying the per se rule to concerted refusals to deal has been subjected to criticism. For example, Professor Handler has written that the Court erred in refusing to discriminate between "those boycotts which are so patently injurious to competition as to admit of no legal justification and those having less obvious anti-competitive repercussions so as to warrant application of the rule of reason in determining their legality."[22]

2. Even if concerted refusals to deal are not per se violations of the Sherman Act, the Supreme Court would probably hold that the boycott of minorities by the Washington REC was an invalid restraint under the "rule of reason." Under the rule of reason there would be introduced into evidence facts relating to the nature and condition of the industry, the extent of the restraint on competition, and any other evidence that would be considered relevant in determining the reasonableness of the restraint.

In this case it could be shown that the members of the REC have control over the entire real estate market in the specified areas, as revealed by the percentage of sales they control as well as by the fact that there have been no or almost no exceptions to their policy of exclusivity. The extent of the restraint on real estate transactions would be established, as discussed above, and these negative effects on competition would probably not be offset by evidence that the restrictive agreements operated to improve competition in any way within the relevant real estate markets. Accordingly, whether or not the *Klor's* holding that group boycotts are per se illegal would be applied in the present context, the concerted refusals to deal in this case appear to violate the Sherman Act.

3. A related contention that the defendants would undoubtedly advance is that no Sherman Act violation occurred, even if there was an agreement to restrict home sales, because the *motive* of the members of the Washington REC was social rather than economic. In other words, it will be urged that the antitrust laws were not intended to reach conspiracies stemming from social or ethnic preferences.

This contention seems groundless. In the first place, although we think of antitrust as being primarily aimed at "economic" matters, the enforcement of competition has always been considered in terms of its intimate impact upon social and political questions such as the scope of entrepreneurial initiative and freedom, the distribution of wealth and the dispersion of power. Questions of economics are so inextricably interwoven with politics and social justice as to preclude any effort to restrict the Sherman Act to purely economic phenomena.[23]

Secondly, there is ample precedent for the application of the antitrust laws to noneconomic or so-called "moral boycotts." In *Council of Defense v. International Magazine Co.*,[24] an organization of patriotic souls was enjoined from persuading retail distributors and the public at large to shun Hearst publications because of Hearst's preference for neutrality in the First World War. In *United States v. Mortgage Conference of New York*,[25] a district court entered a consent decree enjoining the members of an association of mortgage lenders from agreeing, *inter alia*, not to compete for a mortgage or a lease because the property was owned or occupied by "persons belonging to any particular racial or national group."[26]

Third, the decision in the *Klor's* case casts substantial doubt on the vitality of any exception to the antitrust laws based upon the doctrine of "moral boycotts." By relying extensively on *Fashion Originators' Guild of America, Inc. v. FTC*,[27] which held that a boycott to eliminate tortious acts was not justified, the Supreme Court seemed to be rejecting any deviation from the general rule in such cases.[28]

Finally, even if certain noncommercial boycotts would escape the usual rule, as enunciated in the *Klor's* case, there seems no possible justification for the present restrictive agreement under the Sherman Act. Whatever may be the proper disposition of boycotts based upon a particular group's conception of morality or patriotism, leeway should not be granted to a boycott, such as the present one, that is rooted in policies inconsistent with the constitutional policy against depriving minorities of the right to buy and own property on equal terms with all.[29] There is no basis, in other words, to apply any vestige of the "moral boycotts" doctrine to a patently immoral boycott.

IV / Vertical Concerted Refusals to Deal

It might be possible to prove a separate violation of section 3 of the Sherman Act by the members of the Washington REC in the form of a concerted refusal to deal between the real estate brokers and each homeowner who signs a deed with covenants not to sell to members of certain minorities.

In this connection it is useful to consider *United States v. Parke-Davis & Sons Co.*[30] That case held that the Sherman Act prohibited resale price maintenance by a manufacturer of drugs who not only announced its pricing policy and its intention not to deal further with retailers who failed to abide by it, but also actively induced unwilling retailers to comply with the policy. The Supreme Court limited the leading case permitting refusals to deal, *United States v. Colgate & Co.*,[31] to the situation where the manufacturer did no more than announce its intention not to deal with customers who would not resell at stated prices. Under *Parke-Davis*, therefore, if the manufacturer secures his customer's adherence to resale prices by means going beyond a mere declination to sell to uncooperative customers, there is a violation of the Sherman Act.

The *Parke-Davis* and *Colgate* cases involved "vertical" price-fixing, that is, agreements to fix prices between parties not in competition with one another, but rather on different lines of the distribution system. Other Sherman Act violations may involve vertical restraints, for example, division of markets. Thus a manufacturer, as part of his marketing plan, may agree with one distributor not to commission a competing distributor within a prescribed area. Although division of markets among competitors is a per se violation of the Sherman Act,[32] the validity of vertical divisions, such as exclusive dealerships, has not been definitively settled.[33] At present the test of reasonableness appears to be applied to such agreements.[34] In the present context, this theory would bring into issue the agreements between the X Company and each of the individuals who purchased a home from it prohibiting resale to members of minority groups.

Because this appears to be a relatively novel antitrust theory, it is difficult to estimate its force here. Perhaps only certain vertical group boycotts would be struck down while boycotts protecting "lawful business purposes" would be upheld. (This is a standard that has been suggested for exclusive dealerships.[35]) Perhaps the only utility of the theory would be to bolster a case charging a "horizontal" concerted refusal to deal, along the lines discussed in section III of this memorandum, and perhaps it would not be given any weight at all.

The foregoing memorandum was put to practical use. The president of the American Jewish Committee in May 1962 used it as the basis of testimony before the United States Commission on Civil Rights. And on July 1, 1963, Emanuel Celler, Chairman of the House Judiciary Committee, wrote a letter to the Department of Justice, relying on the memorandum and urging "the possibility of the use of the antitrust laws in this field."

The federal government has never invoked the antitrust theory, but several private suits have recently been filed under the federal or state antitrust laws. There has been some progress. The Sixth Circuit Court of Appeals has ruled that the Sherman Anti-Trust Act provides proper grounds for a suit to enjoin a board of realtors from conspiring to prevent Negroes from renting property in white neighborhoods in Akron, Ohio.[36] *On another front, the Federal Trade Commission became the first federal agency to attack housing segregation by attempting to police real estate advertising. In late 1967 the FTC issued complaints against operators of apartment developments in Virginia for failure to disclose in their advertisements that they rent only to whites.*[37] *Although there have been developments in antitrust law since the memorandum was written, the broad outlines of its argument remain the basis of these suits. It is therefore possible that the Supreme Court will soon be asked to speak the definitive word on the application of the antitrust laws to discrimination in housing. Whatever the outcome in the High Court, it is unlikely that major inroads will be made against housing discrimination in the United States except by vigorous enforcement of the 1968 federal fair housing law, the recently resurrected 1866 federal law,*[38] *and similar state laws.*

NOTES

Civil Liberties Fellow Robert E. Burns assisted in the preparation of the memorandum, part of which served as the basis for a portion of the author's "Critique of 'Racial Discrimination in Private Housing,'" published in 52 *California Law Review* 50 (1964).

1. 245 U.S. 60 (1917).
2. 334 U.S. 1 (1948).
3. 334 U.S. 24 (1948).
4. Now 8 U.S.C. § 42.
5. 334 U.S. at 31.
6. Barrows v. Jackson, 346 U.S. 249 (1953); Progress Development Corp. v. Mitchell, 236 F.2d 222 (7th Cir. 1961).
7. 3 *Race Rel. L. Rep.* 693 (Cal. Super. Ct. 1958).
8. See Attorney General's Report on the Antitrust Laws, pp. 132–33 (1955).
9. See, generally, Standard Oil Co. v. United States, 221 U.S. 1 (1911).
10. United States v. National Association of Real Estate Boards, 339 U.S. 485 (1950).
11. 306 U.S. 208, 227 (1939).
12. Theater Enterprises, Inc. v. Paramount Film Distributing Corp., 346 U.S. 537, 540–41 (1954).
13. Pittsburgh Plate Glass Co. v. United States, 260 F.2d 397, 400–401

(4th Cir. 1958), *aff'd on other grounds,* 360 U.S. 395 (1959); Advertising Speciality National Ass'n v. FTC, 238 F.2d 108 (1st Cir. 1956).

14. See Comment, 63 *Yale L.J.* 1124, 1127–28 (1954).

15. See United States v. Reading Co., 226 U.S. 324, 365 (1912).

16. See Klor's, Inc. v. Broadway-Hale Stores, Inc., 359 U.S. 207, 213 n. 7 (1959).

17. See Attorney General's Report, *supra* note 8 at 25.

18. E.g., Northern Pacific Ry. v. United States, 356 U.S. 1, 5 (1958).

19. See Barber, "Refusals to Deal under the Federal Antitrust Laws," 103 *U. Pa. L. Rev.* 847, 872–79 (1955).

20. See Note, 71 *Harv. L. Rev.* 1531, 1536–40 (1958).

21. 359 U.S. 207 (1959).

22. Handler, "Recent Developments in Antitrust Laws: 1958–59," 59 *Colum. L. Rev.* 843, 862 (1959).

23. *Cf.* Northern Pacific Ry. v. United States 356 U.S. 1, 4 (1958).

24. 267 Fed. 390 (8th Cir. 1920).

25. CCH Trade Cases 1948–49, par. 62,273.

26. See also Hughes Tool Co. v. Motion Picture Ass'n, 66 F. Supp. 390 (S.D.N.Y. 1946) (group boycott against organization engaged in allegedly immoral advertising), and Kuryer Publishing Co. v. Messmer, 162 Wis. 565, 156 N.W. 948 (1916) (boycott by Roman Catholics of offensive newspapers).

27. 312 U.S. 457 (1941).

28. See "The Supreme Court, 1958 Term," 73 *Harv. L. Rev.* 84, 202 (1959).

29. Buchanan v. Warley, 245 U.S. 60 (1917); Shelley v. Kraemer, 334 U.S. 1 (1948).

30. 362 U.S. 29 (1960).

31. 250 U.S. 300 (1919).

32. United States v. Addyston Pipe and Steel Co., 85 Fed. 271 (6th Cir. 1898), *aff'd,* 175 U.S. 221 (1899).

33. See Attorney General's Report, *supra* note 8 at 27–29.

34. *Compare* United States v. Columbia Steel Co., 344 U.S. 495 (1948), *with* Boro Hall Corp. v. General Motors Corp., 124 F.2d 822 (2d Cir.), *rehearing denied,* 130 F.2d 196 (2d Cir. 1942).

35. See Attorney General's Report, *supra* note 8 at 29.

36. Bratcher v. Akron Area Board of Realtors, 381 F.2d 723 (6th Cir. 1967).

37. See N.Y. *Times,* December 9, 1967, p. 1, col. 1.

38. Jones v. Alfred H. Mayer Co., decided June 17, 1968.

25

Equality for the Illegitimate

Over the past fifteen years the courts have invoked the Constitution to strike down numerous laws which discriminated against individuals on the basis of race, poverty and other arbitrary classifications. But at least one important form of legal discrimination—that against persons of illegitimate birth—has largely escaped judicial scrutiny. Based on ancestry and penalizing blameless individuals for the acts of others over whom they had no control, such laws are as offensive as those directed against the Negro and the poor.

At common law the illegitimate child was incapable of inheriting and was barred from compelling his putative father to contribute to his support and maintenance. Today, a majority of states deny the illegitimate a right of inheritance from his father. In addition, restrictions exist as to the rights of custody, adoption and visitation. Perhaps most important to the great majority of illegitimate children, discrimination against them has permeated state welfare laws. Several federal statutes also result in discrimination against illegitimate children by referring to state law for a definition of "child." On the other hand, benefits under the Social Security Act, formerly tied to a child's right of inheritance under state intestacy law, are now generally available to illegitimates.

For the most part, discrimination against the illegitimate is the product of an unexamined tradition in the United States and elsewhere. The purported justification for the laws is to control illicit sexual conduct and discourage the bringing of children into the world out of wedlock. Although this rationale has been accepted uncritically for centuries, it is subject to strong objections on both empirical and constitutional grounds, as the brief that follows indicates.

Despite the injustice of the illegitimacy laws, few constitutional attacks on them have been mounted and none has been successful. In one of the first of such cases, the American Civil Liberties Union in 1967 challenged a Louisiana decision which excluded illegitimate children from the benefits of a state statute that granted all "children" the right to sue for the wrongful death of their mother.

The case arose when Louise Levy, a Negro woman, came to the Charity Hospital in New Orleans with symptoms of tiredness, dizziness, chest pain and slowness of breath. The doctor to whom she was assigned purportedly examined her, but he failed to take her blood pressure or conduct any other test which would have revealed her condition, which was hypertensive uremia. The doctor sent the patient home with tonic and tranquilizers. When she returned a week later with more severe symptoms, he merely looked at her, told her she was not taking the medicine and recommended a psychiatrist. Ten days later Louise Levy died.

Her five children then brought a wrongful death action under the statute against the doctor and the Charity Hospital for negligence in the diagnosis and treatment. The Louisiana courts dismissed the action on the sole ground that the children were illegitimate, even though it was acknowledged that they were living with their mother and were supported by her at the time of her death.

The author prepared the following brief in Levy v. Louisiana, *maintaining that it was a violation of equal protection and due process for the state to exclude illegitimate children from the benefit of the statute.*

In reading the brief, two additional points should be borne in mind. The first is that a more direct way of alleviating the plight of illegitimates is through legislation. Although experience in the area of race relations suggests that repeal of statutory reform would not eliminate discrimination against those born out of wedlock and certainly would not do away with their inferior social position, it would help alleviate the economic and psychological damage now being encouraged by states and the federal government.

The second point is that the brief omits a possible constitutional argument based on the 1965 Supreme Court case of Griswold v. Connecticut. *In* Griswold *it was held that Connecticut's birth control law unconstitutionally intruded upon the right of marital privacy, which is part of a protected zone of privacy emanating from the specific guarantees of the Bill of Rights. This theory could be invoked to challenge state regulations of sexual conduct, in particular all prohibitions on private sexual activity between consenting adults. Adultery and especially fornication statutes might be vulnerable, and to the extent they are it will become difficult to justify continued application of the law penalizing illegitimates. Although this line of argument was considered, it was finally decided that it was premature and perhaps overoptimistic to expect the Supreme Court to adopt a theory that would broadly undercut state regulation of sexual conduct.*

I / Article 2315 is invalid under the equal protection clause of the Fourteenth Amendment.

A. *The governing standards*

This Court has employed two well-established and related standards in determining questions under the equal protection clause. The first looks to the characteristic or trait determining the classification. Under it some classifications are by their nature suspect, and may only be utilized if there "clearly appears . . . some overriding statutory purpose . . ." or "compelling justification."[1] The second standard looks to the purpose of the statute and the basis of the classification and requires that the two be reasonably related.

The discrimination against the illegitimate children in this case is unconstitutional under both of these standards. Louisiana, in article 2315, in effect has created two classes of children—one that can sue for wrongful death and one that cannot. The classification, based on illegitimacy, is unrelated to the purpose of article 2315 and is, moreover, by its nature a suspect criterion, the use of which the state has utterly failed to justify. The unreasonableness of the classification is accentuated by the fact that Louisiana is the only state that deprives illegitimate children of the right to sue for the wrongful death of their mother.

In reference to the first standard, this Court has repeatedly affirmed that classifications based on race or ancestry are "constitutionally suspect."[2] According to Black's Law Dictionary, illegitimacy is "The condition before the law or the social *status*, of a bastard; the state or condition of one whose parents were not intermarried at the time of his birth" (emphasis in original). It is obvious that a child's illegitimacy is like his race and ancestry and has nothing whatever to do with his own actions or conduct. As this Court said in *Hirabayashi v. United States,*[3] "Distinctions between citizens solely because of their ancestry are by their very nature odious to a free people whose institutions are founded upon the doctrine of equality."

Thus, attacks upon classifications based on illegitimacy "come to this Court with a momentum for respect lacking when appeal is made to liberties which derive merely from shifting economic arrangements."[4] There is no room for the state to claim that the discrimination here should be sustained if there is any "rational basis" to support it. Accordingly, there should be no constitutional distinction between discrimination based on illegitimacy and that based on race; discrimination against illegitimates should also be "constitutionally suspect."

This is all the more true because statutes directed against illegitimates tend to fall most heavily on Negroes, as in this case, and in some instances may have been designed to achieve this end. Thus, in 1960 Louisiana instituted new measures to penalize illegitimates as part of a large anti-integration package passed at an emergency session of the legislature.[5] It is relevant in this connection that in 1964 a total of 9,567 illegitimate children were born in Louisiana. Of these 8,441 were Negro and 1,126 were white.[6]

The second constitutional standard—a reasonable relationship between classification and purpose—was stated as early as 1896 in *Gulf, Colorado & Santa Fe Railway Co. v. Ellis:*[7]

. . . the attempted classification . . . must always rest upon some difference which bears a reasonable and just relation to the act in respect to which the classification is proposed, and can never be made arbitrarily and without any such basis.

This standard has consistently been adhered to by the Court. As stated in *McLaughlin v. Florida*,[8] the question is "whether the classifications drawn in a statute are reasonable in light of its purpose."

While the equal protection clause does not always require an exact correspondence between the purpose sought to be achieved and the class encompassed by the statute, here there is a complete lack of reasonable relation between the two. Judging article 2315 in light of its purpose and the appropriate constitutional standard, it is plain that it is "arbitrary" and not a "reasonable classification" to deprive children of a cause of action for the negligent death of their mother on the sole ground that they are illegitimate. This will now be shown as to both claims under the statute.

B. *The claim for wrongful death*

The purpose of wrongful death statutes, deriving from England's Lord Campbell's Act,[9] is to reimburse those who stand to lose through the death of another, usually a close relative, whether through contributions based on past earnings or through loss of services, training, nurture, education and guidance.[10] In ruling that illegitimate children could sue under the Federal Wrongful Death Act, the Court of Appeals for the Second Circuit said:

The purpose and object of the statute is to continue the support of dependents after a casualty. To hold that these children or the parents do not come within the terms of the act would be to defeat the purposes of the act. The benefit conferred beyond being for such beneficiaries is for society's welfare in making provision for the support of those who might otherwise become dependent.[11]

Louisiana's wrongful death statute was an "adoption" of Lord Campbell's Act[12] and its traditional compensatory purpose was early set forth by the Supreme Court of Louisiana:

The object of this law was to save [children] harmless during their minority from the loss of benefits (material and moral) which they would have received had their father lived up to the time of their respective majorities.[13]

The purposes of death statutes in general, and of Louisiana's in particular, are wholly consistent with the claim of the children here. They were as close to their mother as any children born in wedlock could be. They were fully dependent on her for the necessities of life, as well as the vital intangibles of training, nurture and guidance. And they are now losing as much as legitimate children would lose in comparable circumstances—indeed, because of the absence of a father, probably more. To lose sight of these facts is not only to ignore the object of actions for wrongful death but to treat these illegitimate children as "constitutional nonpersons" devoid of the equal protection of the laws.[14]

The unreasonableness of the classification here in light of the statutory purpose becomes even plainer when it is recognized that in Louisiana both parents are under a legal duty to support their illegitimate children.[15] Article 239 of the Civil Code provides the rationale for this rule: "[N]ature and humanity establish certain reciprocal duties between fathers and mothers and their illegitimate children. . . ." In this context of a state policy requiring parents to support their out-of-wedlock children, it is surely bizarre to deny them a cause of action against a wrongdoer who caused the death of their mother, on whom they were dependent.

The invalid application of article 2315 is pointed up further by a recent decision of a three-judge District Court of the Middle District of Alabama. In *Smith v. King*,[16] the court invalidated the "substitute father" regulation of the Alabama Department of Pensions and Security, under which public assistance payments known as Aid to Families with Dependent Children were to be terminated if a man lived out of wedlock in their home or had sexual relations with their mother. The District Court held this a denial of the equal protection of the laws because under the Alabama regulation financial assistance is

denied for an arbitrary reason—the alleged sexual behavior of the mother; such a reason is wholly unrelated to any purpose of the Aid to Dependent Children statutes. . . . The punishment under the regulation is against needy children, not against the participants in the conduct condemned by the regulation.[17]

The *Smith* case is directly in point here because in both cases, for reasons "wholly unrelated" to the purpose of state legislation, benefits under the statutes have been denied on the ground of illegitimacy. The present case is an even stronger instance of a denial of equal protection of the laws than the *Smith* case because there not only the illegitimate children were denied benefits, but the entire family—including the mother who was "responsible" for the illegitimacy—while here only the illegitimate children are being denied the right to sue. Moreover, in *Smith* there was not the additional inequity, present here, that denial of recovery permits a wrongdoer to escape any consequences for his act.

The arbitrary character of the ruling below is clarified by its attempted justification in the Louisiana courts. The Supreme Court of Louisiana wrote no opinion, and the sole justification given by the Court of Appeal for interpreting article 2315 to discriminate against illegitimates was that "it discourages bringing children into the world out of wedlock." But the court cited no evidence to support the reasonableness of this means of controlling illegitimate births.

Moreover, the attempted justification of the Louisiana court is offensive to common sense. It would be truly remarkable if persons contemplating or in the process of producing a child out of wedlock would be deterred by the possibility that the child would not be able to recover for their wrongful death. Surely such a fanciful assertion, which is at the root of the decisions below, will not suffice to justify the denial of rights conferred by article 2315 to children who have lost their mother through another's wrongful conduct.

Nor can Louisiana carry its heavy burden of proof by relying on other possible reasons for discriminating against illegitimate children. One argument, sometimes relied on to justify the exercise of state police power in this general area, is the asserted right of a state to regulate sexual activity, and specifically to discourage promiscuity. But as with illegitimacy, neither common sense nor practical experience supports the assumption that discrimination against illegitimate children under article 2315 will deter illicit sexual activity.

Another possible argument would rely on the promotion of family unity. This policy is usually asserted to protect the interests of a parent's legitimate children against the claims of the illegitimate ones.[18] But in this case there are no legitimate children who stand to lose. Moreover, there is every reason to believe that "family unity" will be harmed rather than aided by disqualifying the illegitimate children here from maintaining an action to recover for the wrongful death of their mother. If the children do not recover in this action, they are likely to be split up in different homes or sent to an orphanage, with disastrous consequences for "family unity." If they do receive some money, it is at least possible that arrangements could be made to provide a home for all of them with an aunt, other relative or friend.

C. *The survivorship claim*

In addition to authorizing a claim for wrongful death, article 2315 makes the right to recover damages caused by "an offense or quasi-offense" survive the death of the injured person for one year in favor of certain classes of persons, including the deceased's "child or children." The Louisiana courts also rejected the plaintiff's claim based on survivorship because the children were illegitimate. As in the case of the claim for wrongful death, there is no valid basis for this result.

A central purpose of the survivorship portion of article 2315 is to reinforce the deterrent aspects of the general tort law by refusing to permit a wrongdoer to escape payment of damages through the death of his victim. This purpose is expressed in the introductory sentence of the article, which provides that "Every act whatever of man that causes damages to another obliges him by whose fault it happened to repair it," and it has been explained as follows: "[T]he idea apparently evolved that the person responsible for the wrongful act should pay damages to someone connected with the deceased, whether or not that person was dependent on him."[19]

It is obvious that to deny illegitimate children the right to recover on their survivorship claim when legitimate children could recover is inconsistent with the express purpose of article 2315. There is no reason why they should not be allowed to call to account the "person responsible" for their mother's death equally with legitimate children. Moreover, as with the wrongful death claim, there is no support of either a factual or common-sense nature for the conclusion that individuals will be deterred from having illegitimate children or from engaging in illicit sexual activity by a law barring illegitimates from recovering by way of survivorship for damages incurred by the deceased before he died.

The only argument that might be made here that has not already been answered in connection with wrongful death is that to permit recovery could prejudice the claim of any legitimate children. This argument would be based on the fact that the total amount of the survivorship claim—the pain and suffering of the deceased, valued at $5,000 in the complaint—is fixed and would not depend on the number of children.

But this contention—which the Louisiana courts did not rely on below—is without real substance. In the first place, there are no legitimate children involved in this case. Second, if there were legitimate children, this argument would be questionable even with respect to a survivorship claim from a *father* of illegitimate children who has acknowledged the children. As of 1960, in twenty-one states illegitimates could inherit from their father,[20] and it has been persuasively argued that this result is constitutionally required.[21] Whatever the result with regard to fathers, the argument against recovery is without any force whatever as to mothers of illegitimate children, with whom, as in this case, they will usually have a more intimate relationship. Finally, while there may be an issue of proof of paternity in some cases, this difficulty is wholly absent in connection with maternity, where public records are invariably available.

Recognizing these considerations, forty-nine states and the District of Columbia have accorded illegitimates equal inheritance rights from their mothers.[22] Even Louisiana has gone so far as to permit illegitimates to inherit from their mother if they are acknowledged (however informally) and there are no legitimate children.[23] This situation further emphasizes the irrational nature of the discrimination here because, under Louisiana law, if the deceased mother of the children had collected damages for pain and suffering from the wrongdoer before her death, the illegitimate children would have lawfully inherited this money.

II / The discrimination imposed against the illegitimate children in this case violates the due process clause.

There is a violation of due process in this case because the state has arbitrarily barred certain children from suing for their mother's wrongful death, and state imposition of disabilities "on a wholly arbitrary standard or on a consideration that offends the dictates of reason offends the Due Process Clause."[24]

Furthermore, the decision below is violative of the children's due process rights because it denies them rights on the basis of a condition of birth and a status over which they had no control and which they are powerless to correct. A leading legal philosopher, Professor Lon Fuller, maintains that a rule which an individual has no opportunity to obey is not a law at all but an arbitrary application of governmental force.[25] And this Court has recognized in several contexts that it is impermissible to hold an individual responsible for his status or conduct over which he has no control. *Robinson v. California*[26] involved a California statute making it a misdemeanor for any person to "be addicted to the use of narcotics." The Court ruled that the "status" of narcotics addiction is "an illness which may be contracted innocently or involuntarily," and that therefore any punishment for the condition is invalid as "cruel and unusual" under the Eighth and Fourteenth Amendments. Or, as Justice Harlan said in his concurring opinion, to subject an individual to criminal penalty for a condition which he could not control is an "arbitrary imposition" by the state.[27]

NAACP v. Overstreet[28] is also on point. In this case the Court dismissed a petition for certiorari which earlier had been granted, limited to the question whether the lower court, by holding the NAACP liable "for acts performed without its knowledge and by persons beyond its control," denied it rights secured by the Fourteenth Amendment. Although a majority of the Court voted to dismiss the petition, thereby expressing no opinion on the merits, four Justices through an opinion of Justice Douglas concluded that it violated the Fourteenth Amendment to hold the NAACP liable for acts over which it had no control.[29]

Oyama v. California[30] brings us even closer to the instant case. There the Court struck down California's Alien Land Law that inflicted harm on a child due to the status of his father. In holding that extraordinary procedural burdens could not be imposed on a citizen in providing the ownership of land merely because his father was an alien ineligible for citizenship, the Court reiterated that distinctions based on ancestry are "by their very nature odious to a free people."[31]

Louisiana's imposition of a burden upon children because of the actions of their parents not only contravenes the biblical injunction that "The son shall not bear the iniquity of the father,"[32] but it is inconsistent with an explicit constitutional policy. Article III, section 3, clause 2 of the Constitution provides that "The Congress shall have power to declare the Punishment of Treason, but no Attainder of Treason shall work Corruption of Blood, or Forfeiture except during the Life of the Person attainted." While this provision applies in terms only to cases of treason (which had largely occasioned the historic use of corruption of blood in England), it manifests a broader principle of justice: that individuals should not be denied rights because of the behavior of their ancestors which they could not control. In fact, what Louisiana has done here is similar to the medieval form of punishment by which a "felon's blood was attainted or corrupted" with the result that he could not own property himself, "nor could any heir born before or after the felony claim through him."[33] Indeed, if corruption of blood is explicitly forbidden by the Constitution with respect to the heinous crime of treason, it certainly should not be permitted in lesser contexts.

In sum, as the only state that sanctions the cruel result of the ruling below, Louisiana not only has acted unreasonably in light of the purpose of article 2315, but it has denied rights to blameless individuals for the acts of others without any factual or other adequate justification, and it has flouted some of the most conspicuous decisions of this Court holding that a state cannot harm individuals on the basis of their ancestry. Such action by Louisiana is obviously arbitrary and therefore inconsistent with the due process clause of the Fourteenth Amendment.

On March 27, 1968, the author argued the Levy case in the Supreme Court, and on May 20, 1968, the Court upheld the appeal by ruling 6–3 that Louisiana could not validly deny illegitimate children a right to sue for the wrongful death of their mother.

With the increased consciousness among lawyers of the varied disabilities of illegitimate persons, other litigation on the question can be expected. One important case, Smith v. King, *which is discussed in the above brief, was argued in the Supreme Court one month after the Levy appeal. Another case arose in Maryland (*In re Bridget Cager*), where mothers were first charged with criminal child neglect and then found to be in civil neglect solely because they had two illegitimate children.*

A less conventional issue was raised in two cases where illegitimates sued for damages because of the economic and social disabilities of their status—in effect, a suit for "wrongful birth." In one case the illegitimate alleged that his father, while married to another woman, falsely promised his mother that he would get a divorce and marry her; the plaintiff was then conceived, but the father never fulfilled his promise. In the second case, the plantiff was born as a result of the rape of his mother while she was a patient in a New York mental institution, and he alleged that the state was negligent in failing to protect her against the attack. Both suits were ultimately dismissed, although in the latter case a lower court upheld the claim. The main reasons given for denying a right to sue were the theoretical difficulty of allowing recovery to someone who, if the wrong had not occurred, would not have been born at all, and the practical problem of estimating monetary damages in such cases.

NOTES

Also participating in the preparation of the brief were Adolph J. Levy, Melvin L. Wulf, Robert Pitofsky, Lois P. Sheinfeld of the Hays Program's Project on Social Welfare Law, and Civil Liberties Fellows David Rudovsky, John C. Gray, Jr., and Sylvia Law. Parts of the brief and the introductory note are based on a comment by the author and David Rudovsky, entitled "Equality for the Illegitimate," which appeared in 8 *Welfare Law Bulletin* 13 (May 1967).

1. McLaughlin v. Florida, 379 U.S. 184, 192 (1964); Oyama v. California, 332 U.S. 633, 640 (1948).

2. Bolling v. Sharpe, 347 U.S. 497, 499 (1954).

3. 320 U.S. 81, 100 (1943).

4. Kovacs v. Cooper, 336 U.S. 77, 95 (1949) (Frankfurter, J., concurring).

5. La. Rev. Stat. 14:79.2; N.Y. *Times*, Aug. 28, 1960, p. 62, col. 4. See generally Bell, *Aid to Dependent Children* (1965).

Historically, the children of slaves were all deemed to be illegitimate. See Catterall, *Judicial Cases Concerning American Slavery and the Negro* (1932). Marriages between whites and Negroes were long prohibited in Louisiana and the illegitimate children of miscegenetic unions, like those who were the product of incest or adultery, could not be legitimated by subsequent marriage or formal acknowledgment. Hibbert v. Mudd, 187 So.2d 503 (La. App. 1966).

6. Report of the Division of Public Health, Louisiana State Board of Health, p. 21 (1964).

7. 165 U.S. 150, 155 (1897).

8. 379 U.S. 184, 193 (1964). See also Traux v. Raich, 239 U.S. 33, 42 (1915); Carrington v. Rash, 380 U.S. 89, 93 (1965).

9. 9 & 10 Vict. Ch. 93 (1846).

10. See Speiser, *Recovery for Wrongful Death* iii–iv, 12–13 (1967).

11. Middleton v. Luckenbach S.S. Co., 70 F.2d 326, 329–30 (1934), quoted in DeSylva v. Ballentine, 351 U.S. 570, 583–84 (1956) (Douglas, J., concurring).

12. Cooper v. Blanck, 39 So.2d 352, 359 (La. App. 1923).

13. Eichorn v. New Orleans & C.R. Light & P. Co., 114 La. 712, 724, 38 So. 526, 530 (1904).

14. See Fortas, "Equal Rights—For Whom?" 42 *N.Y.U.L. Rev.* 401, 408 (1967).

15. La. Civil Code, article 240.

16. 277 F. Supp. 31 (M.D. Ala. 1967).

17. *Id.* at 40.

18. See Krause, "Equal Protection for the Illegitimate," 65 *Mich. L. Rev.* 477, 493 (1967).

19. Note, 14 *Tulane L. Rev.* 612, 619 (1940).

20. See Note, "Illegitimacy," 26 *Brooklyn L. Rev.* 45, 76–79 (1959).

21. See Krause, *supra* note 18 at 495–502.

22. See note 20 *supra* at 76–79. New York became the 49th state in 1967. N.Y. Estates, Powers, and Trusts Law § 4–1.1(1) (1967).

23. La. Civil Code, article 918. See Allen v. Anderson, 55 So.2d 596 (La. App. 1951).

24. Schware v. Board of Bar Examiners, 353 U.S. 232, 249 (1957) (Frankfurter, J., concurring).

25. Fuller, *The Morality of Law* 39, 70–73 (1964).
26. 370 U.S. 660 (1962).
27. *Id.* at 679. See also Driver v. Hinnant, 356 F.2d 761 (4th Cir. 1966) ("chronic alcholism" a disease not punishable as a crime).
28. 384 U.S. 118 (1966).
29. *Id.* at 123–26.
30. 332 U.S. 633, 640 (1948).
31. *Id.* at 646.
32. Ezekiel 18:20.
33. Holdsworth, 3 *History of English Law* 69 (1923).

Appendix A

The Arthur Garfield Hays and Robert Marshall Civil Liberties Fellows

1958–1959

Jordan Derwin
Kenneth M. Greenfield
Edward D. Lanford (G)

1959–1960

Julius Berman
Jack L. Kroner (G)
Lewis Stein

1960–1961

Ronald L. Goldfarb (G)
Bernard Mindich
Don Williamson

1961–1962

Jeffrey M. Albert (G)
Robert E. Burns (G)
Joseph E. Downs
Alvin L. Goldman

1962–1963

Nathan M. Greene (G)
George L. Santangelo
John E. Smith (G)
Gerald Sobel

1963–1964

Paul S. Adler (G)
Franklin S. Bonem

Bernard Evans Harvith (G)
Julian K. Melmed
Lawrence D. Ross

1964–1965

John Murphy
Albert W. Overby
Robert J. Rabin (G)
Benjamin J. Zinkin (G)

1965–1966

William E. Crain
Hillel Hoffman (G)
Paul S. Schreiber
Bonnie P. Winawer

1966–1967

David S. Bogen (G)
Norman J. Chachkin
Michael D. Kaufman (G)
David Rudovsky
Robert Van Lierop

1967–1968

John C. Gray, Jr. (G)
Sylvia Law
Ronald Pollack

(G) refers to graduate student

Appendix B

The Advisory Committee to the Hays Program

Hays Memorial Committee

J. David Stern, Chairman
William Abramson
Roger N. Baldwin
William J. Butler
Osmond K. Fraenkel
E. Sheldon Stewart

ADVISORY COMMITTEE

Anthony G. Amsterdam
Charles E. Ares
Leonard B. Boudin
Helen L. Buttenwieser
Robert L. Carter
Edward N. Costikyan
Vern Countryman
Nanette Dembitz
Henry M. di Suvero
Edward J. Ennis
Irwin Feinberg, M.D.
Murray Gordon
Michael Harrington
Paul Hartman
William M. Kunstler
Anthony Lewis
Ephraim London
Edwin J. Lukas
Louis Lusky
Burke Marshall
James Marshall
Will Maslow
Robert B. McKay
Michael Meltsner
Willie Morris
John de J. Pemberton
Leo Pfeffer
Sol Rabkin
Carl Rachlin
J. Lee Rankin
Charles A. Reich
Joseph B. Robison
Alan U. Schwartz
Jack Sheinkman
Rowland Watts
Melvin L. Wulf

Index